RED SEAS

GERALD HORNE

RED SEAS

Ferdinand Smith and Radical Black Sailors in the United States and Jamaica

New York University Press • *New York and London*

NEW YORK UNIVERSITY PRESS
New York and London
www.nyupress.org

Library of Congress Cataloging-in-Publication Data
Horne, Gerald.
Red Seas : Ferdinand Smith and radical black sailors
in the United States and Jamaica / Gerald Horne.
p. cm.
Includes bibliographical references and index.
ISBN 0-8147-3668-8 (cloth : alk. paper)
1. Smith, Ferdinand.   2. Labor leaders—United States—
Biography.   3. African American communists—Biography.
4. Jamaican Americans—Biography.   5. National Maritime
Union of America—History—20th century.   6. Labor leaders—
Jamaica—Biography.   I. Title.
HD6509.S6H67   2005
331.88'113875'092—dc22   2004029622

New York University Press books are printed on acid-free paper,
and their binding materials are chosen for strength and durability.

Manufactured in the United States of America

MC 10 9 8 7 6 5 4 3 2 1

Contents

All illustrations appear as an insert following p. 168.

Preface

FALL HAD JUST ARRIVED in a somber Manhattan in 1944. The arrival weeks earlier of Allied forces on the shores of Western Europe had both given hope that an awful war might soon be ending, while emboldening those whose desire to settle scores with ideological foes had been stalled by Washington's alliance with Moscow. This was the backdrop as the great and the good gathered together in the main banquet hall of a midtown hotel to honor a mahogany-colored man of Jamaican descent, widely viewed as one of the most powerful Negroes in the country.

Besides being second in command of the National Maritime Union, Ferdinand Smith—the man to be honored—was also a leading member of the Communist Party. Well over six feet tall, weighing over two hundred pounds, and then in his fifties, Smith's accent betrayed his Caribbean origins, while his eyes, which resembled slits, could have easily convinced the unsuspecting that his roots were in China. Well-spoken and a fluent writer, Smith also had formidable administrative and organizational skills, which he wielded on behalf of a union of sailors. He supervised a massive staff of ninety-nine, which meant that he may have managed more workers, including white workers, than any other Negro—or Communist—in the nation.[1]

His Communist ties did not prevent two thousand guests from coming to sing his praises "in recognition of his outstanding service to Labor, the Negro people and the Nation."[2] Symbolizing the holy trinity of the liberal left, "a great nine foot portrait of Mr. Smith, flanked by pictures of [President Franklin Roosevelt] and CIO President Philip Murray . . . hung over the speaker's dais."[3] The doyenne of Negro America, Mary McLeod Bethune, was there, along with Basil Harris, president of the U.S. Lines, "the largest shipping company in the world," and William Dawson, the moderate black congressman from Chicago. Joining the chorus of hosannas were the wife of media mogul William Paley; the writer Donald Ogden Stewart; Lester Granger of the Urban

League; the well-connected jurist, William Hastie; the affluent Marshall Field; and actors Paul Robeson and Jose Ferrer. John Davis, a man known to be close to the organized left, commented that "never before had there been such a representative gathering of Negro leaders under one roof." For those who could not come, radio station WINS-AM broadcast the speakers' remarks.[4]

Yet, perhaps sensing the gathering storm that would bar a U.S. president from openly praising a U.S. Communist for generations to come, President Franklin D. Roosevelt's message concentrated more on Smith's union's gargantuan contribution to the war effort than on Smith himself.[5] There was good reason for this hesitation. Hours before the tribute to Smith the front page of the conservative *New York World-Telegram* had excoriated him. An "alien Communist plans to tour the United States and speak for the Roosevelt-Truman ticket, working closely with the CIO Political Action Committee."[6] This would become the opening salvo in a battle that was to conclude with Smith's departure from the United States in 1951 to his native Jamaica where he reemerged as a prominent local, pan-Caribbean and international trade union leader. His departure ultimately also led to the decimation of the union he helped to build, the NMU.

Nonetheless, before he left Smith played a key role in labor and community affairs. One of FDR's close allies, the labor leader Sidney Hillman—with whom the White House reputedly "cleared" matters major and minor—called him "Ferd."[7] Mayor Fiorello La Guardia of New York City owed him a debt of gratitude after Smith attempted to quell a bitter riot in Harlem.[8] Because of his eminence in Harlem, Smith was dispatched to confer with mayors and other opinion shapers in the major West Coast cities of Seattle, Oakland, San Francisco, and Los Angeles which had experienced a massive influx of Negroes during the war.[9]

Even after the Red Scare and Cold War began, Smith continued to be influential. In 1947, *Ebony* proclaimed that "no longer can A. Philip Randolph . . . speak for 'all Negro Labor.'"[10] Smith was prominently featured in this article.[11] Yet, unlike Randolph, Smith was leader of a union whose members were white, not black. Also unlike Randolph, Smith's union was so massive that it could potentially strangle the nation's economy. At its zenith of influence in 1945 the NMU had a membership of some 90,000.[12] With a grip on many of the imports and exports of the nation and with a towering ally in the Communist-led West Coast longshoremen, this union of mariners—which had an "alien Communist" who also happened to be a Negro, as its leader[13]—was formidable.[14]

Despite his power[15] and image—Smith dressed nattily in dark double-breasted suits with freshly starched shirts and fashionable ties—his weekly salary was typically $75 per week. Still, in his office on the sixth floor of a building formerly owned by the telephone company in the Chelsea district of Manhattan,[16] he was akin to the Chief Operating Officer of a major enterprise. There were three to four close aides positioned in the anteroom of his office, assisting him in his duties of negotiating contracts for his members, presiding over meetings, and writing columns for the union press and various Negro newspapers. Terry Penman, who worked with him at the NMU, described him as a "terrific" supervisor, always "willing to listen." He was a "compassionate" and "caring person." He was, she felt, one of the "nicest persons I've ever met."

He was also one of the smartest. Paul Jarvis, who worked closely with him in the NMU, remembered him fondly as "well read" and an "avid reader," often to be found with newspapers such as the Communist *Daily Worker,* the conservative *New York World-Telegram,* or the mainstream *New York Times* tucked under his arm, or perusing the works of Oscar Wilde and Mark Twain.[17]

Intelligence aside, how did a Communist Negro immigrant come to wield such power? This was the high tide of the "popular front," when Reds were at the apex of their influence and were gaining a foothold in the nation by taking a more progressive position on "racial" equality than traditional political groups. Moreover, blacks were beginning to gain some victories in their crusade against Jim Crow. And for some time immigrants had comprised a large percentage of U.S. sailors. That Smith was a Jamaican Negro rather than a native-born African American may also help account for his rise. When James Weldon Johnson, the NAACP official and diplomat, visited Jamaica, he was struck by the presence of "black custom house officials, black soldiers, black policemen, black street car conductors, black clerks in the big shops, black girls in the telegraph office and at the news-stand of the fashionable Myrtle Bank Hotel."[18] Unlike many Negroes, Smith's upbringing was different from that of many in the United States—dark-skinned folk in powerful posts were not new to him. This may have given him a certain confidence.

On the other hand, Smith was a Communist in a country where the phrase "alien Red" evoked the satanic. And he was no low-level Red ei-

ther; he was a leader of a union thought to be essential to the functioning of Soviet espionage in the United States, since union members routinely traversed the globe and had the ability to transport messages and
instructions.[19] In the late 1930s, when hysteria about Soviet espionage
in the United States was almost at its height, William McFee, a mainstream journalist, called the NMU the leaders of "Seagoing Soviets" and
the "real Trojan Horse of America." The "Russian Revolution began in
the navy," he reported, "and it is well to remember that in 1931, after the
British fleet to Kiel, Germany, which was at the time full of Communists, that fleet was the scene of the most serious mutiny since the eighteenth century." The Communists had "learned," he said, "that the merchant marine is more important than the fighting ships. Transportation
of all kinds, as Stalin has kindly pointed out, is the real nervous system
of the bourgeois world."[20] In turn, the *New York Times* charged that
Communists dominated "ship radio posts" which they could use for espionage.[21]

Smith and the NMU did not seek to allay these suspicions. When
Ben Davis, the Negro Communist, was elected to the New York City
Council in 1943, he praised the NMU effusively: "In blazing the trail for
equality of Negro workers in the labor movement," he proclaimed, this
union "planted the seeds for the victory of which my election was a har-
vest." The NMU "provided more than 100 seamen who came to Harlem
and manned the polls on Election Day."[22] When the Red Councilman
from Harlem was reelected in 1945, Smith helped to organize a "truck
trailer which we circulated every day . . . eight hours a day, in addition
to 50,000 leaflets, outdoor meetings and other activities we carried
out."[23] Yet the twin struggles for civil and labor rights came at a stiff
price. The civil rights movement exploded as the most resolute
guardians of the economic well-being of Negroes—left-wing trade
unionists like Smith—were under deadly siege.

In short, the routing of the NMU helped to alter the character of the
Negro freedom struggle. Josh Lawrence, a New York–based NMU
leader, recalled when "back in the thirties and even the early forties . . .
there were only two places in the South where black and white could
meet together—in the black churches and the halls of the NMU."[24] With
members in Norfolk, Wilmington, Charleston, Savannah, Jacksonville,
Miami, Mobile, New Orleans, Houston, Memphis, and a number of
southern river ports, the NMU was a precious link in a chain of resist-

ance to Jim Crow. When this link snapped, Negroes were left not only with fewer meeting halls but also—and more importantly—with a diminished and shrunken leadership. When those who constituted "black labor at sea" were diminished, in a real sense "black labor" itself was "at sea," shorn of its moorings, adrift, unable to anchor firmly the crucial idea that class exploitation was at the heart of "racial" bias. This mattered a good deal in a community that was overwhelmingly working class. This class realignment allowed for the further rise of middle-class clerics and lawyers (who have their own particular class interests) to the forefront of Negro leadership, a position they continue to occupy.[25]

Early in the morning of 16 February 1948, four white FBI men arrived and parked at the corner of 141st Street and Convent Avenue in Harlem. Not long thereafter a tall, well-built middle-aged Negro man emerged from one of the apartments. Two of the men jumped out of the car. They moved hastily toward the house. They stopped the man, flashed a paper, and elbowed him into the car.[26]

    This was the beginning of a chain of events that would conclude with Ferdinand Smith being ousted from the country he had helped build. The day of reckoning arrived on 16 August 1951. After repeated detentions and hearings, punctuated by regular protests and Smith's ongoing activism, he arrived at Idlewild Airport for a flight on Pan-American Airways to London. An immigration officer accompanied him to ensure that he would not miss his flight. Scores of sympathizers were there to bid him a fond farewell, among them his good friend, Paul Robeson. Many slipped rolls of bills and envelopes presumably containing money into Smith's hands.[27]

    Finally, his enemies thought, they had consigned Smith to well-deserved obscurity. They were wrong. From London Smith traveled to Vienna, where the World Federation of Trade Unions, viewed in Washington as a "Communist front," gave him a high-level post.[28] His work sent him to the British West Indies and he wound up returning to Jamaica, where he organized sugar workers and led a left-wing union federation. There in the summer of 1955, Jamaican leader Alexander Bustamante confided to a local U.S. diplomat that he was worried that in the absence of stringent measures Smith could have become a "[Cheddi] Jagan" of Jamaica, referring to the Communist who led the former British Guiana before being unceremoniously ousted.[29]

Yet those stringent measures were taken and when Smith died in Jamaica in 1961, he was far—quite far—from becoming the Prime Minister of the island nation where he was born.

This is a book about Ferdinand Smith. But, as the subtitle suggests, it is also a book about Jamaica, the National Maritime Union (and sailors more broadly), and the Communist Party.

The Introduction sketches Smith's early years in Jamaica and his subsequent beginnings as a migrant laborer in Panama and Cuba before he moved to Mobile, Alabama, as World War I was coming to an end. From there he moved to New York City where a booming West Indian population was coming into conflict with native-born Negroes. Smith worked at various jobs before obtaining work as a ship's steward. In this he carried on a long tradition of black sailors that stretched back to the founding of the United States.

Chapter 1 provides the background on the radicalism that so often characterized seamen, along with an analysis of the Communist Party and the movement led by Smith's fellow Jamaican, Marcus Garvey, two movements which had a significant influence on the Manhattan that Smith came to call home. This chapter also traces sailors' early efforts to unionize and details the career of David Grange, also a Jamaican Negro, who was a key leader of the pre-NMU sailors' union. His presence indicates that Smith's leadership of the NMU was not anomalous: sailors' unions were one of the few places where a contingent of white men were led by Negroes.

Chapter 2 discusses the mercurial Joseph Curran, the chief leader of the NMU, who owed his post largely to Communists—a decision they later were to rue. An effort was made to oust Smith from the leadership on account of his alleged "scabbing" during the epochal General Strike of 1934 in San Francisco. The nature of the shipping industry is outlined here, along with the early relationship between the NAACP and the NMU. Though some might think that a Communist-led union would be antidemocractic, the NMU was the opposite, frequently violating an ongoing principle of unions to this day by airing dissident viewpoints, even those hostile to Communists, in the union journal.

Chapter 3 examines more closely the union's effort to battle "racial" bias at sea, particularly in Gulf ports, where these efforts were severely hampered by legalized Jim Crow. There was at times a striking identity of interest and even membership between members of the Ku Klux

Klan and the American Federation of Labor (AFL). Like most unions, the NMU was not particularly insightful when it came to gender bias, a deficiency underscored by ancient biases against women at sea.

Chapter 4 deals with the consistent internationalism of the union, as sailors were frequently involved in protests in Nazi Germany, Brazil, India, and elsewhere. Exposure to ports like Cape Town and Durban could reinforce preexisting biases or inspire sailors to new levels of antiracist resistance. Smith's own antiracist activism was often expressed through his leadership role in "popular front"—or, as his detractors would have it, "Communist front"—organizations such as the National Negro Congress (NNC) and the Negro Labor Victory Committee (NLVC). The chapter also shows the NMU's massive sacrifices during World War II that in some respects outstripped those of the armed forces.

Chapter 5 focuses more closely on Smith, particularly as he was called on by the city fathers to intervene when the "Harlem Riot," which some saw as a setback to antifascist unity, erupted in 1943. Paradoxically, as his value to the state increased, government surveillance of Smith grew in response to growing concern about Communist influence at a time when Washington and Moscow were wartime allies. This chapter discusses Smith's relations with the Congress of Industrial Organizations (CIO) and his closeness to Congressman Adam Clayton Powell, as well as his complicated ties to A. Philip Randolph, a former NNC leader himself. Finally, internal union problems that exploded a few years later are examined.

Chapter 6 details the beginnings of Smith's travails in 1944, as he was exposed as an "illegal alien" just as he was about to embark on a campaign to ensure the reelection of President Roosevelt. This occurred as the Communist Party endured internal strife of its own, as the conclusion of the war signaled the onset of a new era: the Red Scare and Cold War.

Chapter 7 portrays the ambitious attempt by the NMU and its waterfront and global allies in 1946 to launch a strike that would potentially encircle the planet. Simultaneously the union, a stern critic of U.S. foreign policy, became more heavily dependent on the U.S. State Department to intervene on behalf of its members who often ran afoul of foreign governments. Some sailors began to wonder whether they would be better treated by the consular services if their union was less hostile to the White House.

Chapter 8 explores the uproarious convention of 1947 that marked the beginning of the end of Smith's tenure with the NMU, as he was expelled in 1948 from the union he built and led. Smith's ouster marked the onset of a decline of the union generally and Negroes within the union specifically—a turning point that occurred as desegregation was supposedly creating new freedoms. In short, Negroes took a step back on the "class" front as they advanced on the "race" front. This had a particularly potent impact in the southern ports from Norfolk to New Orleans to Houston where the union had been notably strong. Even so, there was a general perception that the south was catching up with the north, which was standing still.

Chapter 9 follows Smith as he led the Harlem Trade Union Council which fought job bias in Gotham. Also portrayed are the immigration hearings that led to his departure from the United States. Smith's ouster coincided with the "screening"—or purging—of progressive sailors, which had a devastating impact on Negro sailors in particular. The industry was in the process of downsizing, as "flags of convenience"— ships flying under the banner of countries such as Liberia and Panama—increased. Smith's ascendancy was representative of a growing class consciousness among Negroes, just as his fall from power occurred as "racial" gains seemed to increase. This provided the preconditions for a resurgence of black nationalism.

Chapter 10 describes Smith's travels to Vienna to work for the Communist-led World Federation of Trade Unions. With Austria as his base, he sought to travel to Africa and the Caribbean to organize unions and anticolonial protest generally, in addition to mobilizing on behalf of a U.S.-based petition drive to bring the U.S. government into the dock for committing "genocide" against Negroes. These multifaceted efforts attracted the attention of U.S. and U.K. security agencies and ultimately Smith was barred from entering the Caribbean. Stymied, by 1952 he moved to set up residence in Jamaica. There, as chapter 11 suggests, he was viewed as the "evil genius" of communism, as he led the sugar workers' union and left-wing efforts generally. However, when the colonial government refused to recognize his union, his efforts collapsed.

Though Smith was viewed as a vector for the recipient of "Moscow Gold"—Soviet subsidies—it turned out that his opponents in Jamaica were the largest beneficiary of foreign largesse: this is discussed in chapter 12. Also noted here is a circuit of Pan-Africanism that involved the circulation of ideas from the Caribbean to Africa to North America, with Smith intimately involved. Finally, as the colonial government refused to renew his passport, Smith was barred from traveling to Eastern Europe for medical treatment, and died in August 1961.

The Epilogue brings the story up to date and includes final reflections on the matter of blacks sailing the "Red Seas." It was almost as if the U.S. elites felt they had to undermine the entire shipping industry in order to rid themselves of the possibility of a further rising by left-led sailors—burning down the house to roast the pig, if you will. In the aftermath of the terror attack on the United States on 11 September 2001, some began to wonder whether the nation had jeopardized national security by becoming too dependent on poorly paid foreign sailors toiling aboard "floating slums," who were sailing into Atlantic, Gulf, and Pacific ports on a regular basis. Such was the legacy of the ousting of the red sailor, Ferdinand Smith, from the NMU—and the United States—and his repatriation to Jamaica.

Introduction

Sailing from Jamaica

NOT MUCH IS KNOWN about the early life of Ferdinand Smith. He was born on 5 May 1893 in Sav-la-mar in the parish of Westmoreland, Jamaica—an island nation which he later described as possessing "great natural beauty. Its lofty mountains, deep seas and broad valleys, its fertile plains, many rivers and waterfalls."[1] But alongside this prepossessing physical beauty was an ugly Jamaica that W. E. B. Du Bois described as having a "tragedy of poverty almost uncomprehensible [sic]."[2]

This was particularly true of Westmoreland. This parish was formed in 1703 and quickly became a "name synonymous with the busy sugar industry with flat rice lands, with stately old architecture." In 1710 Thomas Mannings gave Westmoreland land and cattle to "endow a free school," which was incorporated in 1738. It was "one of the oldest secondary schools in Jamaica."[3] Partly because Smith's father was a teacher, Ferdinand Smith was able to receive a basic grounding in reading and writing—a literacy that was to follow him benevolently throughout his life. He was lucky. "The census of 1943 showed that of the population over ten years of age, only 2.76% had any secondary schooling."[4]

Smith also came from a mixed family background. His nephew, Earl Smith, claims that his grandmother—Ferdinand Smith's mother— was of European descent.[5] Certainly Westmoreland had one of the largest settlements of Europeans on the island, a result of a "bountied [sic] immigration scheme" designed after the abolition of slavery in 1834 to draw them there. In the late twentieth century there remained "300 descendants of German immigrants there." Westmoreland was one of the few areas in Jamaica where "most of the peasant farmers are fair-skinned, blue-eyed people of German stock."[6] In a Jamaica scarred by color stratification, Smith's brown skin and lighter skinned relatives may have given him an early advantage.[7]

The region was wracked with ferment and conflict.[8] "Major riots occurred in Falmouth and [Sav-la-mar] in 1859."[9] O. Nigel Bolland writes of "at least 16 serious disturbances . . . between 1884 and 1905" in the British Caribbean, "most of them in Jamaica."[10] The historian and activist Walter Rodney was attracted by the "combativeness" of Jamaicans generally, to the point where "I always felt that there must be tremendous revolutionary potential in that island." Jamaica had risen from colonialism and slavery with a "more violent social history and rugged past than most of the other islands. [There were] large scale slave revolts in the eighteenth century." This pattern continued in the twentieth century. In short, there was fierce class, race, and color conflict in Jamaica; according to the Jamaican historian Rupert Lewis, "social differentiation in Jamaica was more marked than anywhere else in the English-speaking Caribbean."[11]

This volatile situation gave rise to sharp conflict. In neighboring St. Ann's parish, the "plantocracy" there was "once described as 'semi-feudal.' One of the estate owners always wore his [pajamas], even when he used a cattle whip on some unfortunate agricultural inspector."[12] Naturally, peasants were treated worse than bureaucrats. The former, according to Winston James, speaking of the time when Smith was departing his homeland, "are still beasts of burden . . . [and] live [like] savages in unfloored huts, huddled together like beasts of the field."[13]

These brutal lords of the land were not restrained by an alert electorate. In 1901 of a population of 756,000, there were only 16,256 voters, and even this skewed pattern was distorted by color.[14] And of course, whether Jamaicans accepted the British royal family as their sovereign was not subject to plebiscite. Government departments were "headed by white expatriates and all other senior positions were filled by whites or near-whites. It was the policy in the civil service that the few blacks and coloreds employed were not to be promoted above a certain level. In practice, the darker the complexion, the lower the category in which individuals were placed."[15]

Children were not exempt from "racial" discrimination. Lady Bustamante—the longtime aide, then spouse to Jamaica's founding father Alexander Bustamante—was born in Westmoreland in 1912. As she recalled it, in schools "unruly children were chastised with the 'wild cane' or a strop. For small offences, such as speaking out of turn, the offender was made to stand for about an hour, face to the wall and with one finger on the lips." Such practices may have been designed to discourage education altogether since the British conceived of the Jamaicans as merely "hewers of wood and drawers of water." She recalled that "men could only look forward to working on the estates, chopping cane or rising to the grade of foreman; carrying bananas hoping to be a tallyman at the banana ports. Women aspired to teaching, nursing or keeping house for others; and some had nothing to do." Before the upsurge of the 1930s, she could not "recall any serious or sustained newspaper writing that would have drawn attention to the plight of the poor." Color prejudice was so strong that "there was hardly a dark face to be seen amongst the workers in the stores or offices in the centre of the town. Certainly there was none in either of the two banks—Barclays and Nova Scotia. . . . Most of the lawyers and other professionals practising in Montego Bay were either white or of very light complexion. . . . Such was the prejudice that if a black person swam down the adjoining Cornwall Beach and happened to put foot on the sands of Doctor's Cave, some of the white members would come out of the water and quickly depart." In Jamaica, "there were more dogs than bones and . . . the meat was being distributed according to colour and class. . . . Even newspaper advertisements for jobs mentioned skin colour as a qualification."[16]

The economy of Jamaica, heavily dependent on sugar, was collapsing when Ferdinand Smith was an infant. A "long sugar crisis . . . began in the 1880s and [there was] overproduction on the world market, which had led to such low prices that West Indian sugar could only be produced at a loss."[17] This encouraged the trade union movement. After 1895 "several attempts were made to create trade unions, most of which had disappeared by the early 1920s."[18]

Smith was a laborer from his earliest years. His friend, Richard Hart, avers that "his first job after leaving primary school was pushing a hand truck on the Smithfield Wharf, Sav-la-mar for one shilling and sixpence a day."[19] He had managed to attend what was called a college for two years but the deteriorating Jamaican economy forced him to quit and find a job. Eventually he was to become a waiter in a hotel—good training for his post as a ship steward—then a clerk and later a haberdashery salesman.[20] Then, in the midst of this economic upheaval and dislocation, Sav-la-mar was hit by a devastating hurricane.[21]

The local economy collapsing around him, Ferdinand Smith walked from Sav-la-mar to the nearest port scores of miles away and caught a boat to Panama.[22] He was not to return to Jamaica until almost forty years later.

∎

The noted Jamaican writer, Philip Sherlock, has observed that although Jamaicans are "island people," "they have no love for the sea. In their history ships were floating tombs and sails on the horizon, invaders or pirates. . . . The sea imprisoned them. . . . Their links are with the mountains. Half their island is a thousand feet and more above sea level."[23] It was the ship that had brought unwilling, enslaved Africans to the New World and it was the mountain that provided refuge. Yet economic distress can convert the most waterphobic people into confirmed mariners. Such was the case with Smith—and generations of Jamaicans. Like him, Panama was often their port of call and sailing the sea was the only way to get there. When he selected the isthmus as the meeting for his Pan American Congress in 1824, Simon Bolivar singled Panama out as the "veritable capital of the world, the center of the globe, with one face turned toward Asia and the other toward Africa and Europe." As early as 1850, fleeing the economic distress of postabolition Jamaica, residents of the island had begun streaming into this "capital."[24]

White workers were considered for canal construction but they "could not be paid enough to induce them to immigrate, nor could they be forced to accept the level of physical abuse that most of the construction tasks demanded."[25] As plans to build a canal went ahead, even more Jamaicans were attracted to what appeared to be a latter-day El Dorado. By the 1880s there were about nine thousand Jamaican laborers there.

Among these foreign laborers[26] was Ferdinand Smith, who stayed in Panama[27] for five years, working variously as a hotel steward and commissary salesman. He had married a woman from St. Elizabeth's parish in Jamaica and had fathered a daughter.[28] Marcus Garvey was also among the Jamaicans[29] who made it to Panama; the conditions he encountered in the region convinced him that Negroes needed to be better organized. Working conditions for these black workers ranged from difficult to abysmal.[30] This was Smith's first direct encounter with U.S.-style Jim Crow.[31] The Canal Zone was then under Washington's jurisdiction. As late as 1948, when Smith was on his way back to the Caribbean, an eviscerating racial segregation continued to persist.[32] Wages were nominal. Working conditions were harsh.

Unavoidably, this exploitative system gave rise to stiff organized resistance. Strikes were regular.[33] As early as July 1913—as Smith was just settling in—plans were made to deport approximately ten thousand workers of all nationalities.[34] U.S. military intelligence took note when "ten thousand employees of the Panama Canal and the Panama Railway walked out. . . . The strike of all Negro employees of these companies having commenced today. This is about seventy percent of the entire Negro force."[35] A few months later a "confidential" memo reported that "Negro laborers on the Canal Zone are disorganized as a total failure of the strike . . . a strike which resulted only in many of them losing their positions permanently. . . . Canal Zone officials have the bridle hand on the Negroes due to the fact that the Panama Canal and the Panama Railroad control all stores on the Canal Zone and all employees' quarters. . . . Any strike attempted by them is bound to fail." It concluded, "There are radical elements in the Republic of Panama which have not as yet come to light."[36]

As World War I came to an end and Panama was convulsed in instability, Smith moved on to Cuba. He had become part of a roving band of Jamaican migrant workers who moved from island to island, job to job, in constant search of a livelihood. Between 1912 and 1924, 230,000 contract workers were imported into Cuba from Haiti and Jamaica— 24,000 Jamaicans in 1919 alone.[37]

This was not the most propitious time for Smith's arrival in the "Pearl of the Antilles." In 1912 a "race war" took place when the pent-up grievances of Afro-Cubans exploded and "government troops massacred thousands of blacks in retaliation." As a result black migration from Jamaica was curbed in favor of immigrants from Spain. There was "much publicized financed expulsions of West Indians," combined with "racist attacks."[38] Smith spent a scant eleven months in Cuba before migrating to the United States. He arrived in Mobile on 19 November 1920, having traveled on the SS *Tuscan* as a steward.[39]

A Negro steward sailing into port was commonplace. The black cook was so ordinary that he became a "stereotype in nautical fiction."[40] Just as the Pullman sleeping-car porter was associated with the domestic vector of communication, the steward was his counterpart in the global arena.

Thus there was nothing particularly unusual about a Negro sailor arriving in a U.S. port. And it was no coincidence that in 1838 Frederick Douglass escaped northward to freedom dressed in sailors' clothes and armed with a free black sailor's pass. "You cannot write the bloody laws of slavery on those restless billows," he proclaimed. "The ocean, if not the land, is free."[41]

Negroes had long seen the ocean as the pathway to freedom. The NMU once "estimated" that in "1850 . . . more than half of the American seamen were colored men."[42] "The sea," said the NMU journal, "offered a haven to the most militant and aggressive slaves as an escape from bondage." Crispus Attucks, whose martyrdom on behalf of the "American Revolution" was inscribed in blood in 1770, was a seamen, as was the rebel leader Denmark Vesey.[43] As early as 1809 the Negro steward of the *Minerva* smuggled insurrectionary pamphlets into Charleston. Vesey read pamphlets like this aloud, thereby spurring the passage of the 1822 Negro Seaman Act, which permitted the sheriff to board any incoming vessel and to arrest any black sailor for the duration of the ship's stay in the port of Charleston.[44]

Because of the "threat of contagion" that West Indian, northern U.S., and Latin American sailors were said to pose, the port of Galveston also required captains to either deny their black sailors shore leave while in port or to place them in jail for the duration of the ship's visit.[45] This was a reflection of the fact that the slave-owning South correctly viewed Negro sailors as a clear and present danger to its way of life.[46] The importance of sailing to Negroes was confirmed further when the "New York African Free Schools . . . established to provide for Negro children . . . introduced in the 1820s the study of navigation, since many of the best pupils subsequently went to sea."[47]

Negro sailors with their steady incomes, "free" status, and worldliness were leaders in their communities. Sailors established contact with slaves in the British, French, Spanish, and Dutch ports of the Western Hemisphere, exchanging information about slave revolts, abolition, and revolution and "generating rumors that became material forces in their own right." Not surprisingly, slaves and masters alike came to see sailors as potential liberators.

Sailors had played a major role in rebellions in the seventeenth and eighteenth centuries. Though it "lasted only ten days, the revolt of Naples in July 1647 marked the first time that the proletariat of any European city seized power and governed alone," and sailors were important players in this rebellion.[48] The "very term 'strike' evolved from the decision of British seamen in 1768 to 'strike' the sails of their vessels and thereby to cripple the commerce of the empire's capital city."[49] Ships spawned radicals, a concentrated forcing house of internationalism and subversion.[50]

Sailing continued to be a stepping stone to better opportunities in the twentieth century. Decades after Frederick Douglass made his escape, William Monroe Trotter, after being "refused a passport . . . obtained in disguise a seaman's passport and took a job on a freighter bound for Le Havre, where he jumped ship" in 1919 in time to crash the Versailles peace conference, where he intended to press the cause of the Negro.[51] Langston Hughes,[52] Ralph Ellison,[53] and Kwame Nkrumah[54] were among the luminaries from the Pan-African world who went to sea in search of adventure—and a livelihood. In an era of circumscribed opportunity for Negroes, sailing provided not only jobs but also the possibility of escaping to a freer world.

This was very much the case for Ferdinand Smith as he made his way from Cuba to Mobile, a deep South entrepot dominated by Jim Crow and uncongenial to Negroes. J. Alexander Somerville, who migrated from Jamaica to Los Angeles as Smith was making his way to New York City, found it hard to believe that lynchings took place: "The whole affair was so ghastly that we simply could not believe it, so we attributed it to the mental aberration of a fiction writer."[55] But this was reality, not fiction, and after landing in Alabama, Smith quickly left for New York.

There he encountered a booming West Indian population.[56] As European emigration was curbed by war and as U.S. production heated up as the nation sold to both sides in the conflict, an economic boom ensued that lured many West Indians northward. Of course, there had been a lengthy intercourse between the Caribbean islands and the country that became the United States, as their common colonial master in London guaranteed frequent contact.[57] W. E. B. Du Bois was among those who pointed to the central role of West Indians in the Afro-American struggle.[58]

By the time Smith arrived in Harlem, West Indians[59] had also garnered a well-deserved reputation for radicalism. Smith was not unique in being a migrant laborer, inveterate traveler, Marxist, and proletarian intellectual. Otto Huiswood followed a similar trajectory: born in 1893 in Surinam, he was the first Negro to join the U.S. Communist Party, signing on in 1919.[60] He had "shipped out on a Dutch banana boat bound for Holland in January 1910." He wound up in Brooklyn where he "jumped ship" and by 1918 was working on a "pleasure boat on the Fall River Line."[61] During his years as a sailor, he "had made many trips to the Caribbean islands including Jamaica, Trinidad, Haiti, Cuba, Curacao, Barbados and British and Dutch Guiana to make contact with labor leaders and report on conditions." Such travels made for a certain cosmopolitanism, a broadened outlook and an acute awareness of exploitation. Together, these traits were a ready recipe for radicalism.[62]

This migration process—not to mention the bracing encounter with Jim Crow—pushed many West Indians to the left and gave rise to a Pan-Caribbean or "West Indian" identity.[63] The stigma attached to being black in the United States caused some to defensively compensate by declaring that West Indian culture was superior to that of U.S. blacks, which led to conflict with native Negroes. That some Euro-American employers favored them over these Negroes did not help matters.[64]

Smith was able to transcend this ethnic divide, while anchoring himself firmly among the burgeoning left. He joined the Communist-led Marine Workers Industrial Union because he was impressed with their antiracism and progressivism.[65] "Soon after being in America," he recalled years later, "I had come face to face with the harsh realities of racial discrimination, of white men brutally trampling upon even the most elementary human rights of Negroes. I had been in the southern states of the USA, and tasted of this bitter fruit of degradation and segregation. I resented it." His attempt to fight back led him leftward—figuratively to the portside—and toward union organizing and radical politics. He kept his Communist "membership secret" for fear of jeopardizing "my job as Chief Steward, a privileged position"—though his "privilege" did not exempt him from "racial" bias. On board ship, he remembered later, "I have often rebelled at the infamous 'two-pot' system, whereby top-grade rations were prepared for officers while the crewmen were fed the meanest of rations. Many and bitter were the battles both verbal and physical waged between other officers and myself (as chief steward)."

Fortunately for him, "the life of a seaman affords a remarkable opportunity to study the life of people in various countries. Within a few years of seafaring," he noted, "I had known most of the world, had spoken to and intimately observed the modes of living of people in North, South and Central America, Britain, France, Germany, Italy, Spain, Belgium, China and Africa among other places." He was notably struck by the "miserable, over-worked, underfed prisoners in their own country I saw in Africa." Like many sailors, Smith's voracious reading and incessant traveling had given him a depth of understanding of human ex-

perience that soared far beyond that of other Negroes, other labor leaders, and, quite frankly, many other intellectuals.

But not all his encounters on his travels were of misery. He also met
those who "received me warmly . . . I soon learned that they were Communists." When he visited "Russia" he was "met by people rich in culture and material goods"—and, like his good friend to be Paul Robeson,
he was won over completely. These struggles on behalf of "workers and
especially for Negroes" led him to the "theory of the class struggle"
which "has been more than demonstrated in my years of working. I
know the class struggle to be true, because I have been an active leader
and participant all my life." He "began a study of Political Economy as
early as 1925" and rapidly became "satisfied with the theoretical justification of Marxism but this I had to check with practical experiences and
observations."[66]

Life at sea provided plenty of opportunity for reading, which Smith
pursued with determination. This gave him an intellectual edge over
others that was not unique to himself; in fact, Negro sailors were in the
vanguard of a trend that has since dissipated considerably—the rise of
the proletarian intellectual, the powerful autodidact and cosmopoli-
tan.[67] All this combined with the horrors of Jim Crow to drive Smith into
the eagerly waiting arms of the Communist Party.

Workers in Hollywood were fond of saying that Walt Disney probably
created more Communists than Karl Marx, because of his onerous and
exploitative working conditions, not to mention the paltry wages.[68]
Sailors, no doubt, would have viewed the film industry as paradise re-
gained compared to what they faced at sea. From the time of the galley
slaves, laborers at sea had faced particularly oppressive conditions. As
Samuel Johnson once put it, "No man will be a sailor who has con-
trivance enough to get himself into a jail; for being in a ship is being in
jail with the chance of being drowned. . . . A man in jail has more room,
better food, and commonly better company."[69] Indeed, the sailing
ship—"the characteristic machine of this period of globalization"—
combined aspects of the jail and the Dickensian factory.[70]

The atrocious conditions on board pre-NMU ships led to "seamen
[having] the highest death and suicide rate of any major industrial
workers." Seamen were particularly "susceptible to venereal disease,
tuberculosis and disorders of the digestive system."[71] Hoyt Haddock,
an early NMU member, recounts an episode that sheds light on the un-

sanitary conditions they had to endure. He was with a "second engineer at lunch one day" who said, "'my god' and took something out of his soup and showed the captain what he had found. . . . The captain said, 'Oh, that's only half of a cockroach' and went on eating his soup."[72]

Gerald Reminick recalled these vessels as follows:

> If you don't mind sleeping in a narrow bunk on a dirty mattress crawling with bedbugs and have no objection to crowding into a dark hole deep in the after peak of a ship, over the screw, where the fumes from showers and toilets permeate the air; and if lack of ventilation or light has no terror for you and you like to take your meals in a smelly messroom just off a hot galley, sitting at a narrow bench covered with soiled oilcloth and facing a blank wall not too clean, with a slovenly mess boy shoving a plate of greasy stew over your shoulder—if these things please you and you are thankful for them and obedient, you are 100 percent American seamen, a credit to your flag and to the United States. On the other hand, if you kick about such things, if you take part in "inciting to riot," join sit down strikes and in that way interfere with the earnings of a run-down cargo steamer, you are a Communist. Living conditions, in brief, are the cause of much of the discontent and rioting we have had . . . along our waterfronts and on board ships.

Furthermore, as one captain put it, "Our ships are infested with thugs, thieves, gangsters, dope-runners, drunkards, racketeers of all descriptions."[73] A number of sailors were on board involuntarily, victims of "Shanghai-ing," kidnapped and placed on board a ship, often headed for China or points unknown. In nineteenth-century San Francisco, men found "guilty of petty larceny" were "given the choice of going to jail or of signing on a windjammer." Negroes were often the victims of such practices.[74]

Just as ships bred radicals, these unhealthy conditions bred illness and disease.[75] But if such a malady befell a sailor at sea, he was generally out of luck, for there were no doctors on merchant ships.[76] When an injury took place, someone had to open a first-aid manual—perhaps "take a stiff drink to steady his nerves" and give the patient a stiffer one—and plunge into the unknown.[77]

On top of it all, there was the mighty and majestic horror represented by Mother Nature, so awesome that it pushed seamen to flights of rhetorical fancy. One sailor recalled when "waves went over us. The decks were solid ice. Whole tractor trailers were washed over the side. A forty-five ton truck crane was loose on the deck like a battering ram. House trailers on the second deck were completely demolished. . . . You cross from awe to terror." It was a "rogue wave, an overhanging freak wave . . . often described as a 'wall of water.'" In a photograph it would appear "to be a sheer cliff of much greater height than the ship from which the picture was taken." It could "break a ship in [two] in one lick."

If this happened to huge ships, the fate that befell the smaller ones was a lot worse. The latter could be thoroughly destroyed by icing. Ocean sprays could freeze and thicken on the deck, with freezing rains adding to the mix. The ice could become so heavy that the ship "almost disappears within it before the toppling weight rolls her over and sinks her" without a trace.[78] This was the difficult environment in which Smith and other sailors toiled and that fueled their protest.[79]

Smith's job as steward was particularly challenging. As he recounted it, "After a couple of months at sea, even the best-cooked food gets monotonous. Someone in the deck gang starts treating the stewards department like 'flunkies.' The cook [or] messman may have gone through this enough times so he starts with a chip on his shoulder anyway, and he gets sore at the deck and black gang. The black gang may be setting themselves apart from both stewards and deck because they think that their work is more technical and therefore more important." Smith saw this as petty divisiveness that ultimately undercut the interests of sailors. "To my way of thinking," he insisted, "it's high time all such attitudes were given the deep six . . . the time is long passed when we can drift along and tolerate the luxury of petty differences."[80]

Smith himself recalled that on pre-NMU passenger ships, the "steward's department" was at work at 5 A.M. and worked without a break until 10 P.M. or midnight, seven days a week, rain or shine. Quarters were "unbelievably crowded, unventilated and filthy. Pay was pitifully small. . . . Conditions under outright slavery could be little worse. . . . As usual, under such conditions, the Negroes in the industry got the worst of everything—inferior jobs in those departments where they were permitted to work, discrimination in hiring, segregated quarters, and even worse abuse than was handed out to the white crew members. They not only got the worst jobs but the worst ships. A Negro couldn't even go on the gangplank of a decent ship. . . . Anyone who tried to take up a grievance with the union agent was called a Communist trouble maker. . . . There was no union organization aboard the ships. Ship's meetings were unknown. . . . What job security there was could only be realized by working continuously, keeping your mouth shut about abuses and never objecting to any form of exploitation, no matter how flagrant the injustice."[81]

A ship's steward had a hard life. Even though he had the crucial job of making sure that the crew was fed, Smith recalled ruefully that the "chief steward is practically a nonentity on board ship." Since stewards were often Negroes, there may have been "racial" reasons for his low status. Then there was the ever-present problem of finding adequate food abroad at reasonable prices. "Most of these countries where the ship puts into port," Smith recalled, "have very little for themselves in the line of any ship of food. . . . When he cannot procure these provisions, they believe that he is [in] cahoots with the captain or somebody, to keep them from getting their just demands." Then, after managing to procure food, the next problem was getting it on board. Because of the endemic problem of smuggling by sailors—even stewards—they had to submit to an intrusive regime of searching and filching by certain authorities. The steward generally "has to see the mate, who in turn wants an o.k. from the skipper (who most of the time is not on board). . . . In the meantime that milk is getting hot on the dock, the longshoremen are using the bread for their lunch, and also rifling the rest of the stuff."

"At most of the meetings on board the ship, both going and coming, the steward is generally the first to be harassed at the beginning, during the voyage and at the end of the voyage." The steward's department "is like no other," Smith thought.

> It is their failure to realize this situation that often makes the steward bitter, antagonistic, and the object of charges when the ship arrives in port. . . . Many voyages, especially lengthy ones, are rife with bitterness, animosity, name calling, which winds up with charges and counter-charges against this and that fellow upon arrival in port.

Moreover,

> where the voyage is long and tedious, and where the majority of the men get sick of looking at one another, nerves get frayed, and the least little touch of spoken word is liable to start an explosion. All of this

stuff generally bounces back on the grade of grub they have been getting lately, which is generally, of course, the harassed chief steward.

The steward, Smith reminded his readers, "is a human being and
should be treated as such. Stewards are getting fed up with this problem being referred to as a laughing matter and the butt of corny jokes
from a lot of our officials."

So how did Smith handle this thankless job? "I make it my business
to tell the membership at the beginning of the voyage, just what we are
in for, and what we might be up against, and then ask for and demand
cooperation." The problem was that a steward—often a Negro—was in
a sensitive position and represented a difficult confluence of "race" and
class. Thus, even after the founding of the NMU, Smith found that "too
many delegates approach the steward in a commanding and disre-
spectful manner in presenting their beefs." Fortunately, an avowedly
antiracist union like the NMU did not automatically oppose the steward. For Smith acknowledged that "this union has a certain amount of
fakers who are lazy, incompetent, overtime hungry and are general nui-
sances aboard any ship. We, as members" he told the rank and file,
"should take immediate steps to weed out, with special emphasis on
the OUT . . . these characters before they put this union into serious trouble."[82] The chief steward was part chef and part counselor. His job represented one of the highest rungs on the socioeconomic ladder that
Negro men could reach during the era of Jim Crow.

The bad working conditions were not the only factor that helped to create seafaring radicals. As Marcus Rediker has observed, the ship

> was not only a self-contained world but very much a world apart. . . .
> The absence of family, church and state—the primary institutions that
> organized social life—created a power vacuum within the wooden
> world. . . . The isolation of life at sea produced within the tar intensi-
> fied awareness of actual and symbolic uses of power and a powerful
> need for self-defense.

The "ethic of egalitarianism both grew from and was nourished by the
manifold vulnerabilities of life at sea."[83]

In short, sailors' work conditions were a far cry from those of their
fellow workers and proletarians. Bertha Reynolds, a social worker who

worked closely with the NMU, recalled that seafaring forges a "sense of group association" because "a ship's crew has to live with one another twenty four hours a day. They must tolerate each other's queerness [*sic*]. . . . They can never ignore the effect on others of what they do, or not do." The rough conditions that sailors faced at sea and on land in dangerous foreign ports steeled them. "Walking the streets all night to keep warm, going without food and sleep. . . . A man who has done that, and knows he can do it again if he must, has an independence that is not frightened by minor catastrophes, nor easily forced to accept conditions for help that seem to him degrading."[84]

In addition, the rolling oceans themselves had a strange impact on the very marrow of sailors. Herman Ferguson, a former sailor, says that men would get on board ship with their hands shaking violently from the ravages of alcohol abuse and the like; some could not pick up a fork and had to eat from a plate like a dog. They would "sit down to eat and take a towel to put around . . . their neck to pull their head down" into the plate as they shook "like a leaf" buffeted by a strong gale. But after a few weeks of fresh sea air, he said, this condition would clear up magically. Ferguson used to wear glasses until he went to sea; after a few voyages and the soothing effects of "salt spray" and "sea air," he was able to toss them overboard.[85] This meant he could read more of the leftist literature routinely found in the small libraries on board.

The group solidarity, the severe setting, the absence of intervening institutions such as the church, perhaps even the bracing sea air, made the sea a happy hunting ground for Communists. Sailors were also notoriously irreligious.[86] As one old salt put it, "a ship's course is not determined by religious beliefs, race worship, personal inclinations or utopian dreams. A ship's course is determined by the navigator's scientific knowledge of nature."[87] The constant challenges presented by nature further reinforced a materialist outlook; when challenged, there were "no prayers until all was lost, because praying was, in a sense, an admission that human effort had failed. The sailor's perspective was formed by "the nature and setting of their work and was based upon [an] essentially materialistic view of nature, a desire to make an omnipotent nature seem orderly and comprehensible, and a need to entrust [to] each other their prospects for survival."

And just as a mutiny could succeed in the claustrophobic environs of a ship "with the support of only 20–30 percent of the crew so long as the majority of the seamen could be counted upon to remain neutral or to join up once the seizure of power was underway," so too the Marxist and materialist ideas of Communists could prevail with a similar level of support—or perhaps less.[88] The atheism, the austere setting, and the travels to all manner of climes made seafarers notably susceptible to radical appeals. Certainly this was true for Ferdinand Smith, coming as he did from an island with a history of volatile militancy and arriving on another island, Manhattan, where a West Indian population was beginning to make a similar mark.

I

Sailing the Red Seas

IN 1875 the marine engineers formalized their Cleveland-based fraternal lodge into a labor union, the Marine Engineers' Beneficial Association. This was quickly followed by the formation of the Lake Seamen's Association, thereby launching trade unionism among sailors. Early on sailors displayed the militancy that NMU and Ferdinand Smith were to exemplify. The Coast Seamen's Union, for example, affiliated with the International Workingmen's Association, a branch of Karl Marx's First International, and was run by an Advisory Committee made up of IWA members, in accordance with CSU's constitution. In July 1891, the seafarer Andrew Furuseth persuaded the various sailors' unions to combine into the Sailors' Union of the Pacific, which was a precursor to the International Seamen's Union (which joined the American Federation of Labor in 1894). Thus began a new stage of trade unionism at sea.[1]

Eight years later the marine firemen, oilers, watertenders, and wipers' union was formed to represent the interests of the unlicensed workers in a ship's engine rooms.[2] As labor was combining, so was capital—the two trends were related. In 1902, the year he founded U.S. Steel, J. P. Morgan also "set out to gain control of liner shipping in the North Atlantic. He created a new shipping company, the International Mercantile Marine (IMM)," which at its zenith "owned 136 ships, or about one-third of all vessels engaged in foreign trade." These "purchases gave Morgan the largest privately owned commercial fleet in the world, one which was equal in tonnage to the entire French merchant marine. . . . At that stage only Cunard, the dominant Atlantic carrier, lay outside Morgan's control." This was the formidable foe faced by sailors seeking to unionize.[3]

As the SUP saw it, there was yet another cloud hovering over the horizon, namely, immigrant Chinese men whom it saw as low-wage competitors for jobs that belonged properly to men of European descent. Andrew Furuseth, the first major leader of sailors in the United

States, "worked to renew the Chinese Exclusion Act and to extend it to all Orientals." Reflecting the prevailing doctrines of white supremacy, "one of his chief arguments . . . was always that, unless white men were brought back to the sea, the yellow race would win mastery of the sea, and, with it, mastery of the world." Fortunately, not all sailors responded to such odious appeals. In 1913 Spanish-speaking firemen left Furuseth's union to join the IWW; the strength of the IWW was underscored when it "gained complete control of the port of New Orleans, where it conducted an unsuccessful strike in 1913."[4]

But Furuseth's men had far more clout in Washington than either the Chinese or the IWW seamen. In 1915 the "Seamen's (LaFollette) Act halted shipping of Chinese crews by requiring that 75 percent of the members of any ship's department be able to understand English."[5] Such discriminatory language requirements did, however, create opportunities for English-speaking seafarers like Smith, especially since Furuseth "never publicly attacked the Negro race," although Negroes were not welcomed into his union either.[6] Indeed, "checkerboarding" or the integration of black workers into white crews, was not permitted, and for decades blacks were excluded from the West Coast unions.[7]

Furuseth's union's capitulation to "racial chauvinism," showed that it was not equipped to cope with the changing dynamics of the maritime industry, which created an enormous opening for the more "racially" sensitive Communists. When Smith entered the maritime industry,[8] "no Black man was assigned as a sailor, an engineer, a mechanic, carpenter, an electrician, radio operator or an officer—no matter what the Black worker's qualifications might be. A Black worker could only work as a cook, messman, waiter or elsewhere in the steward's department."[9] But big changes were afoot in the industry. By the time World War I came to a close, "union membership had grown to 117,000, seamen's wages had risen to $85 per month and seamen serving on the deck for the first time achieved an eight hour workday."[10] As the United States traded with both sides during the conflict, then confronted Germany for its alleged aggression against nonmilitary ships, the maritime industry endured a roller-coaster ride of advance and retreat that morphed into a lingering recession throughout the 1920s. Given what the capitalist economy could absorb at the time, there were simply too many ships and too many sailors—the global economy was slowing down and the need for ships and sailors shrank accordingly. The resultant shakeout in the industry left numerous seafarers in difficult financial straits.[11] After several failed strikes during this tumultuous decade, the membership of the International Seamen's Union plummeted from more than 100,000 to "fewer than 3000 by 1929."[12]

Yet by 1934, 293,000 people were involved in foreign or interstate shipping. Of this total, 145,000 were in foreign, coastal, or intercoastal commerce, 25,000 on the Great Lakes, and 15,000 on inland waterways. This was a major opportunity for radical trade union organizers.[13] And when a "suddenly awakened Congress . . . passed the 'Merchant Marine Act of 1936'" which, inter alia, "closed our coastal, intercoastal routes and those to Hawaii, Porto Rico and Alaska to all but American ships," domestic shipbuilding and the maritime industry generally both received a boost.[14]

Moved by this upturn in the industry and less concerned that militancy would sink the industry further into debt, in 1936 the ISU went on strike against the Pacific Coast employers. It restricted the strike to the West Coast as a matter of tactics, avoiding overextension and perhaps an unwelcome counterreaction by the employers. A group of East Coast sailors—with Ferdinand Smith in the leadership—nonetheless joined in a sympathy strike both to back their comrades out west and to obtain a better contract for themselves, as their wages often lagged behind those of their Pacific counterparts. They wanted to establish a union-controlled hiring hall and to get rid of the "continuous discharge book," which they saw as a means of compelling a seafarer to carry on his person evidence that would allow him to be "blacklisted." They also wanted more safety at sea and improved working conditions.[15] But "the strike . . . formally ended on January 24, 1937. It gained nothing, in increased wages or improved working conditions," wrote Philip Taft, "but the leaders of the walkout boasted that it had discredited the old union officials. The insurgent leaders sought to take over the name of the International Seamen's Union for the new union they were forming but when they were prevented by the courts, they called themselves the National Maritime Union of America."[16]

Meanwhile the rise of the Congress of Industrial Organizations (CIO) was creating a new chapter in labor history. The newly formed NMU demanded and won representational elections and by 1938 was the exclusive bargaining agent for many of the fifty-two Atlantic steamship companies. The ISU remnant became the Seafarers International Union (SIU) representing workers on the Gulf Coast while in the west, the ISU "dissolved into three separate unions that represented unlicensed personnel." While unions in the steel and auto industries were growing in strength, in the maritime industry "competing unions continued to fight each other."[17]

Communist patriarch William Z. Foster, a former sailor himself, was blunt: "Seamen probably know more about imperialism than any other group of workers. . . . They sail the ships that carry the fruits of imperialist exploitation. They sail the ships that carry the guns and men that are needed to subjugate other peoples for imperialist exploitation."[18] Another radical put it this way: "Seamen built the capitalist world; it is natural they should also destroy it."[19] Communists played a dominant role in the NMU.[20] The confined setting, the poor working conditions, the attenuated effect of the church and other mediating institutions, the exposure to foreign lands and ideas—all this and more contributed to the growing impact of the Communist Party among sailors.

The Reds were not alone in seeking to cater to sailors. The Industrial Workers of the World (IWW) organized a Marine Transport Workers Union. A. Philip Randolph's journal, *The Messenger,* described its Philadelphia branch as exemplifying the "ability of white and black people to work, live and conduct their common affairs side by side." During this era of virulent Jim Crow, at MTWU social affairs, "the workers also mingle, fraternize, dance, eat and play together."[21]

Despite the longstanding reputation of maritime workers for militancy and radical consciousness—especially under the leadership of the IWW—the Communist Party[22] "paid little attention to the waterfront" in the 1920s as Smith was moving to join their ranks. However, in 1926 the party formed "International Seamen's Clubs" in several port cities in the United States and around the world. These clubs played a social and educational role, "providing facilities for reading, recreation and dining."[23]

The Trade Unity Educational League (TUEL), which had close ties to the Communist Party, was cooperating with the IWW in "various fields" in 1926. The IWW was suffering "disintegration . . . losing their headquarters"—and many members at this time.[24] This presented an opportunity for the youthful Communist Party—USA, though not without a problem. For one thing the Communists had been slow to organize among the militant sailors because the leaders at the highest levels of the party felt that it was almost impossible to have rank and file democracy in a union when the membership was scattered at sea.

Sailors had a justifiable reputation for rowdiness and dissolute living—having a sweetheart in every port was no exaggeration. There was something about those who sailed the seven seas that inclined them toward the rambunctious. Despite the notable successes of Reds in organizing sailors, this factor seems to have been stronger than they anticipated. Moreover, according to one Red analysis, there was the "beach comber element, the type which is known as the 'lumpen proletariat' and hall loafers" who "conduct affairs and usually conform to the wishes of whatever officialdom dominates. Organizing a left wing and keeping it functioning under such circumstances is a puzzle which we have been unable to solve."

Then there were the anarchists among the seafarers, who had begun "organized violence slugging our left wingers in the Manhattan Branch's meeting." Not all of them were domestic. There were some "French anarchists of recent arrival in America," who—horror of all horrors—"fought . . . against the Soviet power" in the USSR.[25] Before the advent of the NMU, hiring was "done by 'shapeup,'" for example, the boss just "points his finger at men he wanted or via 'crimps'—proprietors of boarding houses who supplied crews to the shipping companies and one way or another did the seamen out of practically all their wages."[26] The setup was unlikely to attract choirboys and boy scouts.

However, the Communists were able to overcome these barriers. The anarchists were in a slow and steady decline in the United States that the boost of the Spanish Civil War could not arrest. The Depression convinced a critical mass of sailors that their lives could only improve with organization. Strong and centralized leadership dealt with the problem presented by the sailors' transience.

The Communists' antiracism—which was so contrary to the general sentiment in the United States—made them especially appealing to Negroes. This did not escape the attention of the New York Times, which noted in 1926, "Dr. Du Bois . . . thinks it is up to white people of America to treat the Negroes better in order to keep them out of the Communist ranks."[27] Yet better treatment would have implied supporting "racial equality" and thus violating a reigning taboo in the United States.

Although the Communists had their own problems, these may not have repelled Negroes. Reds were ostracized by a broad spectrum of people—but so were Negroes, so this was hardly an obstacle to their recruiting Negroes in a place like Harlem. Even Red critiques of would-be allies (for example, the NAACP [National Association for the Advancement of Colored People]), before the "popular front" was proclaimed in the mid-1930s, did not deter Negroes. Though the Communist Party was criticized for sectarianism when it organized unions independent of the mainstream American Federation of Labor, this facilitated the inclusion of Negro workers, which the federation generally ignored.[28]

Not concentrating on the AFL did encourage the Communist Party to focus more intently on other constituencies, such as Negroes. Unavoidably, this brought the Reds into contact with the Universal Negro Improvement Association—Marcus Garvey's organization—which included many West Indians within its ranks. By the mid-1920s, Garvey was on the fast track to being deported and his organization was splintering. The Communist Party sought to work with an "anti-Garvey faction" in the UNIA, which contained "the best and the proletarian elements. New York is the stronghold of this mass movement."[29] Shipping was the stronghold of the Garvey movement, as its "Black Star Line" was a symbol of repatriation and a vehicle for commerce. But because Garvey's ships, such as the *Yarmouth*, were dependent on a "white chief engineer" and a "white first mate" (the former being accused of the "treachery" that led to the Jamaican leader's deportation) the party, which was strong in the maritime industry, could make inroads among Garveyites.[30]

The Communist Party's reference to "proletarian elements" was an indication of its disdain for the "middle class" said to dominate the NAACP. Reds had helped to build the American Negro Labor Congress—a kind of leftist labor-oriented NAACP—in a conscious effort to attract people like Ferdinand Smith. Its first convention, which focused on organizing Negro workers, was in Chicago in the fall of 1925. At that time, the ANLC was far from being reflexively and firmly anti-Garvey. Indeed, it sent a telegram of support to Marcus Garvey, who was languishing in a jail cell in Atlanta, calling his imprisonment "persecution. . . . We demand your unconditional and immediate release," and it criticized his possible "deportation."[31] On the other hand, in 1924 the Communist Party sent a long and critical letter to the UNIA, focusing "on the question of your attitude toward the Ku Klux Klan."[32]

Militants from the ANLC—including a number of West Indians—were dispatched to the UNIA convention in 1926.[33] Like the anti-Garvey faction, the ANLC forces were "stimulating criticism of Garvey and his tactics." This led to a suggestion for a "joint campaign of the UNIA and ANLC" on various antiracist matters,[34] such as antilynching.

Despite its appearance of militant activity, the ANLC's self-importance was exaggerated. A scant year after the founding convention in 1925, the ANLC existed "merely as an office in Chicago with three party comrades . . . supposedly functioning as the directing body." Although "ten thousand" copies of its journal were being printed regularly, "there are not more than three or four thousand subscribers and no payments have been received worth mentioning for the bundles sent out."[35] From Chicago came the news in early 1926 that "total dues received from units of the ANLC for two months is $6.45 or an average of 32½ dues paying members in the entire country. . . . The ANLC seems to have no active membership or functioning groups outside of Chicago, where there is a group of 50 members."[36]

It is easy to understand why and how a Jamaican sailor like Ferdinand Smith was able to rise quickly within Communist ranks. Apart from the fact that he had the proper class background, more importantly he was willing to stick with the Communists at a time when their strength among Negroes was in need of replenishment. Early in the party's history, an internal memo "discussed extensively the question of the dissatisfied condition of the Negro membership both in Chicago and New York which leads to many becoming inactive." There was "'whispered' disaffection" about "supposed or real wrongs."[37] A few years later it was reported that "white chauvinism is still rampant in the districts."[38] Otto Huiswood told party leader James Ford in 1929 that "Negro work" is "very bad" in the Red-affiliated Trade Union Unity League.[39] Even so, as of November 1931 there were 971 Negroes in the ranks of the Reds out of a "total membership" of 8,743.[40]

Despite these glaring weaknesses among Negroes, the party did intermittently devote attention to this critical sector. Just before this membership report was filed, the party decided to "assign an organizer for the West Indies. . . . As soon as possible, a weekly paper shall be started for the West Indies to be centered in Jamaica."[41] Later, on the initiative of the party, the ANLC reached out to the "Jamaica Trades Union[s]" and actively sought "material on the conditions of the Negro masses in Latin America, especially in the Caribbean countries."[42] In 1929 Otto Huiswood instructed his "dear comrades" that "recent developments in Haiti" are "very important." "We are doing everything possible," he declared, "in order to arouse the Negro workers to protest against the action of the American government in the sending of Marines to Haiti."[43] Two years later a "confidential" proposal called on the party to "initiat[e] activities in the British West Indies" by forming "committees for support of the national liberation struggles of the West Indian masses . . . especially in centers of West Indian Population" such as New York City. In Manhattan, despite periodic expressions of white supremacy, immigrants like Smith could be comforted by the presence of at least one interracial organization that was welcoming. The party specifically sought "contact with and organizational work among West Indian seamen and dockers" and work among "Marine Workers Union of the U.S."[44]

Yet at the same time party operatives were complaining about the "neglect of work among Negroes."[45] Recent European immigrants were known to play a significant role within the Communist Party. It appears that the Negroes who played a leading role during the early years of the Communist Party were likewise immigrants—West Indians like Smith.[46] These immigrants' struggles for self-determination in their homelands may have influenced the Communist Party to adopt the controversial thesis that African Americans merited self-determina- tion—a position that led to the criticism that the Reds were espousing segregation. The prevailing notion was that the "hand of Moscow"[47] was at work here, though one of Smith's West Indian comrades, Cyril Briggs, affirmed that he was "inspired, as you have no doubt guessed, by Wilson's Fourteen Points."[48] Certainly Jamaicans like Smith would be more attracted to an organization that was concerned about their homeland and their "race." Such concerns augmented the black ranks of the party in the United States.

Despite its weaknesses, it would be an error to underestimate the im- pact of the party among Negroes, particularly as it was the most pow- erfully organized interracial political force that was so militantly con- frontational about white supremacy. Despite its frailties, the ANLC, for example, managed in 1928 to mobilize "in support of a group of black seamen who came under attack after the SS *Vestris* sank in stormy seas in November 1928. Black firemen on board had worked feverishly for twenty-four hours to maintain steam and pump the bilges; when told to take lifeboats, they nevertheless sought to help passengers first. . . .

Some crew members and passengers perished." Yet "an investigation by the U.S. attorney alleg[ed] cowardice" on the crew's part. The ANLC "organized a rally that attracted twelve hundred people to St. Luke's Hall in Harlem."[49] In 1930 a leading black sociologist noted that "except for" the IWW and the "Communist vehicle, 'the American Negro Labor Congress,' militancy in the advocacy of Negro membership in trade unions has not been a forte of organized labor in America."[50]

Black support for the Communist Party was not confined to the North. James Allen, former party organizer in the South, observes that in the late 1920s and early 1930s "scattered among Southern cities" there were a "few party sympathizers and beached militant seamen" who "carried on some activity in the Gulf ports." Not surprisingly, whatever strength the party had in the South was in the ports and among sailors.

Violence against the Communist Party was well known in the South. In New Orleans, for example, mere "possession" of the party paper "was considered sufficient cause for persecution." It was routine for "meetings of the Communist Party [to be] broken up" in the South and Southwest "because the Communist spokesmen dared to tackle the Negro question and were bold enough to call the Negro workers to their meetings."[51] In response, the party took extraordinary security measures. As a precaution, "each of us left [meetings] singly and at intervals of a few minutes."[52]

In Norfolk, another port city, "most of the white members of a party unit were expelled for refusal to admit the Negro comrades to their meetings."[53] A party report noted that "even members of our party fraction in these unions have the habit of referring to Negro workers in the contemptuous term used by the white bourgeoisie as 'Niggers.' . . . Any party member using this term should be severely censured and if he continues, should be expelled."[54]

Nevertheless, in 1934 there was a strike in Norfolk of "seven or eight hundred, directly under the leadership" of the MWIU. "All the strikers were Negroes and . . . on the first day of the strike there was a mass recruitment of scabs, 90% of them whites."[55] This Virginia city had become deeply divided along class and "racial" lines. After the strike, however, a "Negro lawyer defended white seamen [in] court and the bail for their release was furnished by Negroes. Negro and white seamen marched to the relief headquarters and put up a joint battle for relief and got it." This was an enormous breakthrough, considering in

New York City that same year the Communist Party complained that "many Negro seamen are still discriminated against on relief."[56]

Yet New York City continued to surpass most other cities in recruiting Negroes. In 1930, for example, "114 out of 954 new recruits" were Negroes, though Detroit had an even larger number. The party, it was said, "is still sadly deficient in the work of training Negro comrades for leadership, in the drawing of Negro comrades into active and leading work in the party. . . . In the whole party we have only two full-time Negro work directors (New York and Chicago)" and it was woefully unsuccessful in attracting Negro women.[57]

Even so, in the early 1930s the party boasted mildly that "only in the present year has the party work among the Negro masses begun to have the character of a serious struggle," with unemployment relief and the cases of Angelo Herndon and the Scottsboro Nine being pivotal. This "laid the *first proletarian foundations of the Communist Party in the southern states*"[58] [emphasis in original]. Though the party may have been surging among Negroes, there were still complaints about Communist Party strength among maritime workers: "We haven't paid enough attention to waterfront workers," a report said in 1932, "we haven't been able to get action by deep seamen."[59] Similarly, though there may have been some Communist advance among Negroes in southern states, there were still nagging complaints about the north. In 1934 the Trade Union Unity League (TUUL), closely affiliated to the party, lamented that "at the present there is practically no trade union organization to speak of among Negroes in New York City. . . . At the present time most of the Negroes are organized into churches, clubs, fraternal societies, etc." TUUL had sought to "send our forces inside [the] workers councils" of the National Urban League in order to convey the "correct line" and build the "revolutionary trade unions among the Negroes in Harlem." A leading TUUL member reported that he had "attended two or three meetings of the Negro Clerical Alliance and listened carefully to them outline the program. [They] say the whites will betray you and the only thing is for the Negroes to organize into separate trade unions."[60] This was the hurdle that the NMU would soon try to overcome.

But all was not bleak. In Harlem on a single day in the spring of 1933 the Unemployed Council fought seventeen evictions, returning possessions in three cases; a major Scottsboro meeting was held at the Abyssinian Baptist Church; a Harlem branch of the Food Workers Industrial Union was formed; and three hundred people demonstrated at the home relief bureau, demanding money for rent.[61] It was in this context that the NMU was founded with critical support from Negro sailors—and Ferdinand Smith.

The NMU was formed after a protracted and violent struggle. The incident that occurred on the Gulf Coast in Galveston in late 1936 was typical. An "ex-friend" accused his former comrade of "double crossing the maritime strikers . . . in this strike" referring to "first class 'sell out artists' and natural finks." Moreover, "when this strike is over," he continued, "every Maritime Union is going to have a 'house cleaning' and put real union men in office at the same time that they crowd the scabs out of the industry."[62] Actually, this attempt to "crowd" out the scabs had begun even before the strike had ended. "There has been an unusual outbreak of violence over this past weekend," Robert Gurton reported in Houston in late 1936. "The law has threatened us." On the Gulf Coast, where Negro waterfront workers were prominent, Smith's leadership was even more critical. "The white ILA [longshore] say they will walk out when the Negroes do, and the Negroes say that they will take action when the whites do."[63] This standoff ended in failure for unionizing efforts when "the colored longshoremen after some heated arguments did go thru the picket lines with police protection and worked one of Jimmy Lyke's ships."[64]

Many Negroes felt that the status quo was about as good as it could get. The presence of a Negro—David Grange—as ISU leader, convinced them that those trying to replace him would not improve their position: that was one reason why Smith's very presence was reassuring.[65] The ability to neutralize or in some cases win over the longshoremen, particularly in the south where the ousting of Negro stevedores had not been entirely successful, was essential to the ultimate victory of the NMU.[66] R. T. Moore, president of Moore Mill and Lumber Company in Oregon would not have concurred with this assessment. Most of all, he was concerned about the "strong evidence that the action of these seamen was influenced by Communists."[67]

Mass picketing, tumultuous rallies, hunger, and violence marked the birth of this union. The strike was "very bloody," as NMU leader Joseph Curran recalled it: "Twenty eight of our people up and down the coast were killed. They were found mashed up on the docks, they were found in the river, one was shot through the stomach in the union hall in Houston, Texas. There was all kind of butchery. . . . The gangsters got into the picture."[68] The violence had a sharp racist edge. NMU member Joe Weiner argued that during the strike "the Negro brothers sustained more casualties in dead, maimed and jailed than their percentage in the union. The colored brothers include West Indians, Filipinos and Puerto Ricans."[69]

U.S. Negroes made an enormous contribution to this organizing effort. A "Harlem Group . . . to aid strikers" included Communist leader James Ford and Thyra Edwards of the National Negro Congress (NNC), among others, the NNC being in the vanguard.[70] The party had a unique contribution to make during strikes. They had begun organizing among the unemployed and could mobilize legions of them for picket line duty.[71] Nationally there was sizable mass support for the insurgents. In mid-1936 a "Citizens Committee for Seamen" held a Manhattan benefit featuring Bob Hope, Will Geer, Jack Dempsey, Heywood Broun, and James Cagney. "This is the first time," the *ISU Pilot* reported, "in the history of the labor movement and Broadway that stars have appeared for a benefit for seamen who are blacklisted for strike activities."[72]

This broad support reflected the fact that not only were workers upset with the industry but so were passengers, who continued to rely on ships for intercontinental travel. In the spring of 1936 W. D. Gelsleichter told President Franklin D. Roosevelt bluntly that "within the past two years there have occurred two major sea disasters, involving American ships, causing the loss of lives of several hundreds of American citizens. . . . Little or nothing has been done by the national government to inquire into the causes of these disasters or to institute measures to prevent their repetition. . . . The shipping interests are becoming more and more solidly entrenched in our Department of Commerce." Inevitably, this meant that "riots, mutinies and sabotage are occurring on American ships."[73] The status quo was dysfunctional—but also ripe for radical reform.[74]

Emerging from this conflict was Ferdinand Smith. In these grim days he was one of the nine men elected to the Strategy Committee of the nascent union that spearheaded East Coast organizing of sailors. Smith agreed to be the lone Negro member on this committee, though not without qualification: "I accept on one condition. If we win, the union will not tolerate segregation or discrimination of any sort." The vote for Smith was second only to that of the NMU's eventual leader and Smith's eventual foil, Joseph Curran.[75]

Smith's popularity was understandable for, as noted, he headed the Food Committee of the budding union, an important committee given that sailors, like many others, were suffering due to the economic depression. There was a soup kitchen on the west side of Manhattan that fed an average of seventeen hundred men daily. Downtown at South Street, an average of one thousand men were fed daily. In Hoboken, two hundred men enjoyed three meals per day and in Brooklyn, there were one thousand more. This was a massive administrative, managerial, and organizational project. Smith's ability to solicit funds for food, oversee its preparation, and coordinate its dispersal had won him many admirers among seafarers.[76] Smith arranged to have "waterfront restaurants . . . used to feed strikers" and by late 1936 had organized a soup kitchen, though he complained that "we barely have enough money to keep going from day to day."[77]

In the port of New York alone there were approximately ten thousand men on the picket lines, an estimated three thousand of them being Negroes—and the latter were hungry not only for food but also for representation in the leadership ranks of organizations they had helped build.[78] They found their man in Smith, as his rapidly became the most articulate voice among the leadership against all forms of division among sailors, "racial" or otherwise. "It wasn't so long ago," he recalled in 1937, "that all of us can't remember when the Stewards were played against the Deck and Engine divisions by the shipowners. . . . This craft snobbishness has no place in the NMU. . . . Stewards—more company minded than union conscious—were used by the companies to chisel on the other two divisions. They served bad food and little of it." Stewards were hired by shippers directly while others went through "fink and crimp halls" to be hired. "Because of the nature of their work, cooks and stewards have lagged behind in their development as trade unionists," a condition that Smith was determined to overcome.[79]

Exploration of the divisiveness of the ranks in the maritime trade helps to shed light on why Smith himself became, perhaps, the most powerful Negro trade unionist in the country. For a potent leader of the ISU, perhaps its most visible symbol at the time of its clash with Smith, was yet another Negro, David E. Grange. It was indicative of their historic strength among seafarers that even during the height of the Jim Crow era, Negroes played a leading role in the ranks. Unfortunately, their leader, David E. Grange,[80] was a tarnished relic, though his obvious weaknesses did pave the way for the rise of a Communist-dominated NMU—and Ferdinand Smith. Over six feet tall with a smooth light-brown skin, Grange too was of Jamaican origin; but unlike the more abstemious Smith, Grange favored a cane and spats, fragrant cigars, and a fresh flower in his lapel—not to mention a pistol.[81]

Harlem leader Adam Clayton Powell, Jr. was dismissive of Grange, calling him the "brains directing this false union. As a Negro he has enforced segregation on the Negro members of the union. By his expressed orders no Negroes are allowed in the central headquarters." Yet Powell, the pastor and politician, was disturbed that though "strike headquarters, 164 Eleventh Avenue" was "under the leadership of Smith and [Oliver] Boutte, both Negroes," the "tragic note is that while the white crews are striking 100 per cent [some] Negroes are refusing to strike and acting as scabs and strike breakers."[82] Together with Lester Granger of the National Urban League and Ben Davis, Jr. of the Communist Party, Powell was a leader of the "Harlem Committee to aid the Striking Seamen" and they had to convince Negroes that dislodging Grange would not mean a setback for black sailors.[83] Smith's presence in the leadership was meant to ensure that such a setback would not occur.

Grange,[84] a key leader of the ISU,[85] did not hesitate to deploy intimidating tactics. This may have influenced some Negroes to leave the union.[86] Yet some NMU stalwarts expressed a grudging admiration for him. Clyde Deal referred to him as a "happy go lucky Negro. . . . Papa Dave," they called him: "I liked him immensely." "Papa Dave" was earning a handsome $10,000 per year at a time when many of his compatriots were selling apples for a pittance in the streets. He was instrumental in revising the ISU Constitution to make elections more difficult in a vain attempt to extend his rule indefinitely.[87]

Nonetheless, Negro sailors had good reason to wonder whether their lot would improve if Grange were to be forced out.[88] As Joseph Curran recalled it, the Eastern Steamship Company "had all Negroes in the steward department, [they] had been there many years. . . . They started a vicious propaganda campaign, that if the Negroes voted for the [NMU] they would be replaced by whites." Because of that the Negroes voted against the dissidents. Though the NMU won an overwhelming majority of the elections it contested—and "all the big companies"—it "had pretty tough times in southern ports," particularly Houston and Galveston. Mobile was "not a problem at all. In Tampa, Jacksonville . . . no problem. We had no port in Mississippi." Texas had not only a racism problem but there was also the issue of the IWW, which "wanted a Gulf Seamen's Union," a concept antithetical to the NMU.[89]

But even the most desperate Negro sailors, and particularly those in the U.S. South, worried that dumping Grange and entrusting their fate to the white leadership of a competing union, the NMU, might not be wise; this is why Smith's presence in the leadership was so crucial. In Houston, where the Deep South met the "Wild West," Grange's supporters in late 1936 included longshoremen, "most" of whom were Negroes and "very backward," according to one insurgent.[90] They were "getting more restless daily. Many of them refuse to work at all. Most of those that do work, go through our picket lines with lowered heads and when questioned, admit they know [what] they are doing." Balancing this setback was the fact that "the labor movement in Mexico has just notified us and the whole public that all hot cargo would be boycotted there." But there was another problem. "David Grange was to have a meeting of his Marine Cooks and Stewards today. About 1000 of the members that he is supposed to have expelled were denied admittance. These men formed a picket line outside so no one attended. He as well as the rest of the ISU officials are getting batty. Every move they make the rank and file are a way ahead of them."[91]

In Houston, the press was aghast at an "exhibition of fascism" as "drunk" men, "some with alcohol and others with power . . . slugged and beat, kicked and gouged 1150 men." Using "tear gas, guns, blackjacks and fists, police 'cleaned out' the waterfront . . . sending 18 striking seamen to hospital and beating at least 150 more."[92]

In southern cities like Houston, where the idea of a Communist-led union seemed like hell on earth, the insurgents faced a stiff challenge. The "police department," it was said, "is controlled by the steamship owners." There were "wholesale arrests, when 200 picketing seamen were taken from the picket lines and thrown in jail" and "beaten unmercifully by the police. . . . It has been said, and rightly so, that Texas is a country in itself."[93]

Thus, by December 1936 insurgent sailors in south Texas were almost ready to run up the white flag of surrender. The strike was deemed "ineffective and undoubtedly will fizzle out completely [which] suggests strongly we accept . . . terms and have an 'organized retreat' holding organization intact, then gain further demands by 'job actions' after crews are 100% union on ships. The place to build the unions stronger," the West Gulf Conference stated confidently, was not ashore but "on board the ships and men must be on the ships to do it." Morosely, it noted that "strikers' numbers are declining. . . . To preserve unions they must accept the best terms possible and return immediately to ships. A wise general when he sees his army is being annihilated, withdraws and reforms his ranks."[94]

The insurgents had to contend with another force that may have been far more pernicious for Negroes than even police batons and demoralizing advice. Middle-class Negroes in south Texas were leading an organized movement to frighten black waterfront workers away from the insurgents. It was headed by the Reverend C. W. Rice, who once told his patron, the affluent Joseph Cullinan, "so far I have been very successful in educating my people in this section against radical movements."[95] Rice's view was shared by the Galveston attorney, Lewis Valentine Ulrey, who concluded in the fall of 1936 that "there are not six men in the state of Texas who know as much about radicalism as does the man, C. W. Rice. . . . [He] will cooperate with us in any way. . . . He is as tight-mouthed as the proverbial clam." The latter was said to possess a "Booker T. Washington complex." Yet Rice was swimming in dangerous waters, for the same man who praised him also remarked that "Houston Jews contributed $10,000 each to the Communist cause in Houston," as he sought to link anti-Semitism with anticommunism.[96] Fanning the flames of anti-Semitism in the 1930s could not be good news for Negroes, no matter how conservative.

Cullinan, a founder of the company that became Texaco, adamantly declined membership in the National Conference of Christians and Jews. Why? "I have long since reached the conclusion," he said, "that the Jewish race as such always have been and are now and probably always will be parasites on society . . . [because of] their known centralized clannish and secret attitude . . . their attitude as bankers or money changers . . . their cringing and cowardly attitude toward" the Ku Klux Klan, their "activities against the Arabs." Writing in 1933, he was sympathetic to what was being done to Jews in Germany: "There was and is sound ground for . . . concern regarding the increasing control of the Jews . . . in that nation's financial affairs."[97] These bigoted views could come back to haunt Negroes themselves—even reactionaries like Rice. Texaco, a major user of tankers that employed sailors, was representative of the kind of enemy that the insurgents were facing. Indeed, Curran believed that the oil companies were "our toughest enemy."[98]

Like many southern ports, the insurgents in Houston had to contend not only with Negro stevedores who were accustomed to viewing "whites" as "white supremacists," but also with Grange's allies. The insurgents countered by circulating literature referring to the "shipowners' nightmare . . . colored seamen [and] white seamen" together. Why did Grange "continuously play upon . . . racial feelings" yet ignore the fact that stewards were "working 15 and 16 hours a day?" Grange was called the "Emperor Jones" and was asked pointedly, "What has become of $143,000 of union funds?" Grange, the literature said curiously, "has fallen victim to the Oriental influence. . . . He has begun to think of himself as a Rajah of old. He now has his uniformed chauffer [sic] wearing a white turban." Grange was "nothing more than an egotistical, publicity-seeking bag of wind who will say anything to get his name in print."[99] The literature charged that like the stewards, the Negro stevedores were "almost to a man under reactionary control" and the "white men there are mostly old, with very few progressives among them."[100]

On the other hand, it was striking how frequently Grange was targeted among the ISU leadership. Was this because his flamboyance inflamed the rough-hewn sailor? Or was it because he was a Negro— which could inflame even more? Ashley Totten of the Brotherhood of Sleeping Car Porters was suspicious of the "headline prominence given to the strike-breaking tactics of David Grange, the sole Negro member of the leadership."[101] If the Communists—usually in the vanguard on "race" in the United States generally and the labor movement specifically—objected to what appeared to be invidious "race"-based tactics, the evidence does not survive.

Gaining the allegiance of Negro sailors was a major prize in this struggle, and this, along with the need to put forward a Negro leader who could compete with Grange, propelled Ferdinand Smith to the leadership of the union. As noted, in the critically important New York port alone, about one-third of those on the picket line were blacks. No doubt many had families who asked them why they were walking away from jobs in the midst of an economic downturn and turning their backs on one of the few Negroes who had made it to trade union leadership. How could they be sure that ousting Grange would not lead to their own displacement by whites? But walk away they did. They marched through cold, slush, rain, and snow. And many of them were not too fond of "Papa Dave." "Brother Williams" of the "SS *Pan American* of the Munson Line" who had been a steward since 1924, was withering in his appraisal: "The Negro seamen sailing out of the port of New York have been treated very badly. Disunity was fostered by Grange, who pitted one group against the other." On board ship "we were told to stay below and [not] be seen by the passengers and finally a chain was placed across no. 8 hatch to keep us in the stern of the ship"—a potentially fatal maneuver. But now, said Brother Williams, the times were changing: "The colored men to a man swear by [the insurgents]. For the first time on the East and Gulf the colored and white seamen are marching together."[102]

One reason many of the "colored" turned their collective back on Grange, who was ostensibly one of their own, was because of the contrasting leadership provided by another Negro, Ferdinand Smith.[103] "We are faced by certain disruptive elements within the ranks of the Negro workers themselves," Smith noted in late 1937. "They are simply men who through lack of ability and leadership qualities have had their chances as union officials and have failed." He went on to defend the NMU from the taunts of its detractors. "The malcontents base their accusations against the NMU on two general points—the amount of Negroes shipped through the union hall as compared with white members, and the official jobs held by Negroes in the organization." He pointed out that in the Stewards' Division, which had a disproportionately large number of Negroes, there were 18,000 members, "1800 of which are Negroes." "The Negro disrupters assert that jobs in the union are monopolized by white workers to the exclusion of Negroes." This was not true, he asserted. "In the port of New York, there are 15 delegates. Of this number five are Negroes. . . . If the argument of proportional representation were carried out rigorously along the lines of color, Negro seamen would have less representation in the NMU than they have now."[104] Keep your eye on the prize, Smith suggested. Shippers were using racist politics to disrupt the union: "White crews are encouraged to reject Negro replacements and vice versa. Negro departments on some ships have been fired and all-white crews demanded by the companies."[105]

It was not foreordained that the NMU would emerge from the shards of the ISU. By early 1937 the rebels' energy was flagging and there was a serious movement to call for surrender. According to Curran, even when the NMU was formed that same year as "one big union," including people in the crafts and the unskilled, they continued to be viewed as illegitimate by the National Labor Relations Board.[106]

But the insurgents were able to face down such powerful foes.[107] Ferdinand Smith was able to survive the challenge and emerged as the second-ranking leader of one of the nation's most powerful unions. However, he was probably not surprised when shortly thereafter a concerted attempt was made to oust him from his new position.

2

Perilous Waters

THE BIRTH OF THE NMU with Ferdinand Smith in the number two post meant that this "West Indian Negro" was now among the most powerful men in the nation. With a firm grip on imports and exports, oil tankers, and more this union was essential to the lifeblood of the nation. Smith was uniquely qualified compared to other NMU leaders. For one, he was better educated than they were. This was particularly true of Joseph Curran, the titular leader of the union, who was poorly educated.[1]

The Communist Party, of course, played a pivotal role in organizing the NMU. M. Hedley Stone, originally Hedley Stein, was part of the Red crew. He was born in Warsaw, Poland, in 1897 (though his father served in Russia's military) but was raised in Newark, New Jersey. He was dirt poor, diminutive, and Jewish. "Jewish families," he recalled, "frowned upon a man going to sea." Yet somehow he wound up as a Communist and top leader of the NMU, which gave him a good opportunity to observe the party's pervasive influence.

He was close to Curran initially. "No matter what part of the room I would enter at a top meeting of the NMU or CIO executive board, Joe would find me and sit alongside of me. Then I would whisper in his ear comments on someone who would be talking." Stone, the Communist, confided in Curran, the non-Communist. He "told Joe everything we did in the party," though his comrades "didn't think that I should tell Joe everything." But Stone continued his collaboration with Curran: "Joe and I had an understanding that an issue was O.K. if I talked for it. If I kept my mouth shut, it was no good." Stone believed that he "was as much an influence on Joe as anyone could imagine—not the party." In other words, the vaunted party influence on Curran may have been no more than the unsteady individual influence wielded by Stone. Why Curran settled on Stone to share confidences with is unclear since the latter—like Smith and the other top NMU leaders—were all Communists. Perhaps Curran cunningly sensed earlier than most that he could conceal his lack of support for the Reds through his friendship with the two-faced Stone. Though he subsequently turned decisively against the party, Stone did acknowledge that at the beginning "we [the Communist Party] had the full confidence of the membership. We could get them to vote anything if we recommended it to them," although "most of the policies" were "laid down in the party" beforehand.

The union's high degree of centralization facilitated this process. This was how the NMU sought to overcome the problem presented by a membership that was often scattered to the four corners of the globe. All dues payments went to the national headquarters in Manhattan; all bills and purchases and repairs were paid from there. "Meetings were held every Monday night at the same time throughout the country." The Manhattan office had "teletype machines" so "we could dispatch decisions simultaneously to all of our offices."

When Stone met Curran in the spring of 1936, the latter was so broke that the party paid his rent. The party had good reason to believe that Curran was their man. They felt that "he was ideal, that he was an outstanding fellow." Curran was more than willing to cooperate with the Communists at this juncture, for he had nothing to lose.

Stone joined the party in 1935 when the "headquarters of the seamen's unit of the party was on 13th street." By his own admission, at that point he knew "nothing. Absolutely nothing" about Marxism. He joined the party in part because "at these party meetings there was no discussion of politics. All of the discussions concerned our problems," of which there were many. The idea for the NMU itself came from the party. At that time, Stone said, few sailors had the capability to organize. So, "naturally we got money from the Communist Party. As a matter of fact, it was the party that told us which printer to take [material] to and so on."

"None of us," Stone said, "knew how to hold a meeting" or "how to draw up a leaflet, even how to pass out a leaflet." Stone didn't think the union could have been organized but for the party, "because we had no experience nor understanding of the labor movement." Though sailors "were probably the most advanced and most knowledgeable group of workers in the country"—being "on slow ships for great lengths of time," they had time to read—but "we didn't have ideas on what to do to change our conditions." The fact that they were "the most disgruntled, dissatisfied, abused, underpaid, overworked group of men" made them ideal for the party. For its part, the party, including

Smith, embraced Curran wholeheartedly. According to Stone, "The party said that under no circumstance were we ever to break with Joe: 'Don't ever force an issue on Joe,'" they said.

Curran perfectly reflected the way some comrades in this hyper-masculinist union visualized the proletariat. He was "big," "burly," and "strong." He had "tattoos on the skin between his thumbs and forefingers." Though he had "great native intelligence" and could "speak extemporaneously," he was "not an administrator. Not an innovator of operation." This made him even more dependent on party comrades and heightened the importance of Smith, a good administrator. Stone asserts that he was "as much an influence on Joe as anyone could imagine—not the party," but the Communist Party may have mistaken Stone's influence, given that he was a party member for a while, for its own.[2]

"Dependent" may be too strong a word to describe Curran's relationship to the Communists, though it is easy to see why this was the consensus before the Red Scare. As the waterfront worker Bill Bailey put it, Curran was "cheating the Party of dues by not joining," since "he was always carrying out the 'party line.'"[3] A de facto Red, Curran was a bleak man with "menacing brown eyes and a nose scalloped by repeated fractures" set amidst a head "like a block of granite," graced by a "gray complexion" and "salt water toughness."

Unlike Smith, who was the epitome of the proletarian intellectual, Curran's "critics maintain[ed] that he [was] too slow-witted to be dishonest. . . . Once when he was asked the secret of his success, he said, 'I was too dumb to be racketeer.'" But Stone observed that though Curran was no genius, it would be a mistake to underestimate him—as the Reds discovered to their cost. It was folly to underestimate a labor leader whose "favorite reading," in which he was absorbed "all the time," was Robert's *Rules of Order.* The ins and outs of parliamentary procedure were his "Bible," ingrained "right into my brain." He regarded the *Rules* as a "course in cunning and he read it for amusement as much as for instruction." The Communists were to discover Curran's procedural wiliness when he moved successfully to purge them as the Red Scare dawned.

An only child born on the Lower East Side of Manhattan in 1906 of Irish American parents, Curran spent most of his boyhood in the home of a German baker in Westfield, New Jersey. Curran never got beyond the fifth grade. But although he was a poor speller he was no dummy.[4]

Early on he displayed a hot temper and a thirst for revenge that characterized his post-Communist years at the union. "One day a sister in the local Catholic school hit him across the hand with a brass-edged ruler. The young boy lost his temper. He ripped a nearby telephone off the wall and threw it at the startled nun."[5] This fiery undercurrent was in stark contrast with the cool that characterized Smith.

As a result of his upbringing in New Jersey, Curran "spoke fluent German" by the age of six. In this household "no English was spoken." He "ran with a group of pretty tough little boys" there. He joined the ISU at the age of eighteen and, as he recalled it, "From the time I started going to sea I can never recall anybody aboard a ship saying, 'I ain't going to sail on that ship because you got an Italian, you got a Negro or you got a Chinese.'" Though it was "true that they had some all black ships and all white ships," "that was the owner's policy." He joined the MWIU in 1934 when "there were about 14,000 in this union." At that point, "we didn't know it was Communist dominated." He did realize that "we couldn't ship" with MWIU membership, as "the government [had] authorized the shipowners to take nobody on his ship that didn't have an ISU book." As a result he and many others felt compelled to join the ISU, which ultimately led to the rise of the NMU.

Curran vividly remembered the two leading Red leaders of the seamen: "Blackie" Myers and Smith. He thought the former was "extremely articulate, a real showman, and he was the top-notch guy." As for Smith, Curran's mangled syntax makes it difficult to discern what he actually thought: "Ferdinand Smith, because he was a Negro, you see, was outstanding but not because of being articulate. He was not." Curran seemed to be saying that Smith was "outstanding" but not by the same standards as Myers was, but by a lower standard, "because he was a Negro."

He may have underestimated Smith, as his comrades may have underestimated him.[6] For although Curran was no intellectual heavyweight, after he rose to high office, "after a while, I started studying. . . . I started to read and study trade union tactics."[7]

Hoyt Haddock, a close friend of Curran's[8] from the time the union began, said that "from the first" the jowly union boss was hostile to the Communist Party but concealed his true intentions until the appropriate moment: "He and I started discussing this when we became acquainted with each other." Haddock, who acknowledges his intellectual debt to the ultraconservative writer, "Ludwig von Mise[s]," recalls that "I was in Joe's office when a Negro came in and started ranting and inferred that Joe was discriminating. Joe just got up out of his chair and went over and got him by the collar and by the seat of the pants and moved him out of the door and said, 'Don't ever come back.'" This was not the kind of approach to fighting racism that the Reds would have counseled, yet they supported Curran nonetheless.[9]

Joe Stack, who was not a Communist at the time of the union's formation but joined later, explained that "with all the pressure and propaganda about being Communists, we had to have a man like Curran that we could show was not affiliated with say, the [MWIU] or the Wobblies" and that's why the left backed him. "If you had a contract and the contract was a bum contract," he said, "the party wouldn't let Curran announce the contract to the rank-and-file." No, "it would be Blackie Myers or Ferdinand Smith." however, "if it was really good, Curran was given the [task]."[10]

In the summer of 1937, shortly after the formation of the union, the NMU gathered at its first convention at the Manhattan Opera House. Longtime political prisoner Tom Mooney was chosen as "honorary chair." Joining him on the committee of honor were the "Scottsboro Boys" and "all seamen in jail for union activities." Smith was nominated "temporary chairman" of the convention but declined in favor of Curran. The air was replete with masculine language and repeated references to "brothers." There were also a number of references to history. "The position of the NMU," a speaker said, "is comparable to that of the IWW in 1909. They had led a series of strikes, become powerful and practically absorbed the ISU of that time. Yet despite their power and size at that time, the IWW deteriorated and today consists of a small sect. . . . What is going to prevent this being the fate of the NMU?" The question hung in the air like the cigarette smoke that filled the room.

Curran reported that "our biggest achievement" was to "have won the support of colored seamen," meaning Negroes and Filipinos. This was important because "if they are not with us, they will assuredly be against us." Smith's prominent presence was insurance that they would continue to support the union, or so it was thought.[11]

Yet the ovations and words of praise he received were a false dawn. The insurgents had hardly unpacked their boxes and moved into their new headquarters when they were embroiled in a bitter conflict over Ferdinand Smith's credentials. He was charged with being a scab during the tumultuous 1934 West Coast strike of waterfront workers which had set the stage for the emergence of the NMU itself two years later. On his application for office Smith noted that he had sailed as Chief Steward on the *Horace Lukenbach* from 1930 to 1934. Peter Innes, a bitter critic of Smith, demanded that Smith be publicly tried for claiming exemption from observing the strike based on his ties to the MWIU. As evidence he presented what purported to be a copy of the Department of Commerce, Bureau of Navigation crew list to the trial committee. At this New York trial Smith argued that the MWIU had ordered the crew to take the ship to the West Coast and then strike it. He maintained that striking the ship in San Pedro, the weakest port in the Pacific Coast, would not have aided the strikers' cause.[12] But Smith's opponents disagreed strongly.[13]

In an ordinary union, such charges against a leader may have been peremptorily dismissed. So too in a union said to be dominated by "authoritarian" Reds. But this did not happen. Because the Red-led union was a model of democracy, Smith was subjected to a prolonged and searing inquiry. Indeed, during its first year the union was so insistently democratic that officers were forbidden to lock the doors to their offices or even to lock their desks; any sailor at any time was free to rummage through the officers' desks on the theory that they were merely hired hands and should have no secrets. In those early days it was felt that all administrative decisions should be made at mass meetings. If a top officer wanted to hire or fire a stenographer, the question was brought up at a mass meeting. Then someone would then argue that inability to write shorthand, for example, was offset by the employee's great devotion.[14]

It was this environment of "ultrademocracy," heavily influenced by the anarchism that seemed to inhere in many sailors, that led to an extended and extensive scrutiny of Smith's actions. During the five-day trial "every piece of evidence obtainable" was scrutinized.[15] Smith's opponents clearly wanted to expel him from the union as the first step toward removing all Reds from leadership positions and reversing the gains of the 1936–37 strike. The trial, with Curran presiding, was quite a spectacle. In the early fall of 1938, "every member of the union" who wanted to "hear all the proceedings" could do so on the "second and fourth floors [of union headquarters], where the microphone system is at the disposal of the Trial Committee." Many beached sailors came to watch and hear one of their chief leaders brought into the dock.

Smith's supporters spoke up in his defense as the hearings unfolded. One sailor charged hotly that "the shipowners and their stooges are at this time centering their main attack upon [Smith]."[16] The seamen's branch of the party was outraged by the prosecution of their comrade, sensing correctly that it was just a prelude to an assault on themselves. "By appealing to the prejudices of some of the white seamen against the Negroes, the ship-owners" were seeking to "split the union's ranks."

Smith proved to be a skilled advocate on his own behalf, ensnaring the trial body in procedural claims, continually invoking "point of order" and generally providing an articulate defense. Harry Bridges, the powerful head of the West Coast longshoremen also weighed in on his behalf. Smith argued that a "month before the strike started I sailed to the Port of Seattle. In that port I was a member of . . . MWIU." He wound up in San Pedro where there were "about two hundred police to prevent the longshoremen from striking" and the "port was wide open." As he explained it, "we had not a majority on board on the Luckenbach, even though had we intended to take action in San Pedro it would not be effective." His idea was "to strike in no port where effective action could not be taken. Therefore we decided to go to San Francisco. The Captain . . . anchored out in the bay. The galley was kept up and he sent for armed guards to keep the crew aboard the vessel, and no one was allowed ashore or on board. . . . Immediately after the strike was over we sent a delegate to the strike headquarters. . . . Getting off [the ship] was not going to help the strike on the West Coast." His opponents were "liars," he said vehemently. "Only today we have had word from Seattle that NMU men were dumped there," and this trial was part and parcel of an offensive against the newly formed union.

He sought to provide context by explaining his relationship to the MWIU. "Since 1933, I lined up my Stewards Department and was an acting guide and was secretly organiz[ing] for the MWIU. In my department . . . they were all members of the MWIU and you want to bear in mind that it meant immediate discharge if anyone knew you were a member of the MWIU. . . . In those days seamen weren't certain about unions. It meant death for a seaman then to be a member of a union. . . . All [seamen] wanted was a living. The seamen were so depressed and it was only the highly militant men that would join a union." Thus, "everything I did was done secretly." Where were your MWIU papers then? his opponents asked. "If you know anything about 1934," Smith replied with asperity, "[you know] that there were vigilantes raiding every hall on the coast." So, shot back his prosecutors, "they also raided your papers?" Curran, who stood by his number 2 man throughout this ordeal (for the most part), added that "in 1934 we destroyed all the evidence we had of the MWIU in order to get into the ISU. If we were caught with any book we were thrown out. . . . Mine is at the bottom of the bay." Smith added, "We are not business men; we're sailors" and that's why he did not possess all the documents his interlocutors desired.

Smith recalled his heroism during the 1936–37 strike in order to shed light on why he would not—could not—scab in 1934. "I was the man responsible for pulling the entire crew off the ship, everyone with the exception of the Captain," he said. "Although I had to do it secretly, I led these men off. . . . At that time I was in line for an Assistant Port Steward's job with the company. I refused to go although this was to be my last trip before getting the job. I was called by Grange and he said these damned Firemen and Sailors would use me and then they would throw me out. He said, 'They need you, first because you are a steward, and second because you are a Negro.' I told him—'The hell with you.' I was a worker and my first interest is and would be with the workers. I was the only Negro in that meeting of the Rank and File called by Grange in Cooper Union. After that a few straggling Negroes came in. Then a few meetings later, I was elected to the Strike Strategy Committee and have gone along working diligently ever since."

Given his valor and fortitude in 1936–37, why would he have acted differently a scant two years earlier, he asked. "The organization I belonged to during the 1934 strike was responsible for the organization of the rank and file. I was sick during the strike, very sick. My lungs were almost shot and despite the instructions of the doctor, I refused to leave the front until I collapsed with pneumonia and had to be carried away." Plucking the heart strings like a skilled virtuoso, Smith concluded, "If I were a fink [strike breaker, informer] at heart, I would not have remained working from 16–20 hours a day, trying to keep the soup kitchen going and raising funds for the rank and file. It is necessary to contrast my reputation with that of these men who are maligning me. . . . I never was a fink and never could be one."

Again, Curran leapt to the defense of his colleague. "I don't want you to be framed," he said with sincerity. "I realize that some of the people whose opinions we have received are people who I would not care to wipe my feet on." Why didn't Smith's opponents "submit this information before the elections, if they had it, or even during the balloting, instead of trying to destroy the union like this." Good point, Smith said. "Three months before the Judges of Election reported, this question was raised. I have documentary proof to that effect. I was met at 110th Street in Harlem and told that I was not going to be seated as Vice-President, even though I was running unopposed. This person told me that and I said, 'Go ahead.'" With a mixture of chivalry and noblesse oblige Smith said, "Rather than be an issue which may wreck the union, I would rather get out, but I want my name before I get out."

Though Communists like Smith dominated the NMU leadership, his critics battered him with tough questions. With increasing exasperation he sought to explain the context of a battle between the MWIU and ISU in which the former had been on the defensive. "There was a hell of a fight against the MWIU members going into the ISU. . . . I don't think there were two stewards in 1934 that were members of the MWIU. You'll find sailors or firemen but not stewards." There was a "battle between these two organizations [the ISU and MWIU]. The steamship owners, realizing the militancy of the MWIU, that it would mean money in their pockets immediately recognized the ISU. And there was a battle between these two organizations." On "my vessel," Smith said, "I was the one who was instrumental in organizing my own department. [As a result,] every member of the Stewards department was MWIU. We were given instructions and had to carry them out. There was no other organization except the SUP on steam-schooners." Curran chimed in, adding, "There was a hell of a fight against the MWIU members going into the ISU, as such."

Smith tried to contrast his militance in 1936—when conditions favored the progressives—with the decidedly less favorable conditions of 1934. "I struck two days before the strike was called here in 1936. We didn't have to stay here. And I know it meant black-listing in the ports of the company against me if the strike had been lost, but I didn't give a good God-damn about that. I was a union man and wanted to be one and I was the guy who got the Luckenbach and got the whole crew to come. . . . I had everything to lose and nothing to gain. And my activity during 1936–37 bore this out. . . . I was down here with the men fighting with the members, hunting food for men, hunting clothes and doing all these things."

His critics would have none of this. Smith examined one witness who recounted a conversation with Peter Innes who said, "As soon as we get through with comrade Smith, we'll get through with the others. And we won't be satisfied until we get rid of all the comrades of the union." Smith thought he was putting up a good defense but felt that Curran, chair of the trial body, was hampering him. "Why is it that every time that [I] make a move you want to rule it out?" he asked the NMU leader. Then he asked another witness, "Isn't it a fact that membership in the MWIU meant immediate dismissal, especially a man that was a chief steward, and you would be black-balled by the company if it was known?"

"Yes," came the reply.

Thus, Smith concluded, "I want to state that I did not join the New York [MWIU] local for that specific reason that the ship-owners had spies at Broad Street to watch men who were going into the headquarters. And I joined the Seattle local where I could go in without being spied upon because I was not known by the ship-owners in Seattle. . . . All of us who returned to the vessels at that time sailed with men who according to Lundeberg are finks. But to us [they] were confused workers."

But his explanations seemed to be falling on deaf ears. Irritated, Smith concluded, "In my way of thinking I have submitted enough evidence that would even be accepted in Hitler's Germany," for "certain questions have led me to believe that you came in with unclean hands." Again and again, he played the "fascist" card, stating at one point, "if I get Hitler to testify here, you'll accept it." This "committee is supposed to be an impartial jury, but it seems obvious from the way the committee is proceeding and acting as investigator, judge and jury and everything else, in other words, they're attempting to justify something they have arrived at even before they enter this room." At one point he announced, "I've sat around this comic opera long enough I think. I've had enough of it. This thing is getting to be a farce."[17]

Smith was angry, then outraged. "My name has been bandied around the waterfront as being a fink," he said. "I say I am not a fink. I have evidence and men to prove that I was not." Tossing out an ultimatum, he declared, "I want to state here and now that after hearing the evidence I have in my possession, if this Council decides I am a fink, I will resign without any further cause for disruption in the union." But "if they decide that I am not, they should throw this out of the window and publicize the fact that I am not a fink, just as they publicized the fact that I was."[18] Wilford Caves was one of the many sailors who backed him at this point. "I [was] chairman of the [Sailors Union of the Pacific] strike committee, during the 1934 strike," he said, and "the record of [Smith] is absolutely clear. . . . We advised them to stay aboard ship and support us in every way possible."[19]

Z. R. Brown, secretary of the San Francisco Bay District of the Maritime Federation of the Pacific, also weighed in. A leader of waterfront workers, he reported that "several" of his members "who were in this port and other Pacific Coast ports during the 1934 strike spoke on the [Smith] situation, after which a motion was passed that I inform you that many ships were anchored in San Francisco Bay at the end of the 1934 strike. . . . I have checked with the Luckenbach Steamship Co. and find that the dates given" by Smith explaining his behavior during this contentious time "check in every detail."[20] So Smith was correct in asserting the propriety of his behavior.

As it turned out, Smith stayed the course and was able to survive as a NMU leader. One reason was that he had Curran's support. As Curran observed years later when he was in the process of ousting Smith from the leadership, "I was the one, many years before that, that stood up and defended Ferdinand Smith when he was brought up on charges as being a fink in the 1934 strike . . . to disrupt the union."[21] Curran was not exaggerating. As he told Harry Bridges at the time, "most of the evidence submitted was purely hearsay. . . . The Trial Committee . . . had at least four members who were definitely hostile to Smith and were members of this Mariners Club setup, which although it hasn't so much strength, is a definitely disruptive force." But he conceded that after the "'34 strike . . . I and many others went to the union halls, were investigated and given clearance." But Smith, who in a like manner disregarded his immigration status, "neglected to do this. As he puts it, he thought he was cleared by his union. Then too, Walter Stack points out that the records of the MWIU were destroyed during the raids. We know this to be true."[22] Smith's claim that his ship was "cleared" was "not disproved," Curran contended. The trial was "part of a general plot . . . to destroy [NMU]," no more than a "conspiracy."[23]

Others were less confident that this was so. William Porter of the trial committee claimed that the Communist Party shaped opinion by orchestrating a "flood of telegrams and resolutions from ships of colored departments, all these with the same tone and showing unmistakable traces of the same subversive group's hand. . . . Flooding of the waterfront with handbills signed by the waterfront section of the [party]." The "day that the trial committee was to reach a verdict," he maintained, these radicals "nearly create[d] a race riot on the fourth floor." Moreover, "we heard threats directed at us if we failed to absolve Smith." Porter wondered why Smith "never did . . . appear before an investigating committee on the West Coast in an effort to clear himself, although he sailed to the coast for two years after the [1934] strike." Nevertheless, the fact that Porter's claim of Red perfidy was published in the paper of the very union that was said to be Red-dominated tended to undermine the thrust of Porter's remarks.[24]

After the dust had settled, Smith was "reinstated with back pay." Though the trial committee hearing the matter did not agree, it was overruled by the membership.[25] Ten ports backed Smith: New York, Philadelphia, Baltimore, Mobile, Boston, Jacksonville, Baytown, Corpus Christi, Tampa, and Norfolk. Those that did not included New Orleans, Providence (the only one in the North), Savannah, Port Arthur, Galveston, and Beaumont. A chastened Smith "made an eloquent plea for internal unity and declared that he had no personal animosity against those who brought charges against him."[26]

The offensive against Smith was part of a larger offensive against the NMU itself. Some people found it disturbing that Communists would lead a union that had so much control over imports and exports. In 1939 President Roosevelt received a "very confidential" memo that detailed the "anti-labor policies" of his own "Maritime Commission" on behalf of the shipowners and against the NMU.[27]

But what was happening in government was tame compared to what was occurring in the streets. In 1935, as the idea of a challenge by sailors on the left to the existing union was gathering speed, the Communist *Daily Worker* reported "gangsterism in the ISU. . . . With the aid of police, in gangster fashion these officials raided the hall of the [Philadelphia] local, arrested a large number of members."[28] During the 1936 strike Percy Jenkins, a Negro, staggered into the union hall, his "shirt in ribbons, blood streaming down his face," for "goons [had] jumped him with bailing hooks."[29] In 1938, the same year that Smith was being prosecuted, violent men with baseball bats and chains— union dissidents and their allies—attacked NMU headquarters in Manhattan.[30] That same year Communist leader Al Lannon warned of "cliques in our union" who are "working outside the regular union channels." Upholding the legitimacy of Smith's impending trial, he declared that "every member of the union has and must have the right of his opinion on any and all questions concerning the union, regardless of whether his arguments are right are wrong, provided that these opinions and arguments are expressed through the regular union channels. . . . Every member has and must have the right to disagree or agree with the union leadership and policy." Yet, said Lannon, "when the debate is over and a decision is made by majority vote then that decision is binding on every member of the union. The minority must abide by and carry out the decision of the majority. . . . Anyone who holds himself responsible to any outside persons or groups whose opinions and decisions he holds above the decisions of the union membership and its officials" was unacceptable.[31]

Lannon was referring to the Mariners' Club, composed of dissident sailors and their allies, which was objecting to Reds in the NMU. As Smith was being tried, the union was charging that the Mariners' Club was "financed" by the shipowners. "They put out [an] anti-NMU newspaper, they raised the Red Scare, they broke up meetings with fist fights. . . . They staged job [crew] actions over phony beefs and when all else failed, they got out the baseball bats and resorted to violence." These claims were not exaggerated. Philip Carey of the NMU was "shot and killed" by goons. Bruce Cameron was "brutally beaten to death by a trio of goons headed by Jerry King." In fact, said the NMU, "there was a period in the late summer and fall of 1937 when it was hardly safe for [an] NMU delegate to venture out on the docks below 14th Street without protection."[32] Negroes thought they were a special target.[33]

Shipping was a brutal industry and sailors had to confront violent cultures at home and abroad. Curran recalled that as his U.S.-based ship pulled into an Uruguayan port, there was a strike and the sailors were greeted with rounds of gunfire. Meanwhile, back at home, just after the NMU was organized Curran "was met on the street by a business agent, Gus Brown. He was sitting in the car. He called me over to the car and stuck a gun in my belly. . . . He was very nervous; he was very emotional. . . . I was scared to death." Fortunately for Curran he did not pull the trigger, but other sailors were not as lucky.[34]

Things got so bad that when in 1938 Curran and a group of sailors marched on Washington, and were later invited to a meeting with Secretary of Labor Frances Perkins, he was extremely apprehensive. "Mrs.

Perkins invited" the beefy sailor to tea. "I refused to drink," recalled
Curran, "or even eat the sandwiches for fear they might be poisoned.
That's how ridiculous we were in those days."[35] It was said of the most
determined opponent of the union—Joseph Ryan of the ILA [stev-
dores]—that the "operators had given him money so that he could hire
men and send them down to the docks armed with baseball bats and
loading hooks to drive the NMU off the waterfront."[36] According to
Richard Boyer, the journalist,"labor spies had been hired to break the
union" via "assassinations, murders and kidnappings."[37]

In July 1938 "fifteen men, armed with baseball bats, entered the national headquarters" of the NMU "and raided the fifth floor. They
forced the entire office and clerical staff, including several union officials to vacate the premises. They roughed up several secretaries and
threw them down the stairs. This squad then damaged some office
equipment and confiscated several documents. . . . The goon squad,
with their baseball bats in full view, broke into Curran's office." They
"called for outlawing Communist membership within the union, demanded that the national officers hire a new secretarial staff and called
for *The Pilot* staff to resign en masse," because they were thought to be
committed Communists.[38] They were evicted from the building after a
fierce and protracted struggle.

Who was behind this strategy of terror? To the NMU, the answer
was clear. Confessions by the direct perpetrators named "Frank J. Taylor, President of the Merchant Marine Institute, the late Robert Hague of
Standard Oil, H. M. Singleton of the Luckenbach Steamship Co., Dalton
Mann of the Grace Line and J. A. Jump of the Isthmian Line owned by
the steel trust," as well as the "Railway Audit and Inspection Co., a notorious industrial 'detective' agency."[39]

The union got a bitter taste of its enemy's tactics at the tumult-filled
1939 sailors' convention in New Orleans, which angered many city fathers because of the NMU's reluctance to adhere to Jim Crow norms.
Members started revolting against Jim Crow from the moment the
trains began bringing them to the "Big Easy," rejecting Jim Crow seat-
ing as they approached the Mason-Dixon line. This was a foretaste of
what was to come. As M. Hedley Stone recalled it, "The rule was to
leave the hotel together and to return together, because there was some
waylaying of seamen in the town." This was done by "some of the
Southern group—the opposition group" in the union. The "Jerusalem
Temple, a shriner's temple," where the convention was held, resembled

a nineteenth-century armed fort in a battle with Native Americans. The opposition came armed with "revolvers, brass knuckles, knives, weed chains (used for snow tires)."[40]

The conflicting currents of "race" and class in New Orleans in 1939 almost destroyed the union.[41] The Communist sailor, Paul Jarvis, later recalled that "Curran was standing by a window talking to someone and I was about twenty-five feet away when all of a sudden I saw a struggle going on. In a matter of a few seconds I ended up across the window with Curran's butt in my face. . . . Hippo Russell layed [sic] this fellow that had bumped Curran and continued to bump us, with a bat—a baseball bat. . . . They had fully intended to knock Curran out of the window, there is no question about that."[42]

The NMU had no choice but to counterattack. Smith's triumph was complete when those who only recently had him in the dock and had mounted a brutal offensive against the union in Louisiana were subjected to a grueling though democratically conducted internal trial themselves. In mid-1939, Smith sat with eight other men. He was one of the judges set to try Jerome King on fourteen counts including the "acceptance of money" from the shipowners to wreck the NMU. King was said to have "knowingly confederated and associated with known and subsequently proved spies and secret agents of the employers." Smith's victory was apparent when the first witness, his close comrade Blackie Myers, "testified that after the elections King had told him all the 'Communists' must go."[43] King had allegedly "threatened to kill Tony Lucio," a NMU stalwart in California, and was charged with being on the payroll of the union's fiercest foe—Standard Oil of New Jersey.[44] King was also accused of "working in cooperation with organizers of Father Coughlin's Christian Front. . . . On [Joseph] Ryan's command he ordered his stooges to stage the baseball bat raid in union headquarters [in 1938]" and "associated himself with waterfront gangsters."[45]

Ultimately, "Jerome Medeiros (alias King)" was indicted for the slaying of Bruce Cameron. This murder, said the NMU, "climaxed a series of assaults on and robberies of seamen along the waterfront."[46] The defendant received a ten-year sentence in Sing-Sing prison. According to one partisan source, he "based" his "defense on 'anti-communist' activities" as a "cover" for "gangster tactics on the waterfront."[47]

Part of the reason for these fierce and protracted internal battles was that the sailors' opposition was so formidable. Smith's Communist comrade, Al Lannon, put it succinctly when he asserted in 1947, "When we speak of the shipowners we speak, not of some separate or related grouping of Big Business but of the ruling oligarchy of monopoly capital itself. . . . Eleven steamship companies are tied in with the Morgan-First National Bank financial interests. . . . Four other companies are dominated by Kuhn, Loeb and Company. . . . The directorates of shipping industry interlock with those of the nation's railroads, coal mines, steel mills, public utilities, banks, insurance companies and manufacturing establishments." These eleven steamship companies connected to Morgan-First National Bank were "the most powerful aggregation of financial control in the country, with assets in excess of 37 billion dollars."[48] In short, shipping was an essential bedrock of capitalism.

In 1900 the United States's merchant fleet was approximately the same size it had been in 1807 as most U.S. trade was carried by foreign, especially British, vessels. World War I helped to shake the United States out of its torpor. What followed was an astonishing expansion of U.S. shipping—leading directly to Ferdinand Smith migrating northward—which led to an increase in the amount of U.S. cargo carried in U.S. vessels from a mere 10 percent in 1913 to 35 percent in 1935. This development fundamentally shifted the balance of international maritime power and constituted an important element in the overall U.S. bid for world power.[49]

The Great War exposed the fact that the fate of the United States would rest on shaky foundations as long as its fortunes were tied to the merchant shipping of other nations. U.S. exports were virtually paralyzed during the war due to the dependence on foreign shipping. The drop in cotton exports "from $62.50 per bale in July 1914 to $36.25 in December" was "repeated to a greater of lesser extent in all export commodities."[50]

The expansion of domestic shipping was also helped by lavish government subsidies and a good deal of corruption. In 1935 Senator Hugo Black of Alabama exposed some of the scandals involving the shipping industry. The future Supreme Court Justice called the mail subsidy for shippers a "saturnalia of waste, inefficiency . . . [and] exploitation of the public." The post office "had provided steamship companies with some $200 million under subsidy contracts. This amounted to almost ten times the normal rate for the mail actually carried." The senator from Alabama "strongly advocated outright government ownership" of the shipping industry to stop the waste and inefficiency. This call for public ownership was emblematic of this radicalism that allowed the NMU to flourish. In 1936 "the seventeen existing subsidized lines, together with two that could become eligible for subsidies in the future, had a net worth of $78 million, gross operating revenues of $122 million and a net profit of only $4.1 million." Shipping was "indisputably a small industry when measured by such usual standards as capitalization, total revenue and employment,"[51] though paradoxically it was strategically one of the most important industries in the nation. This combination of small capitalization and huge importance made it particularly vulnerable to a Communist-led union.

The outrageous subsidies the industry received from the government increased public pressure for reform. Some companies received more than the cost of the entire trip for carrying a few pounds of mail. Generally speaking, the subsidized lines received sixty times the actual cost of carrying mail; this scandal led directly to the founding of the governmental Maritime Commission, with Joseph Kennedy as the first chairman.[52] The fact that close friends of President Roosevelt such as Vincent Astor, a director on the boards of the U.S. Lines, the International Mercantile Marine Company, and the Roosevelt Steamship Company, among others, stood to profit from these government giveaways was part of the problem.[53]

The U.S. economy was heavily dependent on shipping, which helped to justify the excessive subsidies to the industry.[54] Ships were the means by which executives imported raw materials for domestic production, exported finished goods, and inspected their investments abroad.[55] A typical voyage on the American President Lines in 1931, for example, went from Los Angeles to Honolulu, Yokohama, Kobe, Shanghai, and Hong Kong, then back to Balboa, Cristobal, and Havana, carrying and dropping off hundreds of passengers along the way.[56]

With its various classes of travel, ships transported the famous and ordinary alike, which guaranteed that this mode of travel would receive intense scrutiny. Among the former were the actress Joan Bennett, traveling to the Philippines in 1931. The future Supreme Court Justice Earl Warren sailed with his children in opulent surroundings as well.[57] Indeed, in the 1930s traveling abroad on U.S. ships was coming to be seen as part of one's patriotic duty. Joseph Sheehan, president of the American President Lines, remarked, "We Americans are the proudest and most patriotic people in the world—until it comes to the matter of travelling on American flag ships. The British and the Japanese are the two most successful and prosperous operators of merchant ships in the world today."[58] As the clouds of war began to gather, traveling on a U.S. ship became more than just a patriotic gesture. It also became safer than traveling on British and Japanese ships, which might be targeted by various enemies. By September 1939, it was reported that "Americans sailing from Europe in foreign ships now want [the] safety of [the] U.S. flag."[59] The apprehension about security gave the U.S. fleet a boost and enhanced the fortunes of selected captains of industry, and also provided the NMU greater opportunities to organize.

The confrontation between a militant Communist-led union and the shipping magnates was bound to be fierce. Shipping interests were controlled by interlocking ties between Bechtel, General Foods, Ingersoll-Rank, Anaconda Copper, and other giants.[60] The stockholders of the American President Lines included the Bank of America, the Du Ponts, the notorious detective-cum-spy agency Pinkerton's, and Socony-Vacuum Oil.[61]

Facing these corporate giants on the other side of the class divide was an assortment of Communists, including Ferdinand Smith. Leo Robnett told Frederick Woltman, a noted anticommunist, that Smith was "undoubtedly a dominant Communist-liaison man in the powerful East Coast [NMU] that controls every ship entering or leaving the Atlantic seaboard—and maintains a 'hiring hall' through which every ship owner has to hire his seamen."[62] Like many others, Woltman found it intolerable that pro-Moscow Reds like Smith could play such a powerful role in the U.S. economy. The House Un-American Activities Committee agreed, calling Smith a "strong party man" and an early graduate after the Reds "organized" an alleged "Red Annapolis" on the outskirts of Beacon, New York.[63]

According to anticommunists, Smith was not the only NMU leader with these party affiliations. In the fall of 1947, as the union was purging itself of these "alien" elements, anticommunists charged that the party had "over 90% of the official posts of the union."[64] Indeed, they asserted that being a Red was a sine qua non for advancement in the union.[65] Furthermore, the party was accused of establishing a "Stalinist" stranglehold over the NMU, suppressing dissent, and forging an internal dictatorship. This was far from the truth. If anything, the NMU may have gone too far in the opposite direction.

The creation of what might be called an "ultrademocracy" went back to the early days of the union, perhaps as a result of Communist efforts. Hoyt Haddock, an early union member, claimed that the Red, Tommy Ray, and himself, "did most of the work on the [NMU] constitution. He was a Communist at the time and I knew it." Haddock and this "little slight man," placed the "AFL . . . constitution" and the "Declaration of Independence" together and "that's what we wrote the [NMU] constitution by." This was not very conspiratorial. It was a hectic time, when the union was taking off. "Our primary purpose," he avowed, "was to give the membership control of the union." Moreover, Curran was consulted throughout: "Everything that we wrote we checked with Joe, everything."[66]

The constitution set the union on a path toward democracy. Thus, the 7 February 1936 edition of the union's newspaper, *The Pilot,* contained a letter that a week later elicited a response suggesting that the letter was little more than "Red-baiting" and should not have been published. An "editor's note" tended to "agree" with the accusation but added: "However, we disagree that such letters as that from the 'Real Seaman' should be omitted. We welcome letters from seamen and don't care whether they are" pro-Red or not.[67] *The Pilot,* an influential organ for a union stretched across the seven seas, took pains to reassure its readers that the fact that many of its leaders were members of a single party was no more consequential than, say, the leadership of other unions belonging disproportionately to the Democratic Party or the Roman Catholic Church. It went to some lengths to comfort another seaman who "asked" if the paper was being "put out by Communists that are trying to get control of the union."[68]

Throughout the era of the Reds' prominence in the NMU, *The Pilot* was certainly more open and diverse than in the period following their ouster. Thus, in early 1939 six NMU members wrote, "I would also like to ask Brother Smith if there is any truth to the many statements going around that he gave concessions away on deck and below in order to get the stewards an eight-hour day."[69] Smith adamantly denied this accusation.[70] This episode pointed to the "free speech" repercussions of Red dominance of the union but also to the fear that the union's number two leader might favor the stewards—who were disproportionately black—who had been his coworkers.

The very openness of the NMU ensured that such accusations would have free expression. Communist Al Lannon in August 1939 declared that the recently concluded pact between Moscow and Berlin put an end to London's "hope to push Hitler to the East in order to get him involved in war with the Soviet Union."[71] Lest anyone think that *The Pilot* was merely a Red rag, it published several letters and articles disagreeing with Lannon's formulations. Frank Staats reminded him of the line from the Spanish Civil War that "We . . . could never fraternize with any fascists." Yes, London and Paris were "selling out," he said, but "that does not give Russia the right to do the same thing."[72] Edward S. Noble of the SS *Camden* reminded his comrades in mid-1940 that a "year ago [you] used to tell us what a horrible thing Fascism was." Now their line had changed, he said, though he had another idea: "Let the membership decide whether this is their opinion. . . . Stop the peace at any price tone and the onesided attack on the Allies." He added, "on this ship we have thrown our 'Yanks are not coming' pamphlets and buttons over the side as they no longer express the opinion of a majority of the crew."[73] Even before this, *The Pilot* published a resolution denouncing the party,[74] just as it routinely published letters condemning "Communist activity."[75]

Their ecumenical approach notwithstanding, the comrades were walking a fine line. While they were trying to assure the rank and file that their ideology, including their alliance with Moscow, would not be shoved down the throats of nonbelievers, they also saw no reason why they should not spread their ideology through different means, nor hide their vision under a bushel.[76] But this was an era when Jim Crow predisposed many—especially African Americans—to view the radical alternatives the Reds proposed favorably. This made it easier for the party to push its agenda. This was an era when friendly exchanges between Communist leader James Ford and soon-to-be anticommunist hawk, NAACP leader Roy Wilkins, were viewed as a mundane part of the landscape. Thus, as the maritime strike was reaching a critical turning point in 1936, Ford reminded Wilkins of his "letter of September 24th expressing pleasure at hearing my radio broadcast over . . . [NBC]" and thanked him "for your kind words. I was also very glad to read your interview with the Daily Worker."[77] Ford had something to offer the NAACP that it did not have—global contacts—while the NAACP had something that Ford desired: a mass base among Negroes. This made for a mutually beneficial relationship (at least potentially). Hence, in early 1937 Ford told Wilkins's anticommunist leader, NAACP official Walter White, that he had "just returned from a two-weeks' trip into Mexico and I plan very soon to take a trip to Spain. While in Europe, I may have the opportunity of contacting a number of Colored people and talking with them about the problems of the Colored people internationally, as well as in the United States."[78]

Given this context, many were open to the idea of Reds in the driver's seat of the union—in contrast to their attitude shortly thereafter. But even during the heady days of the New Deal, certain forces were working overtime to challenge this hegemony. In March 1940, as criticisms of the union's foreign policy mounted, Joe Ryan, the tireless and unreconstructed foe of the NMU and president of the International Longshoremen's Association, forwarded a leaflet from the "waterfront section of the Communist party" to the White House, telling an FDR aide that the Reds were "endeavoring to destroy our organization." Ryan claimed to be standing tall against this onslaught. In case the message was not understood, he attached a *Daily Worker* editorial critical of FDR's policy in Finland and pointed out that "as a reward" for his fealty to Washington "[I] am being persecuted by Thurman Arnold," a Justice Department attorney.[79]

Another opponent of the NMU was a sailor, Joseph Doyle, who in the summer of 1941 pushed for an inquiry into the Reds' ties with Moscow. He wanted leaders, such as Smith, who were accused of being Red, to be placed on trial internally. At an NMU meeting where this measure was considered, "the resolution was voted down with only two votes registered for it among the close to 400 delegates present."[80] Joseph Curran, widely seen as the Reds' "front man," was irate about this attempt to view the union as a tool of actual or potential subversion. "As long as we were forced to work for $35 a month, live under intolerable conditions, eat food that wasn't fit for human consumption and put in 12 hours a day—nobody called us Communists," he remarked. "It was only after we organized into a strong militant trade union and took strike action to improve our wages and working conditions that we became agents of Moscow."[81] But opponents of Smith and the party argued that a nation entering war could not tolerate a strategically important union like the NMU being controlled by Communists. Would Moscow tolerate a union influenced by Washington? they asked.

As for the party, it continued to plug away, seeing sailors as a fruitful target for recruitment. In 1941, Josh Lawrence, probably the second-ranking black Communist in the NMU, reported that a "group of Negro seamen met in Harlem at the invitation of the Waterfront Section" of the party. "The meeting was so successful it was voted to continue such educationals on a permanent basis and to form an active group to lend support to the struggle of the Negro people."[82] This was an indication of the critical role played by Negroes in places like Harlem and elsewhere and the growing support for the party among Negroes. This was precisely why the sailor, Harlemite, and Communist, Ferdinand Smith was a marked man.

3

The Black Ocean

ONE OF THE MOST DIFFICULT PROBLEMS facing Smith and the union leadership was the question of racism. The steel scaffolding of Jim Crow included the law, stubborn attitudes, management manipulations. Moreover, the NMU had members in a number of reactionary places in the South such as Norfolk, Charleston, and New Orleans, and similarly regressive cities in Texas, such as Houston, Galveston, Corpus Christi, and Brownsville. Discrimination was also faced by Filipinos, Puerto Ricans, and other peoples of color. The same factors that could generate radicalism—the confined quarters where radical ideas could circulate easily as a pamphlet passed from hand to hand; the attenuated impact of the larger society; visits abroad, for example to Durban—could also foster racism. This complicated the union's job enormously. It took the question of racism quite seriously and addressed it preemptively; but issues of male supremacy and sexuality were a different kettle of fish.

It would be a mistake, however, to think that discriminatory policies toward Negro sailors were unique to the former Slave South, or to merchant seamen for that matter. Eugene E. Wilson, a former naval aviator and Annapolis graduate, described an incident that occurred while sailors on leave were attending a bullfight in Callao, Peru, during the 1920s. When a black matador entered the ring, "all the latent southern chivalry in our Navy [was aroused], and there was a good deal of it, and they began to jeer the colored matador shouting, 'C'mon you bull, get the black so and so.'"[1] Such racism was typical. When the black seaman, Adolph W. Newton, arrived in San Diego during World War II, "the first thing I did was to ask some of the Negro sailors what life was like for Negroes in San Diego. They said that it 'wasn't shit'; they called San Diego 'Little Georgia.' I went into town and found that they had told the truth." Similarly, on board ship clashes between Euro-Americans and Negroes over music—"boring hillbilly records" versus jazz—were simply the tip of the iceberg in terms of bias.[2]

Although San Diego was bad for Negroes the South was worse still. Norfolk, for example, was a particularly troublesome port for Negro sailors; one called this Virginia metropolis "shit city." Little wonder. In 1943 "every other day there was an incident with white and 'Negro sailors.'" When the Negro sailors "demanded respect" at a local theater, they were "directed to use the rear entrance with the steward's mates." They refused and another row erupted.[3]

Skeptics might argue that bias was not confined to Negroes. Ships were floating vessels of internal combat where conflict was "often based on ethnic differences." Englishmen, "known to hold strictly to the rules of boxing," squared off against "Scandinavians and other nationalities" who "usually allow rougher methods," or "Finns," who "are sometimes charged with using knives more than other nationalities." Class was a factor too. The "peasant who has never the sea seen before" was a "better target for ridicule" than others. The difficult homosocial conditions of sailing, with its complex pecking order, promoted social conflict of various kinds.[4] "Race" was simply another exacerbating factor, or so it was thought.

Nevertheless, interethnic conflicts between Europeans were often eclipsed when other "races" were on board. Nor was this unique to the United States. In Britain, "Chinese, Arab, Indian and African seamen were kept out" of the union "on the basis of race," though there was a viable "Belgian, Danish, Dutch, French, Polish Seafarers Federation." Even after World War II, which was thought to have considerably reduced racist sentiment, "the Glasgow local of the National Union of Seamen reaffirmed its opposition to the hiring of Indians or Arabs, even if they were British citizens."[5]

Black seamen were also frequently viewed as political radicals. The worldliness that inhered in sailing, combined with the harsh working conditions and the fact that it often attracted the brightest oppressed youth (because of a dearth of opportunity elsewhere), resulted in Negroes being the most radical of the seamen. Examples abound. The International Trade Union Committee of Negro Workers, whose formation was supported by Soviet workers, espoused a militant Pan-African platform.[6] The World Unity Congress of the International Water Transport Workers, met in Hamburg—an important city for trade unionism—in 1932 with 173 delegates from thirty nations. "Comrade Kouyate, a Negro comrade from Africa" ranked third in leadership.[7] The International of Seamen and Harbour Workers and International

Seamen's Clubs were closely tied to the left and maintained an office in Freetown, Sierra Leone, and in Manhattan on 140 Broad Street.[8]

Black seamen were among the most radical. *The Pilot* reported that when the Marine Transport Workers of the IWW called a strike in 1923, the "Colored Marine Stewards and Cooks Association sent a committee down to say that while they were not Wobblies [anarcho-syndicalists], they positively would not ship during the strike. . . . When the crew of the 'Diamond Cement' struck in 1933 the shipowners were unable to get a crew to scab. They finally shanghaied ten unorganized Negro seamen who were unaware of the strike. At sea they learned about it and as soon as the ship touched the port of Philadelphia, they jumped off in support of the strikers. The following year, 1934, in Baltimore, Negro and white unemployed seamen marched to Washington to protect the relief system they had fought for two years to win. They resisted all attempts to separate them, sleeping in a hall rather than be segregated."[9] It was astonishing that Negroes would ally with the Wobblies as these radicals were frequently victims of vicious persecution themselves. There were scores of police raids in California alone, which was part of a "coast-wide drive . . . against organized labor."[10]

Despite efforts to oust them, by 1935 Negroes constituted 6.2 percent of shipping crews, and over 10 percent after the advent of the affirmative action-conscious NMU.[11] Looking back, the NMU concluded that "before" its "birth" the "Negro seamen, the largest minority in the industry were subjected to all kinds of discrimination and exploitation. . . . They were segregated aboard ship in a single department, assigned the most menial tasks and generally treated like outcasts." It was the NMU that "dumped the Jim Crow hiring policy" and established a fairer "rotary hiring system" whereby "every member knew that the one who registers first at the union hall is entitled to ship out first." Nondiscrimination was a major priority with Smith not only for U.S. Negroes but also including "Jews, British West Indians, Chinese, Puerto Ricans, Egyptians, Filipinos" and other "minorities."[12]

This bold policy attracted bright and ambitious men from across the planet. Kwame Nkrumah, the first leader of independent Ghana, fondly "recalled his membership in the [NMU] while working in the [U.S.] as a steward on a passenger ship of the Clyde Mallory Line." He "worked on the ship during summer breaks from Lincoln University in the mid-to-late 1930s. He rose from dishwasher to waiter and then messenger," and was able to fund his intellectual and political endeavors as a result.[13] In addition, Ewart Guinier, born in the Canal Zone in 1910, was a sailor at sixteen and went from there to a faculty post at Harvard.[14]

It was fitting that a lineal descendant of a leading Negro politician from the post–Civil War era played an instrumental role in sailors' battles. Revels Cayton was secretary of the "powerful District No. 2 of the Maritime Federation of the Pacific" and formerly a steward with the Admiral Line. A grandson of the late Senator Hiram Revels, a Communist, and a close ally of Smith, he represented twenty thousand waterfront workers, a thousand of whom were Negroes.[15]

Cayton was one of a number of high-ranking Negro seamen. Josh Lawrence, perhaps the second-most powerful Negro in the union, was born in Elizabeth, New Jersey, in 1917; his father was a truck driver and his mother a laundry woman. In his early twenties he joined the NMU and quickly climbed up the ladder of union leadership. He joined the Communist Party when the NAACP dispatched him to a Red meeting to challenge what was going on. He went, listened, thought, then agreed with his would-be opponents and joined their ranks. Unlike Smith, the native-born Lawrence was "more open" about his party ties, according to his widow, Vicki Lawrence.[16] Like Smith, he had roots in the Caribbean: his father was from Jamaica and was a lay minister when not driving a truck, while his mother had family ties in South Carolina.[17]

Melvin Roberts, Jesse Brooks, Albert Smith, Justin Smith, and D. G. Grant—Negroes all—were NMU officials in the port of New York.[18] Also among its Negro leader were Percy Jenkins, an active seaman for thirty years who had joined the ISU in 1913, and Charles Mills, a former president of Shipyard Workers Local 1166 of the AFL in Galveston. John Anderson, another Negro leader, reminded his comrades that "I started going to sea since 1923 and [helped] to organize the NUMAGRO strike of the Munson Line during the 1936–37 strike." H. S. Grossett had "been a union man since 1921," as a "Chief Steward," and "a sailor since 1919." Clifford Harper had served on the Food Committee under Smith's direction during the epochal strike. He led a strike of a Luckenbach ship in port in Philadelphia. For ten years he was Chief Steward for the Mississippi Shipping Company. When Smith faced charges just after assuming office, one of his staunchest defenders was the black sailor Oliver Boutte. He "took the floor and spoke at length slyly stressing racial aspects. . . . He implied as did following party speakers that Smith was on trial as a Negro and not as a fink."[19]

There were others too, but the point was clear: Smith was not an isolated Negro leader, just he was not the sole Red either. However, it should be noted that few of these leaders were from the South, where the bulk of Negroes continued to reside and where the more egregious examples of Jim Crow persisted.[20] And their being ousted from influence indicates that the civil rights movement, which had its most dramatic impact in the South, was not without cost, as it occurred just as Negro labor was being weakened in the North. Moreover, like Smith, a number of these men had Caribbean roots, hailing from a region where anticommunism was not as strong as in the United States and where black majorities reigned.

Consider Hugh Mulzac, born in 1886 in the West Indies. He went to sea in 1907 after graduating from high school in St. Vincent and was a U.S. citizen by 1918.[21] Like Smith, he too was a working-class intellectual. In his classic work of proletarian literature, *A Star to Steer By*, he observed, "One of the advantages of sea life is that you have plenty of time to think. . . . It is impossible for any reasonably sensitive human being to stand at a ship's wheel for two hours a watch, three times a day, week in, week out, in the radiant beauty of a starlit night or surrounded by pure, exquisite colors of a dawn or sunset at sea, without giving some thought to the world around him, his own past and the future of both it and himself." Like many other Negro sailors, he too abhorred the bias he experienced. "A West Indian in the United States quickly learns that he is meant for menial labor. . . . Many of the clerks seemed to take it as a personal affront that I should even inquire about deck jobs, and of course, I never even hinted that I carried a second officer's ticket." When he applied for a job in Baltimore in 1910 he was told bluntly, "We hire niggers only in the steward's department."[22] But Mulzac had grit and was not crushed by racism. To the contrary, this founding NMU member waged a decades long battle to skipper a ship, finally winning out during World War II.

Working with him to reach this goal was Ferdinand Smith. In fact, Smith's detractors claimed that he spent too much time fighting for the rights of Negroes to the detriment of others. Smith was "very active up in Harlem among the colored seamen," where he "was instrumental in opening up the 'Harlem branch' of the NMU."[23] This was a basis for Bruce Nelson's argument that the union's "leadership worked hard to build a racially integrated union." They "waged an extensive educational campaign against racism in its own ranks."[24] L. D. Reddick of the

Schomburg Library of Manhattan praised the union for fighting racism; it was the only union of the eighteen individuals and organizations listed to be named to the Schomburg's prestigious Race Relations Honor Roll.[25]

According to Ira Brophy, by the end of the war—but before the purges that removed Smith from the leadership—"NMU members showed noticeably less prejudice than did the craft union members." Perhaps this was because "only one union had an active program for the elimination of racism in the industry, the National Maritime Union." Brophy concludes that the "artificial situation of shipboard life produces a type of relationship in which a need for acceptance of each individual in the group is supreme." "Stories from the battle fronts indicate that in similar situations—survival situations in which basic and realistic anxieties are invoked—individuals either crack psychologically or seek the solidarity of the group. . . . In such a situation, relationships would tend to be stripped of the social super-structure of values and attitudes that are characteristic of the majority of societal relationships. It would appear that many of our respondents could not afford the luxury of an anti-Negro prejudice while at sea."[26]

Nevertheless, the union suffered from the fact that the structure of the industry promoted retrograde attitudes. A "typical collier," for example, "might carry a deck crew of Anglo-Saxons, an engine crew speaking Spanish and a stewards department which was all black. . . . Implicit in these arrangements was that if a white gang failed to behave properly . . . their berths would go immediately to black seamen or vice versa. . . . It was felt that Southern whites would spontaneously align themselves against 'damn Yankees.'"[27] The bosses played up regional ethnic and racial tensions to benefit themselves. Thus, at the tumultuous NMU convention in New Orleans in 1939 Curran reported that since the formation of the union in May 1937, "at least 1000 Negro members of the union have lost their jobs through no fault of their own in Atlantic Coast steamship and tanker companies. How many jobs have been lost by them on Gulf ships has not been estimated, but it undoubtedly comes to a higher figure. . . . The problem of Negro employment is a serious one." This occurred even though the NMU "insisted" on "complete equality for the Negro in every phase of the new union's activity," as "written into the Constitution." But, "despite the spirit and letter of the Constitution, Negroes have been steadily forced off NMU ships" because "ships were laid up. Companies went out of business.

The transfer of ships from a company which employed Negroes to one which did not. Changes in the classification of ships in a given trade." And "ships' crews [were] refusing to accept Negro replacements."[28]

This charge was well founded. Though the NMU had shown that it was far ahead of other unions in its willingness to accept Negro leadership, the union was not free of bias. In fact, early in 1938 a "Committee for Colored Members" in Baltimore reported that "within the last thirty days on three different occasions fellow workers of the colored race have been forced from ships by members of their union, solely on account of their color." *The Pilot* reported that this had happened aboard ships "subsidized" by the U.S. government and that it was a "federal offense."[29]

Smith agreed. "If a crew is allowed to refuse a union brother due to the color of his skin," he said, "is it too much to say that it is just as reasonable to refuse another brother because of the shape of his nose, the size of his ears or feet, and the color of his eyes or hair?" How could the union bar Negroes when "the membership adopted a policy of taking in seamen who had worked during the last three strikes." When the "problem of discrimination has been solved on ships in the New York and Cuba Mail and Porto [sic] Rico Lines and on other ships where apparently white and Negro brothers work and live in harmony," why not on all ships?[30]

The steward, Albert Clarke, echoed Smith's views. "Negroes and Filipinos and other racial minorities, such as Portuguese Hindus are not allowed to sail on certain lines." "We were told to be patient," and "now we read in *The Pilot* that there must be a period of 'education' as far as the 'white' membership is concerned. This is the same old baloney."[31] Edward Devoe agreed with him. "When we all were in trouble, the white brothers did not discriminate against us on the picket line, we suffered and stuck together."[32]

One trade unionist noted that "some of the Negro brothers feel we give only lip service to the anti–Jim Crow policy of the NMU. One active and militant Negro brother said: 'We ought to clean up our own backyard first. The very guy that eats at the same table, sleeps in the same foscle, and sits right beside me in the meeting passing resolutions against discrimination and applauding speakers who denounce discrimination ignores me on the street an hour later.'"[33]

Though many objected to this "white chauvinism,"[34] others were not moved. When in Beaumont, Texas, the "Negro Vice-Chairman of the CIO County Council had been asked to resign by other members of the Council," the NMU there protested "acceptance of the resignation."[35] But Texas was particularly intractable with regard to racism. During the strike that led to the NMU's formation, "colored" longshore locals along the Gulf Coast had their "charters . . . revoked" and were "given a rough deal . . . abuse from police, company thugs" and the like.[36]

This was no small matter. In light of the traditional fifty-fifty division of jobs between "white" and "colored" longshore locals, the latter were among the more powerful institutions among African Americans. They were being pressured not to align with Reds and radicals even though the left had been their staunchest allies. The policy was successful in that some of the locals were "under company domination" and were considered "company cat's paws" (some of the "white" locals had "no record to brag about" either, though they were outraged by the fact that in pockets along the coast "Negroes" had more than half the jobs: they had "2/3 of the work"). Maritime leader Gilbert Mers described this as "the source of most of our grief at the present time in trying to bring about a solid maritime federation. Hundreds of white men have been driven away from the waterfronts on this account. These sores do not heal in a day or two," he told radical labor leader Harry Bridges.[37]

As Mers saw it, maritime organizing along the Gulf Coast was still hampered by the rancor lingering from the unrest in Brownsville in 1906 when "Negro Cavalrymen stationed at Fort Brown . . . staged a riot through that city. Ever since [then] the populace [has] bar[red] Negroes from the city. When the [longshoremen] organized, whites and Negroes alike were taken in the organization in separate locals. These Negroes live in Harlingen, some 20 miles inland," while "administrations in Port Isabel and Brownsville have refused to allow Negroes to enter the cities." Obviously, this did not facilitate maritime organizing. According to Mers, "There probably never will be colored labor on the docks of those cities, unless shipping interests should be able to prevail on the powers-that-be to use them as strikebreakers in the event of a tie-up." This "racial" divide complicated the efforts of progressive forces, for just as some Negroes feared the coming of the NMU because of their allegiance to David Grange, on the Gulf Coast "race" relations were so ulcerous that "the white workers in Corpus Christi are at least 80 percent" for combining in a "Maritime Federation," while "the Negroes are opposed." Mers thought this was "for no apparent reason," indicating how difficult it was to bridge this divide. Houston faced a similar problem, for "here again, the white men are inclined toward the Federation with the Negroes holding back"—and "Houston is the best developed port at the present time," particularly compared to Pensacola, New Orleans, and Mobile.[38]

On the other hand, Mers apparently had a point when he complained about the "colored" locals. Another source reported that when one of these locals "had the contracts with the intercoastal ships," their leader "had one of the swellest kick-back rackets in the South. He did not accept any wages as President of the local, but each week when the longshoremen [were] paid off, he was there at the table and each man would give him anything from a quarter to fifty cents."[39] Yet this local had to be involved if the NMU was to be launched. How then could it avoid the stain of such corruption? Mers complained bitterly and repeatedly about "the police . . . beating up pickets in earnest" in Port Arthur.[40] This was during the embryonic stage of the NMU and reflected the fractiousness of the era.[41]

It is easy to understand why NMU members felt that Texas ports were the most bigoted in the nation. As the Communist sailor, Paul Jarvis, recalled, "I remember that if you had a black guy aboard the ship he had better be well-protected when you hit the Gulf because they would throw him the hell off the Gulf. . . . The crews of the Gulf were the worst. They drank more, they were wilder. . . . These guys were racketeers and they used the union to protect themselves." The racist atmosphere was compounded by an "atmosphere of anarchy. . . . Because of the role of the Wobblies," a result of the IWW's historic foothold in the region.[42] How could the union be united when one sector was under such clamorous assault?

The union tried to undermine this bias. Although by law union halls in Texas had to have two toilets—"racially" coded—NMU militants would nail one shut. They "did have quite a bit of trouble," as a result of such law breaking, recalled M. Hedley Stone of the NMU. "One time the Texas Rangers came in[to]" a union hall "and chased all of the blacks out." On the other hand, the union's strength ensured that they were "a factor in defeating Martin Dies," the conservative leader of the House Un-American Activities Committee.[43]

There were powerful forces helping the union's opponents. Early on the NMU reported that "small groups on the KKK principle have been organized by the Esso dominated Refinery Workers Federation, a company union." The leading "purpose" of this cabal was to "drive all unions from the Tri-Cities: Baytown, Pelley and Goose Creek." Naturally, "their particular target now, because we're the oil companies' biggest headache, are NMU seamen." The "dollar-a-year Texas Rangers who are directly on Humble's payroll," were central to this process.[44] The Ku Klux Klan was a significant force in the region; early in 1940 they were "on the march again and fiery crosses are being seen on the plains of Texas." The NMU was particularly upset by the "new tactic" that accompanied this upsurge; "in the majority of cases . . . the leaders of those particular Klans are leaders of the trades and labor councils in the American Federation of Labor."[45] There were other complaints from the Gulf Coast. J. B. Baguio, Jr., was concerned about "discrimination in the port of Texas City. So many of the Filipinos . . . are unable to get berths on ships on account of their race. The majority of these brothers have . . . families that are depending solely on what these Filipino brothers take home."[46]

Jacob Joseph, a "colored" NMU member, told his coworkers that "in the Gulf ports . . . we ship in two classes—white and colored. White brothers ship with white crews and colored brothers with colored crews. Some ships may carry both white and colored crews but where this is the case—they are separated by departments; such as having a colored deck crew and a white engine crew. . . . We have a number of light Puerto Ricans and Latin Americans who could be taken for either white or colored. And they take advantage of this fact by shipping on either side as they please. . . . This is really a distinct discrimination against the North American Negroes and against the white brothers." But not everyone agreed with Smith's solution to the problem. Brother Joseph argued in conclusion, "So let's get rid of the 'bad egg' brothers," that is the Latinos![47]

The casual observer might easily think that these divisive disputes were the exclusive province of the South. This led to sharp attacks on the region. Joseph Weddick asked rhetorically, "Where do they come from?" referring to the problem of "racial" animus, then answered: "Up from the nation's number one economic problem belt." Singling out Texas he became more direct, pointing to the "section so well advertised by . . . Vice-President Garner and Biscuits O'Daniels, Martin Dies, etc. . . . some of these corn pone bravos are handling the first folding money they ever saw, wearing their first pair of shoes."[48] But Texas was not unique. Racist battles raged throughout the first year of the union and beyond, though it is true that these conflicts were disproportionately frequent in the South.[49]

Roy Malliky of the SS *Siboney* reminded that "colored seamen only have the Ward Line, Puerto Rico Line and Clyde Mallory Line ships that we can be shipped on through our union, which ships we were employed on before we joined this union." So if the NMU barred Negroes from these ships, the ISU seemed a better bet.[50] In fact, a special meeting was held to resolve this question at which a Negro steward noted that "these Negroes are just about on the verge of desperation and threaten to walk out of the union and get jobs as they can. Some are advocating that we go into the ISU or the AFL."[51]

Yet there were problems on the Mallory Line too. *The Pilot* reported, "The stewards of the SS Seminole, Clyde Mallory Line, went on strike in the port of Galveston." They were ready to accept a deal when the boss said, "To hell with the niggers, we'll take the [bastards] to sea and make them work." After this blunt threat, the entire group refused to work and the Line canceled the cruise. Because the "colored seamen" were concerned that the NMU would not make a real difference, during the 1936–37 strike "few colored brothers came out with us."[52]

On the verge of war in 1941, it seemed to some that little had changed. Black NMU leader Hulbert Warner pointed to the bosses as a major problem, as "the shipowners' parrots . . . when talking to white seamen say, 'the NMU of America, CIO, is a Negro organization.'"[53] While this may have inspired some Negroes, it enraged those who sought to keep them "in their place." Thus, soon after Warner's statement, five white sailors in Norfolk had to be "replaced" as they "had refused to sail with a Negro replacement."[54] From Vicksburg, NMU leader W. F. Wilson made a prescient remark: "Once the position of the CIO is changed and it loses the support of the Negro people, the CIO will become a dead organization, particularly in the Southern States."[55] This was the danger of capitulating to "white chauvinism."

The steady accusations of racism led Howard McKenzie of the NMU leadership to announce in March 1940 that "in principle Negro brothers had the right to sail on any ship." So far, so equal. But his next words seemed to reflect a retreat: "We've got to recognize that this [discrimination] is an age-old prejudice that is ingrained. As an official of the organization, although I might be willing to sleep in the same focsle and give them equal rights, I know realistically that many of the members that I represent are not willing to do the same thing." In one of his weaker moments, Smith seemed to echo these sentiments. He proclaimed, "A small group of members, misguided or otherwise, . . . assume that because the NMU has accomplished so much that it should be able to bring about a utopia in the marine industry and bring about equality of shipping on all vessels without any consideration whatsoever for the attitude of the shipowners or the members of the crew. And, if you are not able to do so, then you are denounced as fakers and everything else. . . . Conditions which have existed in this country for over 300 years cannot be eradicated by one single union of 50,000 seamen in three short years. " He did have pointed words for the "white minority, who, like the ostrich sticks its head in the sand, refuses to see or hear or recognize that there must be changed conditions." He reminded them that "for over 50 years" other organizations had sought to "organize the seaman and gain better conditions and gain better conditions for them and they could not do it. Because of what? Because it blindly followed a narrow policy of segregation."[56]

But bigotry was a threat to the very survival of the union and so the leadership addressed it forcefully. In mid-1940 a lead item on the leadership's agenda was "the question of the Negro brothers in the union" and developing a "uniform and coordinated policy . . . as a working basis for trying to solve the problem of discrimination."[57] Curran "suggested" that "in order to help Negro and Filipino brothers get jobs soon, the union should go to those companies with which the NMU has contracts and request that a certain portion of their ships be allotted for crews of minority groups."[58] Smith concurred, adding that "the Merchants and Miners, the Savannah Line and the Eastern Company gave preference to Negroes because they could pay them less. This policy was pursued by the ISU." However, he thought "there must be a certain amount of positions allocated to Negro brothers." This was not some trendy, premature affirmative action but a matter of survival for the union. As Smith noted, "The AFL is basing their campaign" against the NMU "on winning the Negroes first—creating a split and potential army of scabs." So the NMU "must concentrate on [those] ships that have preponderance of the Negroes and get them into the NMU."[59] With slight annoyance at the anarchist and anarcho-syndicalist trends that continued to characterize the union, Smith asked those who objected to his plans, "Are we running a union or is it being run by every individual ship's crew? I say that you need a little backbone."[60]

By August 1940, Howard McKenzie was able to report some progress. In the past some employers would "only employ Negroes who had light colored skins" but that was history, thanks to the NMU, he announced with pride. "We can say consequently, that there are many Negroes employed today in the Gulf Oil tankers, who, under the old setup, would not be employed." The Pennsylvania Shipping Company "employed all white in 1937. They do not employ Negroes on any of these ships in 1940. However, there are two of the ships . . . which employed a Filipino stewards department." A similar policy—no Negroes, some Filipinos—obtained among Pan American Tankers and B&L Shipping. The Kellogg shipping company had not changed from being "all white" though "we placed an individual colored messman or an individual colored cook on these ships" and "in some cases the crew squawked." The union had made more progress on freighters. Lykes Bros., with sixty-three ships, "did not employ any Negroes in 1937. . . . However, in 1940 the company employs all Negroes in the Stewards Department on 7 of the 43 ships." Before the advent of the NMU, the "New York and Porto Rico Line" had a "white deck department," but after the union "practically all of the freighters then carried a colored deck department." The New York and Cuba Mail Line "employed colored deck departments in 1938" but after NMU lobbying, "the percentage" rose to "rougly 70% Negro and 30% white." The impact of the NMU was revealed when United Fruit said, "We have increased employment for the Negro brothers by at least 200 for the entire fleet. The company has made it very clear that if it were not for the union they would not have permitted this percentage to increase."[61]

According to Smith, the "U.S. Lines informed the union that they would not hire Porto Ricans. After much argument by the officials of the union," they made a slight concession, though "the question of the employment of Negroes in this line is still a sore point." This company was "in the forefront of all the forces that have been trying unsuccessfully to destroy this union and its leaders. They have made [an] effort to wreck this union on [the] red issue and other issues. They have employed stool-pigeons and labor spies to wreck our union—and failed. They are now resorting to the age-old question of racial prejudice."[62]

Despite these gains Smith and his cohorts still seemed like a group of revolutionaries who had seized the wheels of power but had not yet won the complete allegiance of the masses, nor totally vanquished external opposition. Hence, when Smith sent directives for action to various ports requesting their backing for an "anti-lynching bill," thirteen agreed and seventeen took no action. There was an even smaller response when he suggested supporting the beleaguered West Coast longshore leader, Harry Bridges, who had contributed so much to the founding of the NMU.[63] These Reds could not dictate action by sailors.

Thus, Negro sailors were sorely disappointed with the bigotry they had to confront in the union they had helped build. "Since the discontinuance of the Munson, Red-D, Colombian and Fall River Lines," said one group, "qualified colored waiters and assistant (bed-room) stewards have been forced to disintegrate into the ranks of messboys, utility men, etc. . . . such a deplorable condition continues to exist in the NMU and nothing is being done by you to rectify such conditions."[64] The reproach was echoed by the "Algonquin crew" which demanded "more employment for Negro members. . . . Several brothers bitterly assailed the unemployment among Negro members and accused union officials of laxity on this score."[65] Frank Williams asked resentfully, "Was the NMU founded as a democratic organization or was it founded for the purpose of exterminating the black man from the waterfront?" The problem was not limited to the South and it also afflicted stewards, where Negroes had held historic hegemony. *The Pilot* reported that there was a "deplorable" situation in the "Stewards' Department which is mostly Negro," and that it was particularly nasty in New York where "there are over three thousand black seamen in our union."[66] This indictment inexorably was aimed at the top New York–based Negro union official: Ferdinand Smith.

Touched to the quick, Smith railed at "internal dissension" that hampered progress on such seemingly insoluble problems, then went on to indict the "Grace Line" which "refuses to hire Negroes for passenger vessels. . . . The union repeatedly conferred with the operators of the American Republic Lines in an effort to have them assign one of these ships to Negro crews. However, the company refused either to hire complete Negro crews or to mix crews on these vessels." Flabbergasted, he added, "it seems as though [some are saying] the officials of the union were responsible for this discrimination and not the steamship companies." He warned his fellow Negroes that "there are many forces at work endeavoring to use their just grievances as a means of disrupting the unity of the NMU."[67] Yet he also warned his fellow trade unionists that by barring Negroes they were inviting the destruction of the union. "Negro seamen find the companies apparently on their side while fellow workers oppose them," which "makes a mockery of the phrase 'union brother.'" The bigotry was particularly virulent in the "Deck Division" of the union, while the preponderance of Negroes among stewards made for a better situation there.[68]

Finally, at the behest of the NMU leadership in the summer of 1940 Smith "spent some time in the Stewards Dispatcher's cage" to get a bird's-eye view of how bias—which was propelled by management and was not against the law—may have been at work in the union's very own hiring hall, which allotted workers to jobs. He quickly discovered that "in such ratings as utilitymen, messmen, porters, scullions and 4th cooks on passenger ships which required white replacements, members of the union were not available. The jobs were called for hour after hour without any response from the membership for these jobs . . . making it necessary to reissue permit cards to white nonmembers [so] as to fill these replacements. While these jobs were being called . . . with no response from the white members, many colored members, Porto [sic] Ricans and Negroes, asked why these jobs could not be given to them, since no white members were available. In all such cases the dispatcher was forced to reply that either the crew or the company would not accept them. However, in one instance when the dispatcher was pressed by the Company for two utility men, the dispatcher replied that he had no white utility men but could send colored men. The company replied, send anything because the ship had to sail. However, when the dispatcher sent out two Porto Ricans, one light and one dark, the personnel manager accepted the light Porto Rican and rejected the dark one." "Porto Ricans," he added, were listed without reference to "race" while "English speaking Negroes . . . are all classed as colored, whether they are light, black or brown." At times the lighter skinned "English speaking Negroes" were not as dark as favored "Porto Ricans" and were puzzled by the Byzantine nature of "race" construction. This created undue friction between these two important blocs.

But the antipathy was overridden by the fact that "English speaking Negroes and Porto Ricans who have cards as old as four and six weeks are forced to sit by while white permit card holders who have just returned from a trip are able to ship out in one or two weeks and in certain instances, in one or two days, as occurred on Wednesday while

I was in the cage." How could the NMU tolerate this, especially since on the "West Coast" sailors were "able to ship . . . on ships on the rotary system without any regard to color." Of course, on the West Coast "racial" relations were more fluid and less biased against Negroes, which allowed for more flexible arrangements than on the East Coast or the South.[69]

Smith's investigation was followed by forceful action. In 1942 twenty NMU members, including Clarence Brown—a Negro—were traveling by train from Tampa to New York but the Negroes were not allowed access to the dining car due to Jim Crow. When they sued the Atlantic Coast Line Railroad Company, the roadblocks they encountered illustrated how bias inside the union was nourished by bias outside it, which emboldened those members of the NMU who sought to resist the tide of "racial" change. Those who objected to "racial" integration in one union took heart from the court's decision—in the midst of a war supposedly fought against various forms of bias—that found this Jim Crow practice "not unreasonably or unduly prejudicial or preferential." The adjudicating agency stated that "what complainant asks us to decide is in its essence a social question, and not a question of inequality of treatment."[70]

The NMU also confronted bias in criminal cases. In Charleston, South Carolina, gloom descended at union headquarters at 108 Church Street when a "company stooge" who "shot and killed a colored member of the AFL Laborers' Union" was released.[71]

Such civil and criminal rulings were part of the infrastructure of Jim Crow; they could not be dismantled by Smith and the union leadership alone. Moreover, bias was reinforced by the very nature of ships where terms like "niggerhead"—the "name of the drums [that] anchor windlass and capstans"—were commonly deployed. In 1939 when Galveston sailors objected to a ship's library carrying the work of the noted seaman-cum-writer, Joseph Conrad, *Nigger of the Narcissus,* and demanded that the offending word be changed to "Negro," they were accused of being oversensitive.[72] The same was said of those who objected to the logo of the Noxcema Chemical Company. In place of the corporate name, "the letterhead bears a cartoon of [a] Negro sticking his head out from a pile of stove wood, with a caption in large letters, 'Nigger in the Woodpile.'"[73] Nor were Negroes the sole victims of bigotry. As Eugene Gavin, an "American Indian" who was voted off the SS *Motorex,* noted in the fall of 1941, "The crew refused to sail with me, the Negro is not the only group discriminated against."[74]

But some members proposed remedies that were difficult to ignore. The black Communist sailor Jacob Green was part of the "Negro Committee," which proposed

> that every issue of *The Pilot* contain at least one more article on the Negro Question and, if possible, more. That all ships which are working under the checkerboard system be publicized as much as possible in *The Pilot* with photographs of the Negroes and whites working and living together. . . . That on all second, third and fourth class ships . . . the jobs be called without specifying color as is practiced now.[75]

Whatever its weaknesses, the NMU was miles ahead of its counterparts.

There was a glimpse of this in 1941 on "the first CIO Labor Day in New Orleans," an event that "will never be forgotten here," *The Pilot* reported. "Tears of joy filled the eyes of many Negroes who saw for the first time in their lives Negro and white workers marching. . . . The NMU, the oldest CIO organization in the city, turned out in squad formation. . . . Four hundred and eighty members of the NMU paraded, including boatmen and dockworkers."[76] The previous Christmas the NMU in New Orleans "gave Jim Crow forces an indigestible morsel as a Christmas Day present. White and Negro members of the union celebrated the day . . . in a truly Christian spirit by having a joint dinner in the De Soto Hotel."[77] In the following decade this city began to desegregate as the NMU was weakened, which was an advance on the "race" front but a retreat on the "class" front.

It took courage to resist Jim Crow, and the NMU was one of the few organizations willing to do so. Before this Labor Day celebration, the union was instrumental in Jacksonville in the "failure to get that old boss' buzzard Jim Crow to do their dirty work for them. . . . Striking the docks at Jacksonville, the colored longshoremen appealed to the NMU for help in preventing scab longshoremen from boarding the ships to unload. Cocksure that the time worn prejudices of the South would again be successful in beating labor, the bosses hired white men to scab on the colored striking longshoremen. NMU men lined up with their colored union brothers and refused to permit scab work on their ships. Result. The Miami Ship Scalers Union was called in for negotiations."[78]

Even before the civil rights battles in mid-1950s Montgomery, Alabama, the NMU was challenging Jim Crow forcefully.

Smith and the leadership had their hands full: a Communist-led union with Negro leadership in an anticommunist nation which was ruled by Jim Crow was bound to be busy, at times overwhelmed. Occasionally Smith had to stray beyond his already full official duties and intervene on behalf of others, as when a Negro sailor—a member of the Seafarers International Union—was charged in early 1941 in Texas with murder. He thanked Smith "for helping to save my life" after he was freed and "denounced the SIU for failure to take any action in his behalf."[79] Such generosity explains why in 1942 Smith came in second only behind Curran in garnering votes for reelection.[80] As the United States was about to enter World War II, despite its manifold problems Smith and his union had reason to be confident. As he himself put it in his 1941 annual report, "Few unions have done so much for the Negro as has the NMU."[81]

The problem of discrimination was pushed toward resolution by the pressing conditions of war. Weeks after the United States entered the conflict, the government cracked down on the United States Lines in response to a protest from the NMU and "compelled the company to hire 25 Negro union members. . . . The United States Lines, Moore-Mc-Cormack and Grace Lines" were "three of the most important diehards against hiring colored members and have caused many ships to sail shorthanded."[82] Shortly thereafter, the "Matson Company, which has carried on a policy of discrimination against Negroes since before anyone can remember" said that "in the future hiring aboard all ship: . . . will be done on the basis of competency and ability and not on the basis of color."[83] The prospect of defeat concentrated the government's mind wonderfully in ways that apparently were not as compelling during peacetime.

Right after that, in February 1942, President Roosevelt issued the union's "Modern 'Emancipation Proclamation'" when he mandated that race and color should have no place in determining who was on board ship.[84] In Vicksburg, Mississippi, this was followed by the "merging of the Negro and white dockworkers locals . . . into one group [which] was voted unanimously. . . . This was the first joint meeting of white and colored workers since the early part of 1939."[85] There were also encouraging signs on board ship.[86] An attempt by a "ship's officers and a company representative to prevent Negro seamen from shipping on an NMU contract was stymied by the action of the crew and the union."[87] In Kentucky two NMU members sitting on a train—one black, one white—intentionally violated the state's Jim Crow laws: "The whole coach joined in a general discussion on the question of segregation. Some Negro soldiers participated."[88]

Paradise had not yet arrived, however. Elwood G. Swift of Virginia "was so disturbed" by "his inner emotions" after reading of this violation of his state's tradition that he could not rest.[89] In Mobile, the "Alabama Drydock & Shipping Company" was deemed "directly responsible" for "attacks on Negro workers at its shipyards in which 80 workers were seriously injured . . . nearly all of them Negro men and women." *The Pilot* saw this as a direct response to FDR's executive order.[90] In Helena, Arkansas, at the same moment a "mob of vigilantes . . . goons and thugs . . . were waiting there to mishandle CIO organizers who came into town. . . . Law and order has apparently collapsed. . . . The grand jury composed mostly of bankers and large landowners refused to indict the negligent police authorities."[91] Days after the fall of Singapore, when it was thought by some that the era of white supremacy was over, a member of the jury avowed that "no intelligent Negro or white man wants wholehearted race equality. There can never be equality or anything in common between the Negro and white man except working conditions, wage scales and recognition of each other's prowess." In a sense, this was a step forward since he accepted a form of equality at work. But he did not stop there: "to even suggest checkerboarded"—racially integrated—"inland waterway boats is so fantastic as to be almost unbelievable." He thought this was "purely Communistic," which shows why some blacks thought the Reds were their best defenders. "Do you want to eat with them, take them into their homes to socialize with them, their wives and their daughters? Do they believe it enough to want intermarriage and interbreeding between their own daughters and members of the Negro race? This is what racial equality will eventually mean."[92] The elite of Miami Beach seem to have concurred. When Smith inquired about holding a meeting there, "requesting details on accommodations, particularly for the NMU's Negro delegates," the "City Convention Direction" replied curtly, "I am sorry," no Negroes would be lodging there.[93]

Yet the conditions of war had caused a minor civil war to erupt within the union over the question of Jim Crow. Jack Hopkins, a seaman, reported that "after months of riding a tanker carrying fuel to the

Allied armies through sub-infested waters of the Atlantic and Mediterranean and undergoing the hardships of rough seas and cold and fog, after seeing my brother seamen dying in cold waters and calling for help in the pitch black night," he returned the wiser to the United States. "I boarded a train and was promptly Jim-Crowed in the national capital." Then he arrived in Texas where a "Negro passenger who made the mistake of going to sleep on the bus was promptly kicked and dragged and struck over the head with the driver's ticket puncher and put off the bus." Seeing this he had an epiphany: "Then I knew how the people of Nazi-occupied countries feel but they have the consolation of knowing the invader will be driven from their country someday."[94]

Jack Hopkins's experiences of racism and antiracism highlight the contradictory nature of the civil rights movement and its impact. While Jim Crow barriers were being lifted on the one hand, the NMU, which had been instrumental in creating the conditions for this development, was being weakened on the other. Worse, this working class organization was increasingly isolated socially and interracial fraternity was in decline. Ironically, various forms of nationalism accelerated among Negroes just as the formal stumbling blocks to equality were being dismantled.

Though he faced formidable internal and external obstacles, Ferdinand Smith had helped to establish the NMU as a bulwark of opposition to Jim Crow and was a source of inspiration to Negroes. By 1944 there were "Negro ship captains, a large number of Negro ship officers and nearly 8000 Negro merchant seamen." The *New York Herald Tribune* went on to report that Smith claimed proudly that "colored and white members of his union are now able to await jobs in the same NMU hiring places in southern port cities." Such equality infuriated Dixiecrats, who had reason to believe that there was a direct connection between Reds and Black Liberation.[95]

When the King-Innes crowd invaded NMU headquarters with baseball bats drawn in July 1938, they suffered a severe setback. As Curran recounts it, "We were able to rally the rank and file especially on this business of dumping"—assaulting—"women. . . . Among the seamen, I don't care who the woman is, if you hit a woman, you're in trouble. You go out there and show a couple of pictures of women being hurt by some people and they've lost every chance they had to organize them anyway. The seaman had this reputation. A woman might be a prostitute, but you don't do any harm to her, because if you do, the seaman will catch up with you. They think women are just tops. They may mistreat them when they're with them but when the doors are open, they guard them."[96]

Curran's remarks unintentionally reveal the conflicting attitudes of this mostly male union toward women and the fraught question of sexuality generally. Marcus Rediker observes that "some seamen apparently believed that women, like the adherents of orthodox religion, were potential sources of conflict and perhaps an eventual breach in the solidarity order of the ship." The homosocial environment on board ship created a peculiar ethos. "The seaman's labor," says Rediker, "also required a great deal of physical prowess and masculinity and athletic ability were also highly valued."[97] There was a "long-held belief that water is the female element and that women have powers over the sea that are denied to men. This belief dates back to ancient Greece and beyond."[98] As one analyst puts it,

> Nowhere is the feminine as present and as feared as on the sea. The danger seems to be contained in the element itself: currents that cannot be tamed, dangerous depths and reefs, sea monsters devouring hapless sailors, sirens, harpies, sea hags, giant polyps. Terrible beings that stalked and stalk seafarers all the time;

The "association of women with fish" only added to the mythology. Women were barred from ships, particularly because it was feared that their presence would create "conflicts and jealousies among the men."[99]

Sexuality itself was a complicated question for many male sailors; on the ship of the Elizabethan pirate, Sir Francis Drake, one man who "had committed sodomy with two of the ship's boys . . . was hanged."[100] Gender was likewise a complicated subject for many NMU members to contemplate. As with their experiences with "race," their work exposed them to places far beyond the ken of landlubbers, which could expand their horizons beyond the conventional. The sailor Bill Penman was "flabbergasted" upon landing in Vladivostok and discovering "women barbers." Every day he visited a different barbershop so as to experience tonsorial intimacy.[101] Seeing women perform roles abroad that were closed to them at home opened his eyes to the issue of job segregation.

World War II presented a unique challenge to the union's construc-
tions of gender. In May 1941 *The Pilot* featured a revealing picture of
Ann Corio, "celebrated strip-tease artiste" who, it was reported breath-
lessly, "has signed an application for a blind date" with a lucky union
member.[102] On the other hand, when "manpower" in shipping was
strained as men were being drafted, Smith among others rallied to the
support of "our allied seawomen."[103] Bill Penman, perhaps influenced
by his travels in eastern Russia, spoke out against "rank discrimination
of women in our industry. . . . Anyone who has been to Russia before
this war started or to England since, cannot but be convinced and impressed by women's ability to do so-called men's work." Addressing
his brethren, he was blunt: "Let's face the facts [about the] almost complete indifference towards the Women's Auxiliary of our own union. I
know lots of brothers steer clear of this because they don't want the Little Woman to know the real size of their pay envelopes."[104] Nevertheless, many of the women who worked with the union did so with the
NMU's incredibly active Women's Auxiliary. Largely the wives of
sailors, they pursued such traditional maternal goals as seeking funds
for "more nurseries and playgrounds."[105]

There were other economic factors enmeshed with gender. "Some
men expressed fear that women would replace them at their jobs" during the war.[106] Smith rejected such thinking, encouraging those at the
1943 NMU convention to send "telegrams . . . right away . . . regarding
the women going back to sea."[107] They had been "removed from American ships at the beginning of the war, by order of the government." At
the NMU convention a resolution was passed supporting the "demand
of the Seafaring Women for reinstatement in the American Merchant
Marine."[108] By 1946 there were merely 472 women in the union in the
Port of New York—perhaps the largest female representation nationally
in any port—most serving as "stewardess," "waitress," "saladgirl," or
"nurse-stewardess."[109]

Sailors—who were so progressive on so many issues—were not noticeably enlightened when it came to gender. As the union was just beginning, a "group of Grace Line Waitresses" of the "SS *Elena*" "read the
letters from some of our brother seamen. . . . What seems peculiar to us
waitresses is that we have never been approached to join the union.
Many of us would gladly join in your fight."[110] In their roman à clef
Home Is the Sailor, Beth McHenry and Frederick N. Myers write of "a
number of [sailors who] formed a group known as the 'anti-social

league,' a sort of organization of bachelor militants who warred openly on women and the bourgeois influence of home life."[111]

They would have been astonished to meet "Mrs. Georgia Smith," a "Negro woman sea captain" based in Savannah. This "small woman, well past middle age, . . . commanded a full-fledged twenty-two and one-half ton stoop," though she "resigned from the water because a doctor threatened me with a knife." Remarkably, she had a "master's license" and carried people and freight. "I can fix a car as good as anybody," she boasted, "take it apart and put it together again. And I'm a good shot with a gun—only miss about ten out of a hundred." Regrettably, such female talent was sorely lacking on most ships and within the NMU itself, as the union was anything but radical when it came to the "Woman Question."[112]

The NMU was a little better about gay men, though its unstated position seemed to be of the "don't ask, don't tell" variety. The sailor Carl Pandover, who sailed on both coasts, recalled that there were quite a few gay men in the stewards department, many of whom were Negroes. He did not recall any particular problem presented by their presence.[113]

On the other hand, homosexual incidents could roil the waters. William Gomez shipped out as chief cook on the Norton Lilly Steamship Company in January 1944. A few weeks later he was "enticing one William Allison . . . into his room, put his hands on Allison's body and made advances to induce Allison to engage in an act of sodomy. He was unsuccessful." He had bought "four bottles of beer" and invited Allison to his room for a drink—and more. After settling down with the brew, Gomez "closed the door, turned off the lights and . . . placed his hand on Allison's knee and ran it up his thigh." Shortly thereafter, "E. W. O'Connor . . . went to sleep while drunk. . . . At about 2045 O'Connor awoke . . . with a feeling of imminent ejaculation . . . and realized an act of sodomy (oral) had been committed upon him. . . . The room was dark and he felt confused for a moment. Ejaculation occurred and he snapped on his bunk light. . . . He turned on the light and discovered Gomez to be the person who had committed the offense. He hit Gomez with his fist twice and called the watch to arrest [him] but Gomez escaped. Subsequently he discovered Gomez on the ship and again hit him whereupon Gomez produced a knife and O'Connor ran." Gomez was "arrested" and "removed from the ship."

The accused claimed that the charges were false and that he was disliked "on account of his gambling with and winning from them at cards." Although he was convicted, his case should be viewed through the lens of the general unruliness of seamen—the kind that caused some men to invade union headquarters with baseball bats drawn—rather than the prevalence of homosexual rape on board ship.[114]

4

Few Safe Harbors

THE PASTORAL CAMPUS at Tuskeegee featured an impressive statue of its founder, Booker T. Washington, lifting the veil of ignorance from an unnamed Negro—though one may also interpret it as Washington allowing the veil to descend upon him. As Ferdinand Smith arrived on these finely manicured grounds in the midst of World War II, there was no doubt about his intent: he had come to dispel ignorance, specifically to shed light on the connection between a nation fighting a war in the name of the highest ideals while imposing Jim Crow. Thus, at the fifth annual conference of the Southern Negro Youth Congress in Tuskeegee, Alabama, in April 1942, he argued, "You cannot demand of a people that they die for a country which denies them the right to live as free people."[1] These were brave words in a place so close to the cradle of the Confederacy—though the war had made it easier to raise these issues.

The exigencies of fighting an antifascist war created objective conditions that were helpful to Ferdinand Smith, the NMU, and Negroes in general. Their foes, the Dixiecrats and the racist diehards, were thrown on the defensive, as they bore too great a resemblance to the enemy in Berlin. Simultaneously, Black Communists like Smith's comrade Ben Davis rose in public estimation, as he was elected to the New York City Council in 1943 and was reelected in 1945.[2]

These advances came at a very heavy price. The NMU sacrificed a great deal in the war, sailing through submarine-infested waters in order to deliver life-saving supplies to Murmansk and other critical ports worldwide. In the summer of 1942—with three years to go before the war ended—*Life* magazine reported that "from its 4,000,000 men the U.S. army has lost to date 1381. . . . From its 600,000 men, the Navy has lost 3420 sailors. . . . But from its small number of 50,000 men [NMU] has lost 1800 seamen." The "biggest seamen's union in the world" helped bring about the Allied victory with an arduous effort drenched with blood.[3] By war's end, it is estimated that "at least 8651 mariners were killed at sea, 11,000 wounded of whom at least 1100 died from their wounds and 604 men and women were taken prisoner." Dwight D. Eisenhower reflected the feelings of many when he said, "When final victory is ours there is no organization that [merits] its credit more deservedly than the Merchant Marine."[4]

A good deal of this blood was shed by Negroes. In November 1942 Smith affirmed that of the two thousand sailors carrying goods to fight Hitler, three hundred and thirty were Negroes.[5] One reason for this high number was that Negroes were effectively barred from the U.S. Navy, which forced them to look elsewhere. A segregated naval facility opened in June 1942, the "Great Lakes Training Center," named ironically after the heroic Civil War era Negro waterman, Robert Smalls. As late as 1943, 98 percent of those serving in the U.S. Navy were white. Yet somehow the navy registered "surprise at the total lack of enthusiasm for naval service among young black men."[6]

Many Negroes seeking an opportunity to serve their nation at sea looked to the NMU.[7] However, because they sailed to some of the poorest countries in the world union members had "an estimated tuberculosis rate three or four times that of the rest of the population."[8] The war, with its pressing need for ships to carry supplies to far-flung battlefields and allies alike, provided an opportunity for the NMU to expand, increasing the power of an already formidable union.[9] In 1944 the Democratic National Committee remarked with awe that "last year in 1943, over 1800 merchant ships, 19 million tons of them, tasted salt water for the first time. [It was] more than twice the number of ships built in the record breaking year of 1942." By way of comparison, "in 1937 . . . only 18 merchant vessels were built and in 1938 only 25!"[10] Thus, "of the 220,000 workers in water transport in mid 1944 75 percent were organized. Of the 166,000 organized workers in water transportation, 45 percent were in the [NMU]." The union was as essential to the health of the economy as smoothly functioning arteries and capillaries were to the health of the body.[11]

Moreover, this Communist-led union had a very different approach to the war from the common perception. Repeatedly, *The Pilot* expressed views that were critical of the Reds. Thus, in early June 1941 one sailor wrote, "You have in great big headlines a story about the immense increase in wages those who work on the ships going to the war zones receive. On the next page you have a picture of an NMU Peace delegation in Washington with such signs as 'No More Convoys.' In other words, the officials of the NMU are two-faced about their anti-war policy."[12] Other critics wondered how the NMU could reconcile having "played a leading role" at a Chicago conference in the late summer of 1940, attended by twenty thousand delegates, to forge the American Peace Mobilization, when convoys to fuel the war were employing NMU members.[13] This sailor must have been confirmed in his views about the leadership when by early July 1941 the NMU reversed itself and convened a "special membership meeting" which voted "full support of the 'present struggle of Great Britain and the Soviet Union against the forces of fascism.'"[14]

Smith was less susceptible to charges of ideological swings dictated by Moscow, since his anti–Jim Crow message did not begin all at once on 22 June 1941 when the Soviet Union was invaded by Germany. It only picked up the pace. From the beginning of U.S. involvement in the war, Smith argued that the Jim Crow that had caused so much misery for the NMU leadership and Negroes alike could no longer be tolerated because it was severely hampering the national security of the nation. He told his fellow sailors that "we dedicate our lives to the defeat of Hitlerism abroad'" and "we equally dedicate ourselves to the eradication of all vestiges of human oppression from these United States."[15] In mid-1943, dressed in a dark double-breasted suit, Smith joined with Congressman Thomas D'Allesandro and Daniel Ellison, a grandson of Frederick Douglass, in Baltimore as the SS *Frederick Douglass* was launched. "In the Civil War," Smith said, Douglass had argued that "slavery must expand or die. Today, it is recognized that fascism is no different and must be treated similarly."[16]

He repeated this argument throughout the war. Cognizant of his Caribbean roots, he expanded his thesis to include the entire colonized world. Speaking in Buffalo in July 1942 at the Conference for the Full Use of Negro Labor Power, he declared, "As we carry on the fight for the complete mobilization of Negro Americans we must also recognize that in Asia and Africa there are hundreds of millions of colored people available, but not yet fully mobilized. . . . Our country must take the lead in seeing that these colored peoples receive their freedom now." Linking the two struggles, he added, "The successful fight for Negro rights in America will help mobilize these colonial peoples." While he "lauded the Red Army," he criticized "Great Britain" because the "whole United Nations' fight against Hitlerism suffered in Malaya, Singapore, Burma because of the shortsighted British policy of denying to her colonials their natural inspirations for freedom."[17]

NMU members understood this phenomenon well, given their familiarity with the ports of the European colonies in Asia. Moreover, a number of key Negro leaders of the pro-Tokyo movement were sailors—which is how they had become acquainted with Japan in the first place. Robert Obadiah Jordan, head of the Ethiopian Pacific Movement based in Harlem, was among them. Born in Jamaica, he "worked several years as quartermaster on Japanese boats which belonged to the Japanese Mail Steamship Company." As one analyst put it, "Nippon's gigantic plan [was] to muster millions of colored people in the United States who would work as a potential fifth column and would, when the order was given, stir up all sorts of unrest. . . . [Tokyo] recruited several hundred [Negroes]," a number of whom were invited to Japan. By 1942 "ten seamen" were on trial at the federal courthouse in Brooklyn for spying on behalf of the Axis.[18] The union's friend, Paul Robeson, reminded its members in The Pilot, "Don't think that because the Japanese are colored that they are leading the fight for freedom."[19]

Sympathy for Japan among black Americans presented a clear and present danger to the war effort. The eminent writer and Asian specialist, Pearl Buck, addressed a "letter to Colored Americans," asking them not to give up on the United States. "I know that there are among you" those "who . . . say, that it might be well if Japan should win this war. . . . Do not think of vengeance. . . . Certainly it is asking you to be better than the white man has been."[20]

Buck recognized, as did Smith and the NMU, that it would take hard work to win Negroes over to the Allies' cause. Simultaneously, the union and Smith refused to fall victim to the anti-Issei and anti-Nissei crusade that led to the internment of Japanese Americans. Years later, seaman Joe Stack recalled that "the NMU, ILWU [West Coast longshore], MCS [Marine Cooks and Stewards] . . . were among the few unions that protested to the U.S. government against the internment of the Japanese Americans. Also, the NMU had a standing committee, which I was a member of, that pressured the U.S. government to clear many [Japanese American] seamen in order for them to sail on American ships during the latter part of the war."[21] As the hysteria against Japanese Americans mounted, in August 1942 Smith posed in tie and shirtsleeves with "Japanese brother Kaoru Abe," just released from internment. "It was through the efforts of the NMU that Kaoru was finally released," Smith told the seamen. Abe, an NMU member, had been interned after the ship he was on had the misfortune of sailing to the West Coast.[22]

Similarly, in August 1942 Smith told his fellow NMU leaders, "We are pleased to report that the union has finally been successful in bringing about a change in status of Filipino seamen who are now allowed to sail the ships under the same status as American citizens."[23] The NMU had a strong record when it came to scrutinizing Asia or Imperial Japan. Almost a year before the bombing of Pearl Harbor, the union raised searching questions about U.S. "steel for Japan" and "the largest consignment of gasoline ever ordered in this country by the Japanese government."[24] Sailors on the SS *Nemaha* assailed the "criminal actions of Japan's invasion [of China] and war against the people of Japan" and called for a "complete embargo of Japan."[25]

The NMU's far-sightedness was the result of the sailors' ethic of internationalism, their detailed knowledge of global affairs, and their distrust of ultranationalists. Because of their international experience, sailors entered the war with more awareness and discernment than any other union and perhaps, any other group.

Sailors' national origins, however, were more heterogeneous than those of other workers, as Smith's roots in Jamaica exemplified. Andrew Furuseth, an early leader of the sailors' union, was Norwegian. In the first few decades of the twentieth century "every major seaport in the U.S.A. became the home port for a relatively large number of Norwegian seamen" and the "Norwegian fleet became the third largest in the world. Eighty percent of the Norwegian ships were engaged in foreign trade." The Scandinavian Seamen's Club, founded in 1935, led the "first official 'sit-down strike'" in the United States.

They leaned distinctly to the left. In December 1935 a Norwegian ship arrived at pier 7 in New Jersey, just across the Hudson River, and started to load scrap iron bound for Italy. But when the sailors learned of the destination and purpose of the shipment—for the war in Ethiopia—they went on strike. Adam Clayton Powell then leaped in, called the Norwegian consulate and demanded that the ship not be loaded. The ship was detained for weeks before it was able to depart. The seamen also protested in Mobile against sending scrap iron to Japan—because of the war in China—and joined the NMU en masse because of the union's welcome to "alien labor" and their importance in the ranks.[26] As sailors and potential sailors enlisted in the armed forces, the NMU's reliance on alien seamen grew accordingly. In early 1942, the NMU acknowledged that "under peacetime law, American vessels under subsidy are required to carry 100% American crews with the exception that 10% aliens are permitted in the Steward Department on passenger ships. On non-subsidized vessels, 75% of the crew is required to be citizens during peacetime." But "due to the shortage of merchant marine personnel, this law has been revised for the duration" of the war.[27]

As the NMU noted later, "thousands of foreign seamen answered our country's [call]." One of them was Saleh Mirghani, twenty-six, of Egypt, who was "seriously injured in a bombing attack in Antwerp while aboard the SS *Amelia Earhart* in 1945." Desperate for labor, "during the war" the U.S. "government issued urgent appeals in the press and over the radio for skilled seamen to man our merchant fleet." "Aliens in the Army and Navy were eligible for American citizenship after being in uniform for three months."[28]

The "aliens" were joined by U.S. sailors in promoting internationalist causes. As early as 1935, progressive sailors raised the joint slogan, "Defend Ethiopia"—"every worker in the U.S. make Ethiopia his business."[29] That year one sailor was shot and sixteen others were hurt as "Reds" launched a "riot" on the *Bremen* after they tried to snatch the swastika-adorned flag from this German ship. Numerous U.S. sailors were arrested attempting to smuggle anti-Nazi literature into Hamburg.[30] The situation had become so severe that Blackie Myers felt compelled to inform the White House that "it has become the practice to detain American seamen in Hamburg when it becomes known that they are in opposition to the Hitler regime."[31]

The journalist Richard Boyer found that "there were NMU sailors who had been jailed in India for their fight for freedom there," while others were "jailed" in South Africa, Brazil, and elsewhere. "Francis Xavier O'Hallahan who had been jailed by the Japanese in Shanghai in 1938 as a result of his activity with the Chinese people" was among those who had sacrificed for freedom beyond the borders of the United States.[32]

When the Spanish Civil War—a precursor to the antifascist war—broke out, sailors were among the first to answer the call. Indeed, the confluence of the war and the founding of the union harmed the latter in that the sailors' "courage, leadership and expertise . . . bolstered the Loyalists' losing cause but stripped the seamen's movement of many of its most dedicated cadre and hindered the strike effort" and ultimately the union itself.[33] Hundreds of seamen fought in Spain, making a disproportionately large contribution to the renowned Abraham Lincoln Brigade.[34]

After fighting in Spain, NMU member Bill McCarthy "was imprisoned in fascist Italy where he continued his fight against fascism with the Italian underground." Such altruistic selflessness led one writer to argue that the NMU had created a "new kind of American. They know that the world whose seas they sail is one world. They know that what happens in Indonesia or Africa is as important as what happens in Brooklyn or Chicago. They have little division between thought and action."[35] Although seamen were by definition more mobile, more likely to be near or in Spain or other trouble spots than others, which gave them an advantage when conflict broke out, their accomplishment was no less impressive for that. The crew that sailed to Valencia with a hefty $300,000 worth of food, clothing, and medicine for the embattled enemies of fascism was made up of NMU members.[36]

During World War II the NMU refused to staff ships sailing to "Franco Spain." "We owe this to the 900 members of the NMU who went to join the Loyalists," it said, "we owe it to the 300 members who died in Spain."[37] Later Smith joined with the budding choreographer and dancer, Pearl Primus, to raise funds for the Joint Anti-Fascist Refugee Committee in their campaign for a free Spain.[38]

In short, sailors had a sound understanding of the perils of fascism and political repression. What happened in the spring of 1937 as the union was being launched was typical. In Buenos Aires the "crew of the *American Legion* staged a sit-down strike. One of the colored brothers, the Stewards Department delegate, was left behind at Rio," then rejoined the ship. When he went to the purser he was told "no money was coming to him." The crew struck in response and the captain capitulated. The crew realized that "the brother was picked as an example . . . because he was a steward's delegate and a militant rank and filer. The captain, it was reported, thought it would break the solidarity of the crew."[39] Away from the reactionary winds of North America, sailors seemed to be able to pursue their common class interests and put narrow "racial" concerns behind them.

The global nature of the industry forced the NMU to attend to matters beyond U.S. shores. Deteriorating working conditions and wages on foreign ships could—and eventually did—contribute to similar conditions on U.S. ships. This led to the formation of the "Pan American

Department" in 1940, which "served to counteract the tendency of various American shipowners to transfer their vessels to foreign registry, particularly to flags of Latin American republics." The union was "able to organize many of the seamen employed on vessels owned by American interests and flying flags of one or another of the Latin American countries. Today," said Smith, "over 600 vessels owned by American interests are in this category." The battle against "flags of convenience" was an early priority for the NMU. The ouster of Smith and his comrades weakened the union in its fight, leading to its defeat in this crucial battle.

But Smith persevered. In 1940 he was calling for a hemispheric union of sailors, urging the NMU to "establish closer relations with the existing maritime unions of such . . . nations as Chile, Cuba, Mexico, Brazil and Argentina . . . establishment of the 'brotherhood-of-the-sea' as is called for in our Constitution." Smith recalled the "action of the Cuban longshoremen who rallied to our support during our 1936–37 strike; also the demonstrations of sympathy of the Chilean longshoremen."[40] Smith reciprocated by extending the union's solidarity to "rank and file members of the Union Obrera Maritima" of Buenos Aires,[41] just as he periodically conferred with Vicente Lombardo, the Mexican trade union leader.[42] Unlike many unions—and many Reds too, for that matter—the NMU was in a unique position to assess international politics and make intelligent judgments. It was in the NMU's interest to be familiar with the political economy of different nations, so as to better advise its members which ones to avoid, and which nation's sailors might be seeking to undercut the wages and working conditions of their U.S. counterparts. As the union was debating the feasibility of endorsing the war in Europe, it also "endorsed the principle of [a] Pan-American Trade Union. We went further than that. We joined with the trade unions in Chile, in Central America, Mexico and the Argentine to establish a Council in Havana. This Council's job is to bring the unions closer together, especially the maritime unions." "The shipowners in the past," it emphasized, "have recognized that once they got a ship out of New York, they didn't have to worry about it being worked at the other end." But now, with transcontinental organizing, "that time is past." Just as it was "important . . . for the American Bankers Association to have a Pan-American union and for the real estate operators, the sugar plantation owners and the rest of them," so too for sailors.[43]

So, in response to the charge that the Reds were trying to get the union involved in matters beyond its purview, the union argued that enlightened self-interest dictated that it think globally, just as their bosses did. It had to do so because at any given moment its members could be found anywhere on earth. Thus, in late February 1941, Smith was executing a familiar duty: contacting the State Department on behalf of an aggrieved sailor. This case concerned "one Ernst Roth" of the "crew of the SS *Brazil*," who had been "employed as vegetable cook" and was "taken off the ship by the British authorities in the Port of Spain, Trinidad." Roth, "born in Germany," had his "locker . . . searched" and "as far as we know is still being held in custody." The State Department said that since he was born abroad there was nothing the United States could do—but Smith pressed on.[44] Smith reached out to the State Department again in the spring of 1941 after a "request from the crew of the SS Siboney of the American Export Lines" concerned about the "whereabouts of two of our members; namely, Carmel Carvera and Ralph Tucker . . . taken off the ship in the port of Lisbon, Portugal" by police.[45]

At times the union seemed to be no more than a branch of a global federation of seamen, given its frequent defense of foreign sailors and sailors abroad. It helped to form a Committee of European Seamen, comprised of sailors who had fled to the United States after their nations had been overrun by the Nazis. There were a thousand members in New York City alone: "Norwegian, Danish, Dutch, Belgian and French seamen. . . . Even Greek and Yugoslav seamen are joining." In addition to helping them in the United States, the NMU assisted them by raising complaints about wages and working conditions on their ships.[46]

The NMU accelerated its efforts as war approached. It had to confront "quite a lobby in Washington" which favored the Greek and Yugoslav governments setting up bodies in the United States to try and punish absconding and protesting sailors. The NMU took a "very firm stand against any such attempt to acquire extra-territorial rights," since "such a precedent might later develop into an attempt on the part of our own reactionaries to establish similar procedures in foreign countries for American seamen." The "problem of foreign seamen has become a general problem for the union," it reported, underscoring the strong internationalism of the NMU.[47]

The NMU also felt that if it tolerated atrocious working conditions for sailors in one nation the same would happen in the United States, in a kind of "race to the bottom." Why shouldn't those bringing goods to the United States deploy low-wage labor in rusted out "floating slums" if they could get away with it, and what did that mean for the future of the NMU? Thus, during the favorable conditions created by the war the union pressed the British colonial government to improve conditions for Indian sailors, for example. "You have to go back to the last century," said a union spokesman, "to find conditions on American ships comparable to those now prevailing on British vessels employing Indian seamen." Six of these exploited laborers visited NMU headquarters in Manhattan, where they described their $15 per month salaries, seven-day workweeks with fourteen-hour days, no overtime, and no paid vacations.[48]

Another reason the union had to pay attention to global developments was that it had to be in a position to alert its members about unfavorable conditions at different ports. This was particularly true for Negro sailors going to Africa. NMU member Charles Pennick perished when his ship "was docked at the coal pier in Dakar." The "coal dock [was] without a single light for its entire length. The closest shore lights [were] about 100 yards distant from the dock and beyond the coal piles." He faltered in the "almost complete darkness," slipped, and drowned.[49]

In the late summer of 1940 Victor Duran recounted his voyage from New York City to South Africa where the dangers were just as grave as those in Dakar. "There had been the best of harmony between the colored and white members of the crew. . . . However, after arriving in Port Elizabeth . . . the Master informed us that the Port Authorities had ruled that none of the colored crew were to be allowed ashore, although there was no such restriction in Cape Town." This made him suspicious. "All this takes on [the] look of collusion between the company, the Captain and possibly the South African government." For "one of the colored men went down the spring line in Durban and had no trouble going through the gate or in the town." The lesson the NMU learned was that it was difficult to build an island of "racial" equality in the midst of a sea of turbulent bigotry.[50]

The problem of African-American sailors in South Africa was a constant irritant even during the war, as seamen recounted first-hand stories of the precursors of apartheid. Smith protested formally to the U.S.

Maritime Commission and the South African consulate but was informed that "your own house ought to be put in order" first. The Commission "consistently refused to inject itself into the personnel policies adopted by the various shipping companies," including the "American South African Line" which continued to sail to South Africa.[51] Because he felt that "our own welfare here in America is closely tied up with the general advancement of the African people," Smith refused to give up.[52]

Just as foreign travel could enlighten a person, so too could it reinforce prejudice. Thus, at the NMU's behest the State Department decided to "probe discrimination by the Venezuelan government against Negro seamen on board American vessels calling at Venezuelan ports." Smith told Secretary of State Cordell Hull that black sailors were being "refused shore leave," not to mention that "any person belonging to the Yellow race" also was being barred.[53]

These frequent encounters with discrimination helped forge strong bonds across the Atlantic. A. A. Adio-Moses, Secretary-General of the Trade Union Congress of Nigeria, told his friends in the United States that "we have had rather disturbing news of the lynching of Negroes by American whites"; he intended to raise this matter at their next meeting, and requested "suggestions as to what action we could take to help."[54] In turn the NMU crew on the SS *Selma Victory* "voted" to turn over the "ship's fund" to the "Gold Miners of South Africa. The crew expressed support for the gold miners' efforts to obtain better conditions in face of mass arrest and shootings of strikers. . . . The junior third mate, a former NMU member, was given a vote of thanks for getting copies of *The Pilot* for the crew in South Africa."[55] Such mutual reinforcement of each other's struggles was rare among workers and even rarer between the United States and Africa, but was becoming the norm in Smith's NMU.

Bigotry was not limited to Africa. The sailor Raymond Levering observed that "on Christmas day" in 1940 "we were in Panama. Several of the sailors had been friendly for a long time with a Negro longshoreman, exchanging tips on the dog races every trip. When we arrived in Panama, this longshoreman invited three of these fellows to a Christmas party at his home, the host supplying the liquor, turkey and female company (colored of course). . . . A good time was had by all. . . . [Yet] if a Negro replacement should be sent to a ship from the [hiring] hall, one would have a hard time convincing these very men that he should be accepted in accordance with our Constitution. . . . I know that one of these men in particular would raise violent and vicious objections. If Negro workers are good enough [for] white workers to go to Christmas parties with, then are they good enough to work alongside their union brothers on the job? Sure they are." Repeating a union slogan during the war, he said they should end racism so as to better combat "our native American fascists."[56]

But in 1944, sailors were again complaining about Panama. "If the situation as it stands is not corrected," four of them said angrily, then they would get what "the British got from the natives of Singapore or Burma." "On two occasions two members of our crew visited the Balboa clubhouse . . . and were denied admittance to the restaurant and movies." They detected the long hand of Jim Crow in this de facto U.S. protectorate and pointed to the "resentment with which many white Americans are treated by the Panamanian Negroes."[57]

Despite the antifascist atmosphere created by the war, racist practices did not disappear magically at home or abroad. Though leading circles in Britain were touting the "Four Freedoms" and the "Atlantic Charter," evidently they did not intend these promises to apply to their colonies. A. E. Moselle of the United Committee of Coloured Peoples' Association of Cardiff observed that "as a rule colored seamen were given employment only on coal-carrying ships, those with clean cargoes carrying white seamen."[58]

Solidarity was needed because London, perceived as being on the side of the angels during the war, continued its racist policies. In 1944 "several Negro members" of an NMU crew "were refused admission to the dance floor and public ballrooms in an English port." In response, the sailors "sent a committee to interview the manager of the Rialto Ballroom," where they "condemned this white chauvinism."[59] The NMU announced that "unless the U.S. government requests in writing that they be replaced by white seamen, the full Negro crew in the Stewards Department of the SS *West Jaffrey* will take the ship out despite the British Ministry of Shipping."[60]

Smith was no stranger to the Empire given that he was from Jamaica. Despite the widespread perception that Communists like himself held their tongues during the war lest the Soviet Union be offended, this was not so with him. "It would be splendid," he said, "if the voice of labor were raised . . . in a vigorous demand for Independence" in the colonies. He was pleased that "Congress [had] finally repealed the shameful Chinese Exclusion Act" but it "should not delay in granting quota immigration and naturalization privileges to the people of India."[61]

Illustrating how important global issues were in the union, candidates for office in the NMU began to tout their international activism during their campaigns. Thus, when the Negro sailor Leo Stoute ran for union office in 1944, he noted that he was not only "active on [the] Brooklyn waterfront" and had been at sea for two decades, but he had also "organized against the attempt to import strike-breakers in Curacao . . . to replace striking seamen of the Grace Line." He was proud of the fact that he had "worked with organizers in establishing the San Juan branch of the NMU in 1937."[62]

In general, both shipowners and Washington were highly suspicious of the global connections of this Communist-led union, suspecting that such connection would facilitate international working-class— and "colored"—solidarity, mutual support for strikes, and the like. But after the war began, they recognized that sailors could obtain rare and plentiful intelligence useful for the war. When Johnny Vinnaccia went to the NMU hiring hall during the war in search of work, "the p.a. system announced that I'm to go to Blackie Myers' office. Sitting in there are two characters who look like detectives, but better-dressed, smoother, better education written all over them. One says, 'Would you like to go to Italy?' You know, you never knew where you were shipping to, for security. I looked at Blackie, and he nodded to go along with them. Next question, 'you are a member of the Communist Party, right?' What the hell is this? I look at Blackie, a party member like me. He nods okay. 'We're from the Office of Strategic Services. You go down to Baltimore. Find the ship with Captain so-and-so. Tell him I sent you. You'll be in the crew of a ship to Italy. When you get there, contact the Communist Party. When you come back, tell us what you learned. You can also tell the U.S. Communist Party.' Blackie again signalled okay.'" Johnny Vinnaccia was "smuggled across the front and wandered Italy behind the German lines, making contact with the partisans, carrying messages and so forth. This made me overstay my leave and I missed my ship."[63] Such cloak-and-dagger activity was not unusual and sheds light on contemporary controversies as to whether Communists engaged in espionage. Sure they did, and it often benefited the allies, including Washington and, yes, Moscow.

Seamen sailing to North Africa were able to report in early 1943 that the "local French governments are still being administered by Vichyites and that thousands of trade unionists and other anti-fascists are still interned in concentration camps." Sailors were indispensable to the war effort because their global connections were helpful in gathering intelligence.[64]

Smith could often be found in his spacious corner office on the sixth floor of the NMU headquarters in Manhattan. Painted in tasteful off-white tones, the "elegant" office was framed by a "beautiful mahogany" "curved" desk.[65] From here he maintained contact with a global network of sailors and activists, exercising a unique form of power. He was a powerful Negro among powerful Negroes, for, as one of the speakers at the NMU 1941 convention said, "in many unions and other organizations where Negroes are admitted, they usually have little or no say in the running of the organization. Sometimes one or two Negroes are elected or appointed to office to lend an appearance of equality and democracy." However, "the NMU is not such an organization. It not only has Negro officials but the membership sent forty Negro delegates to the Convention, which is the union's main policy-making body."[66]

Because Smith and his comrades recognized that one could not defeat Jim Crow internally without vigorously confronting it externally, instead of working from his comfortable office, he was often in the offices of other organizations. Besides being a Communist, Smith was also a leader of the National Negro Congress, a so-called "Communist front" that in reality was an attempt to establish a "popular front" of left and center forces to destroy Jim Crow. Both the NMU and NNC were formed around the same time and both were scorned for their Red leadership. Smith was also a reliable supporter and contributor to other such efforts, including the Southern Negro Youth Congress and the Southern Conference for Human Welfare. At his behest the union's National Council regularly made sizable contributions to these organizations, helping to keep them afloat and thereby signaling his own importance to the continued health of the popular front.[67] This importance was evident when he "was unanimously elected treasurer" of the NNC, a left-wing challenger to the NAACP.[68]

It was a mutually beneficial relationship. As NNC leader John Davis reminded Smith, "We have been pleased to be of some service to your union both in New York City and on the Pacific Coast. In 1936 I worked with our local council in [San Francisco] to prevent Negro misleaders from recruiting scabs."[69] In return the NNC called Smith "one of the ablest leaders of sections of our population." He was "in a strategic position," it said warmly, "as second highest officer of the union that has done most for the Negro people."[70] NNC literature nationally was often distributed via NMU port agents,[71] and to NMU members.[72] Smith was careful not to confuse his two leadership roles; thus, when the NNC decided to start a branch in Jacksonville, an elaborate protocol was devised whereby its local official was asked to contact the NMU Port Agent "to make a formal request through the National Office of the NMU" for Smith to speak."[73]

The war drove the two organizations closer together than ever before, as openings were created for a new offensive against Jim Crow. In mid-1942 Smith addressed an NNC gathering on what he saw as a critical linkage between "race" and jobs. "Two months ago," he told the audience, "Alderman Earl Dickerson of Chicago and I had a conference with Donald Nelson, Chairman of the War Production Board" about these issues. "These demands are basic, and grow out of the failure of the government to carry through a consistent democratic policy in the treatment of oppressed minority groups." Well aware of the global dimensions of the problem, he compared the "confusion and dismay in the minds of colonial peoples of Asia, Africa and Latin America and the West Indies" over their participation in the war when they themselves were not free with the similar dilemma faced by Negroes. "Full freedom for Puerto Rico" was one of his suggested reforms.[74]

Smith's words were coupled with equally intrepid actions. In Memphis, a bastion of the deep South, the NNC and NMU were working hand in hand to organize Negroes into CIO locals. "About 80% of this new CIO membership is composed of Negro workers," according to NMU leader William R. Henderson, and in turn, "[many] are very much interested in setting up a local branch [of NNC]."[75] This was part of a general upsurge in the South, propelled by the unique setting of the war. Early in 1944 Smith told a CIO conference that "only a few months ago, in the state of Florida where the Ku Klux Klan has been active, Negroes and whites marched side by side on a picket line organized by the Local NMU branch."[76] This was extraordinary in the South at this time.

The NMU's approach to organizing was a labor-community approach that recognized that workers were not only actors in the workplace but also parishioners, parents of students, and neighbors. The NNC included all these categories in its work. Despite subsequent allegations, the funds NMU contributed to this organization were well spent since the NNC was indispensable to left labor organizing, particularly in rougher precincts of the South.[77]

The two organizations also cooperated in other parts of the country. For example, when Anthony R. Lamont, "a Negro seaman and member of the [NMU] died while being held in a prison ward of the Kings County Hospital," Smith was "concerned over reports of police brutality to its Negro members in certain waterfront sections of Brooklyn" and worried that Lamont was its latest victim. He was able to call on the NNC, which was more experienced in handling such matters.[78] Smith's fondness for the NNC and his post as a leading member of its board were apparent when he told Davis in late 1941 that "because of my great interest in the National Board meeting. . . . I have altered my plans to enable me to be present at this meeting. I have arranged to stop off at Washington en route to Detroit to attend the CIO convention and look forward to seeing you."[79]

But the relationship was subject to conflicting pressures. A. Philip Randolph, the feisty labor leader, had pulled away from the NNC not least because he thought it had too many Euro-Americans in key roles. Yet the NMU was striving at the same time to promote "racial" unity. Thus, in the spring of 1940, when Smith forwarded a routine financial "contribution" to the NNC, he informed NNC leader John Davis that he and "another delegate (white) . . . [had been] elected from the port of New York" for an NNC gathering, in other words, the NMU would send a "mixed delegation." "We would be somewhat embarrassed," he added, "if this was not approved by your organization since our membership insisted in not making any distinction in the election. In fact they were definitely for a mixed delegation."[80] Davis responded that he had "no objection," since "the problems of the Negro people are inseparable from the problems of the masses of white workers in our country."[81]

Smith felt so strongly about the NNC that he urged other union leaders to join up as members. In 1944, weeks before D-Day, he told John Green, leader of the International Union of Marine and Shipbuilding Workers, "I sincerely believe that the Congress can be of great value to your union, as it has been so many others, in furthering the cause of unionism among the unorganized Negro people of America. Our Director of Organization has just returned from a field trip to Newport News and other places in Virginia, where your union is currently meeting fierce opposition from the Peninsula Shipbuilding Union—as you know, a company union. Certainly, our reorganized [NNC] councils in that state can be of assistance." Almost as an afterthought, he asked "whether your Executive Board has yet met on our [NNC] request for financial support."[82]

Evidently Smith and his comrades thought so highly of the NNC that they emulated it by focusing more narrowly on the special problems presented by the war. Though some have suggested that the Communists relinquished their struggle during the war in the interests of antifascist unity, this is an exaggeration. Actually, they took the line that "in order for the war to be won most rapidly and effectively, the shackles of Jim Crow must be broken." Smith exemplified this tendency. Thus, in 1942, although overwhelmed by his NMU duties, he took on the added responsibility of acting as Secretary of the National Emergency Committee to Stop Lynching, followed by leadership in the Negro Labor Victory Committee.[83] His analysis of the question of segregated blood banks illustrated his dual approach: "There must be no let up on the protests to the Red Cross against their unscientific segregation of blood donated by Negro people. At the same time, however, we must not refrain from making such donations since the men whose lives will be saved through such blood donations are not responsible for the policy of discrimination practiced by the Red Cross."[84]

As for the newly formed Negro Labor Victory Committee—yet another suspected "Communist front" designed to enlist workers on behalf of the war—Smith told it that the "NMU Constitution forbids direct affiliation with organizations other than trade unions," so "regrettably we cannot affiliate." But he pledged "our wholehearted support and cooperation."[85] He went on to work closely with the NLVC as it quickly racked up an impressive list of victories. In 1943 he told the NMU convention that he was "chairman" of the NLVC, "an organization of 54 CIO, AFL and railroad brotherhood unions, meeting jointly with people's organizations, community groups, etc."[86]

Charles Collins, the NLVC's day-to-day leader, was a trade unionist from Grenada. In mid-1943 he announced that the NLVC had "placed some 6000 Negro men and women in skilled and unskilled positions, where hitherto they had been barred." This amount encompassed 100 merchant marines, though the largest total was 750 warehouse workers and 300 fur workers. When Hugh Mulzac finally received an opportunity to skipper a ship, he had the NLVC to thank.

When unions suddenly initiated antidiscrimination committees in unions, the NLVC claimed responsibility.[87] When the War Production Board decided to train and employ thousands of Negro workers, it did so after a meeting with Smith and Collins.[88] When Harlem tenants faced eviction orders from landlords, Smith counseled the NLVC and asked "whether there is anything the NMU can do to further the interests of the evicted tenants in an organizational way."[89]

Collins, a "husky, handsome . . . ex-WPA actor," lived in the spice island of Grenada until he was sixteen. He taught at a public school at this young age, then went to work in 1927 as a common laborer at a packinghouse. He attended evening high school in Harlem, then City College, before becoming an elevator operator at the Hotel Martha Washington—cruelly, one of the few forms of upward mobility for Negroes during this era. He "broke into the professional stage as a dock-hand" in the proletarian drama *Stevedore*, then played "MacDuff in Orson Welles's production of *Macbeth*." As an activist he led a "fight against railroad Jim Crow which segregated Negro and white actors in 'Macbeth' while on tour." Later he spent "five days in jail for trying to rent a bathhouse at the lily-white Parkway Baths in Coney Island," and was pivotal in the "big organizing drive in 1937 to unionize hotel workers. Out of that campaign Collins became a union kingpin, one of three Negro union officials in Local 6, with 18,000 members. Of these, 3000 are Negroes."[90] He was well situated to aid Smith in building a popular front on behalf of the war and Negro rights.

As its title and efforts suggested, labor was at the heart of the NLVC's efforts. Representation in its higher councils was based on union strength, "unions having 5000 or more members" being entitled to "three delegates." This gave the NLVC connections to unions that were well positioned on behalf of Negroes searching for jobs.[91] This was a bold attempt to mobilize labor against Jim Crow and added wind to the sails of NMU's own efforts in this sphere. Hence by the summer of 1944, Smith was able to announce that "after seven years of unswerving determination," his union had been able to place an anti–Jim Crow clause in its contract with shippers. He was elated. "This is of major significance," he told readers of his column in the Harlem-based *People's Voice*. It had "far-reaching implications for American labor. . . . Remember, on a ship Negroes and whites not only work together, but they eat, sleep, play and study together. The ship is their home. How much easier such unity can be wielded [than] in shoreside jobs!"[92] As he saw it, the NMU victory was a foot in the door auguring better days to come. "Steadily and surely, jimcro [*sic*] is being ousted from our economic life. In many industries Negroes are employed at jobs that never before were opened to them" and "jobs are the key to democracy."[93]

The resounding successes secured by Smith and his union spread like wildfire throughout the land, bringing a barrage of requests to work their magic in other industries. A "Negro woman" writing from Los Angeles had "recently been hired by [longshore] as an organizer." She was now trying to organize a "defense plant" where "250–300 Negro women are employed."[94] Would Smith help? she asked. The request was emblematic of the great impact that Smith and his union had had on the minds of Negroes nationally.

Like the NMU and the NNC, the NLVC weighed in on the reelection of the Communist Councilman Ben Davis. It "unanimously endorsed" him.[95] The American Labor Party, whose line on the ballot Davis also claimed, sent the NLVC a $500 donation since it felt that the organization would help its candidate "get an impressive vote."[96]

J. Edgar Hoover, the director of the FBI, had been paying attention to the NLVC. In 1943 he observed that it was "exceedingly active in holding meetings and agitating among the Negroes in Harlem." It had been brought into existence by "the Negro committee of the National Committee of the Communist Party" with "the objective in mind to counteract the inroads made among the Negro people by the March on Washington Movement." Yes, it was true, Hoover conceded, that the NLVC was "supported by quite a number of international and local unions of the CIO and the AFofL, which are reported to be Communist dominated."[97]

5

Wind in Their Sails

AUGUST 1943 seemed to be proceeding along as a typically warm summer month in wartime Harlem. But by the end of the first week, the Negroes of Harlem had erupted with rage, pushed to rebellion by accumulated anger over continuous offenses, large and small. They were in no mood to tolerate conditions they had endured for centuries in the midst of a war that had promised so much. The "riot" of rage and destruction was prompted by allegations that a Negro soldier in uniform had been killed by police, illustrating the depth of the effect of the war on their consciousness and actions.

One of the leaders called upon to quell this rebellion with assurances that all was well was Ferdinand Smith. Along with Mayor Fiorello La Guardia, NAACP leader Walter White, and a number of other luminaries he rode up and down the streets of Harlem in a sound truck repeating the point that the soldier in question was not killed. Yet even Smith—top trade union leader, local columnist, crusader for jobs and justice—could not stop the "raucous shouts of disbelief" from Harlemites nor the "rat-tat-tat of bricks and bottles hitting the roof of the sound truck."[1]

Working tirelessly through Sunday night and Monday morning, Smith played a leading role in restoring order to a besieged Harlem. He had arrived at the 28th precinct at 123rd Street at 10 P.M. Along with his comrade Max Yergan and a fellow West Indian, Hope Stevens, he demanded "radio time immediately" in order to explain what had happened, and also demanded that all "gin mills" be closed down. He cautioned the police against the unrestrained use of force. All his suggestions were accepted and soon his voice could be heard booming over WOR and WABC.

At 5:30 A.M., after a marathon round of discussions with infuriated Harlemites, he retired to rest. After a couple of hours of fitful sleep he returned to the scene and discovered that the rumors of the soldier's demise were just as strong as before. Finally, he trekked to Sydenham Hospital, a stone's throw from the police precinct and arranged to have the youth who had been assaulted photographed, and the pictures published in the city's newspapers. As *The Pilot* stated proudly, Smith "had worn himself out in the interests of labor, his own people and unity for victory." For his part, Smith made several recommendations to forestall future outbreaks: "Assign Negro and white policemen to patrol the streets in pairs. . . . Police must learn that they are supposed to provide protection for law abiding Negroes as well as white people."[2] The NAACP agreed with Smith on this matter, suggesting that the revolt "showed resentment to soldier treatment," and citing many incidents across the nation involving assaults on Negro soldiers in uniform.[3]

These were wise words, but others were angrier at the Harlemites than at the police authorities. Claude Barnett, the well-regarded Negro journalist, was more critical than Smith. He was among the many who condemned the destruction of property that had ensued. "The plain bold truth," he asserted, "was that this was not a race riot." No, "it was a Negro riot. It was not the better elements. It was the rag tags, the gutter snipes, the vicious. . . . Most of these ignorant, rough, sensitively mean people are products of the South. . . . The South has ruled by fear. Once away from southern tyranny all the mean attributes which have been repressed come out."[4]

Many people agreed with Barnett. "A Group" of self-proclaimed "White People" expressed their outrage directly to the Mayor. "How come that the nigger can afford to dress (and strut) far better than a lot of the whites?" they asked. "One has only to walk down LaSalle to see how poorly the white children are clothed and how decked out with the latest finery the nigger kids are. . . . They are ruining every section of the city and the Mayor encourages it." This was too much, they declared: "WHAT ARE WHITE AMERICANS FIGHTING FOR AND HAVE FOUGHT FOR? TO MAKE AMERICA SAFE FOR THE NEGRO" [their emphasis]. "Is there nothing you can do, as Mayor, about Negroes standing on the corners of white neighborhoods in their ridiculous zoot suits and air of defiance and gaping after every white girl that passes? We are asked to stay out of Harlem." In that case, well, "Keep them in Harlem" was their return slogan.[5]

Intelligence authorities were not too pleased with Smith's high profile either. One senses that they felt it was time to cut him down to size—something they were able to do more dramatically after the war ended. In a "confidential" dispatch the FBI and military intelligence seemed astonished that Mayor La Guardia would introduce Smith, a radical trade union leader, as one of two "leaders of Harlem with whom he had toured the affected district and . . . had been constantly with him that night." Apparently referring to Yergan and Smith, the agent went on to say that "the fact that these two individuals are considered 'leaders' and outstanding residents of Harlem is a reflection of the deep inroads made by the Communist Party into the Negro population . . . and is a presage of future difficulties to be encountered when the 'party line' no longer coincides with the policy of the United States." Already zeroing in on Smith's ambiguous immigration status, it noted that he was "born in the Virgin Islands" and was "reputed to keep his own personal files concerning communistic activities. It is alleged that he is not given full liaison information from the Communist Party concerning their contacts abroad and that [he] is endeavoring to compile his own estimate of this liaison." The authorities perceived that Smith was a "man of great influence in Negro activities, well versed in organizing and controlling committees to solidify the Communist Party in front organizations along the line employed in the early 1930s in so many European communities via the popular front idea." The report concluded, "due to Subject's activities and to his close contacts and past experience in organizing, he must be considered . . . a very dangerous character in the subversive field."[6] In a trend that was to escalate after the war, as "racial" tension rose so too did Red-baiting.

Military intelligence was astonished by the breadth of Smith's political activities. His role as "treasurer" of the NNC "gave him a terrific amount of influence among the Negroes of the country because in many sections the Congress is looked upon with greater favor than the [NAACP]." He was also a "sponsor and padrino [sic]" of "Pubelos Hispanos," "active" in "United Spanish Aid," the "progressive committee to rebuild the American Labor Party," the "Council on African Affairs," the "defense committee" for the accused Communist Morris Schappes, and other so-called "Communist fronts." Smith was "the one who sees to it that the Communist Party line is carried through in the National Maritime Union" and "alleged to be in charge of organizing cells on ships in order to spread Communism. At a meeting of the Communist Party in June 1941, it was decided to take definite steps to bring Negroes into the front organizations and the job of urging the Negroes into such organizations was placed in the hands of [Smith]. His first job was to set up the organization under the name of the Negro Labor for Victory

Committee with himself at the head and, as such, has since then been very active in Harlem amongst Negro seamen." More ominously, Smith was "reported as one of the secret advocates of a labor revolution after the Communist pattern."[7]

As the FBI surveyed the scene, it was simultaneously alarmed and amazed by the influence of Smith, the Communist. In a "secret" report, FBI Director J. Edgar Hoover could not help but notice that Smith's name kept popping up in radical circles. There he was at a dinner of three hundred and fifty at the Hotel Commodore in Manhattan addressing the case of Communist leader Earl Browder, and there he was again at a national emergency committee to stop lynching. "During the month of October 1942," Hoover said, the NMU "continued in [CP] inspired agitation for an immediate western front in Europe. . . . [NMU's] Pan American division has been actively organizing Greek, Chinese, Yugoslavian, Norwegian, Danish and Dutch seamen" at such a feverish pace that it gave new meaning to the well-worn phrase, "workers of the world unite." For the union had "intensified its activity among seamen from India and the British colonial possessions, working closely in this regard with the [CP] in various parts of the British Empire. [NMU] seamen have been making contacts with Communist Party functionaries in foreign ports, particularly at the offices in such ports of the friends of the Soviet Union." The union's radicalism stretched from Murmansk to Manhattan as its "members have been furnished during October with 'strong arm squads' to assist in keeping order at various street meetings in New York and have assisted in the conduct of 'rent strikes' among the Negroes in the Harlem area of New York City."[8]

It seemed to the authorities that the NMU not only had its own unique domestic policy, but also its own foreign policy—and that these were in conflict with what was being decided in Washington. Hoover had little sympathy for the "Joint Anti-Fascist Refugee Committee" but, lo and behold, there was Smith at the Hotel Roosevelt in Manhattan addressing four hundred and fifty people on the subject of "democratic Spain."[9]

The State Department was not too busy in 1943 to pay attention to Smith's letter to them "on behalf of one Guido Fioravanti, founder of the National Federation of Construction Workers in Argentina, who has been a prisoner of the fascist Italian government in the island of Ventotene since 1937."[10] Given Smith's Communist sympathies, it is hard to know whether the State Department was pleased or displeased when

Smith told Secretary of State Cordell Hull that he "wholeheartedly approve[d]" of his policy toward China.[11]

The government's intense scrutiny of Smith and the union went far beyond compiling "secret" and "confidential" reports. Joseph Curran brought the matter directly to the attention of President Roosevelt, claiming that "Members and officials are being shadowed and hounded." Treading carefully, Roosevelt reassured Curran, "I am able to say to you that the [FBI] has not investigated the National Maritime Union," though he left open the possibility that another intelligence agency might do the same thing.[12] But the president found it hard to ignore other information he was receiving about this important union, for example, the "attack made before [the] House of Representatives by Congressman Keefe . . . claiming [the NMU was] dominated by Communists and [the] leadership [was] plotting with Stalin to take over [the] Panama Canal."[13]

Although the scrutiny of Smith increased after his prominent role in the Harlem Riot, he was disappointed with the response to his recommendations for reform. Smith told Mayor La Guardia that "New York police are warning all whites that they enter Harlem after dark at their own risk." "We call upon you," he said, speaking in his capacity as an NNC official, to "institute proper action immediately." In short, "incendiary statements such as this must be stopped." He warned the mayor that "we must never permit a repetition of the horrible Harlem riots which to this day are perhaps the ugliest blot on the history of the City of New York."[14]

Smith was in a unique position to assess the situation in New York City for he had become a key political operative there, as military intelligence acknowledged. In the late 1930s he was involved in the Trade Union Non-Partisan Committee for the Selection of a Negro to City Council.[15] He was also heavily involved with the American Labor Party and critical of the Democratic Party standard-bearer, Franklin Roosevelt. In 1940 he, Curran, and other union officers asserted that "neither Roosevelt nor Wilkie will serve the interests of organized labor." They all backed John L. Lewis's "condemnation and repudiation of the Roosevelt Administration" due to his policy on war, his policy of "transfer of ships to foreign flags," and his "refusal to act on the Anti-Lynch Bill."[16]

However, by the time the next election came around, he and other union officers and party comrades threw their full support behind President Roosevelt. Smith also took a special interest in local politics, often collaborating with City Councilman, then Congressman Adam Clayton Powell, Jr.[17] He recognized that the success of his union could not be divorced from the advance of his community and that what had been won at the bargaining table could be lost in the legislature. Thus, in the summer of 1944 he convened a meeting of CIO and AFL "Negro trade union leaders" to work for Powell's election. He devised ambitious plans to "mobilize 500 trade union members to canvass voters," "to organize a flying squad of 50 Negro trade union leaders to canvass" and "organize five mass outdoor rallies" for Powell and the neighboring Congressman, Vito Marcantonio.[18] Smith took the lead in "mapping [an] all-out labor drive to send [Powell] to Congress."[19] Smith and Powell also collaborated on the massive Negro Freedom Rally held during the summer of 1943 in Manhattan. An NMU committee "headed by Josh Lawrence began holding street meetings in Harlem and throughout the city to spur attendance. . . . A second NMU committee" helped the "rally through the distribution of posters and leaflets."[20]

Smith joined the actor Canada Lee and others in the popular front in the Non-Partisan Committee for the Re-Election of Assemblyman Hulan E. Jack, the African American leader,[21] just as his union "took an active part in defeating arch reactionary 'Cotton Ed' Smith in the South Carolina primary election to select the Democratic nominee for U.S. Senator. That means that Smith will be out of the next Senate, for the first time since 1907."[22]

As Smith noted, he was "in the midst of an effort to unify the Negro people nationally in support" of FDR's "policies for the 1944 elections. . . . We are now organizing labor legislative conferences in many important cities in these areas. . . . Simultaneously we are campaigning for the establishment of military equality for the Negro people."[23] Harlemites "under the auspices of the Harlem Community Council, CIO-AFL are launching their big 'Draft Roosevelt' campaign" which "will involve the signing of a gigantic post card" and "a few brief addresses at an open-air meeting on the corner of 126th Street and 7th Avenue."[24] Smith argued that NNC Board members are "expected to make at least ONE meeting a day for Roosevelt (emphasis in original)."[25] The National Council of the NMU "unanimously passed a resolution" allowing Smith to tour the nation in support of Roosevelt. As *The Pilot* noted, "during the past year alone Smith has addressed hundreds of fraternal, civic, church and trade union organizations." Curran "strongly recommended Bro. Smith as the best man to bring this message to the Negro people."[26] An earlier Smith speaking tour had enhanced "the prestige of the union." This was "unprecedented in labor history," Curran said, for "throughout his tour Smith was able to convince Negro leaders that the Negro could not stand alone."[27]

Smith spent a lot of time on the West Coast, from Southern California to Seattle. He met almost daily with union leaders, Negro leaders, and elected officials, spoke at mass meetings, and held press conferences.[28] In Los Angeles he conferred with the mayor, "who asked that he work out a program of action applicable to local conditions that will prevent a repetition of the recent riots in this city."[29] Smith and Mayor Fletcher Bowron of Los Angeles got "to know each other after a luncheon attended by 60 prominent AFL, CIO and civic leaders." Attired in his dark double-breasted suit, Smith declared that "fomenters of race hatred and bigotry must be dealt with sharply by the authorities. They should be imprisoned if necessary. . . . There should be FEPCs [Fair Employment Practices Committee] in every sphere of activity affecting the well-being of the Negro people."[30]

The union leadership "commended" Smith for his "fine handling of the administrative functions of his office. . . . We are proud that one of the foremost Negro trade unionists in the country is the Secretary of our union. . . . Brother Smith has done our union and our country a great service in the outstanding role he has played in welding white and Negro unity nationally, a tremendous and lasting contribution to the cause of the United Nations and democracy."[31]

Beyond the stated goal of supporting FDR's reelection bid, Smith had a larger agenda as well, namely, to use the occasion to advance his—or his constituency's—agenda. His support for FDR was based on his approval of the president's skill in building an antifascist coalition that included the USSR, and his analysis that "full employment in the maritime industry hinges in part upon the kind of foreign policy we pursue."[32] Thus, while drumming up support for Roosevelt, he was also organizing an "emergency action meeting on the anti-poll tax legislation" that "prominent Negro and Jewish organizations will attend." The "conference will consider also the question of equality in the armed forces, the urgency of which is indicated by the recent uncalled for arrest of Joe Louis at Camp Sibert, Alabama, which is a real blow."[33]

Smith felt that the "enforced backwardness of the Black Belt [in the Deep South] is an unbearable drag on the progress of our country and on the war." Thus, at his behest, the NNC "assigned a full-time organizer, Mr. Oscar Bryant, to the Alabama rural areas" and "formed six rural clubs" there.[34]

Through his newspaper columns and speeches, Smith had become a major interpreter in Harlem of prevailing political trends. He praised the black role and "political maturity" demonstrated in elections of the Negro Communist Ben Davis in 1943 and a "Democratic Mayor in Cleveland" and a "Republican Governor in Kentucky."[35] At the same time, as the 1944 election approached, he was concerned about the "alarmingly small proportion of participation by Negro voters in strategic areas" and "insufficient emphasis upon registration of new voters." Thus, the NNC planned to "launch immediately a nation-wide registration drive, directed to Negroes in key areas."[36]

Smith's praise for FDR upon the latter's death in 1945 knew no bounds. He hailed FDR for his "genius and statesmanship," and commended him for his trip to West Africa.[37] Smith had delivered a radio broadcast, one of many he made under government auspices during the war, calling this visit "an event of great significance."[38] For a while he transferred his approval to FDR's successor, Harry S Truman—and this was reciprocated. When the Missourian was nominated for Vice President, Smith called it "a defeat for the poll-taxers and Bourbons."[39] In the spring of 1945 Truman praised Smith for his effort to "dedicate a recreational hall to the memory of my lamented predecessor."[40]

The war allowed Smith and other progressives to advance their causes. The long-awaited idea of a Fair Employment Practices Committee gathered steam,[41] partly because of Smith's leadership role, as when he chaired a "Negro Freedom Rally" in 1944 in Manhattan "attended by 20,000 Negroes and whites," which led to scores of telegrams being forwarded to the U.S. Senate.[42] Smith and Powell, who had become something of a political couple, pressured FDR to "restate your full support" of FEPC,[43] and exerted considerable pressure on the Senate majority leader, Alben Barkley, as well.[44] These politicians were presented with petitions carrying the signatures of thousands—collected via the NNC's "various branches"—demanding a permanent FEPC.[45]

In addition, the CIO (with a few notable exceptions) was allied with the Democratic Party and the NMU, already suspect to some because of its Red ties. Certainly, the NMU—which, unlike most CIO unions, was not called into being by this federation—was forthright about its differences with the CIO. An editorial in *The Pilot* in May 1941 declared that FDR confidante and CIO leader "[Sidney] Hillman was not put in office to protect labor but to mislead it. . . . Hillman's job is to seduce the less militant unions away from their fellow trade unions, get them to swallow the Administration's war program, sign no-strike agreements and not ask for wage increases."[46] In 1940 Curran exclaimed that Hillman was "ready to sell the workers down the river."[47]

However, the coming of the war and the fact that the fate of the Soviet Union was at stake caused the NMU to switch gears. Soon Smith was reaching out to Hillman's comrade, Phil Murray, addressing him as "sir and brother," asking him to "facilitate an audience with President Roosevelt" that would include the Reverend Powell, the Urban League's Lester Granger, and Smith himself.[48] Hillman—whose importance was underscored by FDR's remark, "clear it with Sidney"—in turn referred to Smith as "Ferd," telling him in 1944 that he "would be happy to attend" a rally in Manhattan that Smith was helping to organize.[49]

By this time, Smith was part of a small number of popular front labor leaders with direct lines of access into the White House itself. He often conferred with Hillman[50] and John Abt—who happened to be a Communist too—from Hillman's staff.[51] Abt and Smith worked together at the highest levels of the American Labor Party, for example.[52] Hillman said he "appreciate[d] the opportunity to talk with a delegation" from the Negro Labor Victory Committee about "means of coordinating our joint efforts."[53]

Smith also became a fixture at CIO gatherings nationally. At the November 1943 convention he was elected to the National Executive Board of this powerful body, after Blackie Myers stepped down to allow Smith to take over. When the resolution on "racial" discrimination was being discussed on the convention floor, "Brother Smith had made a brilliant address to the delegates in praise of CIO policy on discrimination and blasted the AFL convention's evasive handling of the question." Smith observed that "the membership of my union, carrying out CIO policy, has elected me six consecutive years to represent the union membership in the second highest post in our organization. Yet only 10% of the membership of the union is made up of Negroes. . . . The CIO here and now must resolve that [it] is against the principles and policies of the CIO to maintain or establish through action of any affiliate of the CIO any Jim Crow locals, no matter what part of the country."[54]

In the spring of 1944 he was in Detroit where he was "given an ovation at a banquet" that also featured Shelton Tappes of UAW Ford local 600 and other labor leaders.[55] Days later he was "principal speaker" at a rally called by Western Electric workers at a Baptist church in Baltimore; there he assailed a plan for "segregation of lockers and toilet facilities."[56] Dressed in his customary dark double-breasted suit, he was one of 107 CIO delegates at the Illinois Midwest Negro People's Assembly, and "one of the principal speakers" at this conference of five thousand.[57]

Smith was bouncing from one corner of the nation to another, reassuring Negroes that they should not waver in their determination to win the war and that their grievances would be effectively addressed, while seeking to build organization that would guarantee this outcome. Thus, after Chicago, he "sped to Philadelphia . . . to work with labor, civic and government representatives to iron out a transportation strike . . . instigated ostensibly over the upgrading of eight Negro porters to car operation jobs."[58] In 1943 he protested a nasty "race riot" in Detroit. He called on the governor to "arrest the enemy agents responsible for these outbreaks and to bring about the immediate dissolution of the Ku Klux Klan," which was "part of an organized conspiracy to cripple war production."[59]

Such activity underscored Smith's role as a spokesman for black labor even beyond the NMU. He met with Donald Nelson of the War Production Board to "discuss a plan calling for greater use of Negro workers in the war production program." He proposed a "four point program calling for the training of 50,000 Negro workers for war production."[60] He was more than a black labor leader: he was a black leader, as evidenced by his war-time appearance in Cleveland at the convention of the Fraternal Council of Negro Churches in America. Smith was seeking to bring a newer conception of Negro affairs to disparate audiences—a prolabor conception—and vice versa. In May 1942, he told an audience that "the religious concept of the Brotherhood of man is accepted by organized labor as the key to the practice of successful unionism." "Neither organized labor nor organized religion can exist under nazism," he said.[61] The war and the perils it presented allowed Smith to speak his mind directly, as when he told a CIO meeting in Boston that what was needed was "clear-cut demands for centralized control of the nation's economy" and "international labor unity" of the sort that the NMU had initiated.[62]

The NAACP had a star-crossed relationship with the popular front, as the experience of the Scottsboro case in the 1930s demonstrated. For a while the Association viewed the NNC as a direct competitor on its turf. However, this attitude was not characteristic of the war years.

As the NMU and NNC were coming into being in 1936 Charles Houston, the leading NAACP litigator and future attorney for Communist leader Henry Winston, reflected on the competitive pressures compelling the Association to reassess its rudimentary function. He told NAACP leader Walter White that their organization should seek "to do a job for Negro labor similar to the one done by the ACLU. We cannot become labor organizers because we do not have the experience but we certainly can organize a strong group of lawyers and members to back up Negro labor in its fight to organize, to picket and to strike, freedom of speech and freedom of assembly."[63] The middle-class NAACP leadership was responding to the different vision of Negro leadership provided by the NNC—and the embryonic NMU's Ferdinand Smith.

For example, Roy Wilkins of the NAACP informed the NNC that he was upset about a recent NNC gathering at Harlem's Abyssinian Church. "You have quite a task cut out for yourself," he told the NNC's John Davis with a mixture of paternalism and anxiety. Wilkins was concerned about the "distinct note of racialism and anti-white feeling in the speeches of several persons," along with an "outpouring of the old West Indian nationalism, so reminiscent of the Garvey movement." Worse, "all the old myths about the NAACP were paraded last night as truths." Seeking to drive a wedge into the NNC, he declared, "I am sure that the white persons present in the audience last night, and the Negro members of the Communist Party, must have felt something of the same thing I felt. They were being rebuffed and insulted in a boorish manner. . . . The Communists were smart enough to change their line on us and other organizations, not because they love us any less, but because they love victory more. . . . I wonder if the New York unit of the National Negro Congress will be as smart."[64]

While Wilkins was confronting the NNC frontally, other NAACP informants were proceeding through the back door. "Nuffie" told Walter White that she had wandered into the "press room" of the NNC where "I observed some fifteen girls busily engaged at typewriters; about ten of the girls were white and only five were colored. A man came in and asked to speak to whoever was in charge, whereupon a very businesslike white woman came forward and informed him that she was in complete charge." She added sarcastically, "It was rather interesting, especially at a Negro Congress."[65] Strangely, the officially interracial NAACP was upset about the fact that the NNC encompassed the full spectrum of U.S. society.

Wilkins's warm endorsement turned out to be a "false positive" as relations between the NAACP and the NNC deteriorated. Wilkins's increasingly sour view of the NNC was shared by others. A. Philip Randolph, a leading Negro trade unionist on par with Smith, told the Special Committee to Investigate the National Negro Congress and the NAACP that "my advice is for your organization [the NAACP] . . . [to] have nothing to do with the National Negro Congress."[66] Randolph, a former NNC leader himself, had resigned, recalling that "out of some 1200 or more delegates" at an NNC gathering, "over 300 were white, which made the Congress look like a joke. . . . Why should a Negro Congress have whites in it?" But the problem wasn't just that they were "white." They were also "red." "The Negro people," Randolph said, "cannot afford to add to the handicap of being black, the handicap of being red."[67]

Even during the halcyon days of the antifascist alliance, Smith and the NNC constantly had to look over their shoulders lest Randolph, a former NNC leader, were to show up. "I sincerely believe," said one NNC official in early 1944, "that an all Negro conference at this time in our history would be a very bad conference to hold, because such a conference would not be good for the war effort, and we would [be] falling into the program that Randolph is following, I think that white trade unionists should definitely be included. . . . [They] should play an equal role at the conference." It was profoundly ironic that the reviled left-led NNC was a firm proponent of interracialism—the nation's future official creed—while the lionized Randolph and the soon-to-be canonized NAACP dissented vigorously. Although the most powerful patron of the NNC—the NMU—had already made it clear that it did not approve of "an all Negro conference," regardless of Randolph, the wrangling suggested that the NNC had yet to attain complete clarity on this crucial issue of separatism versus inter-racialism.[68]

Randolph turned against the NNC despite Smith's attempts to bring him round. In 1944, for example, he contacted "Mr. Randolph," "asking you to help" with an NNC rally by buying tickets or speaking. "Mr. Randolph" politely declined.[69] In 1945 on the other hand, Randolph could not have been pleased when the NLVC "unanimously decided" to "appeal" to Benjamin McLaurin, a leader of the porters, asking him to "disassociate himself" from the campaign to deny the Communist Councilman from Harlem, Ben Davis, reelection. McLaurin "would win the love and esteem of our people and of labor" if he were to comply, said the NLVC. But McLaurin ignored the appeal and continued to attack Ben Davis, Smith's favorite Communist elected official.[70]

Despite its apprehension about the NNC, the Association had some advantages over the latter. Most important, the NAACP did not carry the taint of being led by Communists like Ferdinand Smith. In any case, the urgency of dealing with the problems of Negroes seeking to avoid lynching and escaping penury did not leave much time for backbiting. Thus, given the historic role played by seamen among Negroes, the NAACP could not avoid addressing their problems, and this drove them toward Smith and the NMU. In 1938 the NAACP was focused on "approximately thirty five or forty thousand colored seamen . . . the majority of whom not only are citizens but world war veterans," yet experienced "discrimination aboard the ships of the U.S. Maritime Commission."[71]

Donald Smith of the Bronx—a messman in the steward's department—echoed these concerns, complaining that "in the hiring hall jobs are called according to race." According to him, "the crux of the trouble, [was] in the union, which has a large rank and file bloc." There were "colored members, who pay dues, strike assessments, etc. [but] are denied the right to get promotions."

This indictment of the NMU and of Ferdinand Smith and other high-ranking Negroes was a reflection of the tenuous hold on power that he and his comrades had in the early days of the union. The problem was addressed at a 1938 meeting at NMU headquarters on the west side of Manhattan, attended by Smith, NAACP lawyer Thurgood Marshall, and George B. Murphy, a radical from the affluent Baltimore family which controlled a chain of Negro newspapers, and a member of the NAACP staff. The "problem discussed was discrimination against Negro members of the union." Marshall sought to make the Association's views "clear to Mr. Smith," while the NMU leader "told Mr. Marshall that the union was faced with severe problems of organization as well as a split in the labor movement between the CIO and AF of L, that it had a bloc within the union which was actively supporting every type of disruptive action," not to mention a "large southern membership." In his "confidential" account of the gathering, Murphy—who was favorably disposed to the left-led NMU—noted that "Mr. Smith gave the impression of utter sincerity."[72]

Soon thereafter, the NMU was pleased to report that the NAACP "has given us excellent cooperation during the course of the tanker strike" and a new level of cooperation seems to have been reached between these two powerful organizations.[73] When Oliver Boutte of the NMU conferred with NAACP leader Roy Wilkins, the Negro sailor was blunt, lamenting that "the union has sent Negroes to fill openings as stewards, deck-hands and in the engine room but that the ship lines have refused to employ them. . . . The Panama railroad steamship company which is owned outright by the government employs no Negroes whatsoever. . . . The Grace Line heavily subsidized by the government, once employed Negroes but is now lily-white. . . . The Munson Line, which has been practically taken over by the government and reorganized into the American-Republic Line, is now lily-white, although the old Munson Line, employed Negroes on two of its four ships running in South America. . . . The American Export Line and the United States Line do not employ Negroes and the latter has many Germans employed in the categories where Negroes could be employed. These Germans are American citizens but most of them live in Hamburg and most of them do not even speak English."[74] This presented a grave threat to national security, particularly as war approached. The pro-German hiring policy, which occurred at the Negroes' expense, was only the most glaring aspect of Jim Crow at sea. Smith acknowledged that "it is essentially true that the United States Line has a practice of hiring German stewards for the last ten years." It was also true that "possibl[y] some of these German stewards are Nazis or Nazi sympathizers."[75]

Smith knew that the situation called for extraordinary measures. Not only had he just narrowly escaped being ousted from office, but there were enormous problems facing Negro sailors. So, in addition to working with the NNC to alter the "racial" dynamics of the nation, he joined with the NAACP to change the racial dynamics of the shipping industry. Arnold Hill of the National Urban League was also involved. As Thurgood Marshall put it, Smith and Boutte proposed that the leading civil rights organizations "join them in bringing pressure to bear through the President and Congress against the National Maritime Commission to break down discrimination against Negro maritime workers."[76] As Smith told Walter White, who was quite nervous about collaborating with Reds, "we want to welcome your cooperation with the [NMU]."[77]

Daniel Ring of the Maritime Commission denied any complicity in discrimination when confronted by Walter White.[78] Thurgood Marshall told Ring that "we are of the opinion that ships operated by the federal government with federal funds should not maintain a policy of discriminating against Negro employees."[79] The NAACP had received "communications from Seattle complaining of discrimination against Negro seamen, so that . . . this situation is not merely a local one but involves the status of Negroes in the entire marine industry."[80] In addition to lobbying the government, the Association considered a "boycott" of Standard Oil because of its attempt to break an NMU strike by deploying an army of "finks, scabs and strikebreakers."[81] This was part of the Association's larger waterfront offensive that included putting pressure on Joseph Ryan of the longshore union about racism on the docks in New York.[82]

But ultimately the NAACP found it difficult to accept the existence of the NNC, which it saw not only as a competitor but as a Red trojan horse as well. In happier days, Roy Wilkins of the NAACP had embraced the NNC warmly. "There were rumors," he remarked in 1936, "that the Congress was financed by the Communists, by the Republican Party, by the Liberty League and others. I am convinced that these rumors are wholly without foundation, because numerous persons from widely separate places have testified to the trickling in of money in small amounts." The NNC "was unusually democratic." He was impressed that the Negro newspaper, the *Chicago Defender*, "gave [it] unstinted publicity, . . . far more than they have ever given the NAACP, even when it has had annual conferences in Chicago." He was impressed that, unlike the NAACP, the NNC "was not a Congress of school teachers, college presidents and others," as some might suggest. No, said Wilkins, this was a Congress "from the so-called working class."[83]

World War II did not bring the NMU and the Association any closer together. Smith was too important to be ignored by this point, so he was invited to the important November 1943 conference at Harlem's Hotel Theresa to formulate a strategy for Negro voters for the next year's election. Although he could not attend, Mary McLeod Bethune, Max Yergan, Walter White, and Thurgood Marshall did,[84] and they promulgated an ambitious list of demands including the right to vote, an end to the poll tax and the white primary, antilynching laws, a permanent FEPC, and a revised foreign policy featuring more global cooperation.[85] Yet already there were signs that the NMU-NAACP collaboration would not survive. Rayford Logan, a scholar close to the Association, was questioned by the FBI about his attendance and specifically about what he knew about Ferdinand Smith.[86]

As the elections of 1944 drew near, Roy Wilkins derided the NNC as a "shadow of its former self. . . . There are one or two, or perhaps a half dozen, live branches throughout the country—certainly not more. However, following the 'line' of the Communist Party, it is quite likely that these people are submerging themselves as organizations and working through other groups. . . . We cooperate with them on specific issues but we have no sort of working agreement."[87]

But the NAACP's shunning of the NNC and its diminution of contact with Smith may have harmed the Association more than the NMU. Smith had become a force to be reckoned with, a power broker who was just as much at home in the corridors of power in Washington as he was in union halls nationally. He was a black leader, a labor leader, and a black labor leader rolled into one. He even appeared to have gained the confidence of his immediate superior, Joseph Curran, who was un-stinted in his praise of him. Curran affirmed that Smith was "at work, constantly, coordinating the various activities of the union." He had "handled . . . communications effectively and efficiently. . . . He has kept the various ports apprised of interpretations of policy and clarifications on various matters affecting the organization. He has kept the Agents and membership informed . . . and has supervised activities dealing with charges, trials of members, etc. . . . [He] has made a study of the minority question in our organization." Smith "should be compli-mented on the way he has carried out his varied and complex duties, at times under very [trying] circumstances."[88]

This last point appears to have been a veiled reference to the effort to oust Smith from his post. Yet Smith seems to have emerged from this in a stronger position, in part because his opponents had been weak-ened. His leadership position in a strategic industry 85 percent of whose workers were organized gave him and his union the power to shut down the nation's economy.[89]

In 1943, Leo Huberman, the socialist writer, wrote that "in the six short years of its existence the NMU has more than doubled the wages of its members, cut their hours and improved their conditions to an ex-tent that is probably unequalled in American labor history."[90] That a Communist-led union had accomplished this in an anticommunist na-tion made this all the more remarkable. Moreover, because this had been accomplished without stinting on the cultural life of its members, with frequent art exhibits, dance concerts, and the like, the NMU was popular not only among unions but among membership associations generally.[91]

During Curran's frequent absences from New York, he showed Smith how much he trusted him by asking him to "take charge of union business."[92] Curran had many qualities necessary for union leadership—he was a master of bureaucratic maneuvering, had a gruff personality that appealed to many members, and also had a fervent desire to stay in power at all costs—but few of these brought home the "pork chops" (or benefits) for union sailors. Thus, it was often left to Smith and his comrades to engage in the heavy lifting of the union's day-to-day operations. It was Smith, for example, who "headed" the team of "NMU negotiators" with the "Collier Owners Association."[93] The union reported that "the smooth draft of the new closed shop collier agreement providing for the highest wages on any coast" was "prepared by our Negotiating Committee under the supervision of . . . Ferdinand Smith."[94]

During one of the union's most difficult battles, namely, the strike against the oil industry, specifically tankers, Smith was often in the driver's seat.[95] The strike was aimed at five companies: Standard Oil of New Jersey, Socony-Vacuum Oil, Tidewater Oil Company, C. D. Mallory Oil Transport, and the Petroleum Navigation Company. About three thousand workers were involved, five hundred of them in Texas ports.[96] Inevitably, the conflict in the southern ports was fierce. There were a "rash of controversies" with "violence flaring up almost daily."[97] The "situation" was "dynamite" with a "lot of imported gangsters . . . some [were] beginning to wonder if Houston is not subject to some of the same stuff that has sorely troubled the Northern and Eastern cities."[98] The authorities responded by "beating . . . a [NMU] picket into unconsciousness."[99]

Fog-bound, cool, and drizzly Seattle faced problems not unlike those of the humid and hot South Texas ports. Allies of the NMU in the West complained that "labor spies [were being placed] in militant unions for the purpose of wrecking those unions so that contracts may be broken or ignored [and this was] another instance of Standard Oil's HUMANE (?) treatment of its employees." But what could one expect, these unions said, from a company that the "Bolivian government had to sue for the recovery of its oil lands after the [company] had defrauded the government of lawful taxes." Standard Oil was also "building ships in the fascist shipyards in Germany and Italy while American shipyard workers are on part time work." Though purporting to be patriotic, Standard Oil operated the "world's largest refinery on the Dutch island of Aruba" that "runs full blast while American refineries are on reduced schedules." NMU's boycott of Standard Oil was a useful means of introducing a sense of realism and compromise to this otherwise obdurate giant.[100]

By 1944 the NMU in this region had made such strides that their leader, Ralph Rogers, observed that the union's detractors "have had to discard the old outworn cry of 'Reds' because it isn't very effective to shout 'Red' at men who are being bombed and torpedoed and dying for their country alongside the men in our armed forces. Besides," he remarked referring to the United States's wartime ally in Moscow, "that label isn't so derogatory these days." The rank and file had benefited from this alliance. The "chief steward, who is the highest paid unlicensed man aboard ship gets 67 2/3 cents" per hour, while "messmen and ordinary seamen, who are the lowest paid, get [35½] cents" per hour. They worked a 56 hour week."[101]

But as the war wound down, the conditions that had promoted the popular front—and tolerance of Reds like Smith in important posts—began to change. Even before August 1945, there were discernible signs that the conditions that had favored Smith were turning against him.

For Smith had differences with John L. Lewis, the crusty, bushy-browed leader of the coal miners. Initially their relationship was cordial, based on their common interest in pouring more resources into union organizing.[102] The Communist, Al Lannon, was Longshore Director of the CIO Maritime Committee (for a while).[103] But this alliance was materially altered by the coming of the war, as Lewis—unlike the NMU—refused to adhere to the no-strike pledge. "NMU declares strikes harm U.S. war effort" was a typical 1943 headline from *The Pilot*. Aimed at Lewis and his union, the denunciation was personally endorsed by Smith.[104] The NMU went so far as to demanding that the Attorney General file "sedition" charges against Lewis.[105] Its harshness was part of a complicated relationship that the NMU had with its ostensible parent, the CIO. As Curran noted years later, the NMU—unlike other member unions—was "one of the few unions that were not developed by the CIO. We developed ourselves; and after we developed ourselves, we then met with the CIO leadership. . . . We were one of the unions that voted to affiliate with the CIO. The other unions were unions that were creatures of the CIO."[106]

On the other hand, when the pressure of the Red Scare mounted, the fact that the NMU never saw itself as a full-blown "creature" of the CIO facilitated purging of the left, as it was not seen as a bona fide member of the federation in the sense that other unions were.

But the savaging of Lewis may have been a maneuver to mask real differences within the NMU itself about the legitimacy of the no-strike pledge. Sailor Stanley Postek recalled that "there were political differences among the thousands of members in the NMU" and the "big issue that created most of the turmoil was the question of the no strike pledge!" The leadership was under pressure to adhere to the pledge in the interests of prosecuting the war, but many ordinary sailors felt that by giving up their most powerful weapon, the strike, they were emboldening shipowners to impose ever more onerous conditions on them. In addition, "the second big issue was the great desire of the membership to get all of the officials to ship out." The "simple matter" of compelling "the officials" of the NMU "to get their feet wet, hands dirty and heads cleared at the point of production, and to elect new leaders fresh from the sea, was blasphemy in the eyes of the top leadership. . . . The issue was never resolved but did create much bad feeling."[107]

Postek's comments explain why Curran was pressing the White House in the middle of the war"for a passport to go to the USSR and British Isles," a request that was not taken seriously on Pennsylvania Avenue. "It is believed," said a bureaucrat, "that there is no real necessity for the trip and that it is being made for Mr. Curran's personal reasons," that is, to show that he still knew how to walk up the gangplank to get on a ship, even if it was not to work but to travel. The trip would also have allowed him to express his sympathy for the large number of sailors lost in the North Atlantic.

But the State Department detected other reasons for Curran's request: "It has now developed that his absence from the country is desired by certain members of the union in order to make a thorough examination of the finances of the union, the gossip being that he and another member have probably misappropriated funds."[108] The fact that the State Department was aware of the union's internal difficulties suggests that the NMU's problems were so immense that they were becoming increasingly hard to hide.

The overriding problem was the atmosphere created by the war. It was true that the antifascist atmosphere had undermined anticommunism, thus allowing a leader like Smith to be recognized. But the war brought out something else too. A major problem faced by the NMU leadership during the war was that the union's National Council would "not allow anything to come to the membership which would allow our war effort to be interfered with in any way, shape or form. On that we unanimously agreed," said an unnamed NMU leader. But this meant that lingering and festering problems were ignored and "the situation became worse." Although this kind of happy-face or "don't worry, be merry" unionism was understandable, given the enormity of the challenges presented by the war, it lulled the leadership—including Smith—into a sense of lethargy and left them unprepared when the political atmosphere changed once more at the end of the war.

After the war, the union finally recognized that "there was disunity in the national office . . . to the extent that unless it was adjusted, it would interfere seriously with the proper functioning of our office." Communist leaders—notably Smith and Myers—were said to have made "individual decisions on organization, negotiations, and personnel questions at variance with union policy." This was "not healthy," the union asserted with gross understatement. "The war strains and the tremendous task of keeping all ships sailing, might be said to have affected the thinking and ability of some of the National Officers. . . . Differences . . . arose over questions of policy, because of the emotional approach of some officers, flamed into actual hatreds, to the extent they were unable to work correctly" and a "breakdown of administration" resulted. The problem was compounded by a lack of respect for Curran, whom non-Communists viewed as a stooge of the Reds and who was not altogether trusted by all Reds either. "The refusal in some cases of officials to accept the President as the executive officer of the union, has been a large and contributing factor" to the mess. The NMU's internal investigation fueled the "rumors and whispers" that polluted the air like stale tobacco smoke. The leadership, pulling and tugging in different directions, had to be reminded, "Once a decision has been reached as a result of collective discussion, it becomes the responsibility of the National Office collectively and individually to put such decisions into effect. In other words, the differences must be forgotten once a majority decision is reached."[109]

After this report was released, Leo Huberman felt free to tell the union why he, a true blue socialist, felt compelled to resign from the staff after three and a half years' service, as the war was coming to a close. His work for the union in the realm of labor education had won wide acclaim. Yet "certain [union] officials without ever having spent so much as two consecutive hours in the classroom, or in some cases, without ever even having set foot inside the door, were determined that this, that, or the other thing must be changed. These officials had their way. . . . Certain changes were made. . . . It was humiliating for me to have to listen to certain officials discussing what the curriculum should be, when they had no earthly notion of what the curriculum had been." That was not all. "I have long smarted under the rule imposed by the national office that I could not buy a suitable poster, or plan an educational program of any sort, without having to get prior approval from a national officer. . . . It is true of every department head and lesser official in the union." Huberman made these comments in a letter to Smith, addressing him as "Dear Ferdinand," and presciently calling this "situation . . . very serious and very dangerous." "No business runs that way. It couldn't." Yet "in the NMU, the six highest officials are so bogged down with detail, so harassed by petty nonsense, that [they have] not time to think of the important problems facing the union, nor can their subordinates function efficiently." Huberman declared, "I am certain that the members of the NMU expect that their leaders will be giving careful consideration at all times to the problems of how to increase the recent $45 wage award to $100, not to whether or not Leo Huberman has spent $5 for a poster." The "national officers have a saying," he concluded, "'never a day goes by without some crisis.' That's true," but it was not inevitable.[110]

Although Huberman's criticisms were valid, he should have recognized that one reason for the crisis afflicting the union was the constant pressure they were under, especially from interested government agencies. Early in the history of the union, Curran criticized Roosevelt for "the Dies [House Un-American Activities] Committee's attack" on the union. "Instead of trying to whip American public opinion into a frenzy of hysteria," he argued, "it would be well for the Committee to look into the activities of the un-American shipowners, who, for years, have been operating a majority of their ships under foreign flags and employing alien seamen, while at the same time accepting subsidies from the U.S. government for their ships sailing under the American flag."[111]

Curran was right. However, it was not accidental that a Communist-led union would find itself under assault rather than management. The kinds of attacks it suffered in the prewar era were mild compared to those it endured afterward.

6

Storm Signals

A PALL DESCENDED over the midtown Manhattan hotel where two thousand people were expected to honor Ferdinand Smith in 1944. As he reached what appeared to be the zenith of his eventful life in the United States, suddenly his career began a steep decline in the wake of the revelation by a local newspaper that he was no more than an "illegal alien," and a Red one at that. In utter disbelief, the *New York World-Telegram* reported on its front page that "an alien Communist plans to tour the United States and speak for the Roosevelt-Truman ticket, working closely with the CIO Political Action Committee."[1]

Basil Harris, leader of the U.S. Lines, the "largest shipping company in the world," was sufficiently comfortable about his place in society to announce, "I don't care if Curran and Smith are Communists, anarchists, rightists, leftists or atheists. . . . What I'm interested in is that the NMU gave a pledge not only to the government but to the mothers of America that there would be no strikes on American ships and no delays during war." So prompted, Curran added that Smith was "one of the outstanding leaders of our organization and one of the outstanding leaders of the trade union movement. . . . The principles of [Smith] are my principles." The NMU assailed the "smear" of Smith but conceded that "charges that Smith under our constitution should not be holding his office, will be examined as is provided for in that constitution. A trial committee has been named according to our constitutional procedure and upon the request of Brother Smith himself."[2]

Not only were the charges a major setback for Smith and the NMU, they were also harmful to the Roosevelt campaign. As the revelations about Smith were capturing the headlines, the *Washington Times-Herald* reported that "into the nine states in which the political experts think that Negro voters will hold the balance of power next November, the battle for the Roosevelt fourth term will be led by [Ferdinand Smith]." The "roars of opposition that went up from the more vociferous anti-Red labor groups when the 'Clear Everything with Sidney [Hillman]' order reached their camps, will now beat upon the fourth term ears over the Ferdinand Smith issue—only louder, if anything." The Smith bombshell was the opening shot in an all-out war against the progressive aspects of the New Deal legacy. But this was not recognized at the time. "There is no doubt that Smith is a darling of the inner-circle of the more radical New Dealers," the journal said, "and that the elder statesmen in the Democratic National Committee . . . see only more trouble and dangerous trouble, in the appeal now to racial groups in behalf of the fourth term candidate by an orator with a violently radical background."[3] Others, including legions of non-Communists, disagreed sharply. "U.S. official praise[s] alien Red at sendoff dinner for PAC tour," and a headline in the anticommunist *New York World-Telegram*.[4]

The Smith imbroglio also gave Curran the opportunity to put some distance between himself and his erstwhile Communist patrons. In an Open Letter he assailed the party, saying they had falsely accused others of misusing funds, then had an "illegal Council meeting" that "voted to turn the funds of this union and all its resources over to the defense of [Smith]." Opposition to this maneuver was "hidden away in *The Pilot*." This was part of a larger Communist subterfuge, he charged: "Small ports such as Cleveland, Savannah and river ports, which have very few or no members available, are made to appear as those that represent a majority of the membership. . . . Baltimore, Galveston, Boston and other ports which rejected these activities and which had present at their meetings hundreds of members, are hidden or left out of *The Pilot*."[5] Curran's attack was the opening fusillade in a far-reaching conflict. He followed up on his letter by ultimately breaking with the party—and taking his powerful union along with him.

Because of Smith's mighty stature, the authorities scrutinized him carefully. His immigration status became a matter of front-page discussion in the newspapers. The authorities discovered that "there is no evidence that Smith is a registered voter." This was in violation of the by-laws of the American Labor Party, which Smith served as Vice-Chair of the New York County committee.[6] An "informant . . . advised on December 18, 1943 that Smith was in financial difficulties and was being sued. . . . A garnishee order would probably be obtained against him."

The FBI office that reported this information had long been aware of Smith's anomalous immigration status. At one point it considered using this information against him in order to make him into an FBI informant. Months before the revelations about his immigration status hit the headlines, an FBI memo stated that "it would be advisable to inter-view Smith regarding his false claim of U.S. citizenship with a view to-wards developing him as a Confidential Informant."[7] But J. Edgar Hoover dismissed the idea, saying that "in view of his extensive Communist connections and his great influence with the colored element in the Communist Party it would appear unlikely that he would be willing to cooperate with the Bureau. . . . In so far as his falsely claiming citizenship is concerned it would, of course, be unlikely that a violation could be established or that prosecution would be authorized. The only false statements established to date were made prior to 1936" and "would probably not of itself constitute a violation of the statute."[8] Consequently, plans to prosecute Smith with a view to making him an informant were scotched.

On the other hand, the FBI had advance notice of the *New York World-Telegram* story on Smith's immigration problems which it communicated to FDR aide Harry Hopkins in a "personal and confidential" missive.[9] Perhaps this signified some bureau collaboration with this right-leaning newspaper; it was an implicit warning to the White House to be wary of its left-wing allies.[10]

Certainly the bureau was not surprised by the press's disclosures. With inordinate speed and glee, it proceeded to wiretap telephone conversations as Smith and his comrades in the party and union began coming to grips with the scandal. At 10:40 A.M. on 20 September 1944, the FBI recorded the following conversation between Curran and NMU leader Hedley Stone. "We spent all day trying to get Smith and we finally got him this morning," said Curran, "and he don't say yes or no. . . . 24 hours have gone by and we get no answer from Smith except that there's nothing to worry about. I got him on the phone this morning and I raised hell with him for not being here yesterday when we were looking all over for him, and [he] simply answers you by saying there's nothing to worry about. . . . Right off the bat you got a violation of your own constitution, don't you see?" An émigré sailor had to have a "legally filed intention, it's very clear on that, I got it right in front of me. . . . It says right in the god damn thing he must have legally filed intention to become an American citizen."

Curran though Smith's approach to the matter was much too casual. "Nobody has slept all night here," he exclaimed, indicating the stress he was under. Stone could only reply, "This is shocking." Curran continued, "There's a double danger in this, now that this thing has come out the way it is, you're liable to have FBI men down here any minute to pick him up for something, you know what I mean? . . . We got to find out about that, we got to find out whether he ever voted [or] anything like that. . . . There's a lot of ramification in this thing." Worry dissolved into resentment as Curran declared, "It could have been avoided if he'd have come to us he should have years ago, see." Then reality descended: "All right, there's much more to talk about, the phone is probably tapped and people getting information, see." Right. But Stone provided the FBI with something else to chew on as he asked Curran, "Have you got your citizen papers?"[11] As the conversation proceeded, like a film dissolve one could see Curran slowly but surely moving away from his alliance with the Reds and becoming increasingly hostile toward them.

The authorities went into overdrive as they dealt with the disclosures about Smith's status. They monitored Blackie Myers's and Smith's conversations with Communist official Roy Hudson, Smith's discussions with Communist leader James Ford, and Ford's conversations with Hudson. And Smith's discussions with Myers. In the process they accumulated a treasure trove of intelligence and raw gossip.

Early in October 1944 Myers provided his comrade Smith with a plausible rationale for abruptly leaving the campaign trail. "The reason you're dropping out of the tour is because of illness as a result of the strenuous trip you've made. . . . And from the reports we've gotten now on the Coast you're getting tireder [sic] and tireder [sic]," he said.

"Yeah," Smith replied coolly, without apparent ardor.

Like Curran, it suddenly dawned on Myers that "these wires are tapped any way."

"Yeah," Smith replied, again with no evident enthusiasm.

Then, recalling a recent trip, Smith told of the "several receptions and a conference" he had. "One," he said, beaming, "was in Hollywood, boy we were represented, all these folks out here, everywhere . . . were terrific."

"Ferd," said Myers, seeking to jerk his comrade's attention back to the unpleasantness at hand, "look it, look see Harry right away," referring to Harry Bridges, the powerful West Coast longshore leader.

"Yeah," replied Smith, once more with little fire.[12]

Smith probably knew what his closest comrades were saying about the mess. Myers expressed his sympathy for Curran's predicament and his attempt to make sure that Smith's status "cannot become an issue and that Ferdinand [himself] will not become an issue. That was his thinking and he made it apparent, and old bull-headed Ferdie made it impossible for him to even, he started to make a suggestion which was what we wanted and Ferdie jammed it right back in his throat, so we brought it out another way but it came out finally. . . . Curran is plenty worried about it, yeah," he said glumly.[13]

Curran apparently wanted Smith to step down immediately, but Smith would not comply. Late one night in October 1944 James Ford talked about it on the phone with Roy Hudson.

Ford, a fellow Negro Communist, came to the point right away: "Well, I don't know, I don't think it is right Roy," he said expressing his opposition to Smith's departure from the NMU leadership. "I think the union will make a tremendous mistake if they don't fight this issue out." Hudson was conciliatory, though vague. "I met with him about three or four hours, him and Blackie. . . . We worked out a strategy . . . that is going to result in the final outcome of it being a big victory for us. . . . Going in there with a head-on fight with Curran . . . would have been disastrous." Hudson and Myers were backing Curran in his desire to see Smith step down but Ford was having none of it. This could easily make a legitimate political difference appear to have "racial" overtones: "I tell you Roy personally I can't afford to go along with that, I'll speak up." Dumbfounded, Hudson replied, "Go along with what, you don't know what you got to go along with yet." But Ford knew.[14]

He took his concern to Smith's fellow West Indian, Charles Collins. "I have just had a long talk with Ferdie," he said, "I told him it would be . . . foolish to step down." He confessed this was placing a strain on him and other Reds. "This thing worries me, it's upsetting you know." Collins agreed, "Yes, it's very upsetting." Part of the worry was that Ford was not convinced that everyone was above aboard and suspected that some were using the matter to unseat Smith. "I've had two talks with this guy, I went up to his house last week and there's some things deeper about it that I think I have an eye on."[15]

Even after Roosevelt's reelection, the frantic postmidnight conversations continued. In one of these, Myers ducked out of an interminable meeting to seek Roy Hudson's counsel. "We're still at it in here," Myers told Hudson. "Ferdinand brought in a lot of legal opinion and he refuses to carry out the decision reached last night, says he's going to fight it."

"Are you adjourned yet?" Hudson inquired.

"No, not yet," Myers responded dejectedly, "I just c[a]me out here to talk to you," but Smith "refuses to listen. . . . He won't even discuss it with me, I'm sitting next to him." Smith was apparently consulting with some of his Negro allies, as Myers had observed his comrade "with a judge all night long after he left us."[16]

According to the FBI, because Curran had not supported Smith during the crisis and also because he was suspicions of Curran's political reliability, Smith wanted to turn the tables on Curran and oust him from the union leadership. "Smith eventually hopes to replace Joseph Curran . . . with a 'party man,'" the FBI said. "Smith does not believe that Curran is an ardent follower of the Communist Party ideology and sufficiently devoted to party ideals but rather is an opportunist who will 'play ball' with the most powerful group regardless of their belief or affiliation."[17] In retrospect, Smith was correct, as Curran was a consummate opportunist. However, Smith was in no position to go on the offensive when he had to fight to stay on in the country.

The storm abated temporarily. But days after Roosevelt's resounding reelection victory, the other shoe dropped: Smith resigned his union post. He had "filed for citizenship in 1920," it was explained "but, just as some other seamen, did not follow through to keep that application in effect. To have gone into any pros and cons on technicalities in the matter could conceivably have caused dissension in the union and have served as a basis for attack from pro-fascist external forces."[18]

"We . . . know and love" Smith, said the NMU leadership. "It is therefore with the deepest regret that we accept his resignation."[19]

Smith was required to leave the country, then return, presumably to correct his immigration status and be reinstalled in the leadership. The FBI followed him carefully as he "signed on the SS *Medina* on February 1945 as chief steward. He sailed for Mexico on February 12 from New York. He had in his possession a British passport."[20] He was gone for twenty days. Upon his return he was declared eligible to "run in the special election then being held for office of Secretary." Curran was publicly critical of Smith's behavior. "Thousands of dollars were spent in 1944 on this case," he remarked.[21]

Disenchantment with Smith was again expressed when Smith was "re-elected" as Secretary, though he got far less than a majority of the votes cast (there were more than two candidates).[22] This was the beginning of Smith's loss of popularity that would eventually cause him to return to Jamaica. Shortly after his reelection, his closest comrade in the union, Blackie Myers, decided not to run for union office after he neglected to pay his dues and was no longer in good standing.[23] In short order the two top Reds in the union were wounded, just as the NMU faced an uncertain future.

These events weighed heavily on Smith's mind for the next few years. February 1948 was no different from previous years, as he sought to fit in a campaign appearance with former Vice President, now Progressive Party standard-bearer, Henry Wallace, then rush to a meeting of his union where he was expected to argue vociferously against endorsement of the Marshall Plan for European recovery. Sitting between Robeson and Wallace, with Congressman Vito Marcantonio nearby, Smith was featured prominently at an American Labor Party rally in Manhattan.[24]

The federal authorities were busy too, trying to keep track of his movements, for a few hours after he had shared a platform with Wallace—and before he could make it to the critically important union meeting—he was detained. He was one of the first victims of the Justice Department's effort to deport Cold War opponents of "alien" descent.[25] The reason Smith was chosen was simple. He was a Communist. He was an "alien Red Negro." He was also the leader of a vitally important union that was helping to keep afloat various allies in the popular front now challenging the White House's postwar turn away from détente and toward Cold War with the Soviet Union. In April 1945 Smith was contemplating a "prospectus" which would increase his union's already heavy contributions to the NNC. The NNC wanted money for the George Washington Carver School in Harlem, an independent left-oriented institution.[26] A few months later the NNC recorded its "sincere thanks for your recent contribution of $2500."[27] Through Smith's good offices, the Negro Labor Victory Committee had also become a key recipient of NMU funds.[28] The Initiators of the Crusade to End Lynching—which included Paul Robeson—gave Smith "most sincere thanks" for the $2,500 he sent them.[29] Through Smith's energetic efforts, the NMU itself "posted a $5000.00 reward for the capture of . . . lynchers" since it was "quite obvious that neither the FBI nor the state has any intention of acting and apprehending [these] criminals."[30] Even the union's humanitarian donations had a political slant, as $11,000 was provided to the Yugoslav Red Cross.[31]

As the anticommunists began to focus on the leadership of the NMU, they were increasingly suspicious of the various activities of the union's number two leader. He was involved with the Citizens Non-Partisan Committee to Elect Ben Davis (the notorious Black Communist),[32] and the Citizens Committee to Free Earl Browder,[33] the Communist Party leader. He was a sponsor of the Joint Anti-Fascist Refugee Committee,[34] a member of the Board of the United American Spanish Aid Committee, and a signer of a declaration marking the anniversary of the Reichstag Fire in Germany. He seemed to be a one-man "Communist front."[35]

As the political climate turned against Smith, his opponents charged that he was using the hard-earned dues money of sailors—not to mention his well-compensated time—to subsidize various "Communist fronts," and that this was misfeasance of the highest order. In return Smith claimed with some legitimacy that the union had always taken a "labor-community" approach aimed not only at bringing better benefits for its members but also at creating a liberalized climate by fighting racism. Moreover, the NNC, the main beneficiary of Smith's largesse, took a particular approach to Negroes not duplicated by other groups. Though it focused on the "entire Negro population," it saw its "main character" as emphasizing the "trade union and working class composition" of the black community—which was why it hired the veteran sailor, Revels Cayton, as its leader in 1946. This guaranteed that the NNC was as much of a "NMU front" as it was a "Communist front"—but its opponents were having none of this.[36]

The NNC's "trade union and working class" approach to "racial" equality was bolstered by Smith and his union. With the ouster of the former and the decline of the latter, this approach suffered as well. Although Negroes could look forward to desegregation in the future, they faced the possibility that they would earn the right to eat at a lunch counter but perhaps not gain the wherewithal to pay the bill. The prospect of middle-class leaders representing a mostly working-class Negro community—and their class interests being dominant—became more likely.

This thought had occurred to Smith and his comrades. As the purges were beginning to bite, a high-level meeting—probably of Communists—concluded that the "successful struggle of Negroes in America will help America in relation to the colored peoples all over the world." An unnamed Red added, "I think Ferdinand is correct in trying to channelize this through the international labor conference."[37] He was referring to the budding World Federation of Trade Unions for which

Smith would work in the immediate aftermath of his departure from the United States. But the effort to "channelize" the "struggle of Negroes" through "labor" formations was Smith's and his party's approach.

In the unprecedented upsurge by labor after the war unions sought to reverse the losses incurred by the no-strike pledge. For his part, Smith's addressed several audiences on the special needs of the working class. Less than six months after the end of the war he was in Pittsburgh addressing "striking steel and electrical workers" in the Central Baptist Church. In a building full to the rafters with "3000 strikers" and their supporters, Smith said that "the church should take a leading role in rallying support for the strikers among their congregations." Mildly criticizing leading Negro clerics, he asserted that "the church has been preaching the brotherhood of man for ages. Organized labor is practicing it. Men and women of all races and creeds are struggling hand in hand, and they should be backed up by their churches." In a direct refutation of his opponents, "Smith stressed the fact that the current nationwide struggle is for restoration of post V-J Day pay cuts, not for wage increases." It is a "fight to maintain living standards in the face of the high cost of living," he explained to the cheering crowd. This "wage fight is not without its political aspect," since "the attack on the rights of trade unions . . . is the spearhead of an all-out offensive by American fascists to stamp out all the democratic rights enjoyed in our country." Smith cited the by now "familiar pattern of the rise of fascism in Germany, Italy and Japan—ruthless oppression of the people that began with attacks on labor." These "same forces [were] fighting against full employment, fair employment practices, unemployment insurance and the minimum wage bill. They are the same forces who during the war did everything in their power to hamstring effective prosecution of the war by our country. They are the forces of American monopoly, who are out to establish this country as the last stronghold of world monopoly. The fight against these forces is the fight of all the American people."[38]

It seemed that there was no fight of the "American people" from which Smith was absent. He was prominent in the "Oust Bilbo" campaign designed to unseat the unpopular senator from Mississippi.[39] He "address[ed] a mass meeting of Negro and white veterans in Chicago, where a national organization known as the United Negro and Allied Veterans of America was formed." There were three hundred people from thirty states and Joe Louis was designated as the honorary chair.[40]

On the international front he joined with his good friend Paul Robeson in demanding "freedom for Puerto Ricans," characterizing the United States's relationship with this former Spanish colony as an "imperialist adventure." While he was at it, he "urged freedom for the people of Indonesia, China, South Africa and India" too.[41] On South Africa, he "protested to H. T. Andrews, Minister of the Union of South Africa against the 'continuation of the pass system, denial of trade union rights and decent living wages to African workers, and the brutal smashing of the African mine workers' strike.'"[42] He told the segregationist Secretary of State, James Byrnes, that he wanted "immediate action to break relations" with Franco's Spain. "The entire membership" of the NMU, he said—not incorrectly given the union's losses on the Iberian peninsula—"is particularly close to the tremendous suffering of the Spanish people under Franco, due to the fact that more than twenty percent of our members originally came from Spanish speaking countries."[43]

Smith saved his harshest criticism for British Prime Minister Winston Churchill and his March 1946 articulation of the Iron Curtain that was said to have descended over Eastern Europe. Being a native of Jamaica where the sovereignty of the Windsors of England had never been subjected to a referendum, Smith felt particularly qualified to comment on this controversy. He condemned Churchill's words as a "smokescreen flung up to involve Americans in preserving the crumbling British Empire, [which] has been the scourge of humanity for many centuries." He assailed "Churchill's inspired appeal to American mothers and fathers to send their sons to die to preserve the 'prerogative' of British lords, dukes and earls, still conspiring in their musty castles, which have never seen the light of day, to suppress the natural inspirations of the Indian, African, Chinese and Indonesian people." This "must arouse the opposition of the American people who, at great cost, have just fought a war to destroy fascism and tyranny." Churchill, Smith said, "throws up a smokescreen by charging the Soviet Union with the 'crime' of aiding Europe's long-oppressed, democratic forces." "We cannot believe that President Truman knowingly lent aid and comfort to the ravings of a cornered Tory." He dismissed the idea that Moscow presented a threat, adding, "We do not believe this Red Army has changed; nor have the Russian people." On the other hand, "the Tories have not changed since the days of George III. The American people [who] remember 1776" should recognize this above all.[44]

These words were followed up with a conference of Negro Trade Unionists attended by three hundred delegates from seventy locals. It culminated in a "Death Blow to Jim Crow" rally in Harlem with two thousand people present. Smith avowed, "We must concern ourselves with the trade unionists of Africa. . . . We must attend the conference called by the West Indian Trade Unionists next month and help them in their fight to establish a West Indian Federation."[45]

But Smith was appealing to an anticolonial sentiment that was in rapid retreat in his adopted homeland, to be supplanted by a fervent anticommunism. And it was this latter that led to his eventual ouster from the United States.

Smith's militant trade unionism alone could have led to his ouster from the United States, but when combined with his party membership, he stood no chance of reprieve. Joseph Curran, who sensed which way the winds were blowing and rapidly denounced the party that had elevated him to the top leadership position, announced that "500 [party] members dominate" NMU, out of "80,000 members" all told, by dint of "tactics 'no different than those practiced by the Nazis when they destroyed the trade union movement in Germany.'" Through the manipulation of "its cells the [party], according to Mr. Curran, was able to take 107 out of 150 elective offices in this union, one of the most strategic in the nation's life."[46]

This sent a chill through Washington and Wall Street. Now that the war had ended, Moscow became the new antagonist, and the Soviet Union's allies, the Communists, were transformed into a satanic force. The union that they led would be essential if the Marshall Plan were to succeed, if troops and supplies were to be dispatched effectively from around the world.

Just as sailors were essential during the war in supplying valuable intelligence from places near and far, their work continued to be important after the war had ended—though their attitude was not as favorable toward Washington as before. Smith received a message from a "friend . . . in the Pacific" who confided that "the real reason for the shortage of ships" was "due to the number of ships and crews now being used to carry supplies and troops to be used against the Indonesians and those being used by reactionary Chungking forces in China." Another letter acknowledged that "the reason for the slow return of the veterans is political and not a ship shortage. That is especially true here in the Pacific where the cup runneth over with the subjected colonial masses really striking out on new paths for freedom and independence."[47]

Smith's detractors knew that he had direct access to sources of intelligence that often contradicted official sources in Washington. Smith and his friends broadcast this information to all who cared to listen, much to their opponents' irritation. Howard Rushmore, the veteran anticommunist, accused the NMU of trying to "spread . . . Red Propaganda" particularly "among Yanks abroad. . . . The Communist Party and the NMU," he charged, "issued a number of pamphlets urging American troops to revolt against the 'foreign policy' of their own Government." Worse, this "drive" was "inspired by Stalin's desire to have a free hand in China and Japan." He had been reading *The Pilot* and had not liked what he saw. The "current issue," he said in early 1946, carried a letter from NMU member Sol Leviton who told of how his ship "the Marine Wolf, landed in Calcutta. We were there to pick up 2500 GIs. We laid over 48 hours which gave us a chance to distribute a few thousand pamphlets on bringing the GIs back home." According to Rushmore, such acts were akin to sedition.[48]

Apart from Smith, suspicion also fell on Eddie Gordon, the union's representative in Cuba and "a graduate of the Communist Party training school in New York"—as was Smith, it was said. Havana was identified as a meeting place for Communists in the hemisphere and a hotbed for Red conspiracies of various sorts.[49] The Communist International—the worldwide group of parties based in Moscow—had never died, as was reported during the war, said one ex-Red in denouncing Smith. Look at Havana, source of a Red virus: "This waterfront section of the Communist Party," said Victor Campbell, "sent bundles of literature, advocating force and violence [to] Cuba and other countries."[50] What would happen if such literature made it to the wrong hands?

In fact, the NMU had long since developed a fruitful relationship with its counterparts in Cuba. NMU sailors often marched in Havana's labor parades.[51] Curran was a frequent visitor to the "Pearl of the Antilles," particularly for meetings dealing with hemispheric labor organizing. In 1941 he was "elected an Honorary President of the National Maritime Federation of Cuba" and struck up a relationship with Jaime Gravalosa of the Cuban Federation of Labor.[52] Union leaders from Cuba, Colombia, Jamaica, and elsewhere had as an "ultimate aim of organizing a Confederation of Maritime Workers of the American nations." This could hinder the possibility of powerful U.S. shipping interests threatening to utilize cheaper maritime labor in the hemisphere.[53]

According to the House Un-American Activities Committee, the NMU was busy establishing "new branches and sub-branches" of the union and had become a major transmission belt for the Communist Party and "Havana" was "the center of operations"—conveniently offshore and distant from the long arm of Uncle Sam. "Four to five ships daily arrive from the Canal Zone," the Committee reported, and "several ships [arrive] daily direct from South American ports." The "Cuban government permits open left-wing activities and copying the mode of Mexico" and "encourages radical unionism. Thus through the medium of ships alone communications can be carried even faster and more regularly than the regular mail routes barring air mail. . . . Any qualified seaman can smuggle a passenger from Havana to Miami without the passenger's name appearing on the passenger or crew list without his being seen boarding or leaving the ship. The same for travel in the opposite direction. . . . The second most important tie-up," said the Committee warily, "is the Clyde Mallory Lines with direct express service from New York to Florida. For this reason the Communists have seen that two of their most important men are assigned to ports which from a union viewpoint are relatively unimportant, Jacksonville and Miami."

There was a northern complement to Havana: "Organization on the Great Lakes has been the concentration of the Communists for a long time dating back to at least 1929." Not only did this region allow for a quick getaway to Canada, "a Lakes strike can effectively cripple the steel industry and ore mining" since the "coal moves North and the ore moves South. It would also seriously hamper the movement of wheat. Rail and road transportation in the area surrounding the Lakes has been largely designed as a 'feeder' system and could not handle the traffic with the Lakes tied up."[54]

An unnamed informant referred to the NMU as the "trojan horse" in the nation. He was worried about the "infiltration of communistic philosophy into crews of vessels operated under the jurisdiction of the United States Maritime Commission." These Reds were holding meetings to discuss conditions on ships and seizing control of radio operations where they could make "frequent reports" to Communist parties abroad. He was also suspicious of Eddie Gordon and the NMU operations in Havana, which "constitutes an intrinsic factor in the dissemination of Communist literature in Central American and South American ports."[55]

Not only were these subversives Red, Congressman Dies was told, but there were other issues as well. "An American Sailor" writing from Newport News observed that "the leftist group are primarily of a foreign type with a pronounced Jewish trend."[56] The NMU was compared to a nasty tapeworm that had invaded the intestines of society with consequences too macabre to contemplate. But ultimately responsibility rested with the Communist Party, whose "personnel" were said to be the engineers of this lengthy train of conspiracy.[57] True believers concluded that only fools, traitors, or, heaven forbid, Communists themselves would tolerate such subversives having a grip on the nation's economy.

Critics deluged HUAC with questions about the advisability of allowing a Red-dominated union like the NMU to continue. Thomas Abello, a seaman writing from Greece to the Chief Counsel of the committee, revealed that people were holding meetings about Red sailors in southeast Europe. When he returned to "the States . . . I will . . . go to Washington and pay you a visit," he said. "I might have some information you might be wanting to hear. Later I'm thinking of going to South America," where he could keep an eye on subversion too. "Please try to find me something to do in connection with your office," he pleaded.[58]

He was probably not disappointed. Less than a year after the war ended, Louis Russell noted that "Communists in the maritime unions" had recruited 237 new members in recent months. Thus, "in a war against a communistic aggressor, communistic control of American vessels on the high seas and the means of communication between these vessels means that no supplies will be delivered to the American army in foreign ports."[59] There was also concern about "communism in the United States Army" and Reds "agitating the soldiers in remote places to strike." Subversive "literature is being sent overseas" to these soldiers "through the use of the [NMU]."[60]

To those with growing concern about the Reds' role in the nation, this kind of news was a nightmare. Congressman John Wood was staggered when Joseph R. Walsh of Long Island told him that in early 1946 he had attended a meeting of the American Labor Party in Freeport, "out of curiosity." An "official" of the NMU told him "how he and his colleagues placed literature and pamphlets on every ship leaving the port of New York. From 500 to 5000 pieces on each ship with instructions to the crews who were members of the NMU to place them in the hands of GIs urging them to clamor for return home" and other subversive notions.[61]

While Washington was talking about an Iron Curtain descending over Eastern Europe, NMU sailors were said to be in Marseilles joining a French strike of "Communist-bred . . . French seamen and dock workers."[62] Meanwhile, back in New York the "first full-scale political demonstration" at the United Nations in Lake Success was spearheaded by "NMU sailors. . . . Ten taxis and seven private cars streamed into the parking lot and pulled up in a semi-circle. Out came the demonstrators, carrying Egyptian and American flags, the NMU emblem," and placards denouncing Britain, the United States' new Cold War ally, because of its policies in North Africa.[63]

The swiftness and intensity of the anticommunist assault overwhelmed Smith and his comrades; they were not prepared for it. The party's new line, enunciated in 1944 by its leader Earl Browder, trumpeting a new conciliation between labor and capital, allowed the organization to be wrong-footed. Its support for Curran came back to haunt it as he quickly became their chief tormentor. To be fair, the comrades may have had good reason to be surprised by Curran's apostasy. After all, he had underscored his "warm affection" for the party's friend, Paul Robeson, "by naming his son, Joseph Paul" in honor of the famous singer.[64] Confirming the warmness of the relationship, Robeson came to the NMU convention in 1943 to confirm that "some of my closest friends are in your union: Joe, Ferdy, Leo. . . . They are very, very dear friends of mine. . . . Today nothing makes me prouder than to be a member of the [NMU]." Then he performed heartfelt renditions of his favorites, including "Joe Hill" and "Peat Bog Soldiers," in a further demonstration of his affection for the NMU leaders.[65]

Since Smith and Robeson, a presumed non-Communist, "became fast friends and supported each other in their wide-ranging struggles for the rights of black workers in the NMU and elsewhere," it had seemed to follow logically that Curran too was an essential element of this powerful triumvirate. After all, Curran had praised the blatantly pro-Stalin, pro-Soviet film, *Mission to Moscow,* in the pages of the NMU newspaper.[66] He had joined with Smith and "all six national officers" of the union in endorsing the crusade of Morris Schappes, the suspended City College of New York professor sentenced to prison for "perjury," although his ultimate crime was his ties to the left.[67] He had written to

President Roosevelt calling for a pardon for jailed Communist leader Earl Browder.[68] He ran for Congress in 1940 on the left-led American Labor Party ticket. He "breezed through the primaries . . . defeating his opponent by a three and a half to one margin" as "forty one union members volunteered as watchers at the polls."[69] Such "pink" tendencies caused CIO stalwart Len De Caux to declare that Curran "was then one of [the] CIO's most outspoken lefts—more so, in fact, than stricter party-liners who might mince words for the sake of CIO unity."[70]

Curran's viewpoint was so close to that of the party that many analysts concluded that he was a Red himself. He waffled on the question of the extent of Red influence in the union he headed. Once he had the temerity to allege—according to one partisan source—that his "union has no Reds."[71] California Congressman Jerry Voorhis repeatedly inquired about Curran's supposed Communist membership. Curran claimed that documents were forged to show such a tie and angrily refuted "broad hints" that he "should be cited for perjury" in light of his fierce denials.[72] These supposed party membership cards were "forgeries—and clumsy ones, at that," he retorted.[73]

However, heated denials alone did not lay the charges to rest. Testifying before the House Un-American Activities Committee, John Frey, President of the Metal Trades Department of the AFofL claimed to have "photostats of Joe Curran's receipts for payment of dues in the Communist Party." "It is definitely known that practically every day Roy Hudson and Joe Curran meet at the Welcome Inn on Sixth Avenue between Ninth and Tenth Streets in New York City." His "party name" was "Jose Narruc"—"if you read Curran backward, it will give Narruc," Frey concluded triumphantly.[74] But Curran was adamant and no doubt accurate when he said at one of his numerous congressional hearings: "I do wish to state for the record publicly, that I have not been a Communist, I am not a Communist now and I do not believe that I ever intend to be a Communist."[75]

This last clause was seen as too equivocal. The Committee questioned him about his vigorous criticism of the anticommunist crusaders who dogged his union. His "criticizing the Dies [House Un-American Activities] Committee's attack on the [NMU]," as he did in contacting President Roosevelt, was not unusual. "Instead of trying to whip American public opinion into a frenzy of hysteria," he responded, "it would be well for the Committee to look into the activities of the un-American shipowners, who, for years, have been operating a majority of their ships under foreign flags and employing alien seamen, while at the same time, accepting subsidies from the U.S. government for their ships sailing under the American flag."[76] Curran said that his union had "been the target of continued slanderous attacks by Congressman [Martin] Dies, his committee and other anti-labor Congressman" who called the NMU "Communist-controlled."[77]

Dies was persistent. He told fellow House members in 1941 that the NMU had "definitely agreed to call a general strike in the event that Harry Bridges"—the alleged Communist longshore leader—"is deported." As for Curran, Dies wondered why he "switched from his critical position" of the party to "following of the party line . . . late in 1936," coincidentally enough as the NMU was being launched with Curran at the helm.[78] This was all very curious, he thought.

The Committee claimed that Curran's union "has become an integral section of the Communist International's espionage and sabotage apparatus now at work in this country." Besides, he was "inordinately vain (there are fourteen portraits of himself in his New York apartment)." The committee did not think—correctly as it turned out—that his preening would withstand a targeted anticommunist assault that could jeopardize his sinecure.[79]

Committee members argued that Curran was under virtual surveillance by the party lest he make a false move. Dorothy Snyder, who worked closely with him at the NMU, was said to be the Red "watchdog placed over him." They maintained that she was only one of many women who were manipulating sailors; these "young 'comrade girls' popped up on the waterfront to exercise their wiles upon the seamen (successfully in some cases)."[80] Such deft deployments explained why "the NMU left underestimated Curran," since they "felt they had Curran surrounded."[81]

Apparently the Reds did underestimate Curran, an obvious blunder given that he routinely pored over *Robert's Rules of Order,* the bible of parliamentary procedure. A former sailor, Johnny Gladstone, asserted in 1982 that "given enough agents spread around, some of them are bound to rise into positions of responsibility in the organization they infiltrate. It's possible," he declared without any supporting documentation, that "Curran could have been an agent from day one." Like others on the left, he had a poor opinion of Curran: "Hamhead—that was our sobriquet for Curran." Still, Curran "could be called many things but he was no fool. He spoke without anger, without wit, without sarcasm. His demeanor was avuncular."

Gladstone recalled the Reds' attempt to repair their rift with Curran. "He said he would like to salvage the situation, but it was out of his hands. He could no longer talk with Blackie . . . or the 'Party people,' the communications were ruptured." Curran cleverly asked "if it was possible to restore unity within the NMU (I had a feeling he phrased that 'within the NMU' carefully) he would agree to meet with [party leader] Foster; but it had to be Foster—the top."

In an atmosphere of high drama, "Curran put down his coffee cup and walked out of the cafeteria. Cheered by the new possibilities, we swung into action. Several meetings were held at the ninth floor of the party headquarters." But the circle could not be squared. Curran had sensed earlier than most that aligning himself with a party tied to the new Cold War antagonist in Moscow was not a wise career choice.[82] But from the point of view of the left, Curran's perfidy was of a piece with his personality. Or so thought Terry Penman, a sailor who "never really trusted" Curran, especially since he "treated" his first wife "shabbily."[83]

Another sailor, Gordon Thompson, argued that Curran merely wanted to substitute the leadership of one centralized body for another. He "very much wanted an Irish mob to run the national office," said Thompson. "Curran, Lawrenson, Duffy, McIntosh, Hanley and Gavin—how Irish can you get?" According to Thompson, Catholic trade unionists—particularly Irish Catholics—began organizing in the postwar era and "they came to recruit guys in the NMU . . . meetings were held on 14th Street and all of the Irish Catholics on the waterfront were literally ordered to go to those meetings. And it was well-known at the time that these guys were going to take over the NMU."[84]

If these Catholic trade unionists had their eyes the NMU, perhaps they were emboldened by the evident turmoil in the party itself. In 1945 the party ousted its General Secretary, Earl Browder, in part because it considered his approach to employers too conciliatory in the new postwar era. Obviously the no-strike pledge would be dropped; so would the idea of cooperation between sailors and shippers. Browder's ouster was preceded by a momentous meeting in February 1944 in which Browder and his comrades maneuvered to liquidate the party—to be replaced by an "association." Their premise was that the war required a new era of cooperation between management and labor.

It is unclear whether Smith backed Browder at this juncture—his presence was rarely noted in important meetings—though the fact that his close comrade Blackie Myers did, suggests that he may have.[85]

To Harry Haywood, the black Communist sailor, then in faraway Cape Town, it looked altogether different. He met a "young white woman" who asked, "What's this I hear about the party in America?" She had heard "over the radio last night that your party is dissolving itself." It "all came as a great surprise and shock" to Haywood. "It was hard to believe."[86]

Smith did not maintain a high profile in internal party affairs. In 1944 when forty members of the influential National Committee were elected, a number of Negroes were among them, including Ben Davis, Pettis Perry, Henry Winston, James Ford, Claudia Jones, Audley Moore, Rose Gaulden, William Patterson, and others—but not the most powerful Negro Communist, Ferdinand Smith.[87]

In any event, the party was under enormous pressure from on high and the atmosphere was not conducive to clear thinking and straight dealing. Whether for this reason or whether on account of his dubious immigration status, he instinctively opted to be a semicloseted Communist. This is not to suggest that he sought to avoid identification with his party. When Browder was imprisoned, he "sent letters to President Roosevelt and Attorney General Biddle in my own behalf and in behalf" of his union.[88] At a rally to free Browder, Smith exhorted the crowd, "Today we are in a greater struggle. America is troubled at heart because we keep a man in jail who should be in the forefront of the fight against fascism. I call upon you, Mr. President, to unchain the heart of the American people by delivering to us Earl Browder."[89] Smith's support of Browder, among other things, made it easy for anticommunists to attack him. Quickly Smith was denounced as one of "two Commissars"—the other was his comrade Max Yergan—playing a leading role in Harlem. As a parting shot he was called a "Stalinist ward-heeler of the [NMU]."[90]

Unremitting pressure leads to errors and testiness. This was what was happening to the Communists. Ben Davis, the Communist City Councilman from Harlem, was not pleased when his "name was not advertised as a speaker" at an NLVC rally and wanted to discuss this oversight with the NLVC "face to face."[91] Charles Collins gently told his friend, "Don't be surprised if from time to time the [NLVC] fails to come out for a very important measure"—even something as basic as backing Davis. Many names were neglected, he said, not just Davis's.[92]

Later, NMU leader Joe Stack maintained that most of the Reds in the union leadership "only knew how to work for," not "against" Curran, and thus were flummoxed by the onset of the Red Scare and Curran's speedy embrace of anticommunism. Blackie Myers "threw in the towel" and resigned, while floating the apocryphal story that a technicality had forced him out.[93] Norval Welch of the NMU concurred, contending that "Blackie was never prepared for the Cold War. . . . He had got by increasingly on his charm, wit and dark good looks—it is easier to follow a line, when you are exceedingly busy than to think for yourself, so when the crunch came . . . Blackie, among others, was not ready."[94] These are harsh words—and perhaps unfair—but the larger point was that Myers's untimely departure left Smith, with his questionable immigration status, further exposed.

The perpetrators of the Red Scare knew that—rhetoric about "Moscow Gold" aside—the National Maritime Union had become a mainstay for the Communist Party and to weaken the former was inevitably to weaken the latter. Earl Browder, then in a bitter dispute with the party, confided that the NMU "has many times made available to the [CP] the strike funds on deposit as collateral for loans to be contracted by the CP. These loans [were] not shown on . . . the financial statement of the NMU."[95] When the Communist Ben Davis ran for reelection in 1945, the NMU raised more money—by a factor of two—for his campaign than other unions, well ahead of the teachers and furriers.[96]

Because Smith was a leader of this key union that was a mainstay of the Communist Party, he was under increasing pressure. Early on the FBI had noted that Smith was "colored, holds a high office in the Communist Party and is second in command of the NMU in the east. He is running for secretary of the NMU although he was told by the Communist Party not to do so. The Communist Party is desirous of getting [Smith] out of the NMU for reasons of their own."[97] Smith, the FBI said, holds "union book no. 2 in the NMU" behind Curran's number 1, indicative of his high-level role; he also "ranks next to James Ford among the outstanding Negro Communists in this country."[98]

In July 1945 the leadership of the party included NMU stalwarts Josh Lawrence, Blackie Myers, and Al Lannon (interestingly, the private intelligence agency that revealed this identified those who were "Negro" but did not identify others by racial, ethnic, or ethnoreligious labels).[99] The Communists remained strong as long as those like Smith remained in the leadership of the still vigorous NMU. A private intelligence agency which monitored a postwar New York meeting of the waterfront section of the party attended by fifty militants noted with concern that "the section is beginning an intensive campaign to get [petitions] signed for the removal of Coast Guard jurisdiction in Maritime matters. The party has a good talking point here inasmuch as they claim seamen have been subjected to double persecution. Any seaman who has committed a crime is punished first by the captain of the ship at sea and then again is tried by the Coast Guard after the seaman has arrived in port."[100] This was the kind of "pork chop" issue—of concern to sailors no matter what their ideological leanings—that enhanced the reputation of the Reds in the NMU.

Negroes had further reason to admire the union. At a time when a good deal of the nation accepted Jim Crow, the NMU had struck out on another path. Patrick Whalen, the union chief in Maryland, "had developed a rough-and-ready approach to integrating waterfront bars. Whalen accompanied by a group of mixed-race sailors [sic] would enter a bar. If the owner protested, that it was a whites only establishment, Whalen would throw a beer mug through the back bar mirror and declare, 'There, you've just been integrated.'"[101] Before the onset of Southern desegregation in the 1960s, the NMU already had begun taking antiracist measures. One of the union's biggest strongholds was in Galveston, formerly a major entrepot for the slave trade. Galveston was a "leftwing stronghold. The 'Daily Worker' was on sale in the union office, clippings from it on the bulletin board." The NMU had helped organize the oil workers and was assisting other workers across racial lines. The union there "strongly endorsed Henry Wallace" in 1948 "with black members in the lead." In neighboring Port Arthur, the NMU "spearheaded local activities" when the antiblack, anticommunist Martin Dies was chased "out of public life." According to veteran CIO analyst Len De Caux, the "NMU's record was due largely to Communist influence. CIO verbally opposed discrimination. But only the left and notably the Communists, aggressively tried to right ancient wrongs and create genuine union and job equality."[102]

This was a major achievement. The NMU had extensive operations in Savannah, Charleston, Houston, Port Arthur, Jacksonville, Tampa, Corpus Christi, and other cities in the Deep South. In their union halls they flouted prevailing norms by showing "anti-discrimination pictures." Their newspaper, *The Pilot,* had a circulation of sixty thousand and a "world network of 150 . . . pick-up spots." Translators on the staff, particularly Spanish ones, were evidence of the NMU's hemispheric concerns. With funds won from their successful defamation suit against columnist Walter Winchell, they set up a "Leadership School" in order to better promote their progressive egalitarian notions. They produced "anti-racist" films with their own "16mm motion picture camera and 35mm sound strip camera."[103] When the union decided to bid for a license to operate an "FM station" on radio, they intended to up the antiracist ante.[104] The union backed up its words with actions, and one reason was the ideological commitment of the Reds.

The Negro sailor Frank Lumpkin agreed. A ship, he thought, was a "bad place to gamble. It was a prison kind of thing. You couldn't go nowhere. You couldn't spend money. So I sent my money *home.*" It was there that he "began a lifetime habit of serious reading. He read to learn, to try to find answers to the questions that swarmed in his mind." The isolation of the ship and his incessant study, along with what he witnessed on board, led him into the arms of the Reds. He joined the party "because Communist seamen were so solid; they were always fighting discrimination. The top and the bottom of the ship were mostly white, on deck and in the engine room. Blacks were mostly in the middle, in the mess room. The Communists were fighting to change that." He appreciated that.[105]

In the minds of many Negro sailors, the symbol of that change was Ferdinand Smith. However, Smith would not be in the union for long—or in the nation.

7

Storm, at Sea

THE NMU LEFT seemed to be in an impregnable position in the early postwar era, sailing along like a formidable battle cruiser. But there were signs that not all was well. *Time,* the popular newsweekly, and no friend of the union, once remarked that "NMU rank & filers had long had a noticeable list to port: some belonged to dockside cells of the Communist Party."[1] A *Time* cover story in June 1946 carried a large portrait of Curran, "boss of the sailors" with the provocative query, "Will workers of the world unite?" The Chelsea headquarters of the union, said *Time,* was "once a telephone exchange which shoulders aside the ancient tenements and sailors' lodging houses" nearby. "On the top floor [was] a big paneled conference room. There hang the photographs of three NMU heroes: Roosevelt, Tito and another Joe—Stalin—in the center place of honor."[2]

Two of these "heroes" already seemed well beyond the ideological pale. Soon the third would be accused of inaugurating "treason" because of his New Deal and détente policies—when that happened the union would be sailing through decidedly choppy seas for months to come.

Like many in the United States at that moment, *Time,* was concerned that the NMU and its longshore allies in the Committee for Maritime Unity would impose a stultifying strike on the nation. That a Communist-led union would do so at a time when the nation was confronting a "Communist threat" abroad was deemed outrageous. Many asked whether Moscow would tolerate such a strategic union being led by allies of Washington within its borders. Yet it would be no mean feat to oust Ferdinand Smith and his comrades from power for they had developed a loyal following, particularly among Negroes who were not attracted to the kind of leadership they saw in other unions. Smith held firm to his stand on the issues, particularly on global matters. Some were not pleased when Smith posed with Soviet maritime leaders at union headquarters as they stared at a large and imposing portrait of

Stalin hanging in the "NMU'S Council Room."[3] Others objected to him soliciting signatures on petitions for aid to Yugoslavia.[4] In the fall of 1945 the NMU sponsored a rally to protest "transportation of Dutch troops on American ships to enslave the Indonesian people." Likewise, the union objected to the "deportation of Indonesian seamen and the barring of liberty-loving Indonesians from returning to Java."[5] Smith himself joined five Indonesian seamen "striking on six Dutch ships." The union donated $500 to this campaign and, together with Robeson, Smith and the union hailed "the people of Harlem who are feeding them, helping them find shelter and providing them with other essential services."[6] The union went further and voted to boycott all ships loading military cargo for the Dutch in Indonesia, leaving foreign policy specialists in Washington to wonder just who was in charge of the nation's external relations.[7] At a time when many in the United States may have thought the word "Indonesia" was an unusual name for a girl and not the largest predominantly Muslim nation in the world, thanks to Smith and his allies Harlemites and sailors knew better.[8]

While Truman was seeking to whip up concern about an alleged Communist advance, NMU sailors were taking a different approach. After returning from southeast Asia, sailor Juan Alejandro declared, "The Atlantic Charter's holy promise of self determination for the oppressed of this world is just so much hokum. . . . The shooting war isn't over in the Dutch East Indies. Nor is all loveliness and light in French Indo-China." Alejandro explained why NMU sailors were able to gain information that others preferred to keep from U.S. audiences. "American NMU seamen," he said, "have a way of getting around on foreign waterfronts. Even if they don't speak the language they still manage to make themselves understood. They learn a lot." Thus he "saw the bayonets in Saigon" and "heard stories in the native marketplace of the terrible atrocities the French had inflicted." But this was not the kind of news that Washington wanted people to have.[9]

Yet with metronome-like regularity, NMU sailors complained about "U.S. aid against Indo-China" and troops being sent to "Batavia."[10] The problem for the White House was not only that the NMU was led by Reds such as Smith but that the union was in a position to contradict—with up-to-the-minute intelligence—the administration on all sorts of issues, including the troublesome matter of China. In the fall of 1946 the NMU reported that there were "great bodies of [Chinese] troops marching through the main streets and soldiers with machine guns at different street intersections. . . . In front of the custom house is anchored an American fleet. Chiang Kai-Shek's government may control the cities, but the country is seething with revolt." In the United States people were not being told that "the presence of our troops here is strengthening those reactionaries."[11]

The union and Smith had more than an intellectual interest in events in China. In the spring of 1947 Smith contacted the State Department about "Julian Larrinaga, ex-crew member of the SS *Morris Sheppard* who was sentenced to one year and nine months in Shanghai for instigating to murder." Smith wanted the "Shanghai consular official" to "conduct an immediate investigation. . . . We feel that unjustified treatment has been rendered Mr. Larrinaga."[12] He had been "arrested . . . on charges of instigating an assault . . . resulting in the death of a local rickshaw puller" and "was found to be drunk at the time of the alleged offense."[13] Smith had to be informed about the chaotic situation then prevailing in China in order to defend the unionist Larrinaga; yet, increasingly, being informed was seen as being part of the problem.

Defending the interests of their members almost inevitably brought NMU leaders into conflict with the U.S. authorities. Greece, a major flashpoint, became the focus for the so-called "Truman Doctrine" that inaugurated a new phase in the postwar battle against communism. The NMU, which did not back this initiative, came into conflict with Greece by the very act of defending its members. Thus, the union "demanded an investigation of the beating, robbing and imprisonment of three Negro NMU members in Piraeus, Greece. The incident was denounced by [Smith] as 'shocking fruits of the Truman Doctrine.'" Smith linked this doctrine to Jim Crow in a manner that was not flattering to the White House. The "U.S. consular officials failed to give proper representation to the seamen," he said bitterly. The NMU delegate on board said, "in my opinion, the reason they have been so harsh with them is because they are Negroes.'" Thomas Groves, one of the jailed men, said a "U.S. Coast Guard officer urged the Greek court to jail him solely because he is a Negro and a union representative on the ship." The "[skipper] did practically nothing to help his crew member and . . . U.S. consular officials failed to give proper representation to the seamen." Shortly before this incident, "some eight thousand Greek trade unionists of all political denominations were arrested, including the president of the Greek Maritime Federation," a NMU ally. Smith contrasted the U.S. consul's inaction on this case with a recent case in Hungary in which a U.S. "policy runner" had been seized for making anti-Semitic remarks and Washington sprang into action to free him.[14]

While Washington wanted to portray Greece as a noble ally resisting the evil encroachment of Communist radicals, the NMU was painting a different picture based on the unfortunate experiences of their members. Since its inception, the NMU had been close to Greek sailors, a number of whom resided in New York City. This incident only brought the two left-wing allies closer together, much to Washington's dismay.[15]

As the NMU and Smith became more unpopular, the State Department became less interested in cooperating with them in rescuing sailors from harm's way. In June 1947 Smith wrote to Secretary of State George Marshall and attached a letter "from members of various unions re: the actions of the American consul in relation to the conditions that seamen are confronted with abroad." Writing from Le Havre, France, "the undersigned" consisted mostly of "NMU members, others are Canadians and SIU. The beef is that the American Consul won't give us the proper help and the food situation is terrible. . . . All of us are getting the runaround from the companies and the American Consul. The Consul is always laughing at the 'beef.' . . . The union should put more pressure on the State Department for every seaman is ignored by the Consul." This was happening not only in France but elsewhere as well: "All the seamen in these foreign countries are getting the same deal that we're having." How could sailors support Smith and his comrades as union leaders when doing so almost guaranteed the noncooperation of a vital agency like the State Department on "beefs"?[16]

In September 1947 Jess Faughtenberg, a sailor, "sought to complain of the American Council [sic] in this city," that is Bahia, Brazil. After he had visited a doctor, he was declared a deserter but when he "called the Assistant Council [sic] up to complain of this doctor he told me to shut up and said if I gave him any more trouble he would put me in jail. The British council [sic] tried to talk to him and he told him to mind his own business and he would do the same thing."[17]

After the end of the war labor and other forms of unrest mushroomed globally. This complicated the lives of sailors traveling to politically unstable foreign ports, particularly when U.S. diplomats were unhelpful. Smith's office received numerous complaints from sailors around the world. Among them was "brother Thomas Hatchet . . . left in Santiago, Cuba, through the fault of the Master of the vessel of the

Company Agents, not posting a sail-date until noon of the same day, which was on a weekend and the majority of the ship's crew was off and no one knew the ship was sailing until that afternoon."[18] Then there was Willie F. Allen of the SS *San Jose,* who complained about the "outlandish conduct of the Honduras police in regard to seamen who miss their ship in Puerto Cortez. It is our firm belief," said Smith, "that this condition exists with the connivance of the company officials, namely United Fruit . . . Company. One of our brothers, a member of this crew, [had] the misfortune of being left there . . . and when we returned . . . this brother was a sight to behold; on top of suffering from swollen feet, he also was suffering from malnutrition. . . . [His] swollen feet came from sleeping on [a] bare concrete floor without any bedding whatsoever."[19]

There were many other cases too. Smith demanded that the State Department "investigate the repatriation rights of Andres S. Martinez, crew member of the SS *Yaque,* United Fruit Steamship Company who was left behind by his vessel in Puerto Barrio" and "denied the customary repatriation rights and was required to return to Spanish Honduras by the local authorities."[20] But why should the State Department help a Communist-led union which periodically criticized it for policies it was pursuing, given all the other demands on its time?

Assistance from the consul was of great importance in the many repressive port cities in which NMU members often found themselves. Smith complained to the U.S. Maritime Commission about what had befallen "the crew of the SS *Gauntlet*" and the "mistreatment of merchant seamen in the port of Lourenco Marques," Mozambique. They were "brutally beaten and thrown in jail and charged heavy fines on the slightest pretense."[21] And in Beira in Mozambique, East Africa, "Brother West . . . an American of Negro descent" contracted malaria and "instead of receiving adequate care" he "was taken to a so-called hospital on the outskirts of town where the patients were all of African descent. . . . There was no clean linen, not even a towel to ensure the most elementary sanitation. The mattress was of straw; and food . . . was unable to eat." Once more, the union was trying to force the United States into a confrontation with one of its chief anticommunist allies, Portugal.[22]

In neighboring South Africa, then in the early stages of apartheid, a NMU member "sustained injury" to his "left eye from slivers." On "arrival at Cape Town arrangements were made" for him to "consult an eye specialist," but he "was chased out of the doctor's office. The doctor told me no black man was allowed in the office." He returned, "accompanied by the steward and one delegate. We were chased from the premises." The union "had a number of these cases from South Africa." Just as the United States was moving to solidify relations with its anticommunist allies abroad and ease Jim Crow restrictions at home, the NMU and its militant corps of well-traveled Negro sailors complicated its strategy.[23] The anomaly of what came to be known as the "civil rights era" was that the United States sent the Negro sailors packing while maintaining alliances—for the longest time with their racist and repressive allies.

The presence of Negro sailors in nations friendly to the United States—though hardly welcome—was not just a problem in Africa. Australia, another U.S. ally, had yet to do away with the officially sanctioned policy of white supremacy, though Washington was seeking to discard this doctrine domestically. This became a source of conflict when Negro sailors arrived at Australia ports. An Australian weekly wrote that Negroes had a penchant for enticing women "down under." They were "sex-crazed and liable to go mad after drinking very little alcohol." Combined with this was the "revolting sight of local girls hysterically mauling black men and begging them with tearful voices to stay." These were some of the weekly's mildest remarks.[24]

Smith was outraged by "this attempt to discriminate against Negro seamen."[25] He was "horrified and shocked beyond credulity at the monstrous libel," "unsurpassed" in virulence.[26] The Australian ambassador promised "to bring this article before the proper authorities in Australia" and added hopefully, "[This] will not be allowed to affect the good relations which exist between Australia and the United States of America."[27] Skeptics, however, wondered why the United States was allowing a Communist to complicate relations between two allies.

Apart from fighting against bias, the NMU also came into conflict with powerful forces for other reasons. Rank-and-file sailors wanted "strengthening [of] South American ties," adding that "the fight of the NMU against phony foreign flag transfers, against the double exploitation of foreign seamen and for keeping American jobs under the NMU banner, requires the support of Latin American workers." To accomplish this task they had to confront "the reactionary leadership of the AFofL [which] has been sending in their agents to disrupt South American progressive trade unionism."[28] The NMU was also active in

Panama. Smith spoke up forcefully in support of union efforts in the Canal Zone to destroy Jim Crow—a subject with which he was all too familiar, given his tenure there—which led to attempts by the United States to destroy the unions.[29]

Thus, when the NMU and its West Coast longshore allies—which also had Reds in the leadership—joined together in 1946 to press a common bargaining and political position, there was profound fear nationally about the future of the nation. The journalist Victor Riesel warned that "the biggest strike machine in history" was being assembled by the Committee for Maritime Unity (CMU), which included the NMU, Harry Bridges' progressive West Coast longshoremen, and a number of smaller unions. "A prolonged shipping stoppage," he warned, "would cripple over 50 big ports, stall food and gas shipments inside the country and perhaps wind up as the world's first international strike." He was struck by the level of organization: "the committee at this moment [could] put up 3000 seamen in private homes" if need be, thus ensuring that sailors would not be stranded away from their home ports. There is an "entertainment committee" and a "legal and medical aid division has lined up 300 doctors, dentists and registered nurses. . . . The Publicity Department will publish a [newsletter]. The Dispatching Committee will coordinate picketing."[30]

The very idea of Communist-led labor unity sent waves of apprehension in Washington, and the nervousness—even hysteria—led to hyperbole, even confusion and misapprehension, on all sides. As one NMU leader put it at the time, "In reading the statements issued by various officials of the union concerning the record of the CMU in recent weeks, it has occurred to me that a future historian of the labor movement will have great difficulty in deciding just what did happen to the NMU during the critical year, 1946."[31] Indeed, the situation was confusing, for the pressure of the threatened job action caused some NMU leaders to buckle, then redirect attention away from their own inaction.

From the point of view of Washington, the timing of the threatened strike was most unfortunate. Postwar Europe and Asia were both in the grip of hunger and homelessness, conditions that the Truman Administration thought provided fertile soil for the rise of communism. The Marshall Plan, it was said, would address this problem. The NMU itself conceded in the spring of 1946 that "a total of 4,209,000 tons of German shipping will be given to the United States by the Inter-Allied Reparations Agency, fifteen allied countries will share 16 almost new ships."[32]

U.S. foreign policy was on "the threshold of a historic change," conceded one business analyst, and "it is clear that the merchant marine
must, therefore, play a far more important role as an instrument of defense and foreign policy under the Truman Administration than in recent years."[33] There had been an enormous growth in foreign trade and
thus of shipping. "Today," the NMU announced at its 1947 convention,
"there are approximately 2350 deep water vessels in service and NMU
alone has close to 1350 of these under contract. Prior to the war, in 1939
and 1940, we had only about 400 contract vessels."[34]

This was why some thought that Communists like Smith who opposed the Marshall Plan were allowing ideology rather than the best interests of the union to guide them. Would not this initiative mean more
jobs for sailors? they asked. But Smith begged to differ. In his view, the
plan would mean more unemployment for U.S. sailors because Washington would turn over its vessels to Europe and allow them to build
even more. Further, the plan would allow U.S. shippers to "set up
dummy corporations in these countries, as they now have in Panama,
Honduras, etc. and operate with foreign crews for the purpose of escaping American wages and working conditions."[35]

Nevertheless, Smith thought the proclamation of the Marshall Plan
would give the union more leverage. "When I picked up the New York
Times and . . . saw the statement by Secretary of State Marshall that it
would be disastrous . . . if any weakening of the American merchant
marine would take place, because it would completely ruin the foreign
policy of the United States . . . and I said further, 'If we don't [take] advantage of that in our negotiations, we are missing the boat' and I want
to repeat that. I say that we are in a favorable position if we act right, if
we maneuver right. So I am not inclined to retreat and I do not think this
Council intends to retreat." He strove for "two weeks to get the National Office to call our Council into session during the period when the
union was in a state of flux" so they could strike—figuratively—while
the iron was hot. It seemed the union was "in a box and we don't
[know] how to maneuver out of it," because of internal opposition. But,
ever optimistic, Smith maintained, "I think we can . . . we can and we
will."[36] In short, Smith thought the left in judo-like fashion could turn
U.S. imperialism's asset—the Marshall Plan—against it.

Of all the threatened job actions of 1946 this was one of the most significant, because it had gigantic domestic and global consequences. In
the port of New York alone there was "an investment of $1 [billion] in

dock, pier, terminal, warehouse and similar facilities." "Some 6000 ocean-going vessels clear the port's 204 deep water piers annually." The CMU was threatening to bring this transport machine to a crashing halt unless its demands for higher wages and better working conditions were met. This would have major repercussions on the U.S. and global economy.[37]

Because so much was at stake, Smith was proceeding cautiously. The idea of the CMU was a sound one, he thought: "Is it not a logical step," he asked, "for the unions in a given industry to act together or unite for their mutual benefit?" However, he was not as confident of the CMU's ability to bend the shipowners to its will. "Relatively, I don't believe that the maritime unions are in as strong a position as they were before the war. I believe that in the United States capital is relatively in a stronger position." But there was another reason why the ruling elite should be challenged. "The seamen lost too many comrades in this war to sit by idly and allow the conditions for another war to materialize. It is no secret that the political tories and the economic monopolists all over the world helped finance and support fascism in Germany and Italy. Having been badly beaten in Europe, the monopolists are doing their dirty work in America."[38]

The CMU "was an attempt by Harry Bridges" of West Coast longshore and comrades like Smith "to address the post World War II collective bargaining issues by recovering the maritime unity that was . . . in existence from 1935 to 1941." Indeed, it was an attempt by labor to unite behind a larger political agenda. It began in 1946 and, according to the ILWU, "in the ensuing negotiations with the shipowners the CMU achieved great gains in wages and working conditions." But the unexpected resignation of Joseph Curran from the CMU in December 1946 changed the situation. His ostensible reason for resigning was that he objected to what he viewed as West Coast domination.[39]

Curran and those who backed him were frightened by the growing strength of Bridges' union, which was widely believed to be as heavily dominated by Reds as the NMU. This led to a number of unsuccessful attempts to deport Bridges, the Australian-born stevedore. But it was not for lack of trying. Repeatedly the authorities asserted that Bridges and "top CP officials" discussed "maritime unity problems."[40] The authorities feared that the CMU represented a further increase of power by the Communists and their maritime allies, and that the planned 1946 strike was their piece de resistance.

Curran may have been frightened by the scale of what the Communist-led CMU was attempting to do at a time of rising concern about the Red Scare, and decided to throw in his cards in response. Victor Riesel was not exaggerating when he suggested that an "international strike" of mind-boggling dimensions was being attempted.

As Curran became increasingly unenthusiastic about the strike, Smith took the lead in mobilizing the troops for industrial warfare. "We are acting as the general staff in carrying out the declaration of war, and as good generals it is up to us to soberly analyze the factors involved in the carrying out of the program that is outlined. . . . Let us analyze our opponents' threats, their resources. Brother Curran pointed out that the shipowners made some two billions of dollars during the war," Smith said in an indirect jab at Curran. "They have, with their resources for attacking us, a friendly Administration and Congress. Last, but not least, they have a controlled press and radio who will carry on a campaign of lies to attack the Maritime workers." Curran sized up the opposition and concluded that the time had come to surrender. Smith said in effect, "damn the torpedoes, full speed ahead." As he noted, "We have, in contrast to what we had in '34 and '36, some kind of treasury. . . . Collectively, we probably could muster a treasury of some five million dollars." This was a lot of money, especially compared to what the NMU had during the strike leading to the union's formation, when it "had approximately $1.35 in the treasury and we were out for some 90 days. But we were not weakened!" Smith said to "loud applause." Perhaps overoptimistically, he also said, "We have a favorable public opinion."[41]

The NMU reached out to its local allies in labor. As always, Smith was mobilizing his allies among Negroes via the NNC, seeking to form a "Labor Committee" within its ranks.[42] He requested that all "join us on this national picket line!" against the "bankers and industrialists who are fat with war profits. The profiteers want fascism for America," he warned in a statement endorsed by Charles Collins, Josh Lawrence, and other close comrades.[43] Smith reached out not just to Negro unionists but also to Julius Emspak, a major figure in the ranks of labor.[44] Smith had to move aggressively, given that his plans were so ambitious. To indicate the utter seriousness of the proposed strike, he suggested a "work stoppage—24 hours or even more, if necessary. A national work stoppage of 24 hours." This would include not just maritime workers but the railways too. It would bring the nation to an abrupt halt, just as fears were rising about a "communist threat."[45]

But the work on the home front paled in comparison with what was being attempted abroad. At a rally in Manhattan "one of the biggest ovations given . . . was for the representatives of 800 French seamen. . . . In their native language, [they] told the NMUers why they'd determined to sail no American ships until the NMU strike was won."[46]

The CMU was working closely with the World Federation of Trade Unions, recently formed in Paris with heavy participation from Communists globally. Louis Saillant, their leader, told Curran and Harry Bridges in mid-1946 as the strike was about to be launched, that "we relayed especially to the British TUC [union federation] and the Norwegian, Swedish, Dutch, Danish, Belgian and French CGT [union federation] your message asking for support and effective solidarity of the seamen of these countries."[47] Louis Goldblatt, the CMU leader, thanked the Peruvian unions for their "splendid gesture of solidarity,"[48] while efforts were made to reach out to the "Japanese Seamen's Union."[49] The Philippine Seamen's Federation needed no such coaxing, informing Curran, "We are willing to take action June Fifteenth."[50] Danilo Jiminez of Costa Rica told Curran that "as a revolutionist and labor leader in my own country," he, along with "the workers of the whole world," "will cooperate with their comrades of the USA."[51] Jack Vinocur spoke in similar terms, stating that the "entire workers delegation of [the] ILO [International Labor Organization] comprising representatives from over 20 countries this morning unanimously adopted the following statement . . . 'that this meeting of seafarers representatives expresses its solidarity with the organizations which [are] striving to improve the working and living standards of their members.'"[52] The patient cultivation of good relations with Latin America paid off as workers in Puerto Rico pledged to "go on strike in sympathy with you,"[53] while the dynamics of the struggle pushed forward the "question of the amalgamation of the waterfront workers of Mexico with the ILWU."[54]

But this daring attempt at global labor solidarity had to withstand the weight of considerable internal and external pressure. Steeling for the battle, the U.S. Navy called "reserves and volunteers to operate ships in event of strike."[55] A cartoon depicted the tension by showing "Casey Truman Now Batting"—the president was portrayed as a right-handed batter swinging at a ball labeled "NMU."[56] Indeed, Truman was bent on pounding the union into oblivion and thousands were cheering for him. A bulging "crackpot file" maintained by the West Coast longshore union contained a letter complaining that "all these strikes are surely breaking all of us little business people." An unsigned note vowed, "You'll never get away with this bunk, not in the USA."[57]

The CMU could have withstood this pressure—when did a strike ever proceed without pressure?—but for the internecine squabbling that erupted, foreshadowing the impending purges of the left. Initially Curran asked why the NMU, which far exceeded in size the other member unions of the CMU, paid more than its share into the organization's coffers.[58] The NMU had an estimated 90,000 members, compared to 25,000 for all the others.[59] From his point of view, the other unions were freeloaders feeding off the NMU. On the opposing side, Smith felt that Curran was finally showing his true colors, seeking to destabilize the CMU in favor of the AFofL. He said that Curran's attempt to dislodge the NMU from the CMU "will cause harmful consequences." Curran knew full well, he asserted, that to reassure smaller unions they would not be "swallowed up . . . it was mutually agreed that all affiliates—small and large—would have an equal vote." Curran "recognized this fact many years ago" and his eleventh-hour discovery of this imbalance was merely designed to mask his support for "the AFL Maritime Trades Department" which "was formed with the avowed purpose of smashing the CMU unions, including the NMU."[60]

This was just the beginning of a series of accusations and counter-charges. Louis Goldblatt of the ILWU asserted in the midst of a particularly contentious CMU meeting that "[these] are not a verbatim set of minutes." Not only did they contain "several inaccuracies," but they were "completely distorted" with "inaccuracies too numerous to mention." Curran claimed that an important "teletype was deliberately not shown to me by [Ferdinand] Smith . . . and indicates shoddy activities—to say the least. . . . I reject these minutes as totally inaccurate and designed for the purpose of creating misinformation to our membership to accomplish some dirty objectives."[61]

The arguments went beyond Curran and his ideological foes; from time to time Smith crossed swords with Harry Bridges,[62] and occasionally he agreed with Curran. Louis Goldblatt of the ILWU tried to conciliate Curran, at one point saying, "I think some of Joe's complaints have a certain amount of foundation perhaps. . . . I think we should make some attempt to remedy the problems that Joe has raised."[63]

Because the stakes involved were so high, it was difficult to accept arbitration—which was what the CMU was pushed toward.[64] It was even harder for some to swallow Curran's abrupt resignation from the

CMU, a maneuver that effectively destroyed the leverage that the NMU needed for further advance. Smith accused him of a "deliberate lie" and more "lies." Bridges thought that "another 1921" or potential liquidation was faced by maritime unions in light of Curran's "burial of CMU." One sailor asked, "You mean to tell me Curran cannot see [this]?" Smith replied, "History alone can answer." Bridges was sober and contrite: "I have done everything I could to work with Curran. I have taken more insults than anybody around here from Curran." Smith had no time for contrition; he was hopping mad about Curran wrecking the CMU, accusing him of "splitting tactics," "confusion of our members," and an "obvious falsehood" and "red-baiting."

Curran in turn had called Smith and his comrades "leaders of the 'trained seals'" operating on behalf of the Kremlin. "That is why I agree with Harry," said Smith. "It is obvious. . . . Curran" and his supporters "are tied up as a committee to destroy, to obstruct, the unity of the merchant seamen with the longshoremen." Bridges reminded those gathered of the crushing reality of it all. "When we adjourn this time the CMU is ended," he said. Smith replied, "Motion to adjourn sine die," leaving open the wildly optimistic idea that another meeting might take place. The more realistic Hugh Bryson of the Marine Cooks and Stewards countered, "Not sine die," adding "the same regret and the same motion." When CMU adjourned an ambitious attempt to organize waterfront workers of the world—nay, workers of the world—with the United States in the lead faded into history. [65]

The collapse of the CMU signaled that a civil war had broken out in the ranks of the NMU. The conflict would end with Smith's expulsion from the union he had built and his ouster from his adopted country. Heedless, Smith blasted away at Curran's sabotaging of the CMU, charging that it would "cause harmful repercussions not only among the affiliated membership of the CMU but among all seamen." It was a "drastic step" and "the membership should have been consulted before he acted," Smith said. Curran knew all along that each union would have one vote irrespective of size and acting as if this fact had just come to his attention was a phony ruse, charged Smith. He wondered how Curran could call for "unity" with their foes among the West Coast seafarers but could not work with their allies among the West Coast longshoremen. Not everyone endorsed Smith's position, including top leaders who had been associated with the left, such as Hedley Stone and Jack Lawrenson.[66]

Curran did not shrink from the battle. He said Smith and his allies had "motives" that "have not been for our union first. They have openly made it clear on the floor that they spoke officially as members of the Communist Party and for the Communist Party." Nor could they charge him with collaborating with the shipowners, given the no-strike pledge during the war when the Reds "promoted collaboration with the employers."[67]

But the National Council, the union's leadership, supported Smith's position by a 20-10 margin. "I respected your authority," he told the Council, "to give leadership to the membership who elected you." However, "Creative minds can create side issues and prevent discussion of the real issues." He relied on the union constitution which called on the NMU to "cooperate" with other "maritime unions."

The destruction of the CMU, which became an all-consuming issue for the NMU, was about more than just bureaucratic maneuvering. It was the CMU, said Smith, that "won for seamen and licensed officers a reduction of the weekly hours of work at sea to 48 hours with overtime for Sunday and a 40-hour week in all ports. CMU for the first time in history, achieved equal pay for equal work for American seamen sailing on vessels from all ports on all coasts. . . . The reasons advanced by Curran to justify his resignation were carefully reviewed by the CMU Executive Committee, and were found to have no substantial foundations in fact."[68]

Actually, Curran may have had another, unstated reason for abandoning the CMU. Since Bridges himself admitted that he was "prepared to merge with the NMU,"[69] another group of radicals would have been added to the NMU ranks at a time when Curran was working overtime to reduce this number. Curran was sending mixed signals, pretending to favor the left but going right. He opposed the idea of "outlawing political parties of any kind [as] a danger signal," although the resolution was endorsed by other NMU officials.[70]

But this attempt to maintain the legality of the Communist Party was undercut by his pressing charges against Joe Stack, one of the top NMU radicals. The measure split the top six leaders of the union. Stack was accused of "actions unbecoming a member and officer" and "misfeasance, malfeasance, and negligence." Infuriated, Stack charged that the union "was getting closer to one-man rule—the thing that killed the ISU."[71] Smith agreed, saying that some of Curran's tactics "would put to shame anything that the old ISU Emperor could have cooked up. . . .

IS HISTORY REPEATING ITSELF—IN REVERSE?"[72] Stack's comrades also supported him forcefully. Joe Wright, a sailor from Houston, observed, "I am quite certain that Joe Curran is not only just finding out that I am a Communist. I think Joe will remember when he sat in a Communist Party meeting at Galveston with me in 1938."[73]

Curran would not back down, again referring to "Smith and the Communists in the union" as "trained seals," and claiming that the Red newspaper, the *Daily Worker* acted for the "Party hacks in the same manner as a shot of dope does to a dope fiend."[74] Curran insisted, "There is no middle road. Either you want Communist domination over our union" or "you will fight to maintain control by its membership *only*." Sure, "the Communists in the beginning of our union helped to build our union but they are not the Communists of today. . . . Their paper, the 'Daily Worker,' which was once a paper that supported labor, is now a vicious lying sabotaging sheet." This "was an all-out war"![75]

Smith was equally outspoken, lambasting Curran's effort to broker an alliance with the Sailors Union of the Pacific which "bars Negroes and Orientals from membership." He was both racist and anticommunist, Smith charged: "A witch-hunt against 'Communists' is the wedge that will be used to splinter the labor movement into helpless parts."[76]

Negro sailors began to fear that since their rise in the union had been closely linked with the rise of Communists like Smith, his fall would mean theirs too. From Mobile in the Deep South, where Smith had entered the United States some thirty years earlier, Negroes let Curran know that "real and rank and file Negroes in the port . . . are denouncing you [Curran] and the phony Rank and File Caucus" allied with him. "Your Rank and File Caucus," they told him, "is holding meetings in every port in the Gulf and we haven't come across one Negro who has been invited . . . because the Caucus holds its meetings in Jim Crow gin mills where Negroes are discriminated against. Caucus meetings in the port of Mobile are held in that manner." Negroes had become fearful about their class position. Just as it seemed that "race" discrimination might be diminishing, doubts rose whether blacks would lose the class gains they had made. "We know if you or any other official of the NMU red-baits, you will also Negro-bait." On the other hand, the sixty-five Mobile sailors—the bulk of the NMU's Negro membership there—charged that Clyde Ganaway, who worked closely with the Southern Negro Youth Congress and the NAACP, was under assault by the pro-Curran forces. "The Ku Klux Klan here has threatened to run

Ganaway out of town many, many times if he didn't stop fighting for Negroes." And if Ganaway was a Red, the sailors concluded, then "Curran and the Rank and File Caucus could use a good dose of Communism."[77]

Curran never convincingly answered this charge, namely, that wittingly or not he had made a Faustian bargain with the most retrograde elements in order to undermine his opponents. According to Thomas Carolan, a sailor, Curran's most avid supporters included "Weaver, a big goon former purser and by his own admission a member of the Ku Klux Klan." Another Curran ally, Blake, said there were "too many Negroes in the NMU." Another crew member averred, "You know what's the matter with the NMU, too many Negroes." Yet another said he "would contribute a dollar to send Smith back to Jamaica." Smith's favorite Congressman, Vito Marcantonio of East Harlem, was said to have brought "all the Puerto Ricans here and put them on relief. At the last ship's meeting, these two characters tried to get a motion through to comply with the non-Communist affadavits of the Taft-Hartley."[78]

George Rasmussen agreed with Carolan. This "so-called Rank and File Caucus," he said, "has been carrying on a campaign of intimidation against the minorities in the union. In the case of the Negro and Latin American brothers, it has been a subtle campaign. However, in the case of aliens there has been an open vicious attempt to scare [them]. . . . Caucus leaders have threatened to put the finger on any alien supporting a resolution or action put forward by the progressives." In response the "aliens" chose to "either abstain or vote against the progressives." But it didn't stop there: then "you must join the Caucus and possibly kick in a couple of bucks. . . . [Then] you must be prepared to take the next step. Do a little red-baiting, come out for the phony Marshall Plan."[79]

Over and over and over again, Smith's supporters alleged that the movement to purge him and other Reds had led to severe collateral damage for blacks and a general suppression of democracy in a union that had been well known for promoting this practice. From New Orleans came the report that "no one can get up and speak" unless the Curran crowd "know what he is going to say beforehand." In a union renowned for infighting, members were "scared to voice their opinions." "Anyone who disagrees with them at meetings gets booed off the floor" and "is threatened with violence." Jobs were being allotted on the basis of favoritism and "men who do their bidding"—and these were jobs that paid "up to $110.00 per week." Moreover, "the Negroes are discriminated against in the Port of New Orleans in such a manner as would do justice only to Bilbo. . . . Crocker, a Negro Patrolman elected by a majority of our voting membership is being discriminated against, dabbed names and called names like 'nigger' 'red' and others." These opponents of the CMU "had the audacity . . . to advocate that no Negro should ever be permitted to work in the shore side gang."[80]

Other, pro-Curran New Orleans Negroes objected to "the lying, libelous statements" spread about the pro-Curran side.[81] These "members of the Negro race, indignantly" decided to "protest against the vile, untrue, slanderous and divisionist [sic] campaign directed against officials of this port."[82] However, they were a distinct minority among African Americans.

The poisonous atmosphere that had come to permeate the union carried over into the meeting of the National Council in the spring of 1947, where tempers ran high and violence almost erupted. Smith was spending his time at one grueling meeting after another. This took such a toll on him that he began one meeting by announcing that he had a "splitting headache." It was so bad that "possibly before I finish reading the report, I may have to call upon one of my side-kicks to finish reading the report for me." But he proceeded thereafter to give his critics a headache, accusing them of "the most vicious kind of red-baiting, twisted around like a pretzel, and as wishy-washy as it can be." They believed "that out of 150 officers in [the] union, 107 are Communists and they dominate the union. For the life of me, I can't see 107 people dominating 90,000 men." Rhetorically waving a bloody shirt, he declared, "I would like to remind the Council that the things you are discussing now were discussed in Italy twenty-five years ago between the left-wing of the Socialist Party and the right-wing Social Democrats. . . . There was a split and while the Social Democrats were pussyfooting around, Mussolini marched into Rome in a luxurious railroad car and took over."

Smith confessed that as he "sat here listening to speeches," the barrage of words "made me feel like Rip Van Winkle who was asleep for years and just woke up. . . . I remember in 1936 when I came off the ship—I was chief steward on a freighter—I was getting $84 a month. A Chief Steward today gets $260 a month—over 200% increase," he said proudly. These wage increases occurred under Communist leadership, so "where is the detriment to the membership of the union?" he asked. "Before the NMU, sailors were kicked around in dog houses, in crimp joints. A guy couldn't marry if he was in love with a girl; he couldn't support a wife, much less kids," but now that had changed under Red leadership. Ditto for the West Coast, where Reds played a prominent role on the waterfront. "The longshoremen on the West Coast can walk around like men and hold their heads up like workers should." Perhaps the pressure of the moment got the better of him, for he proceeded with revolutionary fervor: "I said before and I say it again, the workers can't lose. There are too many of them. To kill them all, you have to kill the world, because you haven't enough reactionaries in the world to kill off that many people. . . . I want to remind you again, I don't know what happened to Hitler, I don't know where he is. But remember, Mussolini was hung up by his feet."

But the times had changed. Smith's adopted nation had fought Hitler and Mussolini—which sealed their fates—but it was leading the conservative charge that Smith deemed the successor of the two dead dictators. Because Curran sensed the new alignment of forces, he was able to outmaneuver those who thought they had him surrounded. He was dismissive of his critics, even telling one of them bluntly, "You are a rat."

Smith replied that he was now incapable of fulfilling his presidential duties. Curran called his bluff: "So make a motion to elect a new President."

"I don't have to do it," said Smith coldly.

Curran responded, "You haven't got the guts."

Smith confidently but unrealistically fired back, "I have the guts. I can do that if I want to."

But he was wrong; he was not able to do so.

One reason for his failure to do so was that he was both a Red and a black. Morton Davis of the southwest understood this. "In my part of the country," he said, "the propaganda goes out that the Communist have nothing to do with the economic way of life. The propaganda goes out about the Communists that they are Negro-lovers" and "that is the only aspect" that his constituency "are concerned with, or know anything about. . . . So when it comes to tossing this red business around loosely, as it has been done, it becomes a dangerous thing." Thus, Smith was known as "a black bastard" in his neighborhood.

Hedley Stone, a former Red, was embittered on both counts, "race" and ideology. He wanted desperately to become a member of the CIO Executive Board but was blocked when Josh Lawrence—a black Communist—objected, because he felt that the union should place a Negro in this post. Stone, prefiguring later anti-affirmative action resentment, said, "But for my color I would have been on the Executive Board." Presumably he would have been less upset if a white man had been chosen instead of him. Such sentiments did not bode well for Smith.

Smith and his comrades may have underestimated the extent to which the Red Scare had taken hold. Hedley Stone, once a Red himself but now smarting over his failure to make it to the Executive Board, now led the charge against the party, complaining about the prominence of the party newspaper near NMU headquarters. "We gave it a position on the newsstand in our lobby. But that is not enough. They have one and two men standing in front of the building trying to sell 'that good paper.'" Harry Alexander felt similarly. "Who are the Council members and have been since 1939?" he asked. "With the exception of Joe Curran and a few more, all of them are members of the Communist Party. That is a fact. . . . They have control of the union. . . . Read the proceedings of the last convention in 1945. All the committees were controlled by the Council members" and they were Reds. This was far from democratic, he thought.

Back and forth they went at this lengthy meeting, with charges and denials of Communist domination. The Reds argued that it was a diversion from more pressing concerns while the anticommunists contended that there could be no progress without a purge. To Howard McKenzie, "This whole red scare, this shrieking about the Communist, is designed for just one purpose—so the membership will be conditioned psychologically to be told: even though you may not think him guilty, based on the facts, you must find him guilty, or else you are voting for the Communist party. . . . We are getting a shellacking from the shipowners, we can't get the shipowners by the throat, so take McKenzie and get him by the throat. All these arguments are based on simple psychology."

Charles McCarthy thought he had some sort of insight into the inner workings of the anticommunists. He considered himself a "personal friend of Joe Curran" in that "there has been a personal contact between Curran's family and me that I don't think any individual has had the advantage of. I lived for three or four weeks in the same house with Joe Curran and his first wife. . . . I know many times members of the Communist Party came to give me anything from 30 [cents] to a couple of hundred dollars to get places to sleep our men." This was during the unrest of 1936 and "Joe Curran knows that," "we all know it." So, what was going on? "A Catholic who was once a Catholic can be one of the most anti-Catholic and most reactionary people. We see it in French history and in the English church." And that, he suggested, was what had happened to Curran and his coterie. "When Curran surrounds himself with such supporters as Charles Keith, an expelled member of the Communist Party; Drury, an ex-party member; with Lawrenson, who pulled out of the [CP]; with Alexander who was in the party"—Curran himself, who he suggested might have worn red underwear at one time, was now strongly anticommunist. But the Red Scare he had played on was designed to "cause confusion."[83]

That it did. The NMU was so caught up in judging ideological purity that it was in no position to assess and address the dramatic changes taking place in the industry. This became even clearer a few months later at the 1947 NMU convention, which brought Smith step closer toward ouster from the union he had helped build. Despite their strength in the National Council, Smith and his cohorts were outmaneuvered here, not least because they were overwhelmed physically. The opposition was also well organized. They handed out leaflets that declared, "You have a right to know who are the Communist Party Leaders at this convention." For some reason Smith's name was omitted from the list of names. "Is it any wonder," the leaflet asked, "why they are afraid to have the Rank and File convention delegates investigate and review their work???? Defeat the Communist Party dictators! Help Return Control of the NMU to the Union Membership—Vote Rank & File."[84] The convention marked the rise of the Rank & File Caucus—dubbed the "Rank & File Circus" by its critics—and the decline of the Communists within the NMU.

The rancor rose steadily in the months preceding and following the epochal 1947 NMU convention. In retrospect it is difficult to describe the mutual and overwhelming anger of the almost eight hundred delegates on both sides of the ideological divide expressed for three whole weeks. "We have already broken the record in several ways," said Curran at one point. "We have here the largest attendance for [a] union at any convention. The only other union that exceeds us in length of time of their convention, is the railroad brotherhood." It was so long that they had to "borrow money . . . to continue the convention." It was enough to make one sick—which is precisely what happened to Smith. He confessed, "I have an awfully bad cold and a headache. . . . I know that the delegates have been in session for ten days and have been bored with a lot of reading and other items." As at the National Council meeting, Smith's body—indeed, his very psyche—was revolting at the situation he was in.

The bitter infighting—and actual fighting—was punctuated by monotonous and repeated shouts of "point of personal privilege" and "point of order"—often by Smith himself. As Frank Bruno of the SS *Huck Finn* put it, "the tone of the Convention was all haywire." Sol Renzi of the SS *Santa Barbara* said, "At the rate we are going we are heading into open destruction of what Einstein calls the fourth dimension." E. W. Thomas of the SS *Exford* thought he knew why: "What I do know is that the members of our union who are Communists don't do much sailing. They sail about three months out of the year and so they have about five times as much time to get around to do the talking with other people." D. J. Gavin disagreed. "No matter how much you tell them that you are not a Communist, as long as you are in the CIO, and still further, as long as you are a member of the National Maritime Union—no matter whether you are registered as a Communist or whether the Communists kicked you out—those attacking progress will still call you a Communist because the program of this union has always been one of the most outstanding for progress in the routes it has travelled."

He must have had Smith in mind, for Smith was an ubiquitous presence at this Manhattan gathering and at the center of numerous controversies. Thus, he charged that "the minutes out of [the] Port of New Orleans" were "doctored." And further, he defended himself against charges of the "mishandling of union funds . . . wholesale robbing of union funds, stealing of union elections." These "assertions, unsubstantiated . . . directed against me," were no more than "outright vilification and lies" from the "so-called Rank and File Caucus."

He took particular offense when a move was made to "liquidate" the "educational program" of the union, "because they contend that you are training commissars and not men to supervise your contracts." This was "all bunk," he said. "Students have come from Columbia, from New York University and many other colleges and universities to see how the NMU schools are conducted, because of the prestige of the NMU educational set-up." "You smell the red herring," he said. Well, "wipe it off. You smelled it in front of your face and in your face. Don't be fooled by the stench of a herring, Brothers."

Curran hooted at this kind of talk as he attacked the Reds in the union directly. In 1944, he recalled, the party had said the "shipowners were our friends and could be worked with," now they're saying the opposite; well, were they lying then or are they lying now? Seeking to outflank his opponents on the left, he asserted, "You cannot get a seaman to join a union that tells him the boss is his friend." He warned against their supposed convention tactics of arriving "early" and staying "late," seeking to use their ability to endure as a precious asset. Worse, "their booing squads harass all non-Communist speakers." And "in a most flagrant manner, they whitewashed and protected the National Secretary who for seven years fraudulently held office in our union." As a "result of this flagrant violation, over $30,000 of the membership's money was spent in special Council meetings and the by-election necessary to fill the vacant office. After making a short trip, the former Secretary was permitted to run again for the same office, again in violation of the constitution. Those who demanded that he be made to live up to our rules, like any other member, were then immediately branded by the party machine as anti-Negro, red-baiters, and fascists and the specific issue of fraud was successfully covered up." Curran alleged that Smith and his comrades were "appealing to Negroes to vote as a bloc" in his election. "They attempted to segregate the Negroes by having special leaflets signed only by Negroes," he charged. Smith should be "censured," said Alex Stecyk of the SS *Sinclaire Opaline*.

Although there were a number of bread and butter issues before the convention the prospects for effectively addressing these important matters were dim. In vain Smith sought to focus attention on the shipowners. The five leading companies—American Export Lines, Atlantic, Gulf & West Indies Steamship Lines, Moore-McCormack Lines, United Fruit Company Lines, and United States Lines—had net profits of $38 million in the first half of 1947 alone. Smith focused on "the trusts" running shipping. "Among the most obvious examples" are "two lines, Isthmian and Alcoa, operated by two of the nation's most powerful trusts—United States Steel and [Alcoa] dominated in turn by the massive Morgan and Mellon combines."

These corporations were raking in record profits, he said, based on a sharp increase of productivity. "Today, one ship and one crew can do what it took 2.25 ships and 2.25 crews to do prior to the war." Meanwhile, "time and time again I have been approached by members' families who haven't any money left after the death of the breadwinner to bury their loved one," asking pitifully, "how can I get a decent burial.'" and "many times the women's auxiliary has taken up a collection to increase the money allotted by this union."

Then there was the ongoing problem of "flags of convenience." William Standard, the union's attorney, said that in October 1946 alone the U.S. Maritime Commission "had approved the transfer of no less than 266 vessels to Panamanian registry." The issue of "alien" seamen continued to plague the union as well. "When the aliens had been removed from the ships, it was impossible to man the ships with competent men and the ships were held up."

Smith, the "alien" black Red who was second in command of the NMU, felt that "no single duty of the Secretary's office is more important than the protection of the rights and interests of NMU's members in foreign ports. . . . In place after place, seamen are thrown into jail, denied consular protection. . . . On March 24, 1947, for example, I was forced to protest to the State Department the treatment of the SS *Henry Headley* at Durban in October 1946. When the crew went to the Consul to ask that additional food be put aboard the ship before it departed for Buenos Aires . . . the Consul replied with anti-Negro comments." The Coast Guard continued to have "control of all safety and disciplinary machinery" affecting sailors, though this had been billed as a wartime measure (previously the Commerce Department was in charge of this). Consequently, "many [NMU] members [were] tried by the Coast Guard's court martials" in "kangaroo court[s]."

The union was "not able to organize in the manner" that prevailed "before the war." Their "organizing apparatus" was "weak" with "strong opposition . . . in the field in the form" of the Seafarers International Union. Due to the union's strenuous efforts, "wages, hours and conditions have improved to such an extent that our unions have made it necessary for the unorganized companies to place into effect the same wages, hours and conditions for the seamen aboard their ships. Thus, these seamen receive[d] the benefits with none of the responsibilities of belonging to a union." Indeed, they told the unorganized sailors that if they joined the NMU, "Negroes will take their jobs." The idea of "winning new [contracts] through the NLRB elections" was little more than "illusions." But how could they organize "from the shoreside alone" when the targets of their efforts were at sea? Smith advocated a "boycott" of the NLRB. No "basic industry in the United States," he said, "is so badly divided and disunited organizationally as the maritime industry." Workers were "divided into more than a dozen unions. . . . The NMU most nearly approaches the industrial pattern but on East Coast vessels is still only one out of at least four and often five unions aboard ship." Because of this the shipowners and anticommunist unions could gang up on NMU members aboard ship and harass them. Undoubtedly the union's adversaries were pleased that as this impending trouble descended on the industry, the union was busy debating who was and who was not a Communist.[85]

This noisy gathering of old salts in dungarees and khakis and work shirts was punctuated by songs by the union's favorite performer, Paul Robeson. He sang some of his favorites: "The Three Mariners," "Waterboy," "Joe Hill," "Old Man River," "The House I Live In," and "Lullaby." It was one of the few positive notes at the convention. "In less than a few months, the immediate quota of $300,000 was raised" for the faltering Sydenham Hospital in medically underserved Harlem. Of this, said Smith, "our union collected over $6000." Smith's words and Robeson's songs were soothing. After each number the union's self-proclaimed best friend was given a "resounding ovation" and "extended applause" greeted him when he spoke. But those who thought this warm reception signaled a restored "red dawn" were sorely mistaken. For a destructive storm had hit the NMU, and Smith in particular, that ultimately was to leave labor, especially black and red labor, stranded at sea.

8

Walking the Plank

IN 1978 HARRY HAYWOOD, the black Communist sailor, recalled the tumult of the 1947 NMU convention. "It was a Curran sweep both locally and nationally, accomplished with the able bodied support of the local police and Curran's own henchman and thugs in the union."[1] Haywood was not mistaken. Because Smith and the Communists dominated the National Council and the leadership of the union generally, Curran and his allies had decided to mirror the image—real and imagined—of those they opposed: a clandestine cadre with tight connections to more powerful forces and license to use violence.

Smith was aghast at what he had witnessed. "For the first time since the Mariners Club," which had tested him so severely in the union's early days, "a dual and secret organization is being established within our great union, complete with membership cards and dues payments. . . . They were promised that there were 170 jobs waiting for them in the union provided they carried out their disruptive work."[2]

Paul Palazzi, an agent in the port of New York and a Smith ally, noticed in mid-1948 that a "number of out of town goons have drifted into this port" for nefarious purposes.[3] Earlier, Smith was so concerned that he felt compelled to inform President Truman directly about "unsafe conditions on the waterfront in the port of New York. Our members cannot safely board ships as a result of gangster tactics employed by employer goon squads."[4] An undated circular spoke of "$320 a day for organized strong arm squads in the port of New York! 32 guys being paid $10 a day to dump members of the union and to terrorize the homes of officials and members who oppose or criticize. . . . Thousands of dollars being spent to transport dumping squads to Boston, Philadelphia, Baltimore and other ports." When the left held meetings, goons arrived "armed with knives, tear-gas guns, revolvers, tire irons, baseball bats, etc. . . . Fighting among men in the street is one thing, but sailors don't go for terrorizing women and children who have nothing to do with the fight of the union," the circular added.[5]

Curran would have argued that violence deployed by his side was simply in self-defense. It was the Red "machine" that brought "300 to a meeting of over 2500 with a deliberate program to disrupt. . . . They screamed and hollered for two solid hours. . . . They intend to do everything in their power to drive this union" in their preferred direction.[6]

But Smith had a radically different perspective on similar events. He thought that New York members were "treated to such arbitrary action and downright denial of the fundamental rights of the rank and file as has not been witnessed on the waterfront since the days of 'Emperor' Grange. . . . Curran and his caucuseers [sic] tried to ram a 2 [cent] increase down the throats of the membership" and "did not allow one rank and filer to take the deck. . . . No vote was taken because Curran adjourned the meeting rather than let the rank and file speak." This was serious, as a good deal of "the membership of the NMU regularly ships through the port of New York." They brought in their supporters from points far and wide to pack the meeting, "then Curran took 40 minutes of that limited time for his own report."[7]

But this time the prevailing winds were in Curran's favor. He dismissed the union's National Council, where the party had influence, as the equivalent of a "party plenum or a Cominform [sic] branch meeting." It was no more than the "last desperate gasps of the dying Communist Party machine," though he did not discount the "rumors that they will try to burn down union halls,"[8] given that, by his account, the party had "attempted to murder National Treasurer [Hedley] Stone by braining him from behind with a chair."[9]

Curran and Smith seemed to be living on separate planets. When Smith sought to authorize funding for an investigation of "racial" unrest in the NMU branch in New Orleans, Curran viewed it as malfeasance worthy of expulsion. As Smith recalled it, when he sought to write a check for this purpose Stone said no check should be honored unless it had his name or Curran's on it. When office staff followed past practice and refused to cooperate with the attempt to hamstring Smith bureaucratically, Curran fired them.[10] Stone then fired another office worker who filed a "false report on the finances. . . . Several girls [sic] in the department have been out sick this week, unable to stand the nervous strain of such hysterical outbursts and the tension of working under conditions of intimidation." The "head bookkeeper whom Stone fired has been under the care of a physician." This tension resulted from a plan by Stone and Curran that "illegally stopped payment on any and

Ferdinand Smith greets U.S. Vice President Henry Wallace in 1943. Smith subsequently campaigned vigorously for Wallace when he ran for president on a third-party ticket in 1948—a development that angered some and contributed to Smith's ouster from the United States. *(Courtesy of Special Collections and University Archives, Rutgers University Libraries)*

During World War II, the Soviet Union was the close ally of the United States, which facilitated the strengthening of Communist leadership in the National Maritime Union. *(Courtesy of Special Collections and University Archives, Rutgers University Libraries)*

Image of a U.S. Merchant ship with a graph superimposed onto it, indicating the number of ships lost after Pearl Harbor and between 1941 and 1944. Note the peak between 1941 and 1942 and subsequent decline. *(Courtesy of Special Collections and University Archives, Rutgers University Libraries)*

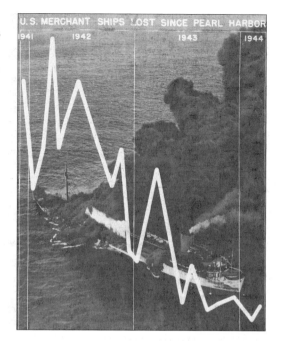

Pittsburgh, 1944. Mayor Cornelius D. Scully, Ferdinand Smith, and Captain Hugh Mulzac, Commander of the *Booker T. Washington*. Pittsburgh was the first city on Smith and Mulzac's six-week tour of the country in which they campaigned for President Roosevelt's reelection. (Seated left to right are Mayor Scully, Captain Mulzac, Smith, and Thyra Edwards, NMU Public Relations assistant. In the rear are former Senator Elmer J. Holland and Charles H. Long, NMU Pittsburgh Agent.) *(Courtesy of Special Collections and University Archives, Rutgers University Libraries)*

Paul Robeson, a good friend of Ferdinand Smith and the NMU, addresses a meeting of sailors in San Francisco in 1945. *(Courtesy of Special Collections and University Archives, Rutgers University Libraries)*

During the 1945 postwar strike wave, NMU members join the United Auto Workers in a picket of a General Motors facility in Baltimore in December. Tempers rose in 1946 when the NMU sought to initiate a global strike. *(Courtesy of Special Collections and University Archives, Rutgers University Libraries)*

Early in 1946 seafaring women join their NMU brothers for a voyage to England. Though an overwhelmingly male union, the NMU did have a contingent of female members. *(Courtesy of Special Collections and University Archives, Rutgers University Libraries)*

Preparing for a voyage, NMU members stock up on books. Sailors, who often had hour upon hour of solitude on the open seas, had plenty of time to read, thereby facilitating the emergence of "proletarian intellectuals" like Ferdinand Smith. *(Courtesy of Special Collections and University Archives, Rutgers University Libraries)*

all checks signed by Smith and McKenzie."[11] It was the prelude to Smith's expulsion from the union.

In a sense Smith was fighting on terrain shaped by Curran. He spent a considerable amount of time refuting or denying the president's tales, leaving him little time to put forward a positive program for union members. Moreover, Curran was an experienced operator in his own right, a master of bureaucratic infighting, who was able to win over a number of Negroes—including H. B. Warner, most likely a former Red—to his side. Smith's allies claimed that these Negroes were all "window dressing" for Curran, but the latter's Negro supporters quickly leveled the same charge at "Josh Lawrence and many other Negroes" siding with the Communist Party.[12] He defeated an ersthwhile Smith supporter, Howard McKenzie, in 1948 for union office.[13]

Curran's ability to co-opt some Negroes in the North while cooperating with Jim Crow advocates in the South, exemplified the flexibility—some might say opportunism—of his tactics. By creating a Communist bogeyman, he was able to avoid dealing substantively with the issues Smith was raising. Smith argued that the "basic question" the union faced was "the role of the National Council" or collective leadership, which is what had inspired the union in the first place. The Marine Firemen, Oilers and Watertenders Union of the Atlantic and Gulf, a constituent element of the old ISU, was angry at the "back talk" of the "rank and file" and had sought to alter their constitution to give top leaders dictatorial powers. "This evil had to be stopped," said Smith. The NMU was formed with the idea of making officers such as Smith and Curran responsible to the NC, with the latter setting policy and the officers executing it. Curran's hidden agenda was to clip the wings of the NC, while Smith wanted to expand their powers. The NC, he thought, "should be broadened out and . . . there should be greater membership participation on it."[14]

Smith also felt that "during the last few years we find that the agents have become so harassed and badgered with directives from the National Office, that it has become impossible for them to do anything on their own initiative."[15] So he wanted more power to devolve from the officers to the port agents too. Curran viewed both moves as a deceitful attempt to strip him of his power under the guise of democratization. Therefore he deftly pushed the momentum created by Smith's proposals toward weakening the National Council, where his influence was weak and Smith's was strong.[16]

Smith's designs, however well-intentioned, could not gain traction and were not in touch with the prevailing climate. Not coincidentally, the first union leader to be indicted under the non-Communist oath requirement of the Taft-Hartley legislation was Hugh Bryson, his old friend from CMU, fellow sailor and fellow trade union leader, of the Marine Cooks and Stewards.[17] In any event, Smith could hardly push for his reforms when he had to spend so much time defending his legitimacy as a Communist trade union leader and beating back the effects of Taft-Hartley. In March 1947 "10 sea unions" called for a "ban on Reds," for example.[18]

Confident that his victory was historically inevitable, Curran did not hesitate to meet with the party hierarchy—who he felt were the real power behind the throne on which Smith sat—to discuss union policy. Besides, despite his frequent denunciation of them, many Communists felt they could—indeed, had to—work with Curran. "I was called to an apartment house in New York," Curran recalled years later, "under the guise of it being a cocktail party and some people wanted to meet me. And they were there in force. All the big guns of the Communist Party were there. There was Gene Dennis, Roy Hudson" and others. They wanted to talk about "peace" but he insisted that the Reds must go from his union. A stalemate quickly set in. Then Communist trade unionists Ben Gold and Irving Potash spoke to him—to no avail.[19]

In the spring of 1947 Curran told the National Council, "In the past two years, I want to tell you boys, I have gone to the top of the Communist Party seven times. I have had seven meetings with them . . . since the convention in 1945 . . . with Foster, with [Eugene] Dennis, with [John] Williamson, with [Jack] Stachel and others." He was "telling them that in my opinion the policies pursued by the members of the Communist Party in the official family of the NMU and on the waterfront generally, [were] dangerous." The Communist leaders could not have sympathized with his main complaint, namely, that Reds played too many high-level roles within the NMU. "The PILOT editor is a member of the Communist Party, the Assistant Editor is a member of the Party and the main staff are members of the Party." This domination had not prevented Curran and many others besides from publishing articles in the union journal scorning the party. The ouster of the Reds from these posts also put an end to freewheeling debate in *The Pilot* and, certainly, the end of any articles critical of Curran himself. At the same time, Curran seemed to be upset that the union journal was not receiving sufficient circulation, despite its supposed domination by Reds. "Some ships have reported where patrolmen came aboard and didn't have a PILOT with them, but they were able to take out of their briefcases party literature. . . . I say that is favoritism."[20]

Curran characterized *The Pilot* as "the sea going edition of the Daily Worker," which devoted too much attention to the "foreign policy of our country."[21] Joe Henderson disagreed, though he concurred that "Communists control the PILOT." However, he added, "I know also that if there was ever a full expression of the sentiments of the membership in any paper, the PILOT has given that and especially in the last few months since Curran gave the death blow to the CMU."[22] This "full expression of sentiments" ended when the Reds were ousted from the journal, to be replaced by homogenized fare dished out by anticommunists.

Nonetheless, the Communists were forced on the defensive by charges leveled against them. Communist journalist George Morris conceded that "one who criticizes Communists—no matter how sharply—isn't necessarily a red-baiter." Something more was required, such as "when one tries to exploit prejudices or a 'scare' against Communists, to settle scores with others in his own organization through befogging the real issues—then it's red-baiting."[23] Whether or not Morris had Curran in mind, his description fits the approach of the NMU leader, whose assault on his union's newspaper repeatedly "befogged" the "real issues." A number of sailors seemed to think so too. The crew of the SS *Zacapa* said they were "damn sick and tired of this continuous red-baiting and disruption" and "baseball bat persuasion."[24] Joe Weiner pointed the finger of accusation squarely at Curran. His alliances with unsavory elements meant that "you, my Negro brothers [are] to be segregated. . . . I know that when a fish begins to decompose, it starts from the head. . . . In order to salvage the body of the fish, the head has to be removed or separated from the body." For those who may not have understood his reference to Curran, he added, "I hope you grasp the meaning and act in time."[25] The crew of the SS *Santa Sofia* seemed to agree with the hoary notion that the "final conflict" would be between Communists and former Communists since those surrounding Curran were among the latter.[26] Being apostates from communism, their opposition to the Reds had an almost religious fervor.

Moreover, they had powerful and influential forces on their side. During the war the shipowners were "getting fat ashore," said the CIO;

their "total assets grew from about $237 million in 1938 to more than $460 million in 1944." Their "net worth increased from about $125 million to $285 million."[27] With so much money involved and with Reds in the postwar era hungering for some of it, intense animosity was inevitable.

Yet Smith's opponents faced a dilemma. Smith's base of support remained among Negro sailors and they connected his demise to their own. At the same time, the national rhetoric responded to Cold War realities[28] by leaning toward "racial" equality, which argued against the kinds of measures being taken against Negro sailors. Thus, Negroes found that their class position was being eroded just as their "racial" status was being upgraded—but this was like *Hamlet* without the prince, for what good were "racial" improvements when one's livelihood was threatened?

This question had particular resonance in southern ports, where NMU had a modicum of strength and where desegregation battles were beginning to erupt just as Negro sailors perceived themselves to be under attack. John O'Brien was horrified when "an elected [union] official in the port of Mobile, one of [Curran's] supporters declared openly that there are too many Negroes in this union. The consensus of opinion among the younger reactionary element now riding the two tankers I have recently been aboard, is that just as soon as the colored brothers and the alien brothers are eliminated, that this will be a union everyone will be proud to belong to."[29] Smith was gravely concerned with the "brutal treatment of John W. Terry, a member of our union, in Beaumont, Texas . . . [NMU]," and pledged that he would "do everything possible as . . . always . . . in the past to fight brutalities against the Negro people and other minorities wherever they may occur."[30] Terry's involvement in the movement for "racial" equality did not sit well with Jim Crow advocates.

As always, Texas was at the epicenter of these postwar battles. Houston, the largest city on the Gulf Coast, was being eyed with favor by the pro-Smith forces and with rising anxiety by his opponents. For "of all the CIO unions in Texas, only the [NMU] raised its full . . . quota" for political contributions and distributed "literature to the general public as well as its membership."[31] This early postwar optimism was to give way to more disturbing accounts. In the Gulf, it was reported, "ports have been thrown into a turmoil of disruption in this critical time by 'caucus' elements assisted by the police and the shipowners."[32]

Galveston was a stronghold for both Reds and blacks and was therefore targeted, illustrating once more the close tie between Red-baiting and black-baiting. By mid-1948 there was yet another "assault of goons on the Galveston hall," as "2000 pounds of allegedly 'Communist' literature were seized after they broke into the desk and files of the port agent. . . . The police put this literature on display at their headquarters, according to front-page stories in the Galveston papers. The literature included books of 50 cent Smith Defense stamps. . . . So-called 'loyalty cards' are being issued by the goons to NMU members who do not actively oppose them. . . . [Others] are arrested and told by the cops to get out of town."[33]

Even after the purges in the NMU, Galveston "remained a leftist stronghold. H. K. Deuchare, a Communist NMU port agent and Wallace agent, was firmly in control." Curran's man, S. D. "Tex" George, responded by developing a "secret alliance" with "the police," a fact that was "crucial to George's eventual success. . . . Seamen in Galveston began arming themselves with brass knuckles, clubs and guns. . . . Tex George himself pistol-whipped two men on a Galveston street with a .45 caliber handgun he always carried. . . . The Galveston police harassed NMU members opposing Tex George." There were "nightly arrests of dozens," who were charged with "vagrancy" and "heavily fined." The authorities "set up a movie camera in an office overlooking the entrance to the NMU hiring hall and photographed everyone entering and leaving. . . . Police then used the lists to periodically round up the men for interrogation and intimidation." The press was essential to the routing of the pro-Smith forces, "consistently referring to the anti-Curran faction, which consisted of non-Communist leftists as well as Communists as a 'Commie goon squad.'"[34] When the pro-Curran faction "lined up with the Klan and the police to eliminate all of the people that were identified as having voted for Ferdinand Smith," this too was generally ignored by the mass media.[35]

This rout was accompanied by the union's retreat from the ideal of equality. In neighboring Port Arthur, "Negro members, no matter how old their cards are, are not shipped, if a white caucus member wants the job. . . . Progressives in Houston are being terrorized. . . . There isn't any more NMU in the West Gulf," declared two seamen. In Galveston, they said, "the patrolman was thrown out of a second story window and the agent was jailed. . . . Throughout the Gulf . . . goons were conducting a reign of terror against the membership and elected officials under the slogan of 'saving the union from the Reds.' . . . The local police of these cities have afforded close cooperation to these gangsters, rounding up honest seamen for wholesale 'vagrancy' arrests."[36]

In Corpus Christi, there was a "big Mexican membership" and a "few Negroes" in the NMU. "Those two are the backbone of our membership," said Norman Gardner. Yet he "was called four times by different Mexicans and Negroes to say that they could not attend the meeting due to the fact that they were intimidated by some of the 'caucus.' . . . This has been going on for weeks. We have slept in our cottage—four of us—with a gun in hand relieving one another," as if this were a latter-day Battle of the Alamo. Even so, he said, "I say that 85% of the membership salutes you, Ferdinand Smith."[37]

Smith was moved by the situation in "the Gulf, where caucus goons have forcibly taken over the union halls and driven out the democratically elected officials, where for a long time certain ports, progressive members and particularly Negro members, have been kept from exercising their rights as union members through open intimidation. . . . Caucus goons in Houston threaten the union dispatcher, brother Jacquette, at pistol point and say, 'We don't want no n-g-ers around here.'"[38] The NMU found it hard to distinguish the violence being inflicted by the "goons" from the violence being used against CIO organizers. "The lynchings, clubbings and torturings," it said, "are a deliberate and calculated weapon of employers to defeat the current CIO drive to organize the workers of the South. . . . Joseph S. Gray, steward on the SS *Nicholas S. Biddle*," was assaulted in a Houston bus by the driver. In words dripping with sarcasm it was said, "Attention Secretary of State Byrnes: While you were whooping it up in Paris for a democracy you wouldn't recognize it if you saw it, down South another Negro member of the NMU was beaten by a KKK goon till he lost sight in one eye."[39]

In the southeast, a few months before these mid-1948 events in Texas, "NMU agent Robert E. Hawkes . . . caused a furor when he asked (unsuccessfully) that two Negro union officials be admitted to the public hearings before the Georgia Senate Judiciary Committee on the white primary bill."[40] In Jacksonville the NMU was "actively backing Wilson Armstrong for City Council," a "member and officer of the Hod Carriers and Common Laborers Union," the "first Negro in 40 years to aspire for public office." The NMU was "distributing leaflets, canvassing," and donating funds to the campaign.[41] Across the South pro-Smith NMU members seeking to advance the battle for equality were met by stiff opposition from pro-Curran backers, bolstered by more powerful forces. While nationally the prevailing rhetoric on equality seemed to be flowing in Smith's direction, in fact, his camp was under attack by the authorities. This apparent paradox formed the template for post-1950s civil rights reform: doors were opened formally, but economic rights were not guaranteed, not least because the radicals who would have spoken out against this anomaly had been purged.

These contradictions were illustrated by J. Skelly Wright, who was courageous enough to confront Jim Crow in New Orleans. Yet as U.S. Attorney he indicted Robert Himmaugh, who worked for the Federal Barge Lines, an agency of the Department of Commerce, on the grounds that he was a Communist—an accusation Himmaugh fervently denied. The "real target apparently was the National Maritime Union," which Wright said was "nothing more than an arm of the Communist Party . . . to be exercised in behalf of Russia in the event of war." When asked in 1983, years later, how he knew this, Wright, then a celebrated federal judge, "could not recall that any evidence was produced to validate that conclusion."[42] In short, Wright symbolized the tensions of a coming era that simultaneously expanded civil rights and restricted civil liberties or the right to association. Yet strengthened civil liberties were a precondition to strengthened civil rights.

Whatever the liberal Wright may have contributed in the realm of civil rights was vitiated by his staunch anticommunism.[43]

In short, New Orleans was rife with "racial" bias, which the NMU left could not ignore. This led to an internal trial of NMU officials thought to be guilty of "racial" discrimination. A "15 man trial committee was elected consisting of 10 men from the Curran caucus and five men who claimed they were 'middle of the road.' . . . The trial committee had refused to hear certain evidence against the accused discriminators. . . . About 15 delegates who sail out of New Orleans tried to get the deck but Curran, as chairman did not recognize most of them." Curran stated that anyone who opposed the accused was supporting a "big red plot," though there was "testimony" available "which proved" that they were "guilty of violating NMU policy" and were "guilty of discrimination." But "Curran as chairman would not recognize" this evidence. "In this red-baiting atmosphere 389 delegates voted . . . not guilty and 308 voted them guilty. . . . Now," said a disappointed sailor, "any official can discriminate and if he is brought on charges, run to Curran and say it is a 'Communist plot' to get rid of him."[44] No wonder opposition to the civil rights movement was so fierce in the South: some had become accustomed to thinking that support for equality was tantamount to support for the "evil empire."

Although the FBI was concerned about these issues, it was indifferent to the victims of bias. Thus, it took note when the NMU "endorsed Reverend L. H. Simpson, Negro candidate for City Councilman at Large, Houston," because his supporters "further followed the Communist line by picketing the steamship MAR-NEGRO, a Spanish ship which docked at Houston."[45] In Birmingham the FBI focused on "Communist infiltration of the National Maritime Union."[46] In Hawaii the bureau was fixated on the NMU "conducting weekly Marxian theory discussion classes at the [NMU] Hall."[47] In Philadelphia it was suspicious because the "the local NMU at Philadelphia has been very active in Negro activities."[48]

An informant told J. Edgar Hoover that "my beef is that we have a lot of sea man [sic] in the NMU that aren't American citizens and don't seem to want to be one either. . . . I believe a little [under] cover work would produce facts." The informant requested, "Please keep my name confidentially, [otherwise] it might cause me to get hurt."[49] But Hoover was already busily hunting down suspected Communists, poring over "confidential" reports from the Office of the Chief of Naval Operations and Naval Intelligence that contained "information" about "crew members of the SS *Veruga*" considered "possible Communist sympathizers." Another report referred to a sailor who "was charged with being a Communist and a party to a 'slow down' strike aboard the SS *Santa Rosa*."[50]

In addition to Negroes, "aliens" also saw a kindred spirit in Smith and like the Negroes, the authorities felt that they too needed reining in. This was apparent from an incident aboard a ship. When "Capt. James Kantsos of the *Newberry Victory*" decided to "split his crew into English-speaking and non-English-speaking groups," he was "sharply rebuffed." "Claiming that members of the crew had approached him on the matter, the captain posted a notice which read: 'Since you are sailing an American ship you must speak only English. Foreign languages spoken on the ship create ill feeling among the American crew members abroad. If you can't speak English well enough, don't speak at all in meeting places on the ship. This is an immediate order! Anyone that doesn't like this can get off.'" A number of Negroes on this ship took exception to this order.[51]

Summing up, Smith was stunned that "instances of 'caucus terror' . . . were mounting" in port after port. In New Orleans, he said, "goon squads of 10 and 15 have been parading daily before the union hall, threatening physical violence to Negroes and aliens who vote against the 'caucus.' . . . In Mobile, Mr. Smith said, 'caucus goons dumped [beat up] a Spanish speaking brother in the union hall.' After the meeting they dumped the dispatcher, Louis Stein. They came aboard a ship covered by Patrolman Von Schmidt on union business and tried to dump him. Tex George, caucus goon leader in the Gulf, gave Bob Greenberg, a rank and filer, 24 hours to leave town. . . . In Tampa, caucus goon squads threatened Sam Albury, Negro port agent. They said they would kill him if he preferred charges against any of the caucus who are carrying on anti-union activity. In Norfolk, Max McLarin, caucus goon squad leader, was responsible for dumping rank and filers, until an aroused membership ran him and his squad out of the port. . . . The word 'commie,' Mr. Smith observed, is affixed to any and all officials and members disagreeing with the policies of Pres. Joseph Curran."[52]

These "racial" and ideological problems necessarily manifested themselves aboard ship. When a German refugee encountered NMU sailors in postwar Germany, a Negro told him, "We does our work and keeps to ourselves and they does their work and keeps to themselves," the "they" referring to whites. In other words, "We don't fuck with them, and they don't fuck with us." Of course, if the captain "fucks with us, the union will fuck with him. We're all NMU," suggesting that even poor "race" relations had not sapped the union's strength—at least not yet.[53] But this was to change.

In August 1948 "charges" were "preferred" by Curran and Stone, calling for Smith's expulsion from the union he had helped build for "misconduct and malfeasance." When Smith ordered an investigation of bias in New Orleans the opposition described it as peculation. Smith and his supporters—Paul Palazzi, Howard McKenzie, et al.—complained that there was no quorum at the trial as one member of the "jury" had resigned. He had objected to being "railroad[ed]." Another had said that nothing that he heard would make him change his mind about Smith. The defendant had requested an adjournment. He had argued that the hearing was closed, and besides there was not enough time to prepare an adequate defense. His argument was rejected.

In a lengthy resolution the crew of the SS *Uruguay* asserted that "the charge" that Smith was involved in "misappropriating . . . union money is only a smokescreen for purging. The money was used to send an investigating committee to the Gulf" to look into charges of bias. It was neither squandered nor spent for personal use. The committee was dispatched southward because numerous members had reported violence, terror, and discrimination there. Smith explained that due to "goon activities in the Gulf area," he and McKenzie had sent Josh Lawrence and Tony Lucio to "investigate." Unfortunately this laudable effort led to the functional equivalent of the death penalty—expulsion.[54]

He was thrown out of office—along with Paul Palazzi and Howard McKenzie—expelled by the "New York membership," 1,462 voting in favor, 523 against: "It was one of the largest meetings in recent years." But Smith was not finished yet. "Three days later this decisive action by the membership was defied by a mob of 250 which invaded union headquarters and attempted to force a special meeting for the purpose of reversing the membership's decision."[55] In their effort to reverse the onrushing pro-Curran tide, Smith's supporters were accused of ever more obstreperous tactics. "They couldn't run it . . . so they wrecked it," according to Curran's supporters. "They stood on their hind legs and hollered, bellowed and grunted. They paraded up and down the aisles, stomped their feet, threatened physical violence."[56] "They" were now increasingly referred to as "com-rats" or "hacks."

An analyst writing in the *Saturday Evening Post* called the ouster of Smith and other Reds from the NMU leadership "probably the biggest single defeat the American Communist Party has ever experienced." It was a "heartening story of the worst trouncing ever inflicted on this country's Reds" and "one of the biggest upheavals in labor history." "Top-secret data on convoy movements and other vital information were streaming into the marine section of the Communist national" office. The setback for the U.S. Communist Party may even affect "Soviet military policy," as Moscow "has consistently sought to dominate the American [maritime] industry. Plans to that end . . . were drafted at a Comintern meeting in Hamburg, Germany in 1930," it was said. Moscow did this "with one eye to a future Russo-American war." From that tiny acorn, a mighty oak grew, as the Reds came to control "107 out of the NMU's 131 elected offices. . . . To this day a big hammer and sickle is prominently displayed in the lobby of the union's headquarters, a six-story building on West 17th Street" in Manhattan." The Reds "used their control of the NMU to stir up trouble in the ranks of the United States Army," given their role in transporting troops back home. "During the wave of Stalinist-run walkouts in France [in 1947] they had the crews of two different American ships stage sympathy strikes in Marseilles."

Then, the analyst said, the Reds declared "war" on Hedley Stone, "the white-haired fifty-one year old NMU treasurer." They circulated rumors that he had received "kickbacks on real estate bought by the union." In their haste to oust him, they forfeited an "opportunity to unionize the 2986 employees and ninety-six vessels of the Isthmian Lines." The writer was particularly happy that Smith's opponents were able to shrug off the idea that "the anticommunists would feel bound to come to Smith's defense. That Smith is a Negro made this seem surer to them. The anticommunists, they thought, would never have the courage to face charges of being both reactionary and anti-Negro. But the anti-Reds took that risk," and succeeded. For Smith "was one of the most active Communists in the drive to cripple American shipping." In 1938 it was Smith who remonstrated Robert L. Desmond "because he refused to join" the party. According to Desmond, Smith said, "I see you're on a tangent. Why don't you join the Communist Party and follow policy." But Desmond adamantly refused and "was never permitted to go back to the sea again." George W. Crosby took a different tack. At Smith's "request" he "did sign up with" the Young Communist League. "At Smith's orders he even distributed Communist literature to soldiers aboard Army transports during the war." Smith was the "key man" and the "Reds lost more ground" when he was ousted.[57]

Another reporter from the anticommunist journal *The Reporter* disagreed. He felt that the NMU, once the "most fiercely independent union in the world" had beaten back the Reds "at the expense of its own democracy."[58] As time passed and the union sank into decline, his opinion seemed more reasonable.

Smith's alliance with the presidential candidacy of Henry A. Wallace—which, like the NMU left, was Red-baited relentlessly—further confirmed the anticommunists in their passionate desire to isolate him and remove him from power. It was not accidental that he was detained by federal authorities after he had appeared at a Wallace rally. CIO official Donald Henderson pressed this issue on the White House, complaining of Smith's "illegal seizure," asserting boldly that "this persecution of Mr. Smith is undertaken because he has raised his voice on behalf of a rival candidate, Henry Wallace."[59]

Yet, when the CIO Executive Board voted in 1948 on whom to support for the White House, the former Vice President received a thumbs-down by a vote of 33-11. Smith was in the minority, along with his comrades from maritime, Harry Bridges and Hugh Bryson.[60]

That even labor liberals were cool toward Wallace was a bad sign. Even liberal Negroes were not predisposed to back Wallace, having made their peace with the incumbent, Truman. Lester Granger of the National Urban League told Max Yergan that he had "been a consistent critic of Mr. Wallace. . . . One [reason] is the lack of attention paid by the Department of Agriculture under his administration to very serious problems of Negro farmers in the South. The whole AAA program, as it was originally established, left Negro tenant farmers holding the bag because of misuse of the Parity Check system. . . . Mr. Wallace's speech in Texas last year when he trotted out the old freight rate differential argument in a palpable attempt to smooth down the feathers of the reactionary South seemed to me an indication that the man will play politics on the lowest level in order to make a point. . . . I would not go on record in support of [Wallace] even if my organization's policies permitted me to do so."[61] The NAACP was equally reluctant to get involved with Wallace, going so far as to fire their aging founder, W. E. B. Du Bois, in part because of his close association with Wallace.[62]

By contrast, the "Maritime Committee for Wallace," in which Smith played a leading role, tried to get the Association to join their campaign to condemn a "recent statement by General [Dwight] Eisenhower that Negro and white people could not live together in intimate circumstance. . . . [The NMU] has proved that Negro and white seamen can live together, work together and face the torpedoes together under the most intimate of circumstances," they argued. But the NAACP was not interested in attacking Democrats or Republicans with designs on the White House. It simply filed away this Smith-inspired letter and continued its open and covert support for President Truman.[63]

Some Negroes who had received concessions from Truman were reluctant to turn against him; some CIO liberals felt they might be bludgeoned if they did so. The White House had powerful levers at its disposal that could be wielded for or against various forces. In the fall of 1946, as the new Red Scare was just taking off, John Owen, Executive Secretary of the AFL Maritime Department, sent a "wire to the President" about an important meeting in New York at which his unit "went on record to notify all shipowners . . . that the U.S. Maritime Commission and the President of the U.S. . . . [decreed] that if any new shipping companies start up on the Atlantic and Gulf Coasts . . . they must negotiate with the AFL all the way through"—not with the CIO's NMU. "If any new shipping operators make labor agreements with the [NMU] the AFL longshoremen will refuse to work these ships."[64] This threat was credible enough to cut off support for Smith's forces and doom them to failure.

As NAACP and NUL officials surveyed the landscape, they felt they had good reason to stand down from the left. Her inquiry bordering on incredulity, Marian Wynn Perry of the NAACP asked Ewart Guinier, "You stated that you had information that persons were being asked whether they invited Negroes to their homes and that the neighbors of federal employees were asked such questions concerning the federal employees being investigated." Federally sanctioned "loyalty oaths" for employees had already created a furor. The kind of race relations favored by the NMU left paradoxically came under assault just as it seemed to become official state policy.[65] The national narrative was being rewritten, and the left was being written out of its historic role.

The purges had a particularly negative impact on minorities. The loyalty oath "layoffs [that] occurred in Cleveland" involved "17 postal workers. . . . Fourteen of the latest group to be suspended are colored; two are white Gentiles; and the other one is Jewish."[66] Viewing such statistics, mainstream rights leaders realized that a heavy price would be paid by anyone bold or misguided enough to veer left and back Wallace.

Leaders had to be careful about the company they kept and it became increasingly difficult to rationalize consorting with Smith and Josh Lawrence, "an important Negro leader in the party although he is not nearly as smooth as nor as important as Ferdinand Smith," in the words of an anticommunist monitor.[67] If they were to violate the informal ban on friendly relations with Reds, they might have to pay a high price. Smith was not alone in his pro-Wallace stance in the union, though Curran was one of Wallace's staunchest critics. However, given the dynamics in the NMU, this recommended Smith even more to the NMU left. Smith solicited two hundred signatures from the crew of the SS *America* alone, urging Wallace to run. "On Smith's desk," it was reported, "are similar petitions totalling 5000 signatures of NMU members who have taken a stand for Wallace so far." A "total of seven ports, 75 elected officials and many ship's crews have thus far given their endorsement" to Wallace. According to Smith, "ports on record backing Wallace on a third party ticket" included "New York, Port Arthur, Providence, San Francisco, San Pedro, Seattle and Galveston" and Savannah. A "majority" of the National Council of the NMU backed Wallace, including Josh Lawrence, Oliver Boutte, Paul Palazzi, and Howard McKenzie.[68]

More people would have supported Wallace but for fear of intimidation by the FBI. They remembered what had happened in February 1948 when "agents of the Federal Bureau of Investigation [began] visiting CIO union offices in New York City ostensibly to verify records of 1946 election contributions by union members," but "actually to pry into current union political activity." This was an "obvious and reprehensible attempt to interfere with the collection and expenditure of voluntary individual contributions for political activity," said the CIO.[69]

The CIO in metropolitan New York City came under strong attack because it was correctly seen as a pro-Wallace bastion. The success of this campaign further eroded Smith's position. "Shouting and a fistfight broke up the first session of a special CIO investigation of charges"[70] brought against the New York affiliate. Curran was at the forefront of this movement, charging that "unless something is done about the CIO Council in New York it will be used as a central anti-body to CIO, there is no question about it."[71]

Above all, CIO progressives had before them the example of Robert New, who, characteristically, suffered the ultimate penalty due to his belief in equality. Chair of the Wallace Committee in South Carolina and Port Agent of the NMU, he "was brutally murdered" in the spring of 1948 "by an anti-Wallace gangster. New was murdered because in the words of his killer, 'he fought for the rights of the Negro people. He was a damned n-g-r lover.'"[72] Shaken by this tragedy, Smith angrily accused his killer, Rudolph Serreo, of being "a self admitted member of the caucus" headed by Curran.[73] With rising alarm, Smith detected a suspicious trend. "This follows the same pattern [as] in New Orleans, Mobile, Galveston, Tampa, Norfolk"—southern ports all, where desegregation was regarded with dread. Wallace hammered away on the issue, with Truman scrambling to catch up without alienating too many Dixiecrats. "In Mobile two weeks ago," said Smith, "caucus goons dumped a Negro committeeman. In New Orleans goon squads of 10 and 15 have been daily parading before the union hall threatening physical violence to Negroes and aliens" and promising "shades of southern justice."[74]

Would other union backers of Wallace have their throats slit and be left to bleed like livestock, as happened to New? Serreo said he had killed New not only because of his enlightened views on "race" but also because he was a "'Communist' and pro-Wallace." Serreo was unrepentant. His lawyer, Thomas P. Stoney, announced that "at the trial I will prosecute Bob New for raising unrest among the colored people in the South. I will prosecute him also as the chairman of the Wallace Committee, and as a Communist." Smith's protest against this outrage was itself the object of protest as an attempt "to spread hate and disunity." He was warned that if he persisted, Serreo supporters would feel compelled to "pay you and your kind a visit . . . in force."[75] Smith was not reassured when Serreo reputedly told Curran, "I did all I can to keep the NMU from going Commie and I'm very, very sorry I can't do more . . . Joe. . . . I know you are behind me, but what about the rest of the 'caucus' guys?"[76]

Not only had this wave of terror swept through the South but it also had reached the Far West where the NMU already faced growing competition from the Sailors Union of the Pacific and the Seafarers International Union. Curran's caucus, alleged Anthony Lucio, an NMU port agent, was "working with the cops." There was "collusion between the caucus, the companies, the cops, the FBI." He attached a transcript of a telephone conversation in which, after one of those speaking referred to San Pedro, California, as "an all Commie port," his interlocutor asked: "Have you contacted many of the companies about . . . a little financial assistance and so forth. . . . The shipowners are giving us a little money too. . . . What about Union Oil? They ought to be good for a chunk of dough." The reply was, "I started meeting with the FBI." When asked about "these Negro guys," the response was "they got 25 active Commies down from L.A.," as if blacks were automatically Reds.[77]

Smith supporters were forced further on the defensive when James Johnson, a Negro sailor, was arrested purportedly because he "answered the description of a burglary suspect." Predictably, there was a good deal of "red-baiting" at his trial. Anti-Curran advocates felt that "such police action is in preparation for police brutality against picket lines, if the unions are forced to strike," with "special efforts to intimidate Negro and minority seamen." Fortunately for Johnson, "the fact that a large delegation was present from the NMU while the case was being heard, no doubt affected the decision to drop further proceedings."[78]

How was it, the Communist Party later asked, that they had suffered such a "crushing defeat" in a "period of three short years" since the conclusion of the war? The party thought it went beyond crude violence. "The bourgeoisie," it said, "sensing the vital importance of maritime and also recognizing the strength of the left as a serious roadblock in their developing plans for a new world war, concentrated upon the maritime unions with an unprecedented campaign." It was in the NMU "in which the progressives had the greatest strength" that "the offensive was sharpest, and the defeat the most severe." On "the west coast," by contrast, "the reactionary offensive moved ahead but at a slower pace." A "large difference" between the NMU and ILWU "was that the progressives held the administration of the union. . . . Secondly, a better qualification of leadership was given with the right issues selected at the proper time . . . unlike a maritime union, in which only a small part of the membership are ashore at a given time. . . . The large Negro core in the key longshore locals, which consistently rallied to progressive policies was also a factor." Of course, the left was not entirely absent from the "administration" of the NMU; likewise, there was a "large Negro core" in the NMU as well. Perhaps the reason the party was ousted from the NMU rather than the ILWU had something to do with the latter being headquartered in a more progressive area—San Francisco—far away from Wall Street, the stronghold of capital, which was within walking distance of the NMU offices. The party correctly pointed out that "unlike a maritime union, in which only a small part of the membership are ashore at a given time," stevedores were relatively stationary, which gave the ILWU more stability than did the NMU. This was one reason the party was reluctant to concentrate on these workers in the first place. The purges also "hit hardest in the Marine Cooks and Stewards, where left strength numerically had been greatest. And in this union, it hit the Negro and other minority members hardest of all. . . . During this time the MCS was undergoing the most sustained and ferocious attack perhaps leveled against any union its size—raids, blatant government interference, lawsuits."[79] This union, which too had a heavy concentration in the Far West, thus suffered from some of the same problems as the NMU, thus underscoring the value of stevedores being relatively stationary.

Surprisingly, the party made no mention of its favorite whipping boy, the Socialist Workers Party, followers of Stalin's enemy Leon Trotsky. The socialists sided with Curran to help him oust Reds like Smith—

then Curran turned on them. But while it lasted, the alliance was quite useful to Curran.[80] Former Reds also helped Curran, reinforcing the view that the "final conflict" would be between Communists and ex-Communists. The *Daily Worker* pointed out that "the main instruments for [Curran's] demagogic campaign were the renegades from communism. Of 32 top officers and port agents elected, 17 are former Communists." The ranks of union progressives were severely depleted by these defections and "6000" sailors "lost during the war," many of them resolute militants, not to mention those who were severely "injured" or "died of natural causes."[81] In any event, the fissures between these left forces were difficult to explain to those outside Marxist circles and contributed to liberal suppositions about their general sectarianism.

The quality of the Communist Party's recruits is also noteworthy. Hulbert Warner, a former Vice President of the NMU, who ultimately directed a campaign to "drive the Communists off the waterfront," was a Communist "at various times from 1938 until 1943." Though he made this admission at a time when it was self-defeating to express any sympathy for the party's ideology, he claimed that when he joined the party he "didn't know a Communist from a Republican."[82] Assuming the accuracy of this statement, it bespeaks certain ideological weaknesses among the Red leaders of the NMU. C. Wright Mills writes that "in the decades before the first World War and again during the great slump, socialist orientation was an important starting point for many union careers." In addition, "as late as the middle Twenties, during the LaFollette campaign, some 42 percent of the labor leaders were affiliated with third parties of one sort or another."[83] Joining the Communist Party back then did not require the same level of ideological commitment it does today; the flip side of this was that the quality of Red recruits was often weak.

Along with the high-level participation of unreliable cadre like Warner, it is also noteworthy that Smith, the top Red in the union and one of the top black Reds nationally, was often absent when high-level meetings were held with leading figures like Bridges or even at meetings of party comrades generally.[84] How could the party carry out its mission of coordinating a common "line" if a key figure like Smith was missing? Perhaps Smith's immigration status caused him to lower his profile within the party. But it is hard to see how he could keep a low profile while remaining a top trade union leader and being shadowed because of his Red ties.

Communists were always a distinct minority within the NMU.[85] When one considers that some of their leading members were government agents, that others were ideologically weak, and that leading figures were often left out of decisionmaking at the highest levels, it becomes easier to understand how and why they could be purged so quickly. Moreover, the drive to oust the Reds from the NMU occurred as the party itself was reeling from the disruption caused by the successful attempt to oust Earl Browder. Inevitably this led to bruised feelings and confusion all around. Charles Keith, the NMU leader, was expelled from the party in 1945, along with Browder. Wounded in Spain, his complete set of Lenin's collected works attested to at least a formalistic understanding of what it meant to be a Communist. Jack Lawrenson, another one-time Red who was expelled, "had a wonderful command of the language and was an excellent speaker," according to Hedley Stone. But he thought that though he was a "well-liked person," he was "lazier than lazy. He arrived at meetings late—party meetings, union meetings, officers' meetings. He lived in [Greenwich] Village and he spent his nights carousing in the Village." Harry Alexander was expelled. Of Russian descent, like Smith he was an "alien" with an ambiguous immigration status, which made him vulnerable to pressure. He was a "pretty good organizer," said Stone, but "was always griping about one thing or another," which demoralized his comrades. Stone himself stopped attending party meetings in the fateful year of 1945. From his perspective, the party "went further and further away from concern with benefits for people. . . . I would compare it to the faux pas made by our country in going to Vietnam. As the union became more and more organized, the party moved away from us. It didn't know how to attach us, to bring us slowly—not immediately—across a wide river."

Even before he left the party, Stone's relations with his comrades were full of conflict. "We used to eat at Bickford's," he recalled, "on the corner of 9th Avenue and 34th Street—the southwest corner. We went in there to eat. I went over and nosed over Joe's [Curran's] shoulder while he was sitting with Smith, Myers and McKenzie. I wouldn't sit down with them." Then he got angry about an officers' tiff over a pay increase. Later they raised the issue at Manhattan Center, close by Bickford's, and the furious sailors "started throwing pennies. The officers had to get off the platform. If one of those pennies hit you, it would hurt you." This was not just a Communist versus non-Communist issue since Harry

Bridges' union "had gotten double what we had gotten. . . . You can imagine how my Communist colleagues felt." Not stopping there, Stone claimed to have been the force behind the effort to oust Blackie Myers from leadership, which hastened Smith's departure. With Communists and ex-Communists back-stabbing and back-biting, it was little wonder that the party lost influence.[86]

The cracks in the popular front also revealed themselves in the deteriorating health of the sailors. Smith's ally, Hugh Mulzac, was hospitalized in Staten Island at this time, "suffering from ulcers . . . due to the exertion and tensions of his duties."[87] Smith himself seemed to take ill during the pivotal and stressful 1947 National Council and convention gatherings. Smith's mental and physical health was affected by his comrades' sharp critiques. Indeed, given some of the strong public criticism, one can only speculate on what may have been said privately. In an extraordinary gesture, the normally discreet party newspaper *The Daily Worker* took him to task in June 1948—just before he was expelled from the union—for "allow[ing]" himself "to be trapped into joining a joint statement" with Curran "surrendering to [an] injunction and calling off [a] walkout without even consulting the strike committee or the council." The newspaper thought this "violated the position of the progressive left unionists in the NMU" and "also sacrificed the interests of the maritime workers."[88] In an equally unprecedented open letter, Josh Lawrence and Paul Palazzi, two of Smith's closest comrades, made a similar point.[89] Beaten down, deserted by some comrades, denounced by others, Smith was ousted from the union he loved in 1948 and faced an uncertain future in the nation he had served so valiantly during the war.

Yet that was not the end of his travails. At the 1949 NMU convention, his and his comrades' dreams of making a comeback were cruelly dashed. There were three identifiable blocs: Smith; Curran; and those tied to the former Communists Jack Lawrenson and Charles Keith. However, since the last group was hostile to Smith, it was clear that he would encounter strong resistance. There had been a precipitous decline from the old NMU which prided itself on its devotion to democracy. This time—according to an account in an anticommunist journal—"identifiable anti-Curran men who attempted to enter the hall had their membership books snatched and were then beaten up in a back room. . . . [The] membership sat silently under [a] pro-Curran chairmanship with police lining the hall."[90]

Although the war in Korea was months away, in the St. Nicholas Arena in Manhattan one would have thought that a dress rehearsal was well under way. Again, an anticommunist journalist observed that "members and officials of other unions who have dropped in at the convention of the CIO's [NMU] . . . have come out shaking their head and saying, 'what a union, what a union.'"

Curran felt hamstrung by the "NMU's ultra-democratic constitution" under which "any motion to suspend the rules to allow a new procedure must have a two-thirds vote and the Curran backers have been unable to muster this." But "most delegates know their Roberts Rules of Orders . . . by heart. Where in other unions the decision of the presiding officer is usually accepted, at the NMU it is open to challenge and vote by the membership."[91] This tradition was on the chopping block in 1949.

Jesse Gray, a future leader of tenants in Manhattan and future member of the state legislature, was upset about the erosion of union rights on board ship in the wake of the purges. He made his feelings plain on the floor of the convention. "If you ask for coffee time, for any time at all not coming to you, you are a Communist. If you press a beef to win overtime you are a Communist. Another brother gets up here to make an amendment about kicking the Trotskyites out. But there hasn't been one who got up and said, 'When you go back to Dixie we are going to fight the KKK.'" Gray could sense that something fundamental had changed in his beloved union. Fighting racism was no longer a leading priority. Fighting Reds was. Gray of the SS *Excambion* rebuffed Curran directly. "The first correction I would like to make," he said, "is to correct the Chair for referring to me as 'Willie' and giving other people names on the floor." In his view this was a racist slur. But this was the least of his concerns. "I make an amendment on the floor as of now . . . that intimidation immediately cease on the floor. I am referring to the intimidation that is being thrown at Negroes and other delegates from the Gulf, who oppose the renegades. Next, I want to point out that they have guys back here, sitting in the middle of the hall, who would like to vote not in favor of Curran . . . but they have a master at the table who tells them, 'You vote our way or you don't come back to the Gulf.' What is this?" he asked. NMU democracy could not survive the arrival of anticommunism. "Epithets" and labels abounded at this gathering—"Hitler," "Hack," "Commie," "Trotskyite," "Comrade," among them.[92]

"Five left-wingers" were "expelled," Smith among them, in a "noisy session marked by loud outbursts and general disorder." The "handling of the cases of the former officials was sprung on the convention in a sudden and surprising manner that caught the anti-Curranists unprepared." "Loud but unavailing protests were made," accompanied by a "great deal of sarcasm and name calling."[93]

A "great deal of noise" had erupted when Smith brought his appeal to the convention floor. His "expulsion from membership" was based on "misconduct and misfeasance." Henry Frierson of the SS *Exchorda* was disconsolate, connecting Smith's expulsion to the deterioration of the situation on board ship. "My salary has remained the same, but my working conditions have not; my beefs on board my ship are not settled." The rapid decline of the party's influence in the union was ratified when Smith's expulsion was upheld, 393 to 146.

From there it was downhill. Clarke R. White of the SS *Gulf Key,* rose to "speak as a Negro brother and I come from Florida." But his "racial" background gave him no moral authority; he received short shrift when he pleaded, "for the sake and protection of those fellows who come from the Gulf or any place in the South, I believe we should have a secret ballot."[94]

Smith and his comrades—and his fellow progressive and Negro sailors—staggered from one defeat to another. Weeks after their defeat at the convention, they suffered another setback. As one observer put it, "On November 16, 1949 at a time when most of the loyal NMU officers were out of town, a group of 400 Communist supporters stormed the union headquarters on W. 17th St. in New York and took over administration of the hall by force. . . . [Curran] recaptured the building in a pitched battle. A subsequent mass meeting called by Curran at the St. Nicholas Arena on Thanksgiving Day was temporarily disrupted by Communist violence."[95] The "Communist supporters" correctly feared that the last vestiges of progressive presence in the union was about to be cast aside and they reacted sharply. Unknown to them, however, their opposition had more weapons than they imagined. When the first signs of trouble started brewing, the "American Radio Association, CIO flashed a message to the crews of all American ships at sea: 'Communist revolution in the [NMU] began Wednesday. . . . Red fascists besieging New York NMU building. . . . On your arrival New York request time off to attend grandmother's funerals. After burying old lady, come down to defend union hall against Commie storm troopers.'" Immediately, "a few men jumped ship and took passage home." For the "next few weeks," the building was "in a state of siege. . . . Goon squads roamed through Chelsea and Greenwich Village and in the seamen's favorite ginmills."[96]

M. Hedley Stone of the union was on a ship sailing to a meeting designed to foil the Communist-led World Federation of Trade Unions. When he arrived in London he received a call from Curran, who told him, "The Kremlin has been captured!"—a strange way to describe the union headquarters he had been heading. Stone proceeded immediately to "Cherbourg," then to "Southampton," "where I was picked up by the U.S. labor attache and put on a plane. I returned to the U.S., and we took the hall back."[97]

Curran and his cohorts did not stop there. After bludgeoning his internal opposition, Curran turned on the progressive Marine Cooks and Stewards. Hugh Bryson, the union's leader, declared, "It is our contention that this charge" of alleged Communist domination "was instigated by certain persons hostile to our organization, and in particular one Joseph Curran." Bryson gamely defended his union. "When we fought [to] put the first Negro stewardess ever to sail on an American ship the other day on the luxury liner *Lundine*, do you consider that in the interest of the Communist Party and against the union?" Curran's other nemesis, Harry Bridges of the ILWU, said Curran was battering his union too, allowing NMU members to "cross the picket line" they had established in Hawaii. Curran, who had been pushed into the spotlight by the Reds, had become their worst nightmare.[98]

Initially, Smith and his comrades had taken a metaphorical beating, then came an actual one, with the none too subtle assistance of the U.S. authorities and Curran. Bruised and wounded, Smith and his supporters limped away from the NMU as the mainstream press stood on the sidelines cheering lustily.[99]

9

Black Labor at Sea

SMITH DID NOT fold up his tent and disappear silently into the night after his 1948 expulsion from the NMU. The next three years were full of angry protests, salacious immigration hearings, and imprisonment. Finally, in 1951 he was forced out of the United States altogether.

After his expulsion from the NMU, Smith, of Jamaican origin, and Ewart Guinier, of Panamanian and Jamaican origin, spearheaded the formation in April 1949 of the Harlem Trade Union Council (HTUC), designed to combat "racial" bias in the sphere of employment.[1] Smith was somber as he cast his eyes over an economically desolate Harlem, a Manhattan neighborhood teeming with Negroes living in intensely crowded conditions. "Unemployment," he said, "has reached 25% among Negroes although the Negro population constitute only 6% of the total population of the city."[2] Addressing this matter was a high priority for him. HTUC quickly placed 250 Negro workers in jobs during the first eight months of its existence. Guinier credited HTUC with opening up "hundreds of jobs for Negro workers in plants and industries from which our people had been previously excluded, including many jobs as technicians in the radio industry."[3]

On one occasion the HTUC invited six breweries and the seven brewery locals to a conference on bias in the industry. Smith appealed to the trade unionists present to embrace "unity without regard to race, creed, color or natural origin." If they failed to do so, he warned, "we would regret being forced to resort to any other method to enforce the just rights of Negro workers."[4]

In case the workers doubted his sincerity about resorting to other methods, they had only to turn from their beer and cast their sights on the docks. There they could see Joseph Ryan, the combative right-leaning boss of the East Coast stevedores who "blamed the conflict" between Negro dockers fighting for their rights and against his union on HTUC. The fact that "many white workers [were] . . . supporting the picket line, proved, he said, that Communists, rather than the members of Local 968, were really behind the protests."[5] Smith decided to join this ferocious battle. There was undeniable racist sentiment in Ryan's ranks: "to a large extent the assimilation of gangsters corresponded with Joe Ryan's presidency of the ILA." The corrupt Ryan "welcomed convicted felons into the union and appointed them as organizers and, in some cases, as presidents and secretaries of locals." Unashamedly, he "admitted hiring convicts to fight Communist influence."[6]

Smith, on the other hand, congratulated Bridges of West Coast longshore for "your decisive defeat" of the "attempt to drive Negro Longshoremen from the Frisco Water Front." He was seeking to deliver a similar result in New York in opposition to the "deliberate and announced policy of the ILA to drive Negro longshoremen from the piers," which was "executed not only against Negro longshoremen but Negro seamen and other Negro maritime workers." He told Bridges, "This is part of the pattern of driving Negroes out of industry at trade union wages and onto the relief rolls from which anti-labor administrators such as New York City Welfare Commissioner Hilliard recruits $25 per week workers."[7] After meeting with the HTUC and the Negro dockers, Congressman Adam Clayton Powell arranged for a congressional committee to conduct a probe into charges of racketeering and discrimination by Ryan's union.[8] But this protest was sidetracked when the press suggested that the twin evils were discrimination and communism. Although it was a step forward in that it targeted bias, it contained the seeds of its own demise in that the focus on Reds distracted attention from the real problem.

Not everyone agreed, however. The *New York Amsterdam News* thought it was "equally unfortunate that Ferdinand Smith and other Communist labor agitators were permitted to horn in on the fight between Ryan and the colored longshoremen. Smith and the rest of the Reds are not interested in helping the workers get justice," it said, "but in stirring up more trouble for the benefit of the Communist Party."[9]

It was a sign of the times when the otherwise progressive Paul O'Dwyer assured the NAACP that the Negro dockers regretted having allowed "Ferdinand Smith and others" to picket. Not comforted by this, the NAACP sternly refused to offer the workers any assistance.[10] Though he had once worked side by side with the NAACP, when Smith and the HTUC brought demonstrators to Radio City in Manhattan to protest the National Broadcasting Company's decision to bar Robeson from appearing on television, the Association likewise steered clear. Undaunted, Smith, "executive secretary" of the HTUC "led the pickets."[11]

The characterization of Ferdinand Smith as a pariah reflected the break up of the popular front he had once led. Negroes were being promised bright horizons if they would simply turn their backs on those they had once embraced, namely, those on the left. This may have "worked" in the South where the decline of the NMU left coincided with the onset of state-sponsored desegregation but this meant only that the South had caught up with other sections of the nation that were standing still or retreating to meet Dixie half-way. This was yet another ironic paradox of what came to be known as the "civil rights movement." In the North the turn from the left led inevitably to ennui and anomie, which erupted in "riots" in the 1960s.

Signs of this trend were evident early on. Communists had been in the forefront of the desegregation of professional baseball. Thus in 1946 Jackie Robinson, a major beneficiary of their activity, scribbled a hand-written note from Montreal to the National Negro Congress to say, "Even though I cannot be present at your meetings rest assured that I'm in my own way working for the same things that you are. . . . Never relent in your fight against Jim Crow. Each of us has a part to play. Let us not leave the burden on the shoulders of a few."[12]

But that is exactly what happened. The "burden" of many protests was left "on the shoulders of a few" as Robinson turned on Robeson and others affiliated with the NNC who had once been in the trenches with him. This weakened the battle against bias in baseball, as the continuing struggle to desegregate managerial ranks suggests, as well as the overall battle against bias in New York. Of course, Robinson was not by himself. Herbert Hill of the NAACP said happily, "I have been successful in exposing [CP] operatives and preventing their participation in legitimate Trade Union and Civil Rights Activities." His work had been used by the "Voice of America," he asserted. He attested to the loyalty of S. Edward Gamerikian, president of the Schenectady branch of the NAACP who "was personally responsible for the expulsion of known Communists." These NAACP leaders took credit for involvement "in the campaign to oust the Communist controlled United Electrical Workers as the collective bargaining agent at the Schenectady plant of the General Electric Corporation."[13]

Such developments put the conservative *New York World-Telegram* in a cheerful mood. In the spring of 1950 it wrote, "Time was when the

Communists running the May Day parades always had the maritime workers proudly up at the head of the line. After them came furriers, office workers then electrical workers. . . . This May 1 the furriers are in the honored first position with half a dozen still dependable locals following before the marine workers start marching."[14] The NMU had borne the brunt of the purges, as their meager number of May Day marchers showed. The larger question, however, was, did Negro workers benefit from these developments? Was Black Labor now lost at sea, adrift, shorn of its moorings?

The NAACP and the NMU seemed to think it was self-evident that these developments *were* beneficial to Negro workers, that Negro Labor was neither at sea nor adrift but firmly anchored in a new national consensus favoring desegregation. After Smith's ouster, the two decided to have "full cooperation and joint action on all issues" where there is an "identity of interest."[15] This "identity of interest" evidently included attacking Smith and his emerging Harlem Trade Union Council. The HTUC, said the NMU, "had no right to use the name of the [NAACP] in connection with its phony charges of discrimination by NMU officials against Puerto Rican and Negro brothers. This was made clear by Roy Wilkins."[16] Reprimand of the HTUC in NMU publications was facilitated by ousting a Smith ally as top editor and replacing him with George Streator, a former *New York Times* reporter and former organizer with the Amalgamated Clothing Workers.[17]

The NMU's and NAACP's attempt to place a cordon sanitaire around Smith to bar the spread of the contagion he presumably carried was not altogether unsuccessful. By 1950 a number of New York City employees were reporting "that we can jeopardize our jobs by affiliation with the New York branch of the NAACP because of its record of cooperation with Communist and Communist front organizations and its infiltration by well-known Communists and fellow travellers." They were horrified that officials of the NAACP branch in New York "spoke at a meeting of the Harlem Labor Council [*sic*]. . . . Its head was Ferdinand Smith, acknowledged member of the Communist Party."[18] Already weak HTUC-NAACP relations deteriorated further. The blockade against Smith was hardly porous.

Shortly thereafter, Hulbert Warner, "Negro Vice-President" of the NMU—and one-time Red and Smith ally—opposed Curran's reelection. He "told of the way administrative campaigners approached people in the union with the line that 'niggers are taking over the union and the big ships are being run by niggers'" and that "new members are all niggers." Warner reported that Hoyt Haddock, NMU representative in Washington, had come to New York to see him. "You know," said Haddock, "army intelligence called me in and [said] that there was a move in [the] union to take over, that the Negroes were given preference and the Puerto Ricans and there is an agent in the union and their finger pointed at you. Well, other government agencies are interested, too," he said. These included "Navy intelligence" and the FBI. Warner, then fighting a losing battle against the slow but steady decline of Negroes and Puerto Ricans in the union they were supposedly about to take over, was beyond rage, calling Curran and his allies "corrupt diseased characters. . . . They have no morals."[19] How could they have morals, he reflected, when the union leadership was "permitting Jim Crow and racketeerism to flourish" while making the spurious charge that Negroes and Puerto Ricans were "being given privileges" and were "taking over the union."[20] Warner claimed to have "sworn statements . . . by responsible officials and members, testifying to discriminatory remarks made by Stone against Negro members in the Port of Galveston. . . . Other affidavits deal with the sale of union [memberships] and permits by officials of the NMU."[21]

Warner was not far wrong. The *New York Times* reported that "the Coast Guard is being guided by the advice of union leaders who had major roles in setting up the screening program in collaboration with Naval Intelligence and Coast Guard men in Washington,"[22] disproportionately excluding Negroes and Puerto Ricans from ships and virtually eradicating a centuries-long trend. Government officials, shipowners, the FBI, the Navy, and Coast Guard—and Curran—met in July 1950 in Washington. Shortly thereafter the U.S. Congress passed the Port Security Act and President Truman issued an executive order authorizing the Coast Guard to screen off the waterfront any seamen or dock workers whose loyalty to the United States it questioned. When Curran and his colleagues met to execute their version of "screening," they were not working from a blank slate. Distressing stories of supposedly unpatriotic sailors—even Negro ones like Ferdinand Smith—dominated the airwaves.

Ultimately trade union militants, in addition to minorities, were targeted under the pretext of "screening." "Experience has shown," said one progressive analyst, "that as soon as a seaman builds a record as a union leader on one voyage, he will be screened off the next." Nevertheless, "about 70% of screened members of MCS [Marine Cooks and Stewards] and 65% of screened longshoremen are Negroes. This is far higher than their proportion of membership of these unions. Most were union members at one time or another."[23]

Juan Mendoza, an NMU sailor, agreed. He charged that there was a "concerted effort on the part of the National office of the union (by Treasurer Stone and condoned by the President) to slander members of the organization who are of minority groups. At present, it is being directed against Negroes and Puerto Ricans."[24] Herbert Hill, the NAACP's leading official in labor affairs who had been prominent in removing leading blacks like Smith from influential positions on the grounds that they were Reds, acknowledged that "the membership composition of the NMU is predominately non-white" and that some questionable things were going on that were adversely affecting their futures. Yet in no uncertain terms he told Walter White, the NAACP leader, "I strongly urge that the Association take no part in the current internal dispute" involving the NMU.[25] The attacks on Negroes and Puerto Ricans therefore continued unabated. Because these minorities had connected their rise in the ranks of the union with the rise of the left, they were predisposed to fight the anticommunist purges—but this only inflamed opposition against them.

Curran's supporters were less interested in the real problems confronting Harlemites. In a Harlem labor conference that kicked off as rumors abounded about Smith and whether he would be shipped back home, a "shipyard worker described the rise of unemployment among Black workers because of the government screening program. He estimated that a staggering eighty percent of those labeled 'security risks' were Black." Hugh Mulzac, Smith's longtime comrade and friend, was among those "banned from ever sailing again."[26]

The ouster of Smith and his comrades did not augur well for Negroes in the union, contrary to what the NAACP thought. To the contrary, African Americans who were reassured by Truman's talk about desegregation were in for a rude surprise. The purges were a signal that it was open season on Negro sailors. Black sailors in the South in particular were faced with the cruel anomaly that just as Jim Crow barriers were beginning to fall in the wider society, they began to reemerge in their union, which had been a premature opponent of Jim Crow.

This could not have happened at a worse time. As the *New York Times* reported, "the year 1949 was the 'worst employment year in the shipping industry since 1923.'" There were "five men for every job available," and the postwar economic downturn meant that the "devaluation of currencies in foreign countries has affected their ability to purchase American goods."[27] The "depression is in full swing," the *New York Times* reported; "in January 1946 there were 70,000 NMU members, a 20,000 dip from the wartime high of 90,000." An NMU leader observed, "We're back where we were in 1936, but it's even worse now because prices are so much higher."[28] In a sense, the purges may be seen as a crude way to effect massive layoffs under the guise of politics.

In this context, other NMU leaders saw Smith's staunch opposition to the Marshall Plan as foolishness. One analysis pointed simply to the "importance of the European Recovery Program" to "American maritime employment," in that "42 percent of all exports from Atlantic Coast ports was ECA financed."[29] On the other hand, the downsizing of maritime employment that was an emblem of the Red Scare may have gone too far, too fast. By 1951 there were complaints about the "lack of seamen" though "cargoes" were "urgently needed by friendly countries in Europe."[30] This "slows foreign aid," the *New York Times* reported.[31] "For the first time in nearly four years," the paper said, "maritime unions are finding it difficult to furnish a sufficient number of adequately trained personnel."[32]

Progressive sailors, particularly those who were black, continued to be expelled, though given the NAACP's position, one might have expected the opposite. Jesse Gray, a close friend of the sailor, Jack O'Dell—the latter went on to advise Martin Luther King, Jr. and Jesse Jackson—charged that Curran was "systematically blacklisting the most militant rank and file union men with the brunt of the attack leveled against Negro and Puerto Rican NMU members." This "brings to a head," he said, "a three year campaign of unprecedented violence, intimidation, terror and murder.... Under cover of the most violent Red-baiting campaign ever conducted in the American labor movement, hundreds of union members were slugged, knifed, and arbitrarily expelled from the union on trumped up charges in kangaroo courts. Through use of hired Ku Kluxers in the South Atlantic and Gulf ports, hundreds of Negro union members were beaten and driven from their union halls. . . . The foreign born membership of the NMU, which at one time numbered 15,000 with a rich militant tradition of helping to build the union, has been driven out in one of the dirtiest, most chauvinistic betrayals in labor history."[33]

Unfortunately, the diminutive, dark-skinned Gray was not exaggerating. A typical incident occurred in New York City in March 1950 when Smith's supporters had to "beat off an attack by Curran's men" as they were meeting. "Some 80 Curran followers came by car and on foot. They carried milk can covers, bricks, tire irons and blackjacks. They smashed the glass door. . . . When it was over the lobby was splattered with blood and broken glass." The observer of this ugly scene noticed that the attacks had a racist thrust. "Curran's strength," the *National Guardian* reported, "lies in the Gulf ports where anti-Negro and anti-Puerto Rican elements swing behind him and where the Negro and the progressives dare not talk too openly."[34] Things were so bad that no one was shocked when "three Negro members of the Stewards Department" of a "Texas Oil tanker . . . preferred charges" against their supervisors after he claimed "there were too many Negroes on this ship."[35]

Another disturbing incident involved Jake Green, a member of the union since it was first organized and a sailor who first went to sea in 1927. He had been elected patrolman in the port of Baltimore in 1944. Yet around 1950 the Coast Guard "informed him that he couldn't sign on" for trips any longer. This Negro "was screened off the ship, under the so-called charge of being a bad 'security risk.' . . . Under the guise of security they have screened thousands of men off the ships and docks of our country." In carrying out these purges, denoted as "screenings," the Coast Guard posed "a lot of questions such as: . . . Do you have Negro visitors in your home?"[36]

Like one hand washing the other, the Coast Guard's aggressive maneuvers were buttressed by those of the union. In 1950 NMU official Neal Hanley sent a mandate to "all ports" that included a "list of names and book nos. that have 'endorsed the programs' of the Communist sheet 'Voice of the Membership' or the 'Independent Caucus.'" There were hundreds of names on this list and the message was clear: they should be ousted.[37]

The Seafarers International Union (SIU), the Pacific counterpart of the NMU, had never been friendly to the idea of equality for Negro members. As the NMU moved steadily away from this goal, the SIU too seized the opportunity to distance itself from this objective. As the screening of sailors gathered steam in the NMU, the few progressives left in the SIU were reporting that it "has not dispatched a Negro to any job in the past 40 years." Still, "approximately 1700 of the 2000 jobs in the stewards department are held by Negroes or Orientals. The objective of

SIU is to replace these workers and make West Coast ships all white." Russel Ryvers had been sailing for four decades from San Francisco, where he resided. "In these 40 years he never saw a Negro in the deck or engine department on any vessel he has ever sailed on." On the ship, the *City of Everett*, the "firemen and sailors ganged up on" a Negro sailor and "walked off the ship" and "forced the company" to dismiss him. On the *President Madison* in Seattle sailors refused to work with Negro "messboys." "Both of them were beaten up before the vessel got to Yokohama; one had his jaw broken." Stewards were earning the then decent wage of almost $700 per month, which was difficult to duplicate onshore. But now that the MCS was being "outlawed" because they were "Communist dominated," their livelihood was in severe jeopardy.[38]

The MCS, a union with an extraordinarily high percentage of Negroes and other minorities, and a close ally of NMU from the outset, was devastated by the change in the political climate. "We helped organize the NMU," said MCS leaders. "Nobody knows better than the charter members of the NMU of the assistance we gave them in their first organizing efforts. It is we who helped organize the tankers on the West Coast and gave up the jurisdiction over these seamen to the NMU, which they later lost to Lundeberg of the SUP [Sailors Union of the Pacific]." Now they were being repaid by Curran, fresh from his victory over Smith, leading the charge against them. This democratic union was about to be expelled from the CIO, though "in referendum elections just completed, the union elected a Chinese-Hawaiian as Honolulu Port Agent, Negroes as Port Agents in Wilmington and Seattle, Jews as Port Agents in San Francisco and New York, a Negro as Seattle Patrolman and a Negro as San Francisco Dispatcher. Of the eight members of the new General Council, five are members of minority national groups."[39]

Members of "minority national groups" were not the only ones being chased out of the unions. Anthony Lucio of San Pedro had stood by Smith while others were deserting him. But by late 1949 he no longer could hold on. "I intend to look for work," he said, "as I haven't made no money [*sic*] nor worked from May, of this year." How ironic that "alien" seamen were being expelled from the union at the very time that so many ships were taking on "alien"—such as Panamanian and Liberian—registry.[40]

Cecil Brooks in early 1951 complained that once the purges started, it became "hard to get beefs settled and open discrimination against members of minority groups intensified." Discrimination was driven by the fact that the "main influence on the officials in the union on policy and other matters came from white southerners in Gulf ports who took leadership in driving progressives, aliens and minority group members out of the union, a drive that found hundreds of Negro brothers expelled in the Gulf, without even a trial."[41] The "United Rank and File Committee" of the NMU, which arose in opposition to Curran, echoed this indictment, charging that "our Negro and Puerto Rican brothers and sisters are the special victim of this 'screening' program. It is no mere coincidence that 75% of all our members being kicked off the ships are Negro or Puerto Rican members, especially those holding key jobs aboard passenger vessels."

In early 1951 it was reported that "two-thirds of the seamen who have been screened by the Coast Guard have been Negro or Puerto Rican . . . in some companies, like Lyke Brothers, the policy is keeping all Negro seamen in the stewards' department," a turnabout from their migration into the engine room when Smith was in the NMU. The same was occurring in the captain's roost. Hugh Mulzac was "screened a short time after he renewed his license. . . . There are no Negro captains able to sail today," it was reported in the spring of 1952. Violence was being wielded not only to disrupt the onshore meetings of those trying to fight back, but increasingly on board ship as well.[42]

Whatever the intention behind Smith's and his comrades' ouster, their departure did not appreciably improve the lives of Negro sailors. As their expulsion was also a prelude to the downsizing of the entire shipping industry via the proliferation of "flags of convenience" and the increasing reliance on low-wage, foreign labor, it is hard to say that this purge helped sailors in the United States.

Ferdinand Smith's detention in February 1948, just after he had appeared at a rally for third-party insurgent Henry Wallace and just before he was to attend a union meeting where he was to speak out vigorously against the Marshall Plan—was only one of numerous attacks on immigrants that characterized the early Red Scare. Radicalism was perceived as "un-American," a foreign import that only quarantine could protect from society at large. Thus, the operative thinking was that the "alien" radicals had to be deported in order to protect the nation as a whole from the danger they were thought to represent. As the anticommunists looked around, they could not help but notice prominent, rad-

ical, immigrant labor leaders such as, Ben Gold, leader of the fur workers, James Matles, who led the electrical workers, Peter Harisides, who
became a Communist leader while an alien, and William Schneider-
man, who became a Communist and then a citizen.[43]

John Santo, formerly secretary-treasurer of the Transport Workers
Union, and Benoit Van Laeken, a longtime member of the Marine Cooks
Union, were among the union leaders slated for deportation. Charles
Doyle, detained with Smith, was a former vice president of the CIO
Chemical Workers Union. He came to the United States in 1924 but was
now married and the father of four U.S.-born children. Yet he was held
for deportation after he had made a trip on behalf of his union to
Canada. When he reentered the United States to go to his home in Nia-
gara Falls, he was arrested, convicted, and subjected to a jail fine of
$500. Michael J. Obermeier, general manager and former president of
Local 6 of the AFL Hotel and Club Workers Union in New York, was arrested for deportation to his native Germany. He had lived in the United
States for thirty-five years and considered himself an American. He had
helped in the war effort among German Americans and made broad-
casts in German for the Office of Strategic Services—but this meant little. Arduilic Susi, an antifascist Italian, secretary of the Chefs, Pastry
Cooks and Cooks Assistants Unions of New York, was arrested for deportation to Italy although he had lived in the United States for twenty-
two years. He had such a sterling antifascist record that Mussolini's
blackshirts had vowed to kill him. Pete Nelson of Everett, Washington,
business agent for a local of the International Woodworkers of America,
was arrested when he sought to return to the United States after a visit
to Canada on union business. This native of Sweden had lived in the
United States for more than twenty years.[44] Thus Smith was not alone
in being ousted from the United States.

That Smith was an "alien," a black, and a Red meant that there were
three strikes against him even before he came to bat. Unlike his comrade,
Harry Bridges, who managed to escape deportation to his native Australia, Smith was not as lucky. Given the prevailing political atmosphere,
it was virtually certain that he would be shipped back to Jamaica. But
this did not occur without a struggle. After being bailed out of government custody as a result of his February 1948 detention, he was arrested
again. While his opposition to the Marshall Plan had hovered over his
first arrest, in June 1949 he was detained "[after] I had organized and led
a picket line of some 12,000 workers around the clock at the office" of

Joseph Ryan, the East Coast longshore leader, who wanted to lift the charter of Local 968, a progressive black local. Again, he was dispatched to Ellis Island, where he spent thirty-seven days and had his bail raised from $3,500 to $10,000 to insure that he would not be speedily released. His third arrest came months later, after he protested the death sentence of Lt. Leon Gilbert, a Negro in South Korea sentenced to death for refusing to lead his men into a suicidal mission. His fourth arrest came in August 1951, days before he was expelled from the country.[45]

Throughout this series of setbacks, Smith continued to speak his mind openly. After his release in August 1949, for example, he declared, "You know why [Attorney General] Tom Clark put me in jail? When I talk, fifteen million Negroes listen. When I talk, six million CIO workers listen. They want to silence me because I am out to expose the failures of the South. They want to impose nightshirt rule on all of New York."[46]

When he was expelled from the NMU in 1948, he did not know that this also would mean expulsion from the United States itself, though many of his supporters feared so. Like a gyrating yo-yo, Smith's final three years in the United States were punctuated by bouts of detention, followed by periods of ever greater activism. The problems facing him in this difficult period were well illustrated by the government's decision to cancel his four-figure bail of December 1948 and set a new bail of $10,000. "The government wanted him to accept the immediate entering of an order of deportation in his case in order to facilitate his departure from this country. [Smith] refused and, on July 6," he was sent to what was becoming his home away from home: Ellis Island.[47]

A month later the judge dismissed the writ of habeas corpus, calling for his release, and ruled that since Smith had applied for permission to leave the country, the government was justified in increasing bail. They would not let him depart, for they suspected that as a veteran courier, as Smith was alleged to be, and a longtime union leader, which he actually was, he could do severe damage to what were perceived as U.S. national interests. His lawyer, Carol King, assured the authorities that "knowing Mr. Smith, I am convinced he will not come back" to the United States—but they were not convinced.[48]

So it was that on 11 August 1949, Smith—ably assisted by the Civil Rights Congress,[49] a "Communist Front" soon to encounter its own Waterloo—was released from Ellis Island after depositing $10,000 bail, "after 37 days imprisonment, but without any other agreements."[50] As

Smith's work with the HTUC gathered momentum—confronting corrupt union leaders on the waterfront, pressuring newly emerging television and radio industries on job bias, seeking to bolster third-party efforts—the Department of Justice stepped in. In a series of lightning "midnight raids" on 22 October 1950, they seized him once more. The war in Korea was heating up, as was concern about Negro loyalty and the presence of radical "aliens." "The newly passed McCarran Act" was "used as a pretext" for these raids.

While in detention on Ellis Island in 1948, Smith conducted a hunger strike in protest. The *Brooklyn Eagle*, a local newspaper, sarcastically called it the "best idea [he] ever had," indicating its wish for his speedy demise.[51] He and George Pirinsky, executive secretary of the American Slav Congress, were kept locked "behind double-barbed wire." Smith recalled that officials "shooed us away" from some sailors "who wanted to talk to us on the one visit we were permitted to make to the canteen." Moreover, "there were some Nazis—White Russians from China"—among the five hundred detained at Ellis Island, who were "allowed liberties such as being permitted to sit outside an enclosure," while Smith, a firm backer of the war, was treated considerably worse.[52]

Smith lost twenty-seven pounds as a result of the hunger strike and the rough conditions he was forced to endure. But his most determined supporters continued to back him, some of them leading a movement to prevent his ouster from the United States. Joining him in the hunger strike were his fellow political detainees, radicals all: Charles Doyle, Gerhart Eisler, Irving Potash, and John Williamson. A circular produced by their supporters referred to Smith as "labor's most prominent Negro leader" and railed at the indignities he had to endure. The five prisoners, all prominent in labor, radical, and artistic circles, "became good friends—real brothers. . . . We read until our eyes burned; we discussed national and international questions." They went on a collective hunger strike to protest the authorities' decision to refuse them bail. "Immediately guards were posted in our cell and stayed with us every second of the night and day—for 24 hours of the day . . . one of the guards accompanying us even if one of us had to go to the washroom and staying in the washroom with us all the time we were there. . . . We suffered great hunger pains and headaches which we tried to fight by drinking water. . . . We began to tire more easily, could not read as much as before and had to lie down more often. . . . The hundreds of letters and wires each one of us received were really . . . a good substitute for meals. . . . On the fourth day of our strike we were taken to a room in the Marine Hospital on Ellis Island." There were many visitors and finally, on 6 March, after about three weeks of detention, they were released on bail.

They wolfed down some "soup and some fruit juice" and then quickly left for Manhattan. "When we arrived in New York a crowd awaited us, among them Navy seamen who gave [Smith] an ovation. That was the only time we saw [Smith] get weak. He could not keep tears from filling his eyes when he was embraced by his fellow workers. . . . The authorities on Ellis Island were worried about the tremendous protest in our behalf," and decided to release them. They were also responding to the fact that their supporters had "picketed the White House."[53] "Six days" with "no food" and the joy of seeing supporters of all nationalities greeting him gripped Smith, known to his friends as "Smitty," as he took the microphone. "I want to get back to my seamen," he told them. He pointed to the irony of starving in a dank Ellis Island jail cell while "only a few steps away" the Statue of Liberty mocked their condition.[54]

An "all-day vigil was held in Detroit" to protest Smith's detention, "with labor, civic and political figures maintaining a 24-hour continuous picketline before immigration offices in support of the imprisoned men," though the "snow and sleet" were "ankle deep."[55] Smith's comrades in the union, together with the MCS and ILWU, issued stamps bearing the slogan "an injury to one is an injury to all" to raise funds for their campaign. Even Philip Murray of the CIO spoke out on Smith's behalf,[56] as did the leader of the New York state CIO and a large number of other AFL and CIO unions.[57] In a tense New Orleans a number of left-led unions, including the Fur and Leather Workers, backed Smith, though Fred Pieper, state CIO Director dissented, saying, "The CIO . . . is not interested" in Smith.[58] Pieper sensed before the others that despite the hunger strike and marches Smith was on his way out.

There were protests from San Francisco and St. Louis, Seattle and Brooklyn. Robeson wrote him words of encouragement, addressing him as "Ferdie," and he commiserated with "My Dear Paul." "I hope that you are well, and not being overworked," Smith, then suffering in prison, asked magnanimously. "I am as fit as can be and in the very best of spirit."[59]

The U.S. immigration authorities were not similarly motivated by magnanimity and, thus, probed relentlessly into Smith's ideology and family life to justify his removal from the country. They sought to destroy his spirit by demonstrating his unfitness. As early as April 1945, they noted that "although Smith is married to a colored woman by whom he has a child, he has been living here in New York City with a white woman. . . . Smith's present wife has filed suit for divorce from him in the Supreme Court at Foley Square and . . . a separation agreement has been signed."[60] The insistent probing into his personal life in the hearings that followed was overshadowed only by the intense scrutiny of his ideas.

Spring was descending in Manhattan as Smith walked into the hearing at 70 Columbus Avenue. Perhaps he looked ruefully at George Hewitt, also known as Tim Holmes, a former Communist functionary who was a chief witness against him. He was really afraid, said Hewitt, that Smith's cronies would exact retribution because his testimony would contradict Smith's own words. Eugene Worthen, Victor Campbell, Enrique Gonzalez, Manning Johnson, Anthony Hennessey, and George Crosby were not as reticent; they contradicted Smith's testimony with gusto. Not only was he a Red, they said—he was in meetings with some of them, they alleged—but he was also a courier, transporting sensitive information across borders for the Communists. Harry Alexander, acting agent in embattled New Orleans, was happy to say that in February 1948, as Smith was languishing in an Ellis Island cell, at an NMU meeting "with over 550 members present, the membership voted with only 18 dissenting votes to support our government in its action against" Smith. "Another resolution introduced to support Smith was rejected" by a similar margin. No tears would be shed at union headquarters if he were to be deported.[61]

Other witnesses were not as convincing as Alexander. Gonzalez was so nervous about discussing his former Red ties that he tied himself up in knots, reducing his credibility as a witness. "I joined" the party "in 1939," he said stumblingly, "I mean 1936; I believe in December or January 1940—I meant January 1937. I mean the end of December 1936 or the beginning of January 1937."[62]

When asked whether he was a Communist Party member, Smith answered bluntly, "never"—he said this more than once. He confessed to having attended "open meetings" of the party at its hall once at 23rd and 10th, then at "25th Street and Eighth Avenue." Choosing his words carefully, he testified, "I have never reported to the Political Bureau or any bureau" of the party. "I have never officiated at any time as chairman or any official capacity" of the party. "I have not attended any waterfront section meetings for the past four years." Of course, "on more than one occasion, yes," he had been asked to join the party, but this "did not come to pass." When NMU members in Baltimore wanted to "make a contribution to the Daily Worker," they were "turned down on the basis of being contrary to the policy of the union."

Immigration authorities did not find his testimony credible. What about his working for the campaign to elect the black Communist, Ben Davis, to his office? "I was never asked nor did I give any authorization to use my name. If it was used, I don't know about it," he replied simply. The "Anchor Club" or the "Seamen's Club" of the party? No, he was not a member. He had not "studied any of Marx's theory" as he was "too busy." He had never subscribed to the party's theoretical journal, *The Communist* and had not read it in "several years." The USSR? He didn't know enough "to render an opinion." His ties to the New York Jewish Communist leader, Israel Amter, were subject to repeated interrogation. Yes, he knew him, but, then again, he knew a lot of people, given that he was the number two leader of one of the most powerful unions in the nation's largest city. An "informant . . . advised" Smith's prosecutors that even Curran was willing to "testify that the subject at [the] time asked him to join the Communist Party." So how could they believe Smith?[63]

Since his rebuttal of his party ties was not found credible, there was added incentive to pry into his personal life. Thus he was asked, "Have you been intimate with, have you had sexual relationships with women other than your wife since you were separated?" "No," he said, though it was true that he was not "living with" his spouse, but "supporting her." What about "Frances Bryant"? Oh yes, she was a "member and official of the union in charge of the women in the union"—ousted from the union for "misconduct" prior to Smith's own forced departure—but, no, he had not slept with her. "It is a very personal question, isn't it? Do I have to answer such personal questions? My answer is no," he testified at one point.

Yet, perhaps unbeknown to Smith, the authorities had spoken to Greta and Barney Lynch and to Leon Luria, the "honorary physician" of the union. Greta and Barney Lynch were thought "willing to give information regarding Smith's relations with Frances Bryant." Though Leon Luria "[knew] something about Smith's relationship" he was reluctant to share what he knew. In any case, the authorities had reason to believe that he was not telling the truth.

How could Smith deny his friendship with this "white woman, named 'Frances,' 32 years old" in 1940, with "brown eyes, brown hair, [and] Christian." Wasn't he aware that "some of the other members are now complaining that she lives in too much luxury" at the tony Tudor City apartment complex close by where the United Nations eventually built its headquarters. Didn't he say that "sooner than give her up, he [would] quit the NMU"? Wasn't her photograph on his desk at the union office as he spoke that very moment?

Although the authorities made several scurrilous allegations they found it hard to rebut the assertion of the woman in question denying "intimate association or cohabitation" with Smith, "at any time or place." Moreover, his accusers' credibility was challenged when they characterized Ms. Bryant falsely as growing about nine inches in height and seventy pounds in weight from the time she testified at the immigration hearing until the time agents chased her down in San Francisco, months later.

Still, they claimed her "character appears to be very poor," though "obviously very intelligent and clever," not to mention "fairly attractive and extremely intelligent." She claimed to not be a party member. Yes, she did work once for the union and yes, she left on less than pleasant terms, accused of misappropriation of funds, but her relations with Smith were above board. In fact, she "had given him a good tongue lashing" upon her departure, presumably for not adequately coming to her defense. Sure, she knew that rumors "circulated" about her by her enemies. Then again, rumors were also "circulated that she liked women and she believed this was started because she had refused to have anything to do with the union heads." Now she was being interrogated relentlessly about a supposed affair with a "union head"— where was the justice? Immigration agents did not believe her anyway. They "gained the impression that Mrs. Bryant was [not] telling the truth concerning her cohabitation with Smith [and] that she was putting on a show of friendly cooperation in order to evade disclosing information of value in this investigation." So they slapped a "mail cover" on her, monitoring those who wrote to her.

Bryant was only one of a number of alleged paramours Smith was asked about, as they painted a picture of him as an aging roué, a stereotypical Negro sailor with an unbridled libido. What about ""Dorothy Greenlee (white)" and "one, Beulah Green (colored)," he was asked. The latter was "at present in love with the subject, but this appears to be a one-sided affection." And what about Ruby Brown, who also used to work at union headquarters but was now working as a dressmaker. Wasn't he sharing an apartment with her at 270 Convent Avenue, #3A at $75 per month? Yes, that was true, he said: "She is the tenant of this apartment and has the lease. She rents a room to the subject for which he pays $8 a week. He occupies the room alone." Her daughter was "19 years old" and "usually lives in the apartment." It was all quite proper. Sure, he knew that she "is the wife of Dr. Amos from whom she is separated."

It had to be painful for Smith when his former wife, Irene Smith, residing at 1077 Boston Road in the Bronx, testified against him. "We just couldn't get along," she now remembered; "there were lots of women." She recalled that Smith conducted himself like a typical sailor, saying he "was out at night on business" but it was not the kind of business that he claimed. "And, of course, I argued with him over it." Immigration charged that Smith came home "drunk" and "taunted" her about his other affairs. "I feel we will reconcile," she said perhaps unrealistically. Yet she did not contradict the central political aspect of Smith's defense: she "[did] not know at all" whether he was a Communist.

Not only was Smith a bad husband, alleged the authorities, but he was also a bad father, typical of the kind of moral degeneracy that characterized alien Reds, polluting the nation and poisoning the atmosphere, or so it was suggested. Writing from the "school cottage" in Mandeville, high in the hills of Jamaica, their unhappy daughter, Stephanie, wrote to "dearest Mommy and Daddy," that "your silence has really made me feel depressed as it [is] not your habit to write for so long, especially Daddy as he always write every week" [sic].

Smith seemed to be taken aback by it all. When "the judge asked my wife had she seen me during the period of our separation," she said, "yes." She wanted reconciliation. The "judge" then "told her that he was going to hold the case in abeyance until she made up her mind what she wanted because in her summons she stated that she wanted to be rid of me forever." Understandably his wife—the mother of his daughter—had ambivalent feelings about him, as he had been a sailor and often away from home. "My daughter and I who are very friendly is [*sic*] trying to patch up my wife and myself. The differences are not serious—just that we do not get along."

The immigration authorities were not buying this. They charged Smith with moral decrepitude. They accused him of "operat[ing] a house of prostitution in Harlem," and "engag[ing]" in the "numbers racket," and, worst of all, of being "intimately associated with a number of white women," including "Madeline Ford," a Communist. "This was common knowledge in maritime labor circles."

The immigration authorities charged that even as Smith was arriving for a hearing in U.S. District Court in mid-July 1949, the activist Abner Green handed him a "sealed envelope," which the security officer present "immediately took." Green told Smith that "the envelope came from a lady spectator." "Ferdie dear," she addressed him, acknowledging that she was "bitter" and "sad" about his looming ouster from the United States. "Maybe we can meet in Jamaica," she said. "If these letters or my calls or anything have created any embarrassment in your present relationship, please forgive me," for "I love you entirely." When "I chose my direction about 13 years ago" it was to be with Smith. She enclosed $25. Unlike his now alienated spouse, "if the FBI could come to get me any time, they might find a sort of tiger."[64]

The FBI thought Smith a veritable reprobate for getting women to swoon over him, risk their well-being, and pledge their undying love. In his defense, Smith charged the United States with violating the Universal Declaration of Human Rights by ill-treating immigrants like himself and his comrade, Claudia Jones. At one hearing Smith refused to testify at all, not wanting to subject himself to further probing and prodding. His attorney, Herman Rosenfeld, called the proceeding "illegal, without effect. . . . I think I would be quoting Mr. Smith accurately if, to use the vernacular, I would call it a kangaroo court."[65] Nevertheless, it was a disastrous encounter for Smith. With his unsteady immigration status, a string of potentially dissatisfied lovers, and a former spouse willing to speak frankly to his prosecutors, Smith was trapped.

Smith probably did not know that government agents were combing through the neighborhoods in which he had lived since arriving in Manhattan some twenty-five years earlier. He had resided at 375 Manhattan Avenue, then at 350 Manhattan, then at 295 Convent Avenue, and was currently at 270 Convent. All his neighbors past and present received pointed visits from white men in cheap suits with probing questions. Most of his neighbors had nothing to say; others were probably afraid to publicly rise to Smith's defense on the picket lines.[66]

The federal authorities had been monitoring Smith's contacts with the Communists for some time. His denial of intimate knowledge of them likely increased their suspicions of him. In the early spring of 1940 they recorded that Smith "and other high executives of the NMU visited" party headquarters "very often . . . had conferences with Roy Hudson who passed orders and instructions." In a gross understatement, the FBI asserted that the "Waterfront Section of the Communist Party is considered by the CP as one of its most important units." Worse, "the NMU is one of [the party's] main sources for recruiting new members." Smith's offenses had not escaped their attention either. Smith "was put in his job of secretary of the NMU by the Communist Party" but "was asked to resign his position by Al Lannon of the CP until his personal affairs can be straightened out but he refuses to do so."[67] How could Smith deny his Communist ties given all this? they asked. They had "raided the waterfront section, No. 28 of the Communist Party of America at 23rd and 7th Avenue . . . at which approximately one hundred and fifty members of the CP were in attendance. As a result of this raid all of the members attending the meeting and the leaders, were taken into custody," including Smith.[68]

The FBI believed they could manipulate the conflicts between Smith and the party. In 1943 they alleged that he was "reputed to keep his own files of Communist activities," which indicated a rift.[69] Smith was "strongly anti-white," J. Edgar Hoover said in a spectacularly inaccurate characterization that casts doubt on virtually all their perceptions of him, not least his supposed love affairs with white women.[70] Such faulty characterizations notwithstanding, the FBI stepped up their scrutiny of him. Despite the wartime détente, the FBI in 1944 "took up surveillance at Smith's residence, 270 Convent Avenue . . . and saw Roy Hudson enter the apartment house about 3:15 P.M." The NMU had a "very heated debate" about "the Smith nomination" after his problematic immigration status was discovered.[71] With such intense scrutiny, government authorities knew about Smith's personal and professional activities and were in an advantageous position to challenge his testimony.

Moreover, they were disturbed by what they found, which only increased their desire to evict him from the United States. "On the waterfront of New York," said the FBI, "the Negroes who are seamen—stewards, cooks, oilers, and wipers cannot ship out unless they pick up a party membership card." Smith, a graduate of "Red Annapolis," a party-administered encampment "only 65 miles north of New York City," was the alleged maestro of this Red orchestra.[72]

Yet Smith denied knowledge of all this at his immigration hearing, though "one witness" was willing to "testify that in 1942 [Smith] was a member of the Communist Party as well as a member of the National Committee of the Communist Party for eight years." He was said to have been present at a "regular meeting" of the party that was "packed due to the interest of the members in the explanations as to the dissolution of the Comintern." Smith persisted in maintaining that the Communist Party was a virtual stranger to him.[73]

The government questioned this claim. Why was he present at a fall 1945 reception honoring the USSR where "toasts were raised in honor of Premier Stalin"?[74] Why, a scant two years later, did he join others in cabling Stalin on his 70th birthday stating, "We united, however, in hailing your leadership in uprooting racial discrimination and oppression from your land of many peoples"?[75] Would anyone other than a card-carrying Red engage in such actions?

Weeks after Smith was first detained in 1948, the FBI was mulling over a persistent "rumor in waterfront circles which appears to be gaining wide circulation. This rumor would indicate that a good possibility exists that Harry Bridges may leave this country for Mexico in the event that strenuous investigation is started aimed at proving that his citizenship was fraudulently obtained. The rumor indicates the possibility that [Smith] might join Bridges and the two would seek to operate an international maritime setup based on the consolidation of left-wing U.S. maritime unions, a proposition which has been widely advocated by the Communist group for some time past."[76] To the FBI this was a frightening prospect, fraught with grave consequences: an alien Australian and his Jamaican comrade operating beyond Washington's jurisdiction, with a stranglehold over U.S. imports and exports, all the while working to advance the goals of communism.

Apart from Smith's political activities the FBI also noted persistent rumors of allegedly illicit business activity, such as running a "crimp joint" for sailors and his supposed plans to "open a restaurant in Harlem." Since he was "by trade a chef or steward," the FBI assumed the venture would be a guaranteed "success." He was said to be "affiliated with a Harlem corporation which was interested in purchasing surplus . . . vessels for use in [the] African river trade."[77] Though the evidence for such assertions was scant at best, the FBI continued to wring its hands over rumors of Smith's involvement in prostitution and illegal gambling.

Nevertheless, the overriding reason for the government's eagerness to deport him was because of his ties to the Communist Party, the importance of which was magnified by his powerful union position. The authorities were disturbed when an unnamed NMU member reported that he had obtained party literature from the union's headquarters and "had with other seamen distributed this literature on ships which were carrying troops to Europe, such as the SS *Santa Paula*, SS *Argentine* and the SS *Uruguay*, but mainly on the SS *Brazil*." He stated further that "he recruited new prospects into the Communist Party in connection with his work as a seaman." This sailor "stated that his assignments on vessels to carry on the Party work were assigned to him by Ferdinand Smith . . . and at various times" Smith "had instructed him to take literature on board ships in a concealed manner and that he should leave it on the bunks of the soldiers on the ship." This literature was said to include "the 'Communist Manifesto'" and other books deemed subversive. In short, as the government saw it, allowing Reds to play the leading role in the NMU allowed for a Red-dominated courier network and the possibility of Reds influencing the military as well. This was unacceptable in its view.[78]

Smith recognized that he was in a perilous position. By now he was fifty-four, a resident of the United States for thirty-five years, "married to an American citizen," according to his official propaganda, "father of an American born citizen and a grandfather." Perhaps he thought that having been "very active in war bond sales . . . I even received a citation, one or two, from the Treasury Department"[79]—might override other issues. Of course, the rapidity with which the political climate changed was stunning. How could he have known that behavior tolerated during the "popular front" would become legally actionable afterwards?

Now he was in a bind. As early as the summer of 1949 he indicated that he would be "willing to consider leaving the U.S. voluntarily if he [could] do so on an unconditional basis." His old friends from the Communist-led World Federation of Trade Unions offered him a job in France, which made the government nervous both about deporting him and not deporting him, as it feared that his sailor connections might contribute to Red courier networks. "Nobody will give me a job" in the

United States, he complained. Since he had come to this country to find work in the first place, why stay? "He had no desire to leave the U.S. but . . . it was necessary for him to seek employment," he emphasized. But what outraged him was the "methods of force and violence against the non-citizen." The people of the United States, he concluded, were being "subjected to an intensive and many-sided attack aimed at the destruction of their rights and liberties. An important part of this attack is the current deportation hysteria set loose by the Justice Department," designed to convince many that the root of their problem was the so-called "alien menace." "The Truman Administration," he said, "is seeking to terrorize the American people and silence opposition to its drive for war and for Wall St. domination of the entire world."[80] Smith was reluctant to allow himself to be forced out of the country, fearing the precedent his case would set for others similarly situated, including "the cases of ninety-eight other alien Communists whom the government is attempting to deport."[81] But ultimately he could not withstand the pressure and was forced to abandon the struggle.

Sailors from the rank-and-file often supported Smith on board ship. But since their protests occurred on oceans thousands of miles away from Manhattan, Smith's opponents found it easy to isolate them from the solidarity of their comrades. Thus, in the spring of 1948 an aide told Assistant U.S. Attorney General Vincent Quinn that "last evening at approximately 6:30. . . . I took a telephone call from . . . Baltimore. . . . [A sailor] stated that he was a crew member of the SS *David Starr Jordan* . . . which was due to sail for Le Havre at midnight and that there had been considerable trouble aboard the vessel between the communist and non-communist factions of the crew revolving about the recent deportation arrest of [Ferdinand Smith]; that there had already been two open fights between these factions and that the Communist faction had attempted to throw . . . overboard at sea if he attempted to sail with the ship. . . . He further claimed that the sailing of the vessel had been delayed from 8:00 A.M. to midnight because of the difficulties described. [Deleted] who spoke with a Negro dialect which was very difficult to understand, stated the purpose of his call was to let [deleted] know of this situation so that should the threats be carried out and [deleted] failed to return from the voyage at least some basis would exist for an investigation into his disappearance. He stated he was not intimidated by these threats and was not afraid to ship on the voyage but intended to do so notwithstanding violence to himself might be involved. He stated he no longer carried a gun but would defend himself otherwise if attacked. I reported the substance of the conversation to [deleted] and then called [deleted] of the FBI. [Deleted] reminded me of the Bureau's policy, with which I was familiar, not to provide police protection where not required in support of federal jurisdiction."[82]

It is unclear how many sailors, anti-Smith or otherwise, may have been "dumped" or tossed overboard but, certainly, his immigration problems created concern globally. In the spring of 1948 "members of the crew of the SS *Veruga*" wrote to the FBI to protest Smith's detention "and the deportation proceedings against him." These were "possible Communist sympathizers," the FBI concluded, implicitly vowing to punish them.[83]

This kind of repression was accompanied by similar actions on dry land. The Black Diamond Steamship Company was one of the employers that began making detailed background checks on sailors. "Why," asked *The Pilot*, "does the company want to know a man's union book number, his race and whether he can read English?" Together with the "Taft-Hartley slave law" and other forms of "blacklisting," this was designed to destroy progressive trade unionism among sailors for all time.[84]

This may have been prescient. Early in 1950, the *New York World-Telegram* noted joyfully that for the first time since 1937 there were no "open Communists running" for NMU offices—though it was suspicious of the candidacy of Jesse Gray, a Negro, a "member who as a delegate to the union's convention last fall, sounded remarkably like the Communist opposition."[85]

Anyone who sounded like Smith would be treated the same way— an eventuality that galvanized protesters and Smith alike. At one notable protest weeks after his first detention in 1948, a "crowd" of two thousand "marched from the offices of the Immigration and Naturalization Service to Duffy Square, marching three abreast in a file of about seven blocks long."[86] After his release Smith spoke to thousands of supporters at Madison Square Garden, a gathering sponsored by the Joint Anti-Fascist Refugee Committee, and to many others at a meeting of the American Jewish Labor Council. He told the latter that "the Jews and the Negroes are always the first victims of reactionary movements. The Jewish and the Negro masses must unite in a fight against the pogrom makers and lynchers." His own Harlem Trade Union Council and the AJLC "have many similarities. . . . Both organizations are stubborn fighters against racial hatred and for friendship between all the nations of the world."[87]

Although these were bold words straight from the hymn book of the old-time religion, they were unhelpful toward his hopes of a future in his adopted homeland. His detractors, on the other hand, were so keen that he depart the country that they overcame their fear that he would help Communist courier networks while abroad.[88]

Virtually until his last day in the United States, Smith was battling for the rights of Negroes. Weeks before his forced departure he attended a packed concert by Paul Robeson to raise funds for and expand the work of the Harlem Trade Union Council. This was during the height of the war in Korea. According to the FBI, Smith "spoke on the question of the Negro as a whole and especially the Negro women who will suffer most as a whole . . . because of the drive toward war." He "mocked" President Truman and derided the war in which the nation was embroiled.[89]

Smith's enemies were elated when he departed the United States. The *New York World-Telegram* commented that "Ferdinand C. Smith finally gets Uncle Sam's Boot as a Red Heel," as the time for his departure approached. It continued to portray this "pleasant though determined man" as being at odds with his comrades: "After the Communists had set things up for him to become a vice-president, he upset them by suddenly announcing that 'my people' insisted that he get the higher post of national secretary. It was Red leader Jack Stachel, now in prison, who gave in and told the other Communists in the union that they must yield to Smith's desires." This was all ancient history, for now "Moscow's loss has been America's gain."[90]

This was Smith's last hurrah, one of the last times he would be derided in the U.S. press. On 15 August 1951 he was at New York's Idlewild Airport. Weeks earlier in "confidential . . . censorship intercepts from WFTU [World Federation of Trade Union] correspondence," the authorities found that Smith "indicates eagerness to come to Europe and states that he has received clearance to go overseas." Because of this "intercept" they could better place a "mail cover" or scrutiny of his correspondents, and even open his mail, as he had asked the WFTU before his departure to send "all official mail" to the HTUC and "all personal mail" to "Edith Roberts, 208 West 151st Street, apartment 26" in Harlem.[91] Hence the FBI knew well in advance when he was leaving and where he was going.

Thus, federal agents were present when about "100 persons led by Paul Robeson" came to bid him farewell at the airport. His good friend Robeson, whose passport was soon to be taken away from him, preventing him from traveling abroad, pressed crumpled currency into his hand. "Thanks," said Smith gratefully, but "I won't starve. . . . I know many English labor leaders, and I'm sure I'll be able to get a berth. I want to work. I am a sailor. If I stay there long enough, I'll be able to work for a labor union. Wherever sailors hang out," he concluded on a poignant note, "you'll find me."[92] He turned away and boarded Pan-American Airways Flight 100 for London, as government agents looked on to insure that he would not slip away.[93] He was never again to reside in the United States, where he had lived for over three decades.[94]

10

Dropping Anchor in Jamaica

THE U.S. AUTHORITIES were in a dilemma: Should they let Smith stay in the United States and continue his union and party organizing, or should they let him depart and carry on his work in Vienna, Kingston, Jamaica or elsewhere? They decided on the latter. Undoubtedly they may have come to regret their decision after Smith went to Europe to work on behalf of the World Federation of Trade Unions. This Communist-led federation had threatened to help the NMU and the ILWU call a global strike in the heady days of 1946.

Smith's comrade from Grenada, Charles Collins, was "the sole American of color" at the WFTU's founding in Paris in 1945. The theme he struck was to animate Smith's subsequent work. "Our own color bars," said the strikingly good-looking former actor, "particularly whether in Cape Town or Charleston, must go if free labor is to live." He had with him a "detailed blueprint for the setting up of a department on Negro and colonial labor with a full time staff to lead the battle against imperialism." This was the unit Smith was to lead.[1]

The WFTU gathering in Paris was timed to coincide with the fifth Pan-African Congress meeting in Manchester, England, in the fall of 1945. At the WFTU, "African and Caribbean delegates saw in a strongly organized labor movement, the only kind of strength which can be used to cut the chains which bind them politically." Though often neglected, labor in the colonized world was a major force against colonialism. In both Africa and the Caribbean, sailors, who had the mobility to travel to Manchester or Paris, were prominent in the labor movement.[2] As the concerns of black labor came to the fore for both the WFTU and PAC, the moment was propitious for the arrival of Smith—the black Jamaican American Communist sailor—in Europe.

London's elites did not welcome the PAC, concerned as they were about preserving colonialism. In a "secret" dispatch, the Colonial Office expressed "interest in obtaining information about West Indians in the United States and American Negro movements generally." It was particularly interested in the "West Indian resolutions" emerging from this gathering. Inevitably, it viewed the arrival of the "West Indian Negro" and "American Negro," Ferdinand Smith, in Jamaica with suspicion.[3]

Like the PAC, the WFTU was not favorably regarded by Washington's allies during the Cold War. In 1953, *The Economist* wrote that it "may already be said to be the Soviet Communist Party's most effective political weapon in the colonies."[4] A report by the American Federation of Labor that year announced that "in the underdeveloped non-industrialized regions, WFTU's working arrangements with a few key individuals may be worth more to the Soviet Union than are, say, seventy-five thousand WFTU members in the Netherlands." "The emblem chosen for the [WTFU's] Third World Congress" in Vienna was "significant. . . . Against the background of the globe, three hands joined fraternally—one white, one brown, one yellow. Communist propaganda," an analyst declared auspiciously, "has usurped the theme of human brotherhood, using the theme to divide non-whites from western whites."[5] During his final years Smith found a palpable fear that the "normalcy" of colonialism was really a cloak for racial tyranny.

But colonial Jamaica was not his immediate destination as he crossed the Atlantic in 1951. When leaving New York, Smith's ultimate destination was the WFTU headquarters in Vienna, the fabled Cold War trip-wire, where he was to work as a leader of this global conglomeration of trade unions. But even before this fateful journey, Smith was trying to bring his pet causes before the WFTU. In 1946 Smith "headed a delegation" from the National Negro Congress "which called upon Louis Saillant, Secretary-General of the [WFTU] . . . to secure his backing and that of the WFTU for the NNC petition to the United Nations" on Negro rights.[6] This gesture and his effort to encourage the WFTU to join a global strike made Washington and London uncomfortable about his presence in Vienna.

Though not fully recovered from the ravages of war, charming, quaint Vienna was awash in old-world charm, replete with coffee bars with delicious pastries, renowned orchestras, and a thriving cultural life. Its formidable and impressive architecture made the "spy versus spy" escapades of the Cold War seem to be unfolding on a lot in Hollywood. Living in Vienna, a crossroads between East and West still full of Soviet troops, would allow Smith to travel and organize in the Caribbean and Africa, and, he thought, would allow for trips in transit to the United States. But his opponents saw this move in the same sinister terms in which they viewed the WFTU. A functionary in the British Embassy in Vienna concluded that "the presence of the WFTU in Austria is a potent danger to Austria."[7] British trade unions cooperated with the British Foreign Office in a united campaign against the WFTU. F. C. Mason of the Foreign Office passed on to A. E. Carthy of the British union federation information from a "confidential source" about the WFTU and requested that it "be passed to the ICFTU"—the International Confederation of Free Trade Unions, sworn foe of the WFTU—"provided no indication of source is given."[8] The Foreign Office was "anxious that every opportunity should be taken of harrying the WFTU and, if possible, driving it well and truly behind the Iron Curtain, where it belongs."[9] This campaign did not bode well for Smith's stay in Austria.

Not surprisingly, upon arriving in Europe Smith immediately sprang into action on behalf of another petition to the United Nations. This one, filed by the Civil Rights Congress, the successor to the NNC, charged the United States with genocide against Negroes. Filed at a time when the Cold War had become hot, the petition questioned Washington's claim to be the paragon of human rights. Days after arriving in Austria in 1951, Smith wrote to CRC leader, William Patterson, on WFTU stationery that he was "having" the petition "translated." Smith, a new leader of the powerful WFTU in which Soviet and other Eastern European trade unionists played a leading role, lamented that "my job calls for more writing than talking and . . . the former is not to my liking." He was writing for the WFTU and other left-leaning organs in the region and the petition was one of his major concerns.[10]

Smith's comrade, Patterson, replied that "it is good to see you so thoroughly involved and with so little loss of time" with the petition, "except I would like to have seen you enjoy a well earned two or three weeks' vacation. Just East of you are a number of magnificent spots," said Patterson, a Communist with no small familiarity with this region, "where a worker can easily rest and enjoy the fruits of labor of himself and of his fellow man."[11] But he should have known that the peripatetic Smith had no time for a holiday. Instead, Smith quickly plunged into a whirlwind of meetings and conferences, which was a tonic as he met many with views as radical as his. "Since I was always an optimist," he told Patterson, "you can readily understand how I feel and how good it is to find others feeling the same way." At one notable meeting "there were delegates from all over the world except, of course, the 'good old USA.'" He was struck by the "Asiatic delegates, particularly the Chinese" who possessed "not merely a question of pride in achievements" but also "a question of confidence." He too was confident, which was why he encouraged Patterson to consider "touring Western Europe" with the petition, "particularly Italy and France" where Communists were dominant.[12]

Such plans eventually led to Patterson's passport being seized, which prevented him from following up on Smith's suggestion—though Smith himself was "among the petitioners" to the United Nations.[13] Soon Smith was reading about Patterson's detention in New York City after arriving from Europe where he publicized the petition. His friend "passed through Vienna like a jet plane," perhaps because of the latter day bloodhounds tailing him. Smith assured him that he had plans to have the petition "widely distributed." "My immediate plans," he said, "call for a quick trip to somewhere in Africa . . . before embarking on the Caribbean tour," including a visit to the place of his birth, Jamaica. But it was Patterson's plight and detention, so similar to his a few years earlier, that concerned him. "All this goes to show," Smith proclaimed, "how desperate the oppressors are. . . . Mr. Truman and his gang" exemplified "the rottenness of the present corrupt, criminal government . . . a gang whose days are surely numbered." On a more pleasant note, he asked that warm regards be conveyed to his good friend "Paul" Robeson.[14]

The U.S. authorities carefully studied these exchanges. One of Smith's letters from Vienna was intercepted by Washington's "Civil Censorship Group Austria (US)." In it he wrote, "I could send the petitions to Paris," to be put before the UN General Assembly. He suggested submitting the document to "Chile, Peru, Argentina, Brasil or one of the Latin or South American countries as second choice." India would be first. "Failing to prevail upon any of these, I would then turn to the East, first to the Arab countries—perhaps Iran or Egypt." Smith was trying to avoid the inevitable claim that the petition was no more than "Communist propaganda," which was why Communist-led nations were not at the top of his list. But, he was realistic enough to recognize that "if no success were achieved" with these nations, all of whom were dependent to a greater or lesser degree on Washington and its allies, "then the Eastern Peoples Republics" should be approached. The U.S. authorities were probably not pleased to read Smith's claim that the petition "is creating terrific furore in this country. I am hoping that . . . more than 100,000 copies" could be sold. "That is our plan and there is every reason to believe it will be carried out. If it is not, the fault lies with us, for the objective conditions are entirely satisfactory," he said, overly optimistically.[15]

Smith may have been unduly sanguine about political conditions worldwide. In the fall of 1951, the United States got hold of a letter he had sent to Communist trade union leader Louis Weinstock. "It made me very happy to note from press reports," said Smith, "that the rally in defense of yourself and other Smith Act victims was such a success. It goes to show that at last the people are waking up to the big lie of the Truman preparation for war. . . . This is no surprise to me." The State Department considered this innocent letter sufficiently important to be forwarded to London, Paris, Kingston, Rome, and Brussels—a sign of the danger Smith was thought to represent.[16]

As it turned out, Patterson's passport was revoked and he was jailed, the petition was buried in an avalanche of Red-baiting, and the promised support did not materialize. Meanwhile, Smith was having his own problems. The U.S. authorities, who were monitoring his every move, were concerned that he was "located in Soviet Zone, Vienna, Austria" at the "Hotel Guldenes Lamm" and for some reason "had frequent contact with CP officials and participated in numerous CP dominated functions prior to departure from the U.S."[17] They were even more troubled when, in 1952, the WFTU dispatched him and Billy Strachan, Secretary of the London branch of the Caribbean Labour Congress, on a tour of the "British West Indies." There the United States discovered it had done its ally in London no favor by forcing Smith to depart New York City. This realization dawned when Smith and Strachan, "two well-known Communists," addressed some ten thousand people assembled in Coronation Market in Kingston.[18]

Speaking to four thousand people at the Kingston Race Course in May 1952, Smith—a celebrity in light of his prominence in the United States—cried, "If there is any boss, you must be the boss, your leaders must be responsible to you." These words resonated in a land where the citizens—make that "subjects"—could not vote on their sovereign. Similarly discomfiting to some were his words that "in the world of today there are two mighty forces—one of these forces is the force for peace . . . led by the great Soviet Union; the other" was the United States, which he viewed as the epicenter of a bellicose imperialism. His organization, the WFTU, which represented some 80 million workers, pledged their solidarity; likewise, he told those assembled to "keep away from this organization"—the AFL affiliated, International Confederation of Free Trade Unions—for it "means the workers no good."[19]

Those seeking to extend British colonial domination over Jamaica, a key producer of the strategic mineral bauxite, were doubtless troubled by his presence. Perhaps this was why the FBI received word that "Mr. Geoffrey Patterson of MI-5 [British intelligence] called. . . . He advised he had received an inquiry from MI-5" about Smith.[20]

Smith was coming to discover that globe-trotting, which his new job required, was not as simple as sailing the seven seas as a steward. When he and Strachan arrived in Trinidad & Tobago, yet another British colony, they were not allowed to leave the airport and were not allowed to visit—though a British diplomat reported with irritation that Smith "found time to address a small group of taxi drivers at the airport on the iniquities of the Governor and the 'glories of life in Russia.'"[21] When he flew across the seas and oceans, government surveillance followed. Thus, in the spring of 1952 the U.S. Secretary of State himself was told by the U.S. consulate in Jamaica that Smith was "scheduled to arrive [at] Idlewild Airport . . . in transit. . . . Recommend surveillance." Anticipating problems, the authorities were instructed in a "confidential" dispatch that "if transportation delays" in New York "should require detention by immigration authorities, recommend that they be sent to England and not (rpt [repeat] not) returned to Jamaica."[22] Thus, when Smith and Strachan's plane left Jamaica for London, proceeding through New York, "the U.S. authorities detained them . . . after keeping them on Ellis Island," then "returned them to Jamaica."[23] This was a rude reintroduction to the United States and a bracing reminder of his last troubled years there.

Smith and Strachan were like men without a country, flying from port to port in search of a place to land. "Smith and Strachan will not be permitted to land in St. Luica," said one colonial bureaucrat flatly.[24] When they "applied . . . for passage to Barbados," the official there inquired, "Will they be permitted to land?"[25] The answer was no. Their entry into the nation that was to be known as Belize was refused.[26] They were initially banned from visiting or inhabiting Trinidad & Tobago[27] and barred from St. Vincent.[28] Smith and Strachan were declared unacceptable for entry into Grenada.[29] Smith's and the WFTU's dream of organizing workers in the region together with a push for decolonization was unfulfilled.

London had grave misgivings about these twin goals. One of their dispatches said, "Smith is reported to be carrying a considerable amount of money."[30] He and his comrade, Strachan, were said to have a thousand pounds in traveler's checks and were correctly assumed to be organizing for the WFTU. It was also reported that they may "intend to use the CLC [Caribbean Labour Congress] as the nucleus" for founding a dreaded "West Indian Communist Party."[31] The British Embassy in the United States forwarded to the Colonial Office a clipping from the black newspaper, the *New York Amsterdam News*, that detailed a plan by U.S. Negro leaders to raise $10,000 to help finance a CLC congress in Trinidad. Perhaps, the British thought, Smith and Strachan were part of a combined "Black-Red" effort against British colonialism.[32] Earlier, Smith had contributed as much as five hundred pounds to Jamaica for hurricane relief, which gave the authorities reason to believe that he might have other funds to dispense for purposes that were not humanitarian.[33]

As some had suspected and others had feared, in exile Smith had become one of many "Red Couriers" bringing cash to the Caribbean for what they considered subversive purposes. The problem was that he was not just an "ordinary sailor" but the high-level leader of a powerful trade union federation backed by Moscow.[34] In addition, London had good reason to be suspicious of the CLC. Richard Hart, the erudite radical lawyer who was to become Smith's closest comrade in Jamaica, played a leading role in this pan-Caribbean organization (it also embraced French and Dutch territories). As early as 1947 the CLC was planning a conference attacking the concept of "imperial preference," which tied island economies tightly to London.[35] In 1950 the St. Kitts-Nevis Trades and Labour Union, a CLC affiliate, decided it would "not handle any cargo originating" in South Africa "on account of deliberate and systematic application of its dreadful policy of apartheid."[36] The CLC had strong support among waterfront workers, who were essential for the survival of these small island nations that imported vital products, and tried to coordinate regionally and hemispherically along the lines of what Smith had attempted with the Committee on Maritime Unity in the United States.[37]

The British had only to look at St. Vincent to get an idea of what Smith and the WFTU had in store for the region. The labor leader there, Ebenezer Joshua, was a constant thorn in London's side and the "colonial regime used every possible lever—rival labour leaders, the police, the legal system, the planters, the press and the colonial bureaucracy—to exert various forms of pressure on Joshua." The "planter class [feared that] unionism would threaten a reduction in their profits. In addition, the planters feared that unionism would unleash forces which would not only subvert the plantation system but also disrupt the traditional patterns of interpersonal relations between the planter and the labourer." Hence the authorities argued that Joshua was an "International Communist" since he attended a WFTU meeting in Vienna. They "claimed that" his union was an "affiliate of the Communist dominated [WFTU]."[38] Actually, after Joshua returned from Vienna "there were hundreds awaiting . . . his landing. . . . The first meeting in Kingstown, the capital city, was attended by over 10,000."[39] By linking labor with decolonization, Smith, Joshua, and others had created a powerful engine for advance. In turn, as Mansraj Ramphal has put it, "the Communist bogey was raised in St. Vincent . . . to scare the wits of a politically uneducated Caribbean people whose minds have been immersed in western propaganda."[40]

London was full of fears of a rising Red danger, symbolized by the presence of Smith's comrade, Cheddi Jagan of Guyana, a U.S.-educated Communist whose attempt to lead his nation was thwarted by Washington and London. Travel restrictions were imposed not only on card-carrying Communists, preventing them from traveling to the far-flung islands and nations of the Caribbean, but also on rather staid leaders like Eric Gairy of Grenada. Even the conservative Alexander Bustamante of Jamaica was hassled when he tried to visit Puerto Rico. Far from being Red, some of these leaders (such as Bustamante) were not even proindependence necessarily. But any self-assertion by the colonized was seen as an attack on colonialism itself.[41] Patterson, under siege himself, rose to Smith's defense after he found himself barred from entering British colonies in the Caribbean. Writing to Smith at his temporary headquarters at the Myrtle Bank Hotel in Kingston, he noted that he had "interceded with the British Ambassador and the State Department. . . . I also immediately cabled Europe . . . calling for protest action by the entire apparatus." Despite the restrictions on Smith, he remained optimistic. "I am sure with a strong leadership the whole of the West Indies would be linked with the Asian forces in the bitter struggle against the imperialist system."[42]

Washington knew that Patterson's dream was not baseless. Frank Elliott of the United States, reporting to the State Department, found himself in Kingston at about the same time as Smith and he was struck by the inequality of income which could portend unrest. "I got stuck with a job down here," he began, but "I don't much like the place. Tourists get off a cruise ship for a few hours or days to gorge on Caribbean fruits—bananas, oranges, grapefruit, pineapples, papayas, mangoes and such and go into ecstasies over the profusion of tropical flowers and trees. From that standpoint these islands are exotic; like the audience's view of a well set up stage. They don't see the tangle of ropes, props, dirt and confusion backstage." The "conditions" in Jamaica were "almost unspeakable; conditions which, in some events, because of Jamaica's proximity, might be dangerous to the welfare of the United States." Echoing other critics in the United States, he blamed the situation on London. "The British have exploited the place—taken out everything, put back nothing." The "Negro population" was "estimated at 65% illegitimate" and "continues rapidly to grow without restraint." There was "chronic unemployment, stark want, downright hunger, with the lowest, most squalid standard of living I have ever seen. This breeds a great social unrest which boils down to the surface in continuous labor difficulties—in many instances violent." He recalled sarcastically how "Eleanor the Great [Roosevelt] used to cry crocodile tears over the lowly state of the American Negro. I can tell you that, as a whole, they fare incomparably better than the natives here." The "thatched roof, tumble down, reed huts—no electricity, no water, no sanitation, set in the midst of all sorts of filth and confusion, plus dirty ragged children are worse than anything I have ever seen in our own South, or anywhere in the world, even the Orient." Jamaica "is a nation of beggars. The mangy, scrawny dogs and cats beg from the natives; the natives beg from the whites and the country itself begs from the Mother Country. All of this poverty has made fertile soil for communistic seeds and those seeds have taken root, cultivated by a rabid local political group. There are two unions in Jamaica—at the heads of which are two gentlemen of color. . . . It's not a rare thing to see the clenched fist Communist salute or hear the 'Internationale' sung at some union gatherings. . . . Considering that this island, the largest of the British West Indies, lies athwart the route to the Panama Canal, and also its proximity to the United States (only 3 hours flying to Florida)," Washington had to take heed. That this letter was forwarded to Secretary of State Dean Acheson suggested that Jamaica would receive high-level attention.[43]

These opinions about Jamaica's plight were echoed by the Reverend Montague Dale of Britain, who "ranged through the tattoo shacks" and was stunned to see "some of the bodies of old motor cars on which cardboard, coconut palms and thin boards are held together with string." He asked, "Where's the sanitation?" The mayor of Kingston responded laconically, "There's none." The Bishop's report "described the inhabitants as 'having their faces haunted with hunger' and being 'depressed below the living standards of animals.' Of Jamaica's population of 1,340,000, no less than 200,000 were estimated to be unemployed in 1951, with many more seriously underemployed."[44]

Smith's mission in Jamaica was to arrest this poverty. But even after he had arrived a report for the BBC indicated that "workers, except Government employees, shopkeepers, contractors, etc. usually get less than . . . 3 [pounds] a week"—or about $6. "There is no unemployment pay, no health insurance and no old age pensions. Many Jamaicans are onlookers in their own home where they see rich Americans and British enjoying the fat."[45] Conditions worsened when in 1950 it was decided that Puerto Ricans were to replace "West Indian farm workers" in Florida and "up the East Coast and to some extent in the Middle West." During the war, it was reported, West Indians had been preferred since they could be forced to go back home since they were not citizens. Now even this small benefit was to be ended.[46]

In partial response to the changing employment situation Jamaican immigrants began to go to the "Mother Country." Yet when their ship, the *Windrush,* arrived in Britain in June 1948 bearing 492 Jamaicans, a "correspondent" with the Labour Party "saw in this influx the hidden hand of 'Uncle Joe' Stalin. 'Do you think,' he confided, 'this sudden influx of 400 West Indians is a subtle move of Russia to create for us in another twenty years time a "Colour Question" here?' . . . Elements in the Home Office were already persuaded that there was 'a large Communist element among the coloured population here and the Communists would no doubt not be slow to make trouble if they could.'"[47] Smith's presence in Europe and Jamaica could do little to assuage this anxiety. Suffering in their homeland, facing barriers to entering the United States, enduring "racial" bias in the United Kingdom, Jamaicans were ripe for the kind of radicalism Smith symbolized.

The authorities' concern over Jamaica's plight did not lead them to be sympathetic toward those who would have liked to have altered the situation. In fact, the British Communist leader R. Palme Dutt asserted in 1953 that "it would be vain to search through the debates of the House of Commons in recent years for any major general debate on the problems of the British Empire as a whole or the impact of these problems on Britain's position in the world and Britain's future. Just as in the old days the annual India debate used to be guaranteed to empty the House, so today a Colonial Affairs debate can normally count on a sparse attendance and the participation of specialists."[48]

Democracy was more of a slogan than a reality in colonies like Jamaica. Writing in 1954, the British writer Jack Woddis observed that "before the Second World War . . . trade unions were illegal in practically every British colony. In fact, the Rt. Hon. James Griffiths, former Secretary of State for the Colonies in the last Labour Government, has stated that in 1930 there were only three registered trade unions in all the colonial territories."[49] Jervis Anderson, a Jamaican American who had an illustrious career writing for the *New Yorker* and other publications, acknowledged the "tenacious grip that British colonial influence exerted upon the psychology of his countrymen" in Jamaica. This "influence" was generated by severe repression. "I read the *New Statesman*," said Anderson, referring to the mildly social democratic journal, "only in the privacy of my residence, as if it were an underground publication. I never took it with me to my office at the *Gleaner*, fearing that Tory-minded overseers might discover and excommunicate me as the carrier of a subversive disease. That fear was not unfounded."[50]

Color prejudice was also a persistent problem. Lady Bustamante, the aide, then spouse of Jamaican leader Alexander Bustamante, who was born in Smith's hometown, wrote that the spouse of Bustamante, who certainly was as conservative as her husband if not more so, seemed to be as irked as a card-carrying Communist by the expressions of white supremacy she witnessed while growing to maturity in Jamaica. Though visiting African Americans routinely marveled at what they perceived as the widespread representation of darker faces at all levels of society on this Caribbean island, she begged to differ. As she saw it, the Jamaica of her early years was comparable to the dankest precincts of Jim Crow in the U.S. As she recalled it, major corporations sited in Jamaica traditionally resisted hiring Jamaicans of an ebony hue, while the leading professions—medicine, law, architecture—were likewise bereft of the melanin rich; meanwhile, the lighter skinned were as allergic to the idea of socializing with their darker counterparts as their comrades on the North American mainland. In Kingston in the 1930s she "began to realize that even newspaper advertisements for jobs mentioned skin colour as a qualification. It was not unusual to read in the *Gleaner:* 'Young lady (white). . . . Respectable young man (fair). . . . Because I was not of light skin, I could not hold a job of any kind in a commercial bank. Though I was proficient in arithmetic and knew how to speak to people, I could not find employment selling cloth, shoes or books in any King Street store.'"[51] Joyce Lindo, an advertising executive in Jamaica, agreed: "I remember that we were the very first agency to use a photograph of a black Jamaican in a *Gleaner* ad. That was in the late 1950s. It had never been done before but we were a young agency and we were looking for moves and methods to prove that we were different."[52]

Jamaica had a long history of class and "racial" struggle, stretching back to slavery, especially among sugar workers.[53] As Smith was growing up in Jamaica, in January 1907 the sixty-five members of the Printers' Union went on strike for higher wages. Between 1914 and 1917 Jamaica experienced a formidable outbreak of industrial unrest.[54] Things were so bad that London concluded, "It was necessary to establish trade unions as a means of controlling the militancy of the working class."[55]

Inevitably the United States exerted considerable influence on Jamaica. According to Jeffrey Harrod, "The association between the civil rights for Negroes movement in the USA and Jamaica has been a constant, if fluctuating, one throughout modern history. . . . The idea of unionism did not come from Britain but from emigrants returning from the USA, Cuba and South America."[56] Indeed, it is remarkable how many Caribbean leaders—including Ferdinand Smith in the 1950s—had been abroad. Jim Headley, a ship's cook, had been active with the NMU and the Young Communist League and the "National Unemployed Movement" in Trinidad. Rupert Gittens was deported to Trinidad as a result of his ties to the Communists in France. Before that he had been in the United States. "where he was influenced by Communist ideas and radical black nationalism." Under his influence, the NUM "was exposed much more to socialist thinking at an international level." The Barbados Labour Party was "started in March 1938" by Hope Stevens, a Harlem-based attorney of Caribbean origins. Hugh Clifford Buchanan, "Jamaica's first active Marxist" had lived in Cuba. Jamaica's first "Marxist group" included Lionel Lynch, a maritime worker, who had been "introduced to Communism while resident in the USA." Arthur Henry, another well-known Jamaican progressive, had worked in the engine room on "Canadian boats." Alexander Bustamante of Jamaica had lived in the United States earlier. The Antiguan labor leader, George Weston, who "subsequently became" an associate of Marcus Garvey, had lived in New York City.[57] Such examples illustrated the dilemma of those who wished to see Smith leave the United States. His departure would not guarantee an end to his activism—only that it would take place elsewhere.

Surprisingly, Smith did not devote much time to his homeland once he had arrived in the United States, perhaps so as not to draw attention to his questionable immigration status. During labor unrest in Jamaica in the 1930s, U.S. sailors were offered "five times what the Jamaican workers were demanding to unload" ships, "but they refused when they received a telegram" from the NMU.[58] Richard Hart, the Jamaican activist, "learned later that the General Secretary of their union was a Jamaican seaman who had been away for nearly twenty years," namely, Ferdinand Smith.[59] During the war Smith spoke to the Caribbean in a shortwave broadcast sponsored by Washington. "The hope of independence for the colonial peoples of the world depend on a United Nations victory. . . . We West Indians are proud to work and fight with other brothers, colored and white of the United Nations."[60] Perhaps due to Smith's influence, in 1943 Joseph Curran "asked the British Ministry of Transportation what it intended to do about the several hundred skilled seamen standing idle in the West Indies because of the discrimination practiced by the employers of the British Merchant Service." Curran "repeated" the NMU's "pledge to support the Trinidad seamen." Curran and his union were "requesting all companies under contract to the NMU to secure their replacements for vessels in Island and South American ports from the regularly established union hiring halls in these ports."[61]

Reciprocally, the presence of a strong left in the region was in the interests of the NMU. Scholar Ronald Harpelle observes with regard to Costa Rica's Atlantic coast that "the only effort to bridge the gap between West Indians and their Hispanic counterparts came with the Communist Party effort to unite [fellow] workers in a struggle against the fruit company."[62] Communists in Cuba, where the NMU maintained an important outpost, "controlled the largest trade unions, which were generally well organized." Unavoidably this attracted Washington's attention. "Witch hunts" for radicals commenced as early as the war, though these were "carried out with a very wide net, not so much to catch actual subversives but to snag political enemies." In the Caribbean there was concern about the spread of U.S.-style "racial" policies, though the popular song "The Best Place Is the U.S." with its refrain, "you can never be in financial jam when you are working for Uncle Sam," was a telling reminder of Washington's gradual displacement of London. In Trinidad alone Washington built roads, dredged new canals that led to new anchorages, built hospitals, and employed thousands to build bases. In short, it did as much to develop the infrastructure and economies of this nation as London had done in decades.[63]

Though they were allies, there was also some friction between London and Washington. As Richard Hart, Smith's Jamaican comrade put it, "The U.S. government had for some time been exerting pressure on the colony-holding European powers to grant political independence to their colonies, as this would facilitate access to them by U.S. investors and exporters."[64] Suspicion was so high between the two nations that when the International Confederation of Free Trade Unions was created in 1949 as a conscious alternative to Smith's WFTU, London was nervous about its U.S. tilt, despite the high stakes involved.[65] After the formation of the AFL-CIO in the United States, the rift continued between U.S. and British labor.[66] A WFTU representative sensed this. Though calling the ICFTU the "scab international," he went on to speak of a "continuous running fight" between labor in the United States and its counterpart in Britain over this federation, which reflected "rivalries between American and British imperialism" over the "colonial question." British labor wanted to "retain control of their colonial trade union movements."[67]

Such squabbling between London and Washington should have been good news for Smith. However, when he arrived in Jamaica in 1952, after a four-decade absence, he found that many Jamaicans were looking to the United States, which not only wished to displace the United Kingdom but was in a financially strong position to do so. Hence his denunciation of U.S. imperialism found fewer and fewer listeners, especially as Washington had plenty of largesse to hand out to its supporters. Moreover, to the unenlightened Smith's anti-Washington line seemed to be an endorsement of London, his vehement protestations to the contrary. His fellow West Indian Communist, Claudia Jones, sensed this. "Many of the present leaders in the West Indies," she said in the 1950s, "look increasingly to the U.S. for salvation. . . . The dangers of U.S. imperialism are not fully grasped" as "the leaning among the West Indian masses [is] towards the more prosperous United States." The "masses" were "in revolt against British imperialism which they see as their ever-present and age-old enemy." She noted that "six times since the end of the war the British found it necessary to send punitive expeditions to 'restore law and order' in the West Indies," including to Guyana to suppress the democratic movement led by Smith's comrade, Cheddi Jagan. In such a context, Washington appeared to some to be a paradigm of progressivism, thus helping to undermine Smith's denunciation of U.S. imperialism.[68] Moreover, as the Jamaican analyst Trevor Munroe has put it, "the development of the Cold War internationally strengthened the right internally and occasioned the penultimate rift" in the progressive forces locally.[69] This too undercut Smith's appeal.

In sum, the environment in Jamaica was extremely complicated. The two major political blocs were represented by the cousins,[70] Norman Manley and Alexander Bustamante. The former was something of a Social Democrat and leader of the Peoples National Party, while the latter was a conservative and leader of the Jamaica Labour Party. Both parties had union affiliates, with the JLP's named after their leader—a conceit reflective of his dictatorial impulses. Smith's arrival on the island coincided with the purge of the left from the PNP. Richard Hart, a learned intellectual, joined with Smith to form a third political formation and union bloc.[71]

Though Communists had a reputation for their worldwide reach, it seemed that the PNP exceeded them in this category. Hart affirms that some British labor bureaucrats "made every effort to persuade trade unionists in the colonies to have nothing to do with politics!" "Our earliest Marxist contacts abroad," on the other hand, "were with Domingo and O'Meally in New York, neither of whom had ever been a member of the Communist Party of the USA. Nor did our subsequent contacts with the British Communists help to enlighten us. . . . Indeed, I cannot recall any assistance from the British CP during our formative period. If anything, it was the other way in the form of information about our struggles for their publications."[72]

On the other hand, Manley was the beneficiary of multiple contacts in the United States, a form of largesse that was the real equivalent of "Washington Gold." When Manley arrived in New York City on one of his frequent trips, NAACP leader "Walter White, a close personal friend of Manley," was present.[73] The NAACP, which had purged the left in its own ranks, contributed financially to Manley and the PNP.[74] Manley had good contacts among the Jamaican expatriate community in New York City, particularly those of means within the "American West Indian Association." On a memorable 1951 visit, to insure a good attendance guests were informed that "the Robinson-La Motta fight will be televised before Dr. Manley speaks."[75]

Washington was not altogether pleased about Manley's U.S. contacts. When he sought to visit with Smith's old friend from Harlem, Congressman Adam Clayton Powell, Jr., "Rockwood Foster of the State Department . . . appeared to think that your programme was too crowded to permit of such a visit." Foster had been "asked" about this visit "on three occasions."[76]

Yet such temporary setbacks did not wreck Manley's support among the North Atlantic powers. The U.S. writer Paul Blanshard, known to be close to influential circles in Washington, was on a friendly first-name basis with "Norman" and his spouse, "Edna."[77] When Manley tried to forge a Caribbean Labour Party in 1956, the British Labour Party "promised us 5000 [pounds] for the first three years," "and that would be an enormous help," Manley confided to Eric Williams of Trinidad in a gross understatement.[78] In fact, though the Communists had a reputation for receiving monetary help from abroad, Manley exceeded them in that regard.[79] Furthermore, seeing what had happened to Smith in the United States, other Jamaicans understood what might await them if they did not toe the prevailing line. Hence, Manley's closeness to North Americans probably helped pull Jamaican politics further to the right, his pretensions toward "democratic socialism" notwithstanding.

Thus, when W. A. Domingo, a leading Jamaican progressive, visited his homeland from his residence in New York City in 1941 he was not as warmly greeted as Manley during his visits to Manhattan. He was "removed from the ship in which he was coming to Jamaica and placed in an Internment Camp," and "detained and imprisoned on a detention order which alleges that he may conduct himself in a manner prejudicial to public safety" because of his notoriety as an activist.[80] Domingo's detention complicated his ability to get a "visa for return to the United States." Domingo confirmed that "Jamaican immigrants to the United States are frequently questioned by immigration authorities at Miami and are warned not to have any connection" with those considered progressive.[81] Yet Domingo was far from being reflexively opposed to London. Indeed, he thought that his "frequent public advocacy of the British cause in the war caused me to be denounced as 'a

British apologist' in a pamphlet published by the Communist Party of the United States."[82]

The different approaches of London and Washington were exposed when the latter began to lionize the NAACP and the former to oppose it. His Majesty's Consul General in New York reported on a talk he had with A. M. Wendell Malliet, a "British West Indian." The diplomat seemed to agree with Malliet's "friends" who "have not always been in agreement with the methods employed by the NAACP and recently stated that colonials in the West Indies, Africa and other parts of the non-white world should be very careful in dealing with the NAACP."[83] London was highly suspicious of any who questioned its colonial domination while Washington felt that ending this "imperial preference" was a precondition to its economic advance in the region. The United States could therefore be more forthcoming toward Norman Manley than the United Kingdom. Thus, London carefully monitored Manley's 1946 visit to the United States, the purpose of which, it thought, was "to raise money, which may well have been for the purpose of providing funds for strikes which have now been called." Manley, London feared, had "made contact with Communist elements during these visits. Members of the PNP have also visited Trinidad in recent months and in view of the strikes in essential services which have recently occurred there, it may well be that the strikes in both colonies have the backing of Communist controlled organizations in the USA."[84] In this case, London's apprehensions about "Communist" influence on Manley may have been an ironic proxy for its fears of U.S. influence upon him.

Not that the United States embraced the Jamaican left—to the contrary. There is no evidence that Washington was pleased when labor unrest erupted on the island in the 1930s. The claim that "Communists," even those from Cuba, were "responsible" for the "riot," accorded with Washington's worldview.[85] Nor was there any evidence that the United States dissented when "the Left Book Club . . . started in 1939 by Richard Hart," an early Marxist group tied to "Frank Hill's printery in Temple Lane," was nicknamed as the "Kremlin."[86]

There is little doubt that London was frightened of Manley, particularly after the labor unrest of the 1930s, and looked to Bustamante as a savior. A U.S. diplomat acknowledged that London consciously backed Bustamante against Manley during the war "and even provided him with ample coupons for rationed gasoline to make it possible for him to tour the country in a campaign against" Manley's party. "It was at this same time," the U.S. official reported, "that the wealthy merchants of Kingston, likewise deciding that Bustamante was the lesser evil, began to pour money into the JLP [Bustamante's party] campaign coffers."[87] The U.S. analyst Paul Blanshard notes that "the whites of Jamaica were alarmed by Bustamante's growth in power, but they were also gratified by his political views," for they feared the mild socialism of Manley. "The Bustamante-white alliance," he observes, "was described by its opponents as essentially fascist in character." Washington had vital interests in the region too. "Although there [were] very few Americans living in Jamaica as permanent residents, American influence [was] substantial for several reasons. At Fort Simonds, west of Kingston, is one of the great air bases of the region. . . . At Goat Island is the nucleus of a strong American naval base."[88]

With his light skin, flowing white mane, and bombastic style, Bustamante was both a demagogue and a reliable defender of British and U.S. imperial interests. He claimed to have been of Spanish origin and to have fought with Spain, but Michael Manley, Norman's son, avers that "it is a matter of record that as of 1938 he had not crossed the Atlantic and certainly had never been to Spain." Fond of alcohol, Michael Manley recalls a meeting at which Bustamante "served an extremely pleasant champagne at ten in the morning."[89] Esther Chapman recalled that "every morning at eleven o'clock" he "was in the habit of taking a magnum of champagne." He was "in the habit of wearing a Spanish cloak which he would fling around his shoulders with all the air of a grand Señor." He was "at his best when dominating simple people" but "abstract discussions on political and social principles are not exactly in his line." While watching a music concert he became "enthralled by the conductor. . . . Perhaps his ancient dreams of dictatorship were echoed in this spectacle of perfect discipline, control and mastery."[90]

Try as she might Lady Gladys Bustamante could not avoid revealing an unflattering picture of her late spouse in her memoir. When she was in London in 1953 for the coronation of the Queen, an "Englishman said to Mr. Bustamante" about her, "What a beautiful African girl that is." "The Chief was not amused" by this reference to her dark skin. Similarly, when they visited Barcelona in 1957, Bustamante—who bragged about his former stay in Spain—seemed strangely unfamiliar with the Iberian peninsula. "He tried, but could not find some of the old familiar places because the massive damage done by bombing during the

Spanish Civil War had turned the place upside down," she wrote lamely.[91]

Though supportive at the time, the Jamaican police officer, David Godfrey, also paints a disturbing portrait of the man known as "Busta." Yes, he was "flamboyant. He was very tall, well over six feet," and charismatic. Yet when he met with him, inevitably his "ever prepared" aide "entered bearing more Red Stripe" beer, "by then [his] third or fourth of the morning. Busta waved the glasses away impatiently. 'Miss Longbridge,' he intoned, 'bring [me] the cases, not bottles.'"[92] The fiery Bustamante's oratory was frequently lubricated—and driven—by liquid spirits.

This man, who claimed to have led Jamaica to independence in 1962 had earlier announced, "Self government means slavery."[93] In 1938 he proclaimed, "I am very glad we are a colony of Great Britain." The "overwhelming majority of his followers were illiterate, superstitious and deeply religious. They had learned to depend on others to make decisions for them and to respect the authority of those in command." In 1945 the union he initiated and that carried his name had 46,538 members. This figure rose to 64,859 by 1951. Correspondingly, Manley's trade union bloc rose from 4,050 in 1949 to 23,312 by the 1950s.[94]

Bustamante simply took advantage of the political disorder brought on by colonialism. Marcus Garvey—whose importance on the island may be understood by the fact that his picture graces the national currency—said in 1930, "I am forced to conclude that Jamaica is indeed an ignorant community; it is limited in intelligence, narrow in its intellectual concepts, almost to the point where one can honestly say that the country is ridiculous." Garvey knew of what he spoke, since his party was allied with the United Fruit Company. But Garvey also served as chair of the "Jamaica Workers and Labourers Association" alongside "S.M. De Leon, secretary. De Leon, who had been 'one of the first West Indians to go to Moscow for training in the twenties' . . . [then] became a Garveyite." Garvey's newspaper printed articles by Smith's Communist comrades such as James Ford and displayed a "sympathetic attitude" toward Moscow. "They have stirred India and are now stirring Africa," he said. Though accepting of Communists, "the cult of Ras Tafari in its most fundamental form was not accepted, however, by the majority of Jamaican Garveyites."[95]

The Cold War was a godsend for Bustamante, just as it proved to be poison for Smith. Trevor Munroe writes that from the 1930s forward, a

"Communist faction with significant influence over the masses" developed. But "the years 1950–52"—the period of Smith's arrival—marked the beginning of the end of this influence."[96] This was a regional trend. When Cheddi Jagan of Guyana backed Richard Hart "against efforts" to "oust him from the Caribbean Labour Congress," an important regional formation, it was a "major factor" in a "strained relationship" between Hart-Smith and Jagan on the one hand, the United States on the other.[97]

Norman Manley, Bustamante's antagonist, also had a checkered background. His mother, a "near-white woman . . . lost all her friends when she married a Negro." Manley escaped to the United Kingdom in 1914 and discovered that "it was impossible to [be] in England and not be aware of the problem of colour. You were immediately aware in a thousand ways that you belonged elsewhere but not there." At Oxford, the sensitive Manley "detected an anti-Indian sentiment which became even more marked and obvious after the [Great] War." Returning to Jamaica and establishing a formidable reputation as a lawyer, Manley sensed that by the late 1930s "the Garvey Movement was a quite negligible factor in Jamaican life," as labor was eclipsing "race" as an organizing principle. Manley, who was actively involved in these epochal events, was struck by the "strong tendency . . . among the workers . . . to resort to violence under provocation and to resist by violence any tendency among themselves to make strong workers' action futile. Quite the most remarkable feature in the expansion of trade union activity in Jamaica has been the rapid acceptance of the idea that you do not break strikes by resort to the large and increasing number of workers who are unemployed."[98]

Smith was caught between these two larger-than-life symbols of his homeland—the demagogic Bustamante and the vacillating Manley. Smith's options were becoming ever more limited. Flying from Europe to the Caribbean via New York could mean detention in Ellis Island, with no guarantee that he could gain entry anywhere in the Caribbean other than Jamaica. He assumed that he could draw a stipend from the WFTU if he chose to reside in Jamaica. This sealed the deal: he decided to live permanently in Jamaica.

When he arrived on the island in 1952, he was impressed. As Richard Hart recounts it, "We had set up this People's Educational Organization which was to be a Marxist educational organization and was going to sponsor the formation of a bookshop, distribution of literature, educational lectures and so on." Smith was welcomed as "this new, very forceful character."[99] But, just as Smith had decided to settle down in Jamaica—after his plans of organizing for the WFTU in the region had been thwarted—he found himself in the midst of a major agitation about Communists. Unlike Richard Hart, who could argue credibly that he was not a member of a Communist Party, Smith was a flesh-and-blood, avowed Marxist-Leninist of the card-carrying variety.

Perhaps drawing a lesson from his U.S. experience, where his personal escapades had been used against him politically, Smith, in his mid-50s by now, settled down to a life of domesticity. He married Sonia Jackson, a woman many years his junior, and ultimately fathered four children (who succeeded his daughter Stephanie from his first marriage): Margaret, Pauline Francis, Ferdinand Pat (named after his comrade William Patterson) and Stalinova (named after Josef Stalin).[100]

Yet these domestic developments were to unfold slowly over the years. During the summer of 1952, writing from the home of "Mrs. Hazel Foster" at 24 North Street in Kingston, Smith told Patterson, "With my running around from place to place so fast . . . I needed some relaxation and nowhere is better for that than in [this] warm climate! I have been here since July 27th and expect to be around for at least three more months. This should be long enough for me to get fit. . . . It would do you good if you could get some of this tropical heat into your bloodstream once in a while." Already he was experiencing one of the downsides of residing on a small island, lamenting, "there is a kind of blackout of progressive news out this way, both local and foreign, so I am without info. . . . Would like, much, to get news of what is cooking your way." He was a vagabond too, which was not conducive to relaxation and reflection: "I am not living at the above address," he said, "since I am going from place to place."[101]

Smith's meandering journey to the Caribbean was a mirror image of what happened to his political project in Jamaica. The left forces he aligned himself with were chased from pillar to post as a Red Scare—smaller in scale but every bit as potent as that he had experienced in the United States—got under way. It had its origins in the split in the Jamaican labor movement, personified by Bustamante, the conservative, and Manley, the Social Democrat. The latter was allied with the so-called "4 Hs": Richard Hart of the Caribbean Labour Congress, Arthur Henry, organizer of the railway workers, Ken Hill, organizer of postal and telegraph workers, and Frank Hill, who worked in various spheres.

All formed the left wing of Manley's political party, the PNP. Beginning in 1946 they organized a Trades Union Congress that challenged Bustamante's federation. In 1949, under relentless pressure from the right, Manley and his allies forced the TUC to withdraw from Smith's WFTU. As Smith was settling down in Jamaica, these political tensions were about to explode, as Manley—still dissatisfied with the direction of the TUC—tried to organize his own National Workers Union and Ken Hill began to wilt under the pressure. Backed by the "Caribbean regional leadership" of the International Confederation of Free Trade Unions, the nemesis of the WFTU, he blocked Hart's effort to bring the TUC back into the WFTU's fold. In a preview of the political violence that was to rock the island two decades later, "there was a physical clash of opposing forces as a result of which Hart and other progressives were prosecuted . . . and credentials of the progressive delegates were disallowed." Then there was yet another split, as Hart's ouster led to the founding of the Jamaica Federation of Trade Unions, which Smith ultimately headed. Though the JFTU was perpetually scorned for receiving funds from Vienna—and presumably Moscow—Ken Hill, who was Catholic, received a healthy "subsidy" from the International Christian Federation of Unions.[102]

This internecine squabbling on the left was propelled by the challenge posed by Bustamante. As Norman Manley put it in 1947, "Busta . . . is driven to campaigning black against brown and black against white in the most vicious way."[103] Though both were light-skinned, for some reason "Busta" was perceived as the champion of the "blacks," while Manley was perceived as the leader of the lighter-skinned "browns." This was a conflict that was to rage throughout Smith's tenure in Jamaica. Being so primordial and basic and so rooted in economic inequality, it proved to be a difficult problem to solve. It also impelled other ethnic conflicts on the island. As Busta was fanning the flames of resentment, Manley was being told by a "Party worker" that "it was a shame 'that when we are fed we are fed by the Chinese and when we are clothed we are clothed by the Syrian.'" Manley wanted "this matter brought to the notice of the [Party] Executive" for it was "worse than ever to find that supposedly responsible party people are stirring up a type of race talk that is absolutely contrary to party policy."[104] Manley had reason to sound an alarm for, as he himself noticed, "Busta" and "his minions are waging a bitter race campaign throughout Kingston. Day by day they are inciting violence on the issue of black against brown. It is a miracle or sign of the decline of his strength that race riots have not already eventuated."[105]

The disorder in the streets was reflected in similar disarray in the PNP. Manley was bitter about the "protracted campaign of the *Gleaner* against the Party with an incessant charge of Communism."[106] The "Colonial Office," he announced, "has decided to back Bustamante," though they had already supported him so much that "they can't do more to give more backing now than they have steadily done" over the years.[107]

Norman Manley was torn. When his son arrived on the island after study abroad, he was confronted by this bitter, contentious debate. "Night after night," said Michael Manley, "discussions would take place at my father's home. . . . Many hours of hearings were conducted." Years later, he still recalled the "wrenching, traumatic scene" that led to the expulsion of Richard Hart and others deemed too far to the left.[108] Manley and his party could not withstand the pressure: they surrendered to the anticommunists in a replay of what had befallen Smith in the NMU.

As an official internal investigation of the controversy explained, "some element of the Party had been engaged in teaching Communist doctrines." TUC leaders were also said to be involved. There was "instruction and training of persons in the Party and TUC to follow and carry out the Communist policy" and a "discrediting of the PNP and its socialist policy in furtherance of Communist doctrines." Of course, "the Party . . . always recognized that it is possible and indeed some think necessary to be a Marxist in the broad sense of that term and to be a democratic socialist at the same time," though it had to distinguish itself from the USSR and the Soviet Communist Party.

Though just settling in, Smith found himself at the heart of this controversy. A 9 November 1951 letter from Austria written by Smith and addressed to Ken Hill was treated as damning evidence. "Dear Brother Hill," said the note, "you have received contribution in the sum of five hundred pounds made by the Secretariat of the WFTU to the TUC fund in aid of workers who have been victims of the recent hurricane in your country." It was tragic that this poor island of Jamaica was locked in dispute about a donation to victims of a natural disaster. Why was there "retention of funds coming from that source," the PNP asked sharply. It objected to the TUC getting donations from Smith's WFTU "or from any communist country," though it was willing to accept "contributions" from "well known English or American trade unions with one or two contributions from unions in the Dominion or Canada and Australia." The PNP, it said, "must take note of the fact that there are loyal Party members who genuinely fear that the Left will eradicate them if and when they are strong enough to do it." So in order to forestall this unlikely event, the left must be purged. The party had to be weakened in order to save it.[109] Manley was reflecting party sentiment when he wrote to F. L. Walcott of the Barbados Workers Union that he was in mortal combat with "extreme left-wing elements of the party including a lot of half-baked young Communists."[110]

Almost half a century after he was purged from the PNP, Richard Hart was "re-admitted." He acknowledged then that his ouster and that of his cohorts "came at a time when Jamaican independence hero Norman Washington Manley, the party's founder wanted desperately to placate the island's then colonial ruler, Britain, and the United States."[111] The United States was skeptical of Manley's articulation of "democratic socialism," which sounded strangely suspicious to Washington. Manley's grandson Douglas conceded about the same time that his father Michael Manley had felt that the purges were a "great mistake."[112]

George Woodcock, a British union official, confided that the expulsions had created one "hell of a mess."[113] Woodcock felt that "so much energy" had been "dissipated on these activities that there is nothing much done, or attempted to increase the living standards of the people."[114] Trevor Munroe, the leading Jamaican intellectual, concluded that after the purge Manley's forces "lost its most active organizers. . . . Working class organization fell into disarray and the dominance of middle class moderation in the councils of the party was firmly established."[115] The same fate had befallen black America at the same time and for similar reasons, Smith being a factor in both cases. Certainly, the ouster of those to Norman and Michael Manley's left made Michael Manley more vulnerable when he sought as prime minister to move aggressively against transnational corporations in the 1970s. On the other hand, these purges probably strengthened London's and Washington's position in Jamaica.

Richard Hart felt that he and others in the left were railroaded and ousted through sham and corrupt tactics. At a pivotal meeting, "a number of persons were recognized by the President as delegates who were not elected," while "a number of branches favourable to the 'Keep Left' view-point were wrongly informed as to the number of delegates they were entitled to send." The specter of violence also dominated Jamaican politics. "A 'strong arm' group was stationed at the outer gate of the conference hall," Hart said, the memories still fresh in his mind. "Delegates and observers favourable to the 'Keep Left' viewpoint were prevented from entering and in three cases had their credentials snatched from them. . . . The conference room was packed with political supporters of the President from West Kingston, most of whom were not members . . . at all. . . . When the President rejected my point of order concerning the illegal composition of the conference, I and a number of the delegates withdrew." Once evicted, Hart and his comrades saw no alternative to forming a "new trade union movement" and making a "request [to] Mr. Ferdinand Smith" to head it.[116]

Smith and Hart suffered another devastating setback when Frank and Ken Hill, fellow victims of the purges engineered by Manley, in turn ousted Smith and Hart. As Hart later recalled, "Delegates and observers known to be opposed to the Hills' policy were intimidated at the outer gate of the Conference Hall by a group of paid gangsters, one of whom had a knife and one a cow-cod and other bottles and sticks. Credentials were snatched away from some persons who were pushed back into the street." "During the scuffle Richard Hart received a slight cut on the arm." An outraged Smith declared, "What happened today should open the workers' eyes. We now have to take the struggle to the streets, fields, villages and to work doubly hard as the vanguard of the progressive element. . . . We should have a union [movement] now, not an organizing committee. But the form should be federal. There should be unions based on industries federated to the central body."[117]

The group led by Smith quickly made an impression on Washington. A "confidential" dispatch from the U.S. consulate in Kingston noted that "the authorities felt until recently that the Communist threat as such was negligible." "In recent months, however, and more especially since the arrival from Vienna of [Smith] . . . there has been noted by the authorities a much intensified Communist effort to penetrate trade unionism and other activities." The movement led by Hart and Smith had "500 active registered members," the consulate reported in late 1952. "The authorities look upon Smith as a keen, thoroughly doctrinaire Communist whose presence has inspired the sudden surge of Communist activity. The development is looked on seriously," for "the Communist element [is] deserving of serious attention."[118]

London was similarly worried. The colonial governor noted that Smith and Hart were "hard at work," "fomenting trouble." He believed there was "continued evidence of their liaison with Chinese . . . and attempts to associate Chinese with Jamaican Communists." Reflecting on their internationalism, he noted that "some use was made by them of the situation in Kenya. Smith, at a street meeting organized by the CLC, declared that the Governor, as representative of the British regime, was the real enemy, and not Bustamante, as some might suppose."[119] "Hart, in association with [Smith] is gathering round him an increasing number of Communists and fellow travellers. . . . Reports have been received that a number of . . . the professional class . . . not previously known to have [had] any association with communism has attended private meetings."[120]

Worried diplomats and bureaucrats were not the only ones transfixed by the specter of communism in tiny Jamaica. Vere John, writing in a local paper, demanded that Communists in the region be banned. "I think it is high time for Government to keep out of this country certain Communist literature," specifically that from the WFTU. "I think the PEO Library at 64 Barry Street with its Communist literature and hung pictures of Lenin and Butcher Stalin should be immediately closed by the police and all that inflammatory stuff burned—including the two pictures. . . . [There] should be a law making it punishable by imprisonment for anyone here to be in possession of any banned literature. Special attention should be paid to Chinese Communists in Jamaica," yet another reference to the fact that there was a sizable Chinese community on the island. "Ferdinand Smith has gone to Vienna to soak up more Red poison and he should be notified by Government that he will not be allowed to re-enter Jamaica, birth or no birth. Let Moscow welcome him—he has forfeited the right to be a citizen." And deport Hart while you are at it, John concluded.[121]

Barred from the United States and the surrounding islands and under constant surveillance, Smith had to endure the added indignity of having his WFTU literature "banned, so afraid are the imperialist governments," said Jack Woddis, "of the helpful advice which these publications can give to colonial workers."[122] The larger problem for Smith was that this split in labor and the concomitant Red Scare was not just a pan-Caribbean matter, it was a global question.[123] But on a small island like Jamaica which reflexively tended to mirror what was perceived to be popular in the metropole, Smith may have been at a greater disadvantage than he had been during his last difficult years in the United States.

Thus, Bustamante seemed to exceed even his U.S. counterparts in proclaiming his fierce hatred of communism. "I am not a Communist," he assured the few who might have thought otherwise. "I cannot divide completely. If I have one pair of shoes," he said with his own unique logic, "I cannot give you one and keep one."[124] But as Smith began to spend what would be the last decade of his life in Kingston, Jamaica, he hoped that not everyone on the island shared Bustamante's logic. As a jailed cleric observed in a novel by the leading Jamaican writer Roger Mais, "Why do you think Communism grows and thrives among the underprivileged people? . . . We are all fools. We are smug and satisfied, and let the Communists beat us to it everytime."[125]

11

On the Beach

JAMAICA WAS AN ISLAND of untold riches filled to the brim with poor people. Smith's mission was to try to alter this imbalance and improve the lives of those who continued to live in dank hovels and thatched huts without paved roads, sidewalks, or running water. Unfortunately the anticommunist bogey foiled his best-laid plans.

George Padmore, the Trinidadian activist and writer, once said that "the West Indies could briefly be described as the sugar section of British imperialism." In Kingston there was a "government of sugar for sugar by sugar."[1] This was an exaggeration to which the banana and coffee planters would have objected. Bananas, for example, "accounted for 55% of the values of domestic exports" in 1937, "while sugar accounted for 18%."[2] In later years, the tourist industry would become sizable, while the growing importance of aluminum meant that bauxite had an increasing share of exports.[3] Nevertheless, the fact that London could buy Jamaican sugar at 32 pounds per ton—France, for example, paid 60 pounds per ton—shows how profitable this industry was for the empire.[4] The wider point was that like many colonized nations, Jamaica was dependent on raw materials, whose prices could be kept low in the absence of bodies like the Organization of Petroleum Exporting Countries (OPEC). Jamaica was also trapped in an iniquitous circle since the finished goods they had to purchase—tractors, autos, televisions, and the like—continued to rise in price. As a result it was under a crushing debt burden that fell disproportionately hard on those at the bottom of the food chain, such as sugar workers.

The workers that kept Jamaica's economic engine running earned a pittance. Even before Ferdinand Smith arrived on the scene, a number of Jamaicans had objected strongly to this state of affairs. Hugh Buchanan, "general secretary" of the sugar workers union and a "longtime Marxist . . . had attended a meeting of the Communist International held in Hamburg in the early 1930s" and "had made a good impression among the comrades in Hamburg as a promising torch-bearer in the English-speaking Caribbean."[5] Now the authorities detected in Smith's arrival a revival of the radical left, particularly among sugar workers.

There was an "expanding Communist movement in Jamaica," according to U.S. authorities. "Eighteen months ago, the Communist movement in Jamaica was of no serious concern to constituted authority. Evidence points clearly to an important intensification in the movement in Jamaica and apparently in the Caribbean area." "The 'shifting of gears' is associated with the arrival of competent Communist leaders from Europe in the Spring of 1952." Smith, who had bested the best the United States had to offer could hardly be matched in Jamaica. "The Communist movement in Jamaica moved from the loose and 'passive' stage into a dynamic period shortly after the return to Jamaica . . . of [Smith] from Vienna." He was "able, intelligent" and a "thoroughly doctrinaire Communist with a keen understanding of Communist organizational techniques" with an "aggressive spirit." He was "well supplied with funds" and was in a "furious mood" after he was "taken to Ellis Island" and "returned to Jamaica" while in transit on a recent flight. Smith had proved to be a force for unity. The "current efforts, presumably led by Smith, to effect a rapprochement of local Communist groups with Jamaican Chinese Communist elements are meeting with far better success than has been thought possible," while "professional persons and other higher-class intellectual types are coming more into the open in expressing Communist sympathies." Thus, "the pan-Caribbean movement is paralleling the local change of pace" and "deserves the close attention of the U.S.," not least since the "possibility that the important bauxite reserves under exploitation by North American companies may ultimately be placed in jeopardy."[6]

The authorities' dismay about Smith's arrival increased when the Communist, Cheddi Jagan, seemed on the verge of coming to power in 1953 in the nation that was to become Guyana. The U.S. authorities thought Georgetown would "now lift the ban in British Guiana on entry of" Smith and Hart and "will now probably be [the] meeting ground of Communist personalities and [the] center of activities."[7] Already, a U.S. labor official was linking "Communist plots in Brazil and British Guiana." The U.S. Consulate thought that such a linkage "might be considered out of place at a union meeting in Jamaica" but was justified, given that Smith's union federation was "growing" and "taking hold in Jamaican country parishes." This was a "discomfiting observation."[8] In fact, Washington thought that "Jamaican leftists are linked with the international Communist movement to a greater degree than those in British Guiana" because of Smith's tenure in Eastern Europe. The fact that Smith was "an adviser . . . in British Guiana" only increased the worry in Washington.[9]

Smith had assumed the image of the "evil genius" of global communism "right in the heart of [the] city of Kingston," for there the "most dangerous organization in Jamaica lurks." Accompanying this hyperbolic article in a local newspaper was an unflattering picture of Smith, "the brain"—a "man with cold, steel-like nerves and a brain that is as shrewd and calculating as the best in Jamaica." In his "room on Barry Street, two long benches and a solid cheap table with a little book case are the only furniture." There Smith worked in this "unpretentious and seeming harmless atmosphere . . . but hanging on the walls are the scheming, impassive and relentless countenances of foreign Communist leaders and agitators." Worse, Smith's union had a "membership of 10,000 sugar workers in the island."[10]

Jamaica was both titillated and intrigued by the presence of a bona fide Communist celebrity, a man who had arguably been the most powerful Red and most powerful Negro in the United States. Interest was reflected in press coverage of him, which inevitably drove some closer to him even when the articles were critical. Smith was termed one of "Freedom's Assassins," one of the "bringers of darkness [who] claim to be bearers of light." Smith's "peaceful, Jersey-bull-like manner camoflagues smouldering volcanic resentments against modern society's constituency." Fortunately, the colonial government "shadows him around the clock." Despite this negative press, not everyone was displeased about his arrival. The paper *Spotlight* observed that "some Jamaicans, without being disloyal or favouring Communism, think it is good for Communism to be around somewhere if it can be controlled. They see Communism as society's conscience, as a sword of Damocles ready to fall if conscience becomes anesthetized into indifference. . . . They argue, with some justification, that until Communism became a world threat, the ruling powers merely used their colonies as hewers of wood and drawers of water, taking all and giving back nothing."

But now, with Smith's arrival, things were changing. "Under the scraggly Red banner which flies over [his] headquarters at 64 Barry Street, a motley crew of mostly young people gathered . . . when a sad-faced giant of a Negro arrived in Jamaica." Crowds were a common occurrence. "Success had been small" previously but "Smith took over and revamped the strategy." He wanted to "win mass membership by forming new trade unions, infiltrate or capture existing ones in whole or part." Like a soccer coach assigning his best defender to shadow the other team's striker, the empire had brought in one of its "crack undercover agents" to confront Smith. The "Commies' Enemy No. 1" was Joseph Kealy. "Irish born," he had joined the Colonial Police Force at the age of sixteen and served in troubled parts of the world, including Egypt, Sudan, and Syria before being transferred to Jamaica. He was now the "well-tempered spearhead in Jamaica's anti-Communist war." Kealy said confidently, "British, American and Jamaican governments work closely in that connection with good results."[11]

Maybe. But if Smith was being neutralized, the press coverage he received gave no indication of it. "TIME magazine," said the *Spotlight*, "once described [Smith] as 'a devouring locust.' Why? Smith is a Communist. Not the garden variety type; but a top-level operator, rated and registered at Moscow." Appropriate measures were being taken, the *Spotlight* informed its readers, for he was "virtually a prisoner in Jamaica—few Caribbean countries will have him as [a] transit passenger. A big, heavy-set man with a sad, deep-lined face, he may be seen any day in Kingston. He moves quietly. His voice purrs or booms, depending on how intensely he feels on a subject. . . . [The authorities] know everything he does. They are amused, not alarmed."[12]

Perhaps. But in their confidential communiques the authorities were not reflecting the official optimism. For already the "number of Communist cells in Jamaica is increasing, especially in rural areas, naming Spanish Town, Race Course, Mandeville, Ocho Rios, Savanah-al-Mar [sic], Clarendon, Lucea, etc." The "attempt [to] form [a] cell at Montego Bay failed," though the "effectiveness of Communist propaganda is increasing, noticeably along [the] Kingston waterfront." How did this happen? How were Reds able to gain such a toehold on the island, particularly after the PNP and TUC were purged?

The fact that Smith's arrival coincided with this alleged Red revival was not seen as a coincidence. He was "reported to be in control of organized communism in [the] British Caribbean and to have ample funds from sources in Vienna." There "are now 500 Communists in Jamaica," said the U.S. consulate, "of which 200 are quite active."[13] They feared that both his funding and the number of Communists would increase, because Smith had "apparently . . . visited Bulgaria." "His activities will be observed," the consulate reported.[14] He was said to be planning to "take Jamaica workingmen to [a] WFTU meeting," abroad, that is "representatives of Jamaican seamen, longshoremen and fishermen."[15] The consulate thought this could only heighten radicalism on the island.

Smith did little to assuage the fears of the U.S. authorities. Sounding bitter, Smith asserted, "When the U.S. Department of Justice began to persecute me, many, many Americans looked back upon the war days when I assisted in keeping the war effort going; when my services were sought on government boards; when mayors appealed for my assistance to quell racial disturbances; when I toured the States broadcasting and lecturing to prevent race riots." But "today, at sixty years of age, I believe more confidently than ever in the ideals that made me a Communist. . . . Wherever working men are struggling, there you will find Ferdinand C. Smith."[16]

The authorities were probably less concerned about Smith's praise for communism than about his union organizing. Manley and Bustamante, the powerful duo of postwar Jamaica, had developed unions that were basically their lengthened shadows and vote getters for their political machines. At a 1954 meeting of SAWU—the Sugar and Agricultural Workers Union, the union Smith put together—someone asked what the "difference [was] between a trade union attached to a political party as against a union unattached to a political party." "Comrade Smith replied that the SAWU was a union unattached to a political party and was therefore distinct in its difference from other unions in Jamaica." As his friend and comrade Richard Hart, recalled, Smith "had revived a concept of what the structure of the trade union movement should be which had been abandoned by the TUC [Trade Union Congress] in 1948, when its separate affiliated unions had been merged into one general workers union like the BITU [Bustamante's federated unions]. He had also introduced a new concept with his advocacy that the workers in each industry should be united regardless of any differences of political beliefs or affiliations which they might have."[17]

The Sugar and Agricultural Workers Union, an affiliate of his Jamaican Federation of Trade Unions (JFTU), was formed in 1953. A "well attended meeting" of SAWU of "over 5000 workers . . . was described by local residents as 'the largest public meeting held here over the past two years.'" When SAWU was formally established on 26 September 1953 at the Magnet Theatre in May Pen, Clarendon, there were representatives from Frome Estate in Westmoreland, Worthy Park Estate, and Bybrook Estate in St. Catherine, Vere in Clarendon, Appleton Estate and Balaclava in St. Elizabeth, Logwood in Hanover and St. Thomas. Weeks later, the *Jamaica Times* reported that "Communist infiltration into the island's sugar industry, led [by] Ferdinand Smith . . . top international 'Red' Executive in the British Caribbean area, has moved from the insignificant stage. While the Bustamante Industrial Trade Union still commands overwhelming support among sugar workers and [Manley's] National Workers Union has minority following there . . . the newly formed Red-led Jamaica Federation of Trade Unions is gaining a toe hold in the industry at the expense of the TUC."[18]

One solid reason for the spectacular rise of the unions organized by Smith was his focus on issues beyond the workplace. Thus, he launched a campaign to strengthen the "local insurance and social security" system, with financing from the government and the employer class. The purpose of his most recent trip to Vienna was to gather ammunition for this battle, one of the first battles of his Jamaica Federation of Trade Unions, involving mass meetings, mass leafleting, and the like.[19]

Though Smith's travels within the Caribbean were circumscribed, London could not prevent his ideas from reaching these shores. In neighboring Trinidad and Tobago a campaign for social security was launched simultaneously with that in Jamaica, "the first of its kind in [the] country." There were also "unemployment demonstrations" held "as a means of stepping up the struggle for the Social Insurance and Social Security" system. Because the WFTU was involved, both nations were able to draw upon the expertise of "L. V. Soloviev" of the USSR— yet another reason for London to complain about how Smith's presence had opened the door to Soviet penetration of the Caribbean.[20]

But West Indians were not dependent on the Soviets for ideas, as Smith, who had been in charge of social measures for thousands of sailors, had plenty of his own. Based on his "personal investigations" and "on the contributions made to the local Social Security Conference, attended by some 200 people of all sections of the population," Smith determined that "the concept of social welfare" in Jamaica was "that of charity and not of right." "There is no provision whatsoever for . . . old age pensions," to cite one example. "In this respect Jamaica is even behind Barbados, Trinidad and Guiana." "Under exceptional circumstances of destitution arising from drought, epidemic disease or such like causes the Parochial Board of any parish . . . 'may afford temporary relief.' . . . But it must be borne in mind that even this relief is limited by the inadequate provision of funds by the government for distribution in this way."

Smith focused on the inadequacies of the system and pointed to the areas in which reforms were necessary. "There is no legislative provision for any benefit during illness or disability except in the case of work injuries." "Limited numbers of workers have subscribed to Benevolent societies whereby out of their own meager savings they provide for themselves," and "a similar service through the trade unions is also in operation." Although there "was legislation for compensation for injuries suffered in the course of employment in Jamaica" it was "totally inadequate." There was "no provision in Jamaica [for] assistance to women who are unable to work while they are pregnant or in the period immediately following childbirth." As of 1949, Smith said, "there were 369,000 children between the ages of 4 and 15 or 264,000 between the ages of 7 and 15 but there was only accommodation for 137,000 children in schools. The situation is relatively the same today." Actually, it was getting worse. "When the [British] Prime Minister came to Jamaica recently, a young member of the war veteran's organization, who, in spite of the promises made during the war, lived in utmost misery, tried to speak to the Minister, but he was arrested by the police. The second time he succeeded but was again arrested. This incident should have opened Churchill's eyes but he did not want to bother. . . . The situation was so serious that a law has been proposed to prohibit any demonstrators to come within 500 yards of parliament."[21]

It was becoming difficult to dismiss Smith as a Red provocateur when all he was doing was fighting for basic provisions for the elderly, disabled and pregnant women, and the unemployed. Initially, London thought that Bustamante, the titular leader of the nation, was not doing enough to confront this new "threat." Bustamante "was not greatly concerned about the activities" of Smith and Hart, said the Colonial Office, "as long as their efforts were directed to establishing the Peoples Educational Organization." But given the "attempt by . . . Communists to obtain trade union support amongst sugar workers" he should be on high alert. The Colonial Governor was "reluctant" to bar Reds—of course, Washington had no such qualms—but "the danger of the spread of Communist influence is real" and "if extreme action is to be taken . . .

better to do it now."[22] Sounding urgent, the Colonial Office asserted that "for nearly 3 years we have been pressing Jamaica to get out of the 'it can't happen here' frame of mind," for "unless [there is] a proper Emergency Powers Ordinance [Jamaica] will be almost powerless to deal with militant communism."[23]

London's response was to encourage the newly formed International Confederation of Free Trade Unions—ICFTU—as a "counter" to Smith's WFTU. But the ICFTU had the temerity to speak of "anti-colonialism." Although the British trade unions were a "moderating influence," it was to the ICFTU that the Colonial Office looked for help. It had to be treated gingerly, as opposition to it by the Jamaican government could "only increase" the "anti-colonial bias of that body and do more harm than good."[24]

U.S. diplomats concurred with this analysis. "Communism," they proclaimed, "has been slowly and methodically setting in Jamaica the past year and has now reached the point where it cannot be safely ignored." "Rather than let the situation get out of hand in Jamaica, it appears desirable to outlaw communism outright."[25] Smith's JFTU was able to provide strike pay, a major difference between it and other union federations. "JFTU tactics making headway," said a U.S. analyst, as Smith and Hart were "now spending entire time travelling in [the] sugar producing area."[26] The JFTU, the U.S. analyst reported, agreeing with the Colonial Office, "is attracting [a] following to much larger extent than authorities expected, partly due to neglect by Chief Minister Bustamante of sugar workers in his own constituency, Parish of Clarendon."[27]

These diplomats' assessment was accurate. Smith was pushing to "reunite the 'left' now," arguing for a "joint conference of the members and supporters" of the forces grouped around Manley and himself.[28] Hart reported that on a "recent visit to Sav-la-mar," Smith said that "several persons influential on [the] waterfront . . . report that the workers are hostile" to the Bustamante forces. A "private meeting [with Smith] has been requested by influential persons, with a view to discussing the possibility of our organizing the workers there."[29]

Smith was also reaching beyond Jamaica to his old haunts in Cuba. As Fidel Castro's forces were electrifying the nation with their audacious guerilla attacks, Smith was meeting with a delegation from Cuba. Since the "principal industry of both countries is sugar," it was necessary to coordinate bargaining strategies and the like; they pledged to supply each other with "details of the wages, hours of work and conditions of work," the price of sugar, and so on.[30]

Bustamante did not need much prodding to take action. Soon he was trying to impose legislation that even the Colonial Office found draconian.[31] In an abrupt turnabout, he was outraged with what he considered London's soft line against the Reds.[32] "This beautiful and sunny island needs help to rescue it from Communism," he declared.[33] Soon the U.S. Consulate was reporting that Bustamante "advocates outlawing communism" and "shows quite a different understanding from a bare two months ago when he stated, 'the few Communists around— mean nothing.'"[34] Bustamante moved quickly to ban "eight Communist publications."[35] Soon Smith began to grumble about tampering with his mail.[36] Bustamante pressured the Colonial Office to outlaw communism altogether—whatever that meant—but the British were reluctant to deploy what they called "fascist methods," although they agreed that it was "important to strangle communism in Jamaica in this early stage rather than wait until it has got a hold." "Police searches of Ferdinand Smith's house and of his union HQ" went forward as London observed that "U.S. interest in these events is to be noted."[37] Soon the press was ablaze with stories of the "raid on Jamaica Communist chief" and the important "documents seized."[38]

"American security forces are keeping a strict watch on the growth of Communists in Jamaica," the *Yorkshire Observer* reported.[39] Though Britain was ostensibly the colonial power in Jamaica, Washington was playing an increasing role in Jamaican politics. It was naturally dismayed to see that Ferdinand Smith, the man it had chased from U.S. shores, had not been driven into political oblivion. Writing in late 1953 from 40 Longston Road in Vineyard Town, Kingston—a working-class community—Smith sounded far from discouraged by his ejection from the United States. "The fight is on, my friend," he crowed, "and we need the help of all those we can call on. Busta, sensing the will of the workers to throw him overboard, is trying to use the power of government to hold on to the trade union movement, from which he derives his real power." He thought Bustamante was on the defensive, while he, Smith, was on the offensive, moving forward. "Despite the fact that we have the government, employers, and the labor fakers arrayed against us, the workers are in a fighting mood." The "sugar season is just about getting started" and "if [the workers] are hungry when they are working, what do you imagine they are like when there is no work?" Smith added, "No matter how bleak I paint the picture, I couldn't paint it as realistically as it really is!" "Here is a government openly using its power to suppress a union which is the creation of the workers themselves, in support of a union which [is] the creature of the employers." The political climate on the island was becoming so repressive that Smith told his correspondent, "Don't use my name or put your address on the envelope."[40]

Although, looking back David Godfrey, a leading member of the Jamaican Constabularly, was dismissive of Smith's forces, his own words are indicative of the impact of the former sailor and the left in general. When Godfrey began in 1950 the police force had "fourteen staff" but "when he was transferred ten years later, there [were] over sixty police at various ranks and the Force had been completely Jamaicanized." One reason was that "serious riots occurred with regrettable frequency," many of them labor related—a situation not helped by the fact that "the local constabulary in those days were pro-JLP," that is, pro-Bustatmante—"for the most part." Godfrey made no connection between this fact and what he termed the "small and ineffectual Communist Party in Jamaica." Smith, he recalled, "eventually managed to establish two feeble organizations," though "the Jamaica comrades never presented a serious security problem." The "police Special Branch had an intelligence-collecting and collation function" that targeted Smith's "ineffectual" band with one of the "most sophisticated technical operation[s] ever mounted in Jamaica up to then." The Catholic Church was co-opted for this operation. The police also maintained "deep cover informants" within Smith's ranks. Smith was also hampered by the fact that "the Jamaican telephone system was notoriously unreliable in the country parts," as even "the officers had to speak quite loudly to each other while the phones alternated between gradual fades and loud static." This facilitated bugging.[41]

Smith was not overstating the veil of repression that had descended on Jamaica. He forwarded to his comrades in the United States an article that claimed that the island was the "missing link in the red chain." In it Victor Riesel, the veteran U.S.-based Red-hunter, spoke of a concerted Communist crusade to seize control of trade unions "from Iceland to South America (through the WFTU)" with Jamaica being the key link and Smith being the key man. "The Communist drive is directed by the ex-New Yorker Ferdinand Smith," who from Jamaica was "directing the WFTU activities throughout the

Caribbean area." "Once let [Smith] obtain a stranglehold on these . . . lifelines of Jamaica's existence, and not only trade unionism here but the country as a whole is doomed." He concluded, "I agree with Bustamante—STOP HIM NOW."[42]

Riesel was preaching to the choir, when it came to Bustamante and his backers in London. The Colonial Office was struggling to prevent a replay of what was occurring in British Guiana and what seemed to be happening in Trinidad & Tobago where "the Communist led unions . . . are established, efficient and strong. . . . One of our main objections [in] refusing to deal with Communist-led unions in Trinidad was that the policy just would not work. That objection does not hold in Jamaica," it was said confidently in early 1954, "where it is quite possible in practice to get along at present without dealing with Communist-led unions but it might not be so in the future if the unions are allowed to grow." The aim, in any case, was to "kill" the union federation before it became as strong as in neighboring Port-of-Spain and Georgetown.[43]

Wading forcefully and publicly into the controversy, Governor Hugh Foot addressed the Chamber of Commerce at the Myrtle Bank in Kingston in March 1954. "I . . . describe the Communist threat," he instructed his attentive audience, "by referring to the old story of the Trojan horse. . . . The difference between ourselves and the Trojan defenders of old is that we know in advance that . . . inside the belly of the beast there are sworn enemies of all we believe in . . . few in number maybe, but . . . armed with all the paraphernalia of treachery and trickery and treason and tyranny. The Moscow horse has arrived in Jamaica. . . . It is foreign to . . . every good tradition which has grown up in the island. . . . It depends on foreign money. If the Communist movement in Jamaica depended on the subscriptions of Jamaicans there would be no danger," since "the subscriptions of Jamaican Communists would not pay the wages of the office boy." This was a curious charge as Sir Hugh must have known how generously Manley's efforts were being subsidized by various entities in the United Kingdom and the United States. But he concluded, "I think we are right to ban the poisonous Communist literature. . . . I see no reason why we should facilitate the travelling of Communists to their headquarters in Eastern Europe"—a reference to Smith's visits to Vienna.[44]

Hart averred that "Governor Foot knew that his allegation that the union and its leaders were being financed by foreign Communist funds was false. . . . Foot was aware of this because the correspondence of persons suspected of leftist sympathies was being illegally opened by the so-called security police and information [about] the receipt of any remittances of foreign funds would have been available from the banks. The Governor knew that the trade union movement's financial resources were so limited that at that time it depended for transport mainly on" himself and his "second hand Hillman Minx motor car and . . . could afford one poorly furnished room . . . at Barry Street for an office." "As he had always done, [Hart] served this and all other causes without payment or reward. Ferdie Smith had only his modest salary as an Assistant Secretary of the WFTU and, after his retirement, a pension and lived very modestly, unable even to afford his own car." Still furious years later, Hart charged that "it is more difficult to conceive of a more blatant and dishonest abuse of his official position by a colonial governor than that of Sir Hugh Foot in making this speech."[45]

The crackdown on Smith and his supporters was successful. Richard Hart lamented in 1953 that "it is now fairly obvious that we are no longer in the strong position we were right after the split in the PNP. . . . For at least six weeks after the split the PNP leaders could not get a hearing on the streets of the city and suburbs except in Eastern St. Andrew. They were howled down by the people. The masses were with the . . . 'left' who had been expelled from the PNP. . . . [The] monster demonstrations we had last year" were "over four times as large" as this year. Part of the problem, he thought, was his erstwhile comrade, Ken Hill, and his "consistent refusal over a number of months to meet Ferdinand Smith . . . the most experienced and distinguished West Indian in the trade union movement today." Hill also prevented Hart "from speaking at public meetings . . . because of my public affirmation that I am still a Marxist and am not alarmed when I am called a 'Communist' or 'Red.'"[46]

The Jamaican left was split time and again, with "Social Democrats" giving in to anticommunist pressure to purge those to their left, who in turn felt compelled to purge others to their left. And while the left was forming a firing squad by forming a circle, those they claimed to represent were suffering. Michael Manley, Norman's son, recalled that "as late as 1952 I can remember employers who thought they were entitled to abuse their workers in the most shameful way"—the way household help was "brutalized" by employers, for example, "beggared description," while those who opposed such maltreatment were denounced as Reds. "I came to be known in certain employer circles as a Communist," said Michael, an eminent Social Democrat, "because I unswervingly asserted the proposition that employer and worker are essentially equal. . . . So deep were the class attitudes in Jamaica that this unoriginal and ideologically pedestrian notion was enough to stamp me at best a dangerous radical and at worst, and more probably, as an out and cut Communist."[47]

Bustamante, the sugar barons, and London worried that Smith's union organizing efforts had struck a chord among workers. Smith noted that the sugarcane the poorly paid workers chopped was shipped to "refineries in [the] U.K., which ships [the] refined product" back to Jamaica, "where it is retailed at a higher price than that which British workers pay," despite the fact that the "cost of living" was "higher than in Great Britain."

Since its creation in 1953, the sugar workers' affiliate of Smith's JFTU had faced "prison, tear gas, bullets and even death." Disorder erupted in early 1954 when this union organized job actions on a number of estates and confronted the economic giants of the island. Though the unions tied to Bustamante and Manley refused to cooperate, "for the first time in [the] history of the island," workers chose to "raise their demands before the cutting of the crop and to ask for a wage increase."[48] Smith and his comrades distributed a leaflet to the workers. It included a quote from the powerful Vernon Tate, chair of the West Indian Sugar Company, who noted ecstatically that in "1953 both our factories surpassed their previous production records," generating record profits. "Yes, sugar workers," said these trade unionists, "there you have it." For the 1954–1955 crop, "let your slogan be: not one stalk of cane will be cut until we have a signed agreement."[49]

Smith, the chief organizer and theoretician of the Sugar and Agricultural Workers Union (SAWU), said the union was "engaged in a number of strikes in Hanover and St. Elizabeth to win increased wages and improved social conditions" in the face of the "policy of the employers" which was "to starve these workers into submission."[50] SAWU was on strike at the Raheen Cane farm, attached to the "Wray & Naphew-owned Appleton Sugar estate" and was battling "strong intimidation by the Police and the strike-breaking activities" of Manley's union. However, encouraged by "Busta" himself, the pro-Bustamante planters flatly refused to negotiate with Smith's union, thereby effectively defeating SAWU.

Manley's ascent to power in 1955 did not change things much. Having just replaced Bustamante as Chief Minister, Manley was told that "he, as head of a 'socialist' government, [should] call upon the police force to cease intimidation of the strikers."[51] An outraged Smith found it hard to believe that Manley's NWU "issued instructions to the workers to ignore the strike appeal." He demanded "that you immediately call upon your officers to desist from these strikebreaking tactics which are only designed to confuse and divide the workers and aid the bosses in their campaign of exploitation."[52]

Smith's global contacts helped the sugar workers. When they met in late 1954 they received messages of solidarity from the Indonesian Plantation Workers, Rumanian Agricultural Workers, Japan Peasants Union, St. Vincent Federated Industrial and Agricultural Workers Union, St. Lucia Seamen and Waterfront Workers, and other unions too numerous to mention. Addressing the assembled workers, their hands calloused from field labor, their brows furrowed from worrying about their survival, Smith praised Cheddi Jagan, now under siege in neighboring Guiana, and congratulated the workers whose struggle for an old-age pension had forced the government to consider the measure. "He exhorted [the] conference to be proud of the name 'Red' as it was a badge of honour."[53]

Smith was hoping to organize both the employed and the unemployed by attempting to erode the "reserve army of labor," a powerful tool for employers. Smith moved that a "provisional chairman and secretary be elected" of "unemployed regional councils to be established on the same basis as the SAWU."[54] He was simultaneously leading marches for "work or unemployment pay" that worked their way through downtown Kingston, going from the Ward Theatre, along King Street and North Street, and down Duke Street.[55]

In addition to marches, Smith and Richard Hart held a "weekly 'News Forum' . . . every Monday night at King Street" at which "foreign news" was featured "each week" about progressive breakthroughs in Kenya, Vietnam, and elsewhere in the colonized world. To that end they also "held one public meeting, lecture, symposium or debate per week," thereby sharpening skills for which Jamaica was already well known.[56]

While Smith was helping to organize sugar workers, his "Peoples Education Organization" was engaging in grassroots education of all, employed and unemployed alike. Addressing a crowd at 64 Barry Street in Kingston at the convention of his umbrella federation, the Jamaica Federation of Trade Unions, he cited Frederick Douglass's proposition that "where there is no struggle, there is no progress." Speaking simply and carefully, "he dealt with practical trade unionism which comes from the every day contact with the workers and showed that, while theoretical knowledge was necessary, emphasis should be placed on learning practically from the workers." Popular with the workers, Smith was "unanimously approved" as president of the JFTU that he had helped found.[57]

Smith's activism dismayed the U.S. authorities, who had thought they had exiled him permanently to a kind of political Siberia. Smith was "making slow but steady headway," they said. He "has announced intention to make trip to unspecified part of Africa during the summer." He has "full-time, influential individual supporters in many isolated rural districts." The "local authorities" were "astonished and puzzled by Smith's activities in isolated areas," particularly on sugar estates which employed thousands of workers.[58]

As Jamaicans began to flee the poverty of their homeland for the better opportunities they hoped to find in the United Kingdom, Washington alleged that Smith had "planted among the 680 Jamaican job-seekers who left . . . a few unidentified Jamaicans who will take up Communist training in London." Moreover, "local Communists in Jamaica have formed a 'death squad,' a strong-arm group of about ten persons headed by Mr. John Roland Simms." Washington conceded, however, that this was in response to similar groups that had arisen among forces allied with Manley and Bustamante.[59]

Washington's growing unease was apparent when Smith reached out to William Patterson, his old comrade from the U.S. Communist Party. "Pat," he said, "maybe you can find a reliable 'cover,' non-political, where I can write you. Should you find this, you may send it to the same address where this letter was sent. . . . She is my niece and is quite reliable. The powers that be haven't the remotest idea of my even knowing her. We have kept it that way." He was eager to reach out to "Fast," Howard, the prolific Red novelist, and "Field," Fred, the progressive philanthropist. But "the problem has been: how to reach them without informing our enemies?" The net of surveillance that dogged his every step hampered his ability to form alliances and simply keep abreast of developments on a poor island with an underdeveloped telecommunications infrastructure.

But Smith was not deterred. "Pat," he exulted, "you can't imagine to what degree the West Indian people are moving toward winning their freedom. I tell you, the whole area is like a [smoldering] volcano. The imperialists know this, that is why they have been sending their big guns down here so frequently. First Churchill, then the Queen a few weeks ago [and] the Archbishop of New York. They are trying to hold onto what can't any longer be held! [I] often wonder if our people—the fifteen million Negro Americans—realize how important to their own freedom would be the winning of independence by the three million West Indians? What they should also realize is that while they are struggling as a minority, against the oppressing majority, we are in the more favorable position of being a vast majority. It is this fact which has forced the colonialists [to] place so much emphasis on the winning of stooges in our ranks." He assured Patterson that he was still "concerned about our friends' struggles in the U.S. The fact is that I am in daily touch with all your activities, through the press and otherwise." He suggested that Patterson get in touch with Stephanie, his daughter, who lived in the Bronx, as a conduit to further communication.[60]

Smith did not mislead. Though besieged on all sides, Smith's union still found time to make "demands" for the "return of Paul Robeson's passport."[61]

These events were unfolding as the Cold War was getting more intense and opposition to Communists like Smith and those sympathetic to the Communists was growing stronger. The British union federation decided to provide a "grant" of five hundred pounds to the unions tied to Manley in a maneuver to counter Smith's JFTU.[62] With "the help of a grant" from the unions of Cuba, Manley's National Workers Union "established a bridgehead in the sugar industry of Jamaica," which it conceded was not "traditionally" its "stronghold." After receiving another fifteen hundred pounds from London, the NWU admitted that "it is safe to say without foreign aid we could never [have] contemplated, much less achieved our present position," given that they were fighting Smith's forces on the left and Bustamante's on the right.[63]

Not surprisingly, these London-based unions chose not to contribute to Smith's JFTU, although the JFTU was organizing workers and seeking to improve their well-being. They refused on account of the

JFTU's Red affiliations, even after Smith made an appeal in the midst of a strike at the Appleton-Raheen Estates in St. Elizabeth and Hanover that was "now in its twentieth day."[64] According to Manley's comrade, F. A. Glasspole, the strikers had "made considerable headway . . . and have been able to close down by strikes two estates one of which is the second largest sugar factory in Jamaica." This was a significant achievement, given that since sugar employed "approximately 50,000 workers and is the key to industrial power in Jamaica."[65]

Meanwhile, as the strike was unfolding in 1954, Norman Manley visited the United States and obtained "funds" from "certain unions."[66] This was a sound investment, counseled F. A. Glasspole. If Manley's forces could prevail, they would have a "profound effect on the whole British West Indian political and trade union development." Indeed, if the PNP and NWU had been in "BG [British Guiana], the situation would never have been allowed to drift" as in Jamaica. Thus, Cuban unions, about to be transformed by Fidel Castro's triumph five years hence, pledged another $5,000 to the NWU.[67]

Smith pleaded in vain for aid to the thousands of sugar workers on strike for sixty days despite "police intimidation and wholesale arrest," "Red-baiting," and "heavy court fines."[68] Smith's assessment of the widespread impact of this job action was sound. Sir Hugh Foot, London's man in Kingston, announced that with the strike "the Moscow Horse has arrived in Jamaica" and that an appropriate response was required.[69] In a "personal and confidential" dispatch, the avuncular Sir Hugh acknowledged that "we have been concerned in the past few weeks about the strikes in several . . . farms." He thought Smith "makes an effective appeal to the rabble amongst the sugar workers, particularly as his new union does not ask for payment of union dues." As such, he was "considering the very awkward question of what further action can be taken to check Communist activity," especially as Smith had "been very active among the sugar workers and danger that he will receive increasing support in the sugar areas is real."[70]

In mid-June 1954 the British held a tense meeting in central Kingston. As they were gathering, the U.S. Supreme Court ruled that Jim Crow was no longer the law of land, fulfilling one of Smith's longtime wishes and giving the besieged left hope that they could look forward to further advances. Given this situation, Sir Hugh admitted that "the activities of Ferdinand Smith and Richard Hart were causing genuine anxiety." Hart, a lawyer known to be one of the most talented thinkers and organizers in Jamaica and Smith, the veteran union leader, made for a formidable team. London's local men knew this well. Smith and Hart "had already succeeded in organizing effective strikes on . . . two sugar estates and, although these had been broken, it [may] not be difficult for them to find opportunities to dislocate parts, or even the whole, of the sugar industry in the future, or, indeed, to break into other industries." Sir Hugh therefore circulated a "secret draft" on "Jamaica Anti-Communist Legislation" to prevent such an eventuality,[71] and warned publicly about the perceived Communist threat in the region.[72] All the while London was gathering large amounts of information on the role of the WFTU in Jamaica,[73] including "minutes" of their meetings[74] and "industrial relations in the sugar industry,"[75] and mulling over the "annual report of the sugar industry labour welfare board."[76] This feverish activity led ultimately to the de facto outlawing of Smith's organizing efforts and strong antileft sentiment in Jamaica.

But while Smith was being squeezed by Manley and Bustamante at home and London and Washington abroad, the Colonial Office had its own difficulties. It was justifiably concerned that the United States was unenthusiastic about British colonialism and feared that such stringent anticommunist legislation in Jamaica would give credence to the seditious notion that the empire should allow Washington and not London to lead the battle against the left. Moreover, the British legation in Washington revealed that the U.S. "press" had a tendency to "exaggerate the magnitude of the Communist element in Jamaica and that this tendency should be combated lest it might deter tourists and would-be investors in Jamaica." It referred to a recent *Saturday Evening Post* article discussing Smith ("a lean, ascetic Negro . . . well received by a small nucleus of left-wing sugar workers") and another piece in a more obscure periodical that also targeted Smith. He is "working again . . . for the Kremlin," said the article, "and in a spot where he can create serious headaches for the U.S. as well as Britain." "The years of valuable labor organizing experience he gained in the NMU will now stand him . . . and Moscow . . . in good stead as he goes to work in co-operation with the hundreds of other trained Kremlin agents now operating in the Caribbean and Latin America year." This being the "backyard" of the United States, which had a large number of Social Democrats— viewed widely in Washington as junior Reds—U.S. authorities feared London was simply not up to the challenge provided by someone like Smith.[77]

Moreover, the United States's move away from the now discredited ideas of "racial" supremacy was problematic for the United Kingdom, as these ideas were an essential part of the colonial enterprise. Even Walter Hood, the British trade union leader, was so disconcerted about meeting with Kenyans that "he refused to talk to some of the African unionists until they got a scrubbing brush and washed themselves."[78]

However, too much should not be made of these U.S.-U.K. tensions for the two powers were generally united on anticommunism. Certainly neither London nor Washington were comforted when Smith and Hart presided over a ceremony that "mourned the death of Stalin" and "two flags at half-mast" were hoisted at their headquarters. "One was the Communist flag and the other the Red Chinese flag."[79]

While they may have been united in their joint hostility to Smith, the tricky Bustamante—when not in an alcoholic stupor—sensed that he could play upon the tensions created by a declining London and a rising Washington. "Busta," said one U.S. diplomat, "invariably tells every American visitor that although he is devoted to the royal family and to his British allegiance, he is intensely pro-American. This assertion is reiterated (and he is much given to repetition) as though it were a paradox hard to believe and almost self-contradictory. Lounging in a colorful shirt on his verandah and refilling our glasses with Mumm's Cordon Bleu . . . [he] dwelt at some length on his stay in the United States" for "eight years . . . posing as Puerto Rican." Busta waxed eloquently about how "if he had any choice over his place of birth, he would have chosen to be born in the United States." No fool, Busta realized that the winning ticket for the rest of the century lay with Uncle Sam.

As so often happened, the conversation between the U.S. representative and Bustamante moved quickly and abruptly to their object of immediate obsession—Smith. "Smith was now a very sick man with relatively little power to make trouble but, said Bustamante, events might have turned out very differently if his government had not taken the action they did. When, early last year, Smith succeeded in getting the workers at the Appleton Estate to go on strike, he [Bustamante] had told Governor Foot that it was essential that the government should freeze out Smith's union by refusing to give it any official recognition. He said that Sir Hugh had objected that this would be inconsistent with democratic practice, since the Sugar and Agricultural Workers union was a duly registered trade union entitled to the same privileges as others under the law." Such even-handedness only confirmed Washington in its view that London was not up to the Red challenge, and that the United States had to displace its erstwhile ally. Bustamante earned Washington's affection when he forcefully told Sir Hugh, "Either you refuse recognition to Smith's union or I'll become a dictator."

Happily, Bustamante's U.S. interlocutor reported, "This seemed to settle the matter." Bustamante then "told Mr. Roy Lindo," of the [sugar] estate, "that he was to have no dealings" with Smith or his union and "Lindo complied, leaving for a vacation in Europe. . . . The Appleton workers drifted away from Smith's union and the strike collapsed." Though satisfied with Bustamante's anticommunist fervor, Armistead Lee, the consular official, was stunned by his "vanity and ambition" and the fact that "union dues" of poor workers from the trade union federation that carried his name had contributed to "his personal wealth." No one mentioned how this federation was threatened by Smith's organizing. Skillfully playing on Washington's ambitions, Busta said that but for his decisive action, "a Jagan could easily have arisen in Jamaica" in the form of "Ferdinand Smith." Busta now felt that Washington owed him one and he fully expected to collect.[80] Sharing Busta's sense that the United States would be playing a key role in the region, N. N. Nethersole of Manley's party was "advis[ing] a revolt from sterling to a U.S. dollar domination" as early as 1952.[81]

Bustamante argued that he had faced down Smith and his trade union organizing simply by ruling his action illegal and spearheading "raids" on his headquarters and home, which "yielded names, accounts, stacks of Red literature," and the like.[82] When the Ministry of Labour announced that it would "not deal with unions associated with Communists or other Communist influence," it inflicted a death blow on Smith's organizing. True, Smith's union was able to secure increased wages for workers, but in the long term the red bogey succeeded in undermining his efforts. Smith received the bad news directly when he and representatives of the sugar workers arrived "at Prospect Farm at the appointed time." The management representative "Mr. Clare met them and offered them a drink but told them that he could not negotiate. When asked why if this was the case, he had brought them all this way, he said that he had invited them only to get to know them! Sadly, the union had no alternative but call . . . workers out on strike," a maneuver that ultimately proved not altogether successful.[83]

From a promising beginning in 1953, Smith's unions—SAWU and the federation to which it was affiliated, JFTU—were driven to launching a series of punishing strikes. Although they made some gains, the costs were high, particularly since union members were so poor. Richard Hart described what happened as "political murder." Meanwhile, the unions tied to Manley and Bustamante, Hart noted, held no "regular meetings at which the workers sit down and discuss their problems. . . . All decisions are made at the top. . . . Workers . . . regard a trade union as something belonging to one or other of the political leaders as a sort of business or political investment. This has caused a very cynical attitude towards trade unionism." Because Manley and Busta were threatened by the rise of the JFTU, "they quickly made common cause to prevent it from spreading," using "every form of police persecution and intimidation."[84]

Ironically, although London was quick and eager when it came to handicapping the left, it was not as enthusiastic about Bustamante's stratagem of simply refusing to deal with Smith and his unions. "That step," wrote the Colonial Office, "was not taken after consultation with HMG [Her Majesty's Government] and was contrary to the general tenor of our advice."[85] A "prima facie case could be made out," said a bureaucrat, "that Government of Jamaica was not acting in accordance with the spirit of Article 18 (h) of Convention No. 82 in that it has decided to have no dealings with the JFTU."[86] London wanted to rein in Bustamante's galloping anticommunism, yet London also knew that doing so would only drive him closer to Washington and accelerate the inevitable—the decline of the United Kingdom and the rise of the United States. So while London was concerned about the de facto illegality of Smith's unions, it felt that some way must be found for Kingston to confront the Reds. This was not an easy square to circle.[87]

Meanwhile, Washington was delighted with the deflation of the "Communist threat" in Jamaica. In the spring of 1955 the Kingston Consulate was celebrating the revelation that "neither Frank nor Ken Hill were Communist." Both were "thoroughly disillusioned with the Com-

munists now and . . . their logical resting place would be in the Bustamante fold." Though Washington had "great respect for their intelligence," it thought they were "essentially opportunists." Now Washington wanted to keep Smith and the left prostrate, for if the JFTU were allowed to bargain for workers, "the picture might very well change. In
such a case, left-wing dissidents" once tied to Manley but "dissatisfied
with the moderate policies of the PNP government, might easily turn to
the Communists if they are the only alternative." Continuing to interfere in Jamaica's internal affairs, the Consulate thought "there may
be . . . a real advantage in keeping . . . [Hill's] TUC alive as an alternative non-Communist haven." Washington was aware that the "present
division of organized labor" was "certainly harmful. It is putting a premium on extravagant wage demands, as each group bids for the mass
following." It failed to mention that division of labor by definition hampered unity and reduced the possibility of attaining these "extravagant
wage demands."[88]

Meeting with Ken Hill, a former left-winger himself, in October
1955 in a "private conversation," a U.S. diplomat was keen to observe
that he "discusse[d] his political odyssey with a disarming candor. . . .
Hill agreed that Jamaica could very easily have gone the same way as
British Guiana had the movement of economic protest and nationalism
fallen into the hands of Communist leadership. As it was," Hill told his
U.S. interlocutor, "the Communists arrived relatively late on the scene;
it was not until March of 1952 that Ferdinand Smith came with some
money and extravagant promises of more from the WFTU. Had they really had substantial funds," he said, acknowledging the fallacy of a direct flow of funds from Vienna and Moscow to Kingston, "they could
have built up a real organization at one time, for none of the other
unions had sufficient resources for effective organizing. Now it was too
late for them." Some of the news was almost too good to be true. Frank
Hill, once a feared leftist, had "been to overseas conferences of Moral
Rearmament and is looked upon by influential MRA circles in Jamaica
as a most promising recruit," quite a coup for this religious group. "On
one point all observers seem to agree. . . . Richard Hart has been the key
figure in Communist activities over the years," though it was no coincidence that the "rapid enrollment of sugar workers in the SAWU during
the period from October 1953 through February 1954" dovetailed with
Smith's increased activism. But now, radical activity was "at its lowest
ebb." Smith was living "obscurely in Kingston, though he has just had

a heart attack." But vigilance was still required, as "it must not be sup-posed that the average Jamaican worker would be immune if there were a well organized and well-financed Communist effort." If the left had not been defeated, "the Guatemala situation might well have been reproduced," that is, there may have been a progressive government not unlike that overthrown by Washington in a bloody coup a year ear-lier.[89]

12

The Final Voyage of Ferdinand Smith

BY THE MID-1950S, Smith's union organizing drives had begun to falter, as the government flatly refused to deal with organizations they considered "Communist." He was now over sixty years old and not in the best of health. Though the weather in Jamaica was superb, it was an underdeveloped island with few of the amenities to which he had grown accustomed during his long stay in Manhattan.

Yet he continued to work, now leading the Peoples Freedom Movement (PFM), a new political party whose "founding conference" in 1955 "was attended on the opening day by 35 people and on the second day by 49, representing 5 parishes." Combating unemployment and fighting fare hikes on buses were its chief issues, but anticommunism derailed the PFM just as it had the SAWU, JFTU, and other organizations Smith had nurtured.[1] Moreover, Smith was beginning to show signs of fatigue. "Our need is so urgent," he moaned, "I have been carrying the load on all fronts . . . I am all spent."[2] He also complained of being cut off from vital sources of information, which could impair his judgment and lead to poor decisions. "I am longing to get some news about [the] Western Hemisphere, etc., etc.," he said in the spring of 1958.[3]

Though Smith's organizations were not exactly flourishing, the authorities continued to monitor him and his comrades relentlessly, as if the revolution were nigh. In late 1955, the Constabulary acknowledged in a "secret" report that the JFTU was "limited to the sugar and agricultural workers and the seamen's association. The union has concentrated on St. Elizabeth and Hanover, and to a lesser extent Clarendon. . . . Smith's annual salary is about 1000 [pounds] while another 2000 [pounds] is said to be for general expenses. Both sums are supplied by the WFTU." This confirmed the fact that the authorities knew where his funding came from and how much there was. They also knew that "Mr. Rodwell Samuel Atherly, a British Communist Party member and a native of British Guiana, whilst on his way to British Guiana was found to be carrying a letter from John La Rose to Mrs. Jagan in which proposals for concerted action among the Communist bodies in Trinidad, British Guiana and Jamaica were set forth." They also kept their eyes on Smith's spouse, "Sonya Jackson," an "East Indian" who has "been very active among the East Indians of Western Kingston and St. Andrew. . . . Lectures are given by Ferdinand Smith. In addition they are taught to read and write." They engaged in a number of activities thought typical—"Gramaphone records of Paul Robeson and China propaganda have also been imported in limited quantities"—though there were "about 10 returned Jamaicans who were British Communist Party holding members." Yet, for all that, the authorities well knew that "Communism is at low ebb in Jamaica," hampered by a "chronic lack of finance."

However, increased spending on surveillance was justified on the grounds that "fertile soil can clearly be seen by the rapid growth of three PFM groups in the matter of two months and the increase of Chinese Communist literature."[4] This was why there was a "long drawn out battle . . . to recover a film projector and speaker sent as a gift from [East] Germany to [Smith]" which had been confiscated by the authorities on the basis of "customs law."[5] Indeed, the colonial government was so insecure about its position that it even suspected a nascent religious group of subversion. "I do not suppose," said a British official, "that there is anything of Communism in these Rastafarians as yet, but," he added realistically, "the great wealth and abject poverty . . . in Jamaica are all that is needed for genuine trouble."[6]

Washington, which did not have the burden of administering Jamaica, could afford to be more balanced in its evaluation. Its assessment was that Smith's party's "influence" was "strongest in a few rural pockets of large sugar estate country where certain union leaders . . . follow the lead of [Smith]" and "have long been established and have a personal following." It thought their "influence" was "negligible in the urban area." It also thought Smith's party was "stronger when running against [Bustamante's party] alone than when a [Manley-backed] candidate is in the field." It was confident that "The overall influence" of Smith's party "has declined during the past year."[7]

Richard Hart did not disagree, acknowledging that "by 1957 the SAWU no longer had sufficient strength to call a strike and was soon unable to keep any organizers in the field." Unlike Washington and London, however, Hart believed this development had both external and internal causes. SAWU and JFTU "began to have immediate success due to its correct policy of uniting the workers regardless of political affiliation and its militant agitation." So challenged, Manley and Bustamante "joined forces with the colonial officials to smash the new union."[8]

The difficulties Smith faced were illustrated by the 1956 visit to the island by William Worthy, the progressive Negro journalist from the United States, later scorned by his government for his controversial visit to "Red China." No doubt Smith was expecting to find in him a willing and sympathetic ear. He would have been surprised by the dispatch filed by the U.S. consulate. "He told us," it said, that Smith and Hart "were most bitter over the Government's continued non-recognition of their trade union and blamed this for their failure to make more headway. They described the PNP Government as having 'sold out.'" Evidently, Worthy told the consulate that Smith had asserted that "the only help now received was his own salary of . . . 90 [pounds] paid by the WFTU." Had Smith known about this conversation, he would have been dismayed that even U.S. progressives—inadvertently or not— were conversing with U.S. diplomats and sharing intelligence about his situation.[9]

On the positive side, unlike his U.S. comrades who were deprived of their passports, Smith was still able to travel, albeit with some difficulty. In early 1955 he returned from Vienna "where he attended a meeting of the WFTU General Council." He was "originally booked to leave London on BOAC [airlines] on 3 January but was unable to take the flight as the Bahamas government informed BOAC that he would not be permitted to land there. . . . He travelled via Amsterdam, Iceland, Montreal, Havana and Curacao, a trip of over two weeks."[10] His ability to leave the island was circumscribed further in early 1957, when he was "refused passport renewal" as a "bad security risk."[11]

Despite these problems, Smith continued to persevere. In vain he demanded that British unions break their ties with Manley's forces as they "actively and publicly support strike breakers . . . in the name of anti-communism." He argued that Manley's PNP and NWU had "refused to recognize the right of workers to belong to unions of their own choosing."[12] Like many others, Smith expected at least a slight turnabout in Kingston's policy after Manley came to power. Even some of Manley's men were skeptical of the ban on Smith's union. "In a private conversation on this subject with Mr. N. N. Nethersole" of the Manley Administration, one of them "remarked to the reporting officer that"

Smith's request for a negation of his union's illegality "had created an embarrassing situation and that legally the [JFTU] was probably right."[13] But Manley's government refused to budge from this anticommunist position.

From 1955 through 1959 Norman Manley, a Social Democrat, was in power (though sovereignty continued to rest with the colonial power in London), ousting his longtime rival, Bustamante. Those to his left, like Smith, who expected political repression to stop were bitterly disappointed. As Richard Hart recalled later, "Passports were denied to them or issued in a severely limited form. Their letters were opened, their movements were monitored and they were harassed . . . by the Police Special Branch." According to Hart, Manley wanted "to convince the British and American governments that his new policy of close co-operation with them would be permanent and that his many years of collaboration with the Marxist 'left' would not be repeated."[14] Hart's analysis has great merit. When Manley was swept to power in the 1955 elections, repression was no longer needed to thwart Smith and the left. Manley's PNP garnered 18 seats, Bustamante's party got 14, while "the two Communist candidates of the People's Freedom Movement lost their deposits."[15]

And though there was constant talk about "Moscow Gold" flowing to Smith's coffers, in fact it was Manley who was the principal beneficiary of foreign largesse. He knocked frequently on the door of the British Labour Party, requesting that they "assist us" and suggesting a "very much closer association."[16] Manley was "tremendously pleased" with the "magnificent contribution" from Labour and expected to "get some help" from the United States too; he was "deeply moved and impressed by the generosity of the assistance."[17] John Hatch of Labour offered the "Caribbean Socialist Federation," a group of parties that included the PNP, "the sum of [2,500 pounds] in 1956, [1,500 pounds] in 1957 and [1,000 pounds] in 1958."[18] Since London was paying the piper, it insisted on calling the tune. Thus, Hatch objected to admitting the Bahamian Federation of Labour into the group, preferring the Progressive Liberal Party, though he conceded that "the extent of their socialism I do not know."[19]

But however much money the PNP received from across the Atlantic, it never seemed to be enough. In a "begging letter" to Labour—which admitted that a similar appeal was being "written separately to the German party"—Manley's men requested a "couple of mobile cinema units. . . . Volkswagen vans or cars fitted with loud-speaking equipment and tape recorders."[20] At the very same time Kingston was confiscating a film projector, a gift from East Germany to Smith's supporters on the grounds that it was an unconscionable interference in the internal affairs of the island. Such generous funding simultaneously boosted Manley and drove Smith's forces further into decline.

It was hard for Smith to accept these political setbacks. Still, his family life in Kingston was like a soothing balm. In his last years he was settled in domesticity with a young spouse and younger children. His alienation from his first wife continued, though his daughter, Stephanie, remained in touch. "My dear daddy," she said gently at one point, "I have a feeling that you are not well as you would have answered my letter and a birthday card. . . . But then, you are a busy person and might have been away from Kingston." Her daughter—his granddaughter—"did us all proud last week by winning a New York State College Scholarship for four years totalling $1400. . . . She graduated with honors from High School, the only Negro girl in a class of 51." Stephanie was buoyed by this news. "This past week," she said, "has been the happiest days of my life. It has been a long, long time that I have been happy. I don't know what else could happen to equal what I felt this past week as I told you she [was] admitted to Barnard College. . . . That old saying of yours that beauty and brains don't go together is all wet for she has developed into a very lovely young lady."[21]

Her news to "my dear daddy" ranged from mild remonstrations—"have not heard from you quite a while"—to news about his granddaughter: "She came in the upper part of 10% of all that took that test that date" and was that rare Negro student admitted to both Columbia and New York University.[22] In another letter she wrote: "I guess you feel that I don't remember you anymore but far from it. You are constantly in my thoughts and more so these past few days."[23]

Her aging father was beleaguered on all fronts—trying to keep a new family afloat on a meager income in a small house, under constant surveillance by the government, and coping with a dwindling political following. Smith was desperately trying to keep it all together, even seeking to revive contacts in the United States that had grown dormant given the logistical hurdles. He was trying to lure his old friend Paul Robeson to the island for a fund-raising "concert under the most impressive sponsorship possible."[24] William Patterson, plagued with his own difficulties, encouraged him to move forward with the Robeson concert. "Any appeal from foreign sources for him to appear," he said, "can only help the movement here. If the appeal comes from official sources or from well established cultural bodies, it will more readily find outlet through the metropolitan area. The campaign has got to be of international scope." He wanted Smith to write an article on "Bandung," the epochal 1955 gathering of mostly African and Asian nations in Indonesia, as its "attack on racism was visible on its face. . . . The maintenance of the color-bar in any phase of economic, political or cultural relations violates the spirit of Geneva and the letter of the UN Charter." The other news was bleak. Their mutual comrade, Claudia Jones of Trinidad, was "sick" and, like Smith, was about to be ejected from the United States—a sober reminder of the obstacles encountered by the hemispheric left.[25]

Smith was seeking "assistance" that was "promised sometime ago" from his U.S. friends. But his comrade, Ben Davis—the black Communist he helped to elect before he was jailed on political charges—hastened to remind him that "on this as on all such matters, you are acquainted, I'm sure, with the fact that I'm isolated from the heart of things because of the severe and unjust restrictions maintained against me and my co-defendants." In sum, Smith would have to look elsewhere for "assistance," for the outlook for his U.S. comrades was as bleak as his. "In a word," said Davis glumly, "it's quite clear that though Geneva has reduced international tensions, this is not yet felt in a big way on the domestic front."[26]

Although Smith was as concerned as the next Red with the global situation, the "assistance" he wanted was simple, centered around buying a car. "To show how important this question of a car is to us," he said, note that "the plan for the SAWU's Annual Conference to take place October 28th had to be postponed to November 18th because the friend who was to take me in his car couldn't take off from his job at the time and I cannot yet take the rough trail."[27]

Though Davis was "somewhat reassured concerning [Smith] personally," given "many reports concerning your condition"—evidently "exaggerated"—he was compelled to tell his comrade that the U.S. party was "in critical condition and this situation has soaked up all our energies and resources." So he would have to look elsewhere for an auto. Yet, despite these internal problems, Davis wanted to fight for a "fundamental change in the attitude we have displayed in the past toward the Caribbean area." He "turned over a copy of [Smith's] letter to me to Cyril Phillips who is undertaking to raise funds to get a car" for his Jamaican comrade's organizing. Davis was "overjoyed at the report of [Smith's] own splendid leadership. . . . Pat remarked on the number of fine young people who form a collective around you, and especially did he mention the young Negro women. One, he said, was another Claudia."[28] Davis knew that in the United States "we are woefully neglecting West Indian work," which was why he was seeking Smith's continued counsel.[29]

But Smith was not altogether in agreement with their counsel to him, for many U.S. Communists could not understand why their counterparts in the Caribbean seemed to resist federating the numerous tiny, postage-stamp sized islands that dotted the region. Still, Smith's correspondence with Patterson and Davis—and his naming his son after Patterson—showed that in terms of the conflicts that wracked U.S. Communists in the late 1950s, Smith's allegiances, like those of most Negro Communists, were decidedly with those identified as "hard-liners."[30] Their principal target was the editor of the party paper, John Gates. Smith thought that his "going from the paper, and I hope all influence in the party, I think was a good thing [for] international co-operation and solidarity. Our mistake was that he was not taken head on at the last convention. Unity is always a most desirable thing, but unity at all cost can be a mistake of the first order." Among other things, they denounced Gates for wanting to put some distance between U.S. Communists and Moscow. But Smith was not only a "hard-liner" on matters concerning Moscow. His dealings with Manley had embittered him immensely. He suggested that the forces that the recently installed Chief Minister were said to represent—the middle classes-should also be viewed with caution in the United States. That, said Smith, was "the meaning of Little Rock" and the contentious school desegregation struggle that engulfed Arkansas in 1957. "Don't negate the role being played by native stooges," counseled Smith, in a frequently repeated refrain. The lesson of Montgomery—the desegregation battle that made Martin Luther King, Jr. a household name—"should be re-learned again," he advised. Above all, these contests "showed that the 'all-powerful whites' [aren't] all powerful in the age of the Sputniks, and long before that. There can be no room for the 'moderates'—meaning the crawlers—this is the time to fight or die on your knees."[31]

If there was one change in Smith it was that he seemed to have become more militant, particularly on "race" matters, after his arrival in

Jamaica. Perhaps this was a result of being forced to deal with the obscenity that was colonialism, with its crude denial of sovereignty and belief in white supremacy. Perhaps it was the peculiar "racial" climate in Jamaica where those who were the darkest were often at the bottom of the socioeconomic pyramid and "brown man rule"—domination by those who were lighter—was so feared that some passively accepted continued domination by London. Perhaps it was the terrible underdevelopment of Jamaica, the result of this lamentable state of affairs, that caused him to think more deeply about basic questions. Whatever the case, over time Smith became a more vehement critic of the empire and what it had wrought. Though Winston Churchill was celebrated in Washington, Smith viewed him as one of the "imperial boys" who had engaged in the "mass slaughter of our people." "We have lived through Churchill's 'freedom' for three hundred years," he said tartly, and "find ourselves in the paradise of poverty."[32] "The Anglo-Saxons, U.S., Britain and the white dominions—are not only arch-imperialists but are arch-racists." "Why," he asked, raising a question that needs to be answered to this day, "are there the smallest Communist [parties] . . . proportionately, in these countries compared to other European countries." It was "in this, that we must search to find the reason for some of the behavior we find hard to understand. People do not live in vacuums!"[33]

No doubt the awful economic situation in Jamaica lay behind Smith's increased militance. While he was speaking out against Jim Crow in the United States, the Kingston government was negotiating with Washington to send poor and bedraggled Jamaicans to U.S. farms and plantations to work for a trifle under agonizing conditions. It took U.S. unions to raise questions about these practices, as Horace Mitchell of the AFL told the Jamaican Minister of Labor that "contracts made with employers of [Jamaicans] are in some respects inferior to those of the Mexican workers." He felt this was undercutting U.S. labor. But he apparently could not see how U.S. labor's backing for Manley and/or Bustamante undermined U.S. labor in the long term.[34]

Even the U.S. consulate in Kingston, so instrumental in destabilizing Smith's labor organizing, was a bit puzzled by the often lame approach of Manley's forces to labor. When the National Workers Union, the union arm of Manley's party, began negotiating with Reynolds and other bauxite companies with the assistance of the U.S.-based United Steelworkers there was a "pleasant surprise to the management of

Kaiser" when the unions "deliberately asked for joint negotiations with all three companies at the same time." Management "had expected that the NWU would bargain separately, playing one company off against the others." Although the consulate was at a loss to explain why, it had an inkling. "The union is far more determined to achieve substantial raises for the skilled workers and to widen the margin above the laborer's rate. This is symptomatic, in the trade union field, of the PNP's tendency to speak for the skilled workers and the professional and clerical classes, while the Jamaican Labor Party [of Bustamante] bases its strength on a combination of the rural peasantry and the unskilled workers (e.g. the cane cutters) together with the urban mercantile community." Smith's JFTU was uniquely positioned to bridge this gap and to demand, as the consulate suggested, "across-the-board" raises for all. But it was unable to do so.[35]

Likewise, there were problems in the rapidly growing tourism industry. In early 1956 the U.S. consulate reported that "Jamaica's Tourist Board continues to be under pressure to make special appeal to colored tourists in the United States" but "publicity emphasis on the 'quaint natives' (e.g. market women with baskets on their heads) was no way to appeal to prospective Negro tourists." On the other hand, "unquestionably, many of the Montego Bay hostelries are fearful of the effect on their limited and fashionable clientele if too much publicity is given to Jamaica's [nonsegregation]." In sum, this industry was trapped between the changing situation in the United States, where "nonsegregation" would create a more affluent class of Negro tourists, which in turn would give the tourism industry a boost for years to come, and irk the old Jim Crow crowd who violently resisted such change.[36]

The rise of the U.S. Negro and the related attention to Jim Crow had the potential to impact Jamaican politics, just as it helped to liberalize the political atmosphere in the United States.[37] Jamaican readers were no doubt appalled to see an article by Rene MacColl in 1956. "I'm just back from Kentucky—frankly I'd rather live in Russia," reported the writer in the *Star*, referring to "the difference in treatment he experienced as a reporter in Petropavlovsk, Russia on the one hand and Sturgis and Clay, Kentucky and Clinton, Tennessee on the other hand." Similarly, during the crucial year of 1956 "Jamaican trade unions" were "unable to agree on protest over Soviet action in Hungary . . . since the Trade Unions Congress [*sic*] wanted to include protest against British action in Egypt."[38]

This was part of the changing environment that had pushed Busta-mante out of power and brought Manley in. U.S. diplomats, who had done so much to crush militant class-based activism, were now nerv-ously eyeing the militant "race" activism filling the vacuum. "A recent jury verdict of acquittal, in a rape case brought against a black Jamaican chauffeur by the Crown, on complaint of a socially prominent white American married woman resident in Jamaica" was sparking unease over "racial" matters. But this case was not unique. "Mrs. Manley . . . finds it necessary, probably for political reasons, to frequently insist publicly that she is really colored. Beggars who are refused alms usu-ally berate the white non-giver by slurring reference to color rather than economic status"—had they done the latter, the consulate would have been complaining about "communism." "Store clerks frequently turn their backs on a white customer and walk away. Most North Shore lux-ury tourist hotels practice a subtle but effective discrimination against Negroes. This is generally known by the Government which, for eco-nomic reasons, chooses to ignore all but the most vociferous com-plaints." Washington was beginning to worry about its handiwork for as independence approached "resentments" were "bound to be trans-ferred from the English to Americans and perhaps intensified."[39] Belat-edly Washington recognized that there was a price to be paid when it surpassed London in the Caribbean.

These were some of the reflections that accompanied the arrival of Jamaican independence. But ironically, all the second thoughts were generated by U.S. diplomats. Smith's comrades in the United States found it hard to believe that he did not support federation among the former British colonies in the region. Patterson, said Davis, "raised some very important questions which none of us felt adequate to dis-cuss intelligently. . . . He said that you were against the Federation idea but he, Pat, was not sure why." Nor was a doubting Davis. "We are par-ticularly interested in Harlem," Davis reminded Smith, "since this, as you doubtless know, is quite a topic in the West Indian community."[40] The comrades did not grasp that Smith was not opposed to federation, just the form it was taking.

Harlemites, who were trying to build a broad front among Negroes irrespective of class, based on common opposition to Jim Crow, found it hard to understand how radicals like Smith saw their fellow "Ne-groes" in Jamaica, a majority black island, as the enemy. Smith was un-usually blunt, contending that "imperialism's mid-twentieth century approach toward maintaining their dominance over those they would continue to oppress and exploit is to create and develop a class of 'native' with whom they can work in their game of imperialists [*sic*] domination."[41] From his perspective, federation was simply a way to consolidate neocolonial rule in the region and submerge local radicalism in places like British Guiana, where Communists were dominant.

"Remember," Smith told Ben Davis, "there are 1,500,000 people" in Jamaica alone who could be part of this grouping. "95% are Negroes. Every political party [is] forced, whether they like it or not, to call themselves Labour or Socialist. It is easier for a 'dead cat to get elected than an Englishman'—all whites are classed as English—so that the only way they can rule the masses and rob them of their very lives, is through stooges. That is why stooges [are] at such a high premium today in these parts. BUT THERE WILL BE SOME CHANGES MADE! Familiar, eh?" Maybe so. But Davis and Smith were living in separate realities. Davis would have been happy to cooperate with Negro Social Democrats in the United States, while in Jamaica Smith saw the Negro Social Democrats as the chief oppressor. This was one reason why he staunchly opposed the form of federation that had evolved.[42]

William Patterson, an analytical attorney like Ben Davis, found Smith's reasoning problematic. "Is the size of Jamaica," he inquired, "the economics, national resources, capital accumulation and related questions of such a character that they cannot be worked out in the federation somewhat as Great Russia worked out its relations with the rest of the former Czarist empire?"[43] Patterson sought to impress upon Smith the point that poverty-stricken Jamaica had insufficient resources to make it on its own. When he traveled to San Juan, Puerto Rico, he found it "far and away above Kingston in its development. There are housing projects everywhere . . . and an airport that is magnificent. Really am surprised at the rate of growth here."[44] But Smith's unfortunate experiences with Manley made it difficult for him to accept federation, an idea championed by Manley. Ironically, Smith found himself on the same side of the fence as the demagogic Bustamante, who too had few good things to say about it and who claimed that it would lead to smaller islands, draining Kingston's treasury.

The prominent Trinidadian writer and intellectual, C. L. R. James, collaborated with Manley on the idea, however. The West Indian Federal Labour Party, which included Manley, the corrupt Vere Bird of Antigua, and James and Eric Williams of Trinidad, was a precursor of federation. Manley was willing to commit the "1200 branches" of the PNP to the cause.[45] He wooed James, telling him, "I am very happy to count you and your wife among my friends,"[46] and issued an invitation, saying, "I would be happy to put you up while you are here" in Jamaica.[47] James, in turn, offered to conduct a "lecture tour" on behalf of these ambitions.[48] Evidently the authorities did not think he posed enough of a "threat" to warrant depriving him of his passport, unlike Smith and Robeson, for example.

Manley began to worry about Smith's opposition to federation in the belief that "Communist inspired leaders are deliberately working on the people to get them to burn cane and argue that . . . they will drive the Company out of Jamaica and the people will get the land."[49] Then a supporter sent him a piece of propaganda from Smith's party with the accompanying note, "It looks to me like a plot to overthrow our party." Their fears were prompted by words from the Smith brochure that appealed to Rastafarians, a new religious-cum-political organization: "The anti-federation struggle must also absorb the demand of the racial groupings of being repatriated to Africa. . . . [Such a grouping] constitutes a large section of the people and . . . their demands fall within their rights of racial origins. Though it must be understood that repatriation to Africa can never be a reality without freedom from imperialism."[50] To Manley it seemed that Smith had crossed the line from antifederation politicking to something approaching sedition.

The presence of the Rastafarians was one more indication that Jamaicans—residing on a small island where imports were a literal lifesaver—could not be indifferent to the larger world. This was no revelation to Smith, of course, a sailor and frequent flyer who had logged hundreds of thousands of miles of travel during his career. Smith also felt the need to continue speaking out on controversial global matters, which did not endear him to Washington either. Even when Smith's JFTU was in decline in 1957, it issued a call to "put an end to mass destruction by banning [atomic] bombs and guided missiles."[51] Smith contacted Bustamante directly and demanded that he endorse JFTU's resolution calling for a halt to nuclear testing. With a magnanimity that he knew was futile, Smith told his fellow Jamaican leader, "If it is your desire to act independently we certainly would have no objection to such a move." Predictably, Bustamante was unmoved though Smith reminded him that "in many wars, particularly the last two world wars . . . many of the valiant sons and daughters of the West Indies have perished without knowing for what they gave their lives." The resolution was a direct challenge to London and Washington, urging that "funds at present spent on arms [be used] to help under-developed countries" and demanding "the withdrawal of all foreign troops to their respective countries."[52]

Smith took his role as a spokesman for what came to be known as the "Third World" seriously. He bitterly assailed the U.S. invasion of Lebanon in 1958. "The Anglo-Saxon imperialists—colonialists," he charged, were "a predatory breed if there ever was [one]." From their perspective, he asserted, "peoples of colour" were "fair game, to be killed if they refuse to or reject the European imperialists ever so kind offer to carry their burdens."[53]

Smith and his comrades objected strenuously when George Padmore, the Trinidadian-born activist and intellectual, "expressed the view that what [had] saved the Gold Coast [Ghana] from the fate of British Guiana was that [Kwame] Nkrumah . . . did not align himself with any section of the European 'left' but 'placed emphasis on Nationalism rather than on Socialist and Marxist aspects of the anti-colonial struggle.'"[54] Padmore's argument was to become quite popular, particularly in North America. This was further evidence if any was needed of the existence of a circuit of Pan-African ideas that coursed through Africa and the Caribbean and the Americas generally. Smith, who had stared down the best that the United States had to offer, commanded respect in these circles, but at the end of the day even he could not prevent Padmore's idea from gaining adherents, most notably in the United States.

Smith coupled his speeches with concrete efforts to build global solidarity, particularly of the kind that would redound to the benefit of Jamaica. The WFTU remained his main global touchstone. In the fall of 1960 he briefed Giuseppe Casadei, WFTU Secretary in Prague, that "organizing the unorganized remains our biggest problem. Of a labour force of nearly 800,000 less than 25% is organized." There had been "victimization of scores of our members. . . . As soon as they show some militancy, down goes the axe!"[55] Although he continued to rely heavily on the WFTU and its network, he went beyond it too. In the run-up to the Cuban Revolution, Smith and the WFTU were both monitoring the volatile situation and protesting human rights violations there. Before the government refused to renew his passport, he attended the "Working Women's World Conference" at Budapest in 1956. He told "Sister

Xemtsova" of the Soviet Agricultural Workers and Employees Union that "we here in Jamaica know that women in the Soviet Union are truly free in every sense of the term. . . . We unfortunately cannot say the same thing about women in Jamaica."[56]

Smith's overall analysis was shaped by what he saw as the toxic effluvium of anticommunism. As he saw it, it was anticommunism that hindered his union organizing and therefore harmed the standard of living of Jamaican workers. As he saw it, it was anticommunism that hindered the life chances of so many. Consider Ken Jones, for example. In 1960, as he told Premier Manley, he was "granted . . . [a] fellowship tenable in the United States" but was "informed that the U.S. Consulate here" in Kingston "could not grant [a] visa because they had information that [he] might be a security risk" as he had "advocated left wing politics while in the PNP about 1950." Minister of Home Affairs, W. M. Seivright, told Manley that "under an arrangement with the United States authorities, the Consulate General has been permitted to consult local security concerning local residents." Of course, Jamaican authorities had no such reciprocal right vis-à-vis U.S. residents. Seivright attached a "secret" document which said that Jones had "associated with" Ferdinand Smith in past years. Manley told Robert McGregor, the U.S. Consul General, "I know a good deal about this case. Eight or nine years ago it is correct that Ken Jones was closely associated with some Marxists in Jamaica" but he had not done so in "five years" and wasn't there some sort of statute of limitations when it came to Red ties? It was "very harsh," thought Manley, to block him now. Jones was compelled to sign a "declaration" asserting, "I have never been a Communist . . . I was a member of the Peoples National Party—the only political organization in which I have ever held membership." No one ever confronted the larger question: why should mere association with Ferdinand Smith block anyone's career?[57]

But it was not necessary to ask this simple question because its anticommunist predicates and premises had been swallowed whole by so many. As Smith was dying, the Houston-based Christian Anti-Communist Crusade exploded in indignation with what it saw in Jamaica. "Communists are permitted to operate openly in Jamaica," it reported. "Communists magazines and textbooks are banned in Jamaica by law. Newsstands are not loaded with Communist agitational material as in Mexico," it said in relief. "However, there is one Kingston bookstore where 'cultural literature' from Communist China and Africa is sold."

No, this was not Smith's doing. This store was "in the center of the Ras Tafarian colony, a religious group which Communists are believed to be exploiting." This "Red-Rasta" alliance was scary. "In the event of a revolution, some well placed ganga and a little agitation by Communists could bring on violence against the police as well as Christians. We have already seen an example of this tactic in the massacring that has been going on in Angola." So, this was also a trans-Atlantic phenomenon—but who was responsible for this sad state of affairs? "In light of the close tie between labor and politics it may be significant that one of the organizers of the labor movement in Jamaica was a deportee from the United States because of Communist activities—Ferdinand Smith."[58]

The Cuban Revolution and Jamaica's proximity to Cuba only increased the hysteria about Smith and the alleged red tide sweeping through the Caribbean. As a correspondent in the newspaper there put it, "If Guantanamo Bay and/or Chaguaramas is evacuated that would not then leave us at the complete mercy of the Communist plan for taking over the Caribbean area."[59] That same year, 1960, H. Vincent Clark, writing in the *Gleaner,* recalled that "about eight years ago . . . I read with admiration and pride of Sir Alexander Bustamante's demand upon the British Government for a loan of . . . 20,000,000 [pounds] to keep Communism out of Jamaica," but now the tumultuous events in Cuba had made him "a witness to the growth of this dreaded ideology here in Jamaica."[60]

Curiously, the apprehension about communism in Jamaica arose when the island's leading communist representative, Ferdinand Smith, was anticipating death. Billy Hall, also writing in the *Gleaner,* was not persuaded by this point. "Jamaica is standing on the edge of a seething volcano," but all too many were sadly "unaware. . . . Communism is right on our doorstep, what are we going to do about it? Already there are six Communist publications in Jamaica. The police recently reported finding local correspondence with Castro officials." This was part of a grand scheme, a conspiracy so immense that it boggled the mind. "The Communists have a plan to put a dictator in Washington before 1973 and are boasting that they are five years ahead of schedule. With Jamaica only 90 miles from Peiping-controlled Cuba," this diabolical scheme would be easier to accomplish.[61] "Cuba has made Jamaica a Quemoy," a reader of the *Jamaica Times* noted, and "this evil that is knocking at our back door and in fact may already have a foot inside the gate," if one would only pay attention to Smith.[62]

Thus coaxed by Washington and some of his constituents, Manley felt incapable of protesting what was happening. But this should have surprised no one. After all, when Smith needed a passport to travel abroad for medical care, he was similarly obstinate. In the spring of 1957 Richard Hart reported that Smith "has been ill for the past eighteen months." He was "suffering from a tired heart" and his "doctors have recommended complete rest."[63] Smith was "endeavoring to seek medical aid," but the Kingston government was balking at renewing his passport. Said Hart, "The government is therefore saying that [Smith] should remain in [Jamaica] and to suffer and even die."[64]

Smith, who had been ousted from the United States, was now being prevented from leaving Jamaica. In "an open letter to the people of Jamaica" his comrades recited the sad litany of Smith's travel travails, his de facto "imprisonment in Trinidad," and how "the puppet government of the Leeward and Windward Islands, and the then British Guiana Government acting on the instructions of the Colonial Office proceeded to 'ban' him from these islands. Even Grantley Adams, then Prime Minister of Barbados, after declaring that such things could never happen there, later went back on his word as he usually does, and denied Smith entry . . . on what he called 'security grounds.' . . . Exactly what is meant by 'security,'" they asked. And what about the ease with which some miscreants entered and exited Jamaica. "Remember not so long ago," they said, "that the Rodeo Circus, of 'Big Sid' fame who during their operations here robbed several people in the island and went away without punishment after being allowed to enter like a king? Was not President Entime [former Haitian President] allowed to land without difficulty while seeking refuge from the wrath of the people he had robbed as leader of his own country?" The "thief is welcome," but "the honest man is unwelcome." They reminded Jamaicans of Smith's yeoman duty for the nation and the region, donating "handsome sums of $10,000 raised in 1947 on behalf of the PNP towards the Montego Bay Caribbean Labour Congress and [500 pounds] which the WFTU donated to [Jamaica] in 1951 to help the sufferers of the hurricane of that year."[65] And were denial of a passport and deteriorating health the thanks he received?

Blocked at home, Smith reached out abroad. He contacted Kwame Nkrumah, leader of Ghana, asking him to "use your good offices with the Jamaican Government" and added a stinging reproach of the Kingston regime.[66] But no passport was issued.

One reason for the decline of left-wing trade unionism in Jamaica beginning in the late 1950s was therefore the decline in health of Ferdinand Smith. In his last year, his close friend and comrade Richard Hart sent out a special appeal, reminding one and all that Smith "was in his day the most prominent Negro trade union leader in the USA. . . . He is now in hospital having for the third time suffered a stroke and somehow survived. It is touch and go as to whether he will recover. Unless he is able to go to a colder climate before the summer of this year, his chances of survival are small." Smith was "suffering from chronic disease of the arteries affecting mainly those of the brain and of the heart (two attacks of cerebral thrombosis, one of coronary thrombosis) causing degeneration and weakness of the heart muscle . . . a regular deterioration of his general condition and a considerable increase of both cerebral and cardiac symptoms during the warmer season of the year." In January 1955 his "passport expired, and in December 1956 he applied for a new one. Early in 1957 he was informed that his application had been refused on 'security grounds.'" Even the United States had allowed Communist patriarch William Z. Foster to go to the U.S.S.R. for health reasons. Was Kingston going to be more unbendingly anticommunist than Washington?[67]

Evidently so. Manley said that "one of the reasons for Mr. Smith's application" being turned down was "that he wanted to go to China in 1960." Not so, said Hart, but the *Gleaner* refused to publish this correction.[68] Similarly, Manley refused to grant Smith a passport regardless of whether his proposed travel was for political or health reasons: in both cases the answer was a firm no. This, despite the fact that in November 1960 Smith "suffered two successive strokes, temporarily losing the power of sight and speech and the control of his limbs." His "speech slurred, his eyes dim, his hands unable to guide a pen," Smith was in terminal decline. This was "murder by political means," charged Hart hotly.[69] Manley would not budge.

The prime minister staunchly refused to give Smith documents to travel to Eastern Europe. On 14 August 1961 at 11 P.M. Ferdinand C. Smith died. He was "buried at his new home in the little mountain village of Mocho in Clarendon, a stone's throw away from the partly finished house into which he had moved to get away from the heat of

Kingston, a mere two weeks before his death." Manley had eventually relented and granted him a passport renewal in early August and Smith was scheduled to leave for Europe by mid-September—but it was all too little too late.

Speaking at this graveside on 16 August, his anguished comrade, Richard Hart, sadly recounted Smith's decline, which was congruent with the decline of the left-wing movement in Jamaica. The JFTU, for example, had been "reduced to little more today than an educational and agitational role." But, thanks to Smith, it had begun to lobby for a "cooperative housing scheme" to alleviate the horrendous living conditions to which so many in Jamaica were subjected. A staunch Communist to the very end, Smith's "last wish" was "that some of his comrades who might be present sing at the grave the traditional working class hymn, 'The Red Flag.'" So prompted, those assembled lustily sang, "the peoples flag is deepest red. It shrouded off our martyred dead and [as] their limbs grow stiff and cold, their life's blood died [sic] its every fold."[70]

Epilogue

FERDINAND SMITH'S OUSTER from the NMU—and the United States—did not appreciably improve the lot of sailors or the industry which they served. By 1995, this union, which had once claimed a membership close to 100,000, had dwindled to a mere 7,000.[1] The "screening" or purging of sailors and the proliferation of "flags of convenience" were among the factors responsible for this decline.

Of course, there were larger trends at work nationally that were also responsible for the decline of an entire industry. The Inter-State Commerce Commission has been accused of favoring railroads over shipping. The "wages of railroad employees rose more slowly than those of seafaring personnel" after 1945, as an "upward spiral in the foreign-trade operations drove the wages of seafaring personnel to record highs"—not to mention the impact of a threatened global strike. Then the government began to subsidize the construction of a massive interstate highway system, which further challenged the role of interstate shipping.[2]

"Flags of convenience" or registering ships in Liberia and Panama and hiring cheap international labor increased after the decline of the NMU, thus confirming the value of Smith's internationalism and his desire to organize and if necessary strike across national boundaries. By 1999 the U.S. Communist periodical, *People's Weekly World*, was reporting that the NMU and "other U.S. seamen's unions have had little success in stopping the reflagging of these ships. Today," said the newspaper, "there's only one U.S. flagged passenger ship in operation in Hawaii, and that ship is about 40 years old." As a sad reminder of Smith's legacy, it said that "the most exploited people on the ship are members of the Stewards Department who serve the passengers. . . . They work long, long hours. It's common to see the same waiter—who serves three or four tables with about 20 passengers three meals a day— waiting on passengers at a midnight buffet." Worse, their overall income depended heavily "on tips." These conditions were reminiscent of the pre-NMU era when the fear of labor organizing at sea and the communism it was said to bring led to the delirium of a "passenger [who] claimed that the letters in the alphabet soup he was served spelled out Karl Marx."[3]

Lest anyone think that such reports were special pleading by the left, these allegations were confirmed in broad outline by the *New York Times* in 1999. The *New York Times* reported that laborers on a cruise ship out of Miami work "as long as 18 hours a day, seven days a week, most galley workers are paid $400 to $450 a month. . . . Most are from Third World countries, working for months without a day off, living in shared quarters with little or no access to the ship's public areas." They faced the "threat of being fired without notice or cause. . . . The Carnival Corporation with 45 ships, the world's largest cruise company, is averaging $2.8 million a day in profits this year, almost all tax-free because the company, which is based in Miami, is registered in Panama." Consistent with the growing trend in the United States, this company, like so many others, was "inside our waters and outside our laws." One of the "earliest written codes, the Rules of Oleron, dating from 13th century Europe, required ship owners to provide free medical care for sick or injured seamen." But in this brave new world of post-NMU decline, even this ancient edict was being undermined.[4]

Unfortunately, the decline of the lot of seafarers was not just a U.S. phenomenon. London's *Financial Times* reported in 2001 that "the International Transport Workers' Federation" had "exposed a worldwide scam to fake certificates for ships' crews and officers." A person could be granted a certificate to "navigate a ship" though he or she possessed next to no "seafaring experience." There were a whopping "12, 653 cases of certificates forged by criminals or maritime authorities," particularly in Panama, which registered 10 percent of the global fleet. With typical understatement the *Financial Times* said that this "practice endangers thousands of seafarers" and placed "cargoes . . . at risk."[5]

Like phony certificates, registering "flags of convenience" also endangers international peace and security. According to *The Economist*, "Osama bin Laden, intelligence sources would have us believe, is, among other things, a shipowner with a fleet of over 20 ships, probably flying flags of convenience." Belatedly, the United States, "spooked that terrorists might turn ships into floating bombs and sail them into American ports" is now trying to reform practices it helped create decades earlier. For as *The Economist* delicately put it, "it was America, after all" that "in the late 1940s . . . switched their tanker fleets to Liberia to avoid high labour costs at home" and, in turn, "Liberia's success spawned many imitators" in search of phony registration of ships. Now, it seems, the "Americans were serious about destroying the monster they helped to create."[6]

Perhaps. But if so, this showed just how far the U.S. authorities had gone to rout the "high labour costs" brought about by the militance of a Red-led sailors' union, the NMU. For "at the end of 1946, 2342 American cargo ships carried roughly 45% of all imports and exports involving the United States." But a scant forty-four years later, "360 vessels were in service." In 2000, "about 250 U.S. flag vessels hauled only 3% of the country's imports and exports despite the nation's phenomenal growth in foreign trade." What was the impact of this trend on national security, asked the *Los Angeles Times.*[7]

It was not as if the U.S. authorities were unaware of the value of the shipping industry. In 1961, Vice Admiral Ralph E. Wilson, a member of the Federal Maritime Board, averred that "in the Cold War, in the conduct of peace-time trade and commerce, our ships become our 'first line of defense.' . . . They are the sure guarantee for the principal movement of our imports and exports." Moreover, during war, the "American merchant marine inevitably becomes the fourth arm of national defense." Defense specialist Hanson Baldwin added, "Airlift, vital for quick reaction and military flexibility, cannot compete with sealift in the transport of bulk cargoes, heavy arms and equipment, fuels and large numbers of ships."[8]

So, who or what is to blame for the deterioration of the shipping industry in the United States? The answer to this question is inseparable from tracing the decline of the NMU left, as symbolized by Smith's ouster from the nation he had served so valiantly. The purges of the union weakened it tremendously, creating a vacuum, eroding the countervailing power provided by the NMU, and unduly strengthening the shipowners who proceeded—predictably—to seek the cheapest labor, which led them to register in Liberia and Panama. Cheaper costs also help to explain the decline of the shipbuilding industry in the United States. This was all part and parcel of the "hollowing out" of the industrial base of the nation, a process which had the added "benefit" of "hollowing out" powerful CIO unions such as the NMU.

Ultimately, the effect was felt far beyond issues of national security. As the historian, Joshua B. Freeman, put it, concomitant with the decline of the NMU, "ships began docking at New Jersey piers far from Manhattan and staying only a day instead of the better part of a week." Thus, "many sailors stopped going into the city at all, depriving it of a presence that went back to the colonial [era]. The ship chandlers, rope works, and saloons that had lined the shores of Brooklyn and Manhattan since the days of Melville disappeared. The maritime unions imploded, as containerization and the end of the passenger lines drastically diminished the need for sailors as well as longshoremen, and more and more shipping lines used foreign crews." The Brooklyn Navy Yard was closed in 1965. "At its height in 1944 [it] employed seventy-one thousand men and women, making it the Navy's biggest shipyard and the largest industrial enterprise."[9]

The losses were incalculable. There was the obvious blow to the economy, as the shops that profited from the presence of so many wage workers closed down. The trade union movement in the nation was deprived of its most class-conscious proletarians when the NMU was downsized. African Americans, likewise, were deprived of jobs that had sustained them since the era of slavery. For blacks, the gains brought by the civil rights movement were bitter-sweet indeed, as they gained the right to eat in restaurants just as their means to pay the bill deteriorated. By 1967 few were surprised when "seventy thousand marchers," including "large contingents from the National Maritime Union," marched in support of the war in Vietnam, which was to claim the lives of so many sailors and sons of sailors, just as it compromised the ability of the nation to fight a "war on poverty," victory in which would have benefited so many African Americans.[10]

Though once in the vanguard of internationalist unions, the NMU swung sharply toward national chauvinism and global reaction. After Smith was ousted, the NMU, which had once sought to bolster sailors' unions abroad so as to prevent shipowners from taking advantage of lower wages abroad, to the detriment of U.S. seafarers, moved in the opposite direction as it sought vigorously to destroy the progressive Canadian Seamen's Union.[11]

The decline in internationalism flowed in more than one direction. Smith was repatriated to Jamaica. His NMU comrade Hugh Mulzac moved back to the Caribbean after he was called before the House Un-American Activities Committee.[12] But just as Smith took the lessons he had learned from the NMU and applied them in Jamaica, others also continued to act progressively, though deprived of the anchor of a progressive sailors' union. Jesse Gray, who stood with Smith to the bitter end, "starting in 1959 . . . organized a series of highly publicized protests against Harlem landlords and city housing policy, repopularizing [*sic*] the use of rent strikes."[13] His friend Jack O'Dell became a top advisor to both Martin Luther King, Jr., and Jesse Jackson after he was ousted from the NMU, which brought him to the attention of the FBI and President John F. Kennedy.[14] Jim Peck, former NMU member, became a leading organizer in the civil rights movement, just as his NMU comrade Bob Kaufman joined the front ranks of poets.[15] On the other hand, by 1952 Blackie Myers had become a "ship clerk" in Harry Bridges' union but he never "recovered from the stifling effects of McCarthyism."[16] By the late 1990s, Paul Palazzi was a broker in the red-hot Manhattan real estate market.[17]

As these NMU militants were being swept out of the union, Joseph Curran in turn was profiting handsomely. The union purchased his "tailor-made suits, size 46 extra long, size 13 and shirts, 36 sleeve length," among other goodies.[18] In 1979 he was sued by a rank-and-file NMU member who charged that he and his successor as union head, Shannon Wall, "had taken hundreds of thousands of dollars in the form of unauthorized perquisites and cash payments." Judge William C. Conner of Federal District Court referred to their rule as "a sorry chronicle of the arrogance of privilege and callous betrayal of trust." The lead plaintiff, Jim Morrisey, charged that when he joined the NMU in 1941 it was a "damn good union. They reacted quick to seamen's complaint[s]. You were free to talk and criticize." That was during the much reviled reign of the so-called "Stalinist" leaders of the union. But once the "Stalinists" were booted out, corruption and dictatorial methods became the rule of thumb.[19]

According to one analyst, Curran was deft in "disqualifying or eliminating oppositionists, transforming the union press into propaganda organs and instilling an atmosphere of physical terror" and "rigged elections."[20] Curran had erected multi-million dollar buildings named after him. He was "protected by an army of private guards." He was "an absentee boss remaining for the most part, in his 'winter residence' in Boca Raton . . . or in his 'summer residence' in Dutchess County, New York." He was notorious for signing multiyear "no-strike" accords. NMU officials, once elected by union members, were now appointed by him.[21]

Curran had been able to maintain his dictatorial rule by using the same kind of sledgehammer tactics that he had deployed so adroitly against Smith. He had taken to heart the chilling words of the Confederate naval officer Raphael Semmes, who once said, "Democracies do very well for the land, but monarchies, and . . . absolute monarchies at that, are the only successful governments for the sea."[22] Harold C. Nystrom, Acting Solicitor to the Secretary of Labor during the Eisenhower Administration, was amazed that at an NMU election "ballots were numbered in such a way that, by [comparing] the signatures contained in a Registration Record Book, it is possible to identify voters with the choice expressed by them," which violated "the Union's own constitution," not to mention elementary due process. A candidate for office "who had protested some election irregularities and some of his sympathizers were assaulted by a rival candidate and other union officials."[23] In 1960 James Mitchell, the Secretary of Labor, asked a federal court to invalidate this NMU election, which involved Curran and seventy-four other officers.[24] Curran's questionable methods may have been exceeded by those of Wall, one of the few labor leaders to back the election of Ronald W. Reagan for U.S. President in 1980 who, in putative payback, was "eyed for [the] Labor Secretary post."[25]

Blacks in labor had not benefited much from the purge of the left. In 1957, A. Philip Randolph, a former antagonist of Smith during his tenure as leader of the union of sleeping car porters, was perversely compensated for his truculence when he was actually barred from some AFL-CIO meetings with the ICFTU because of the objections of the latter.[26] "Who the hell appointed you the champion of Negro workers of America?" asked AFL-CIO boss George Meany. The AFL-CIO claimed that Randolph's union was the "sole 'racist' union" in the federation because almost "all the porters" were Negroes![27]

As the twenty-first century dawned, the shrunken NMU, reflecting its decreased relevance to the political economy of the nation, had reverted to its origins somewhat, as an Afro-Panamanian, Rene Lioaenjie, took the reins of leadership. Lioaenjie confirmed once more the preeminent role that men from the African diaspora have played in sailing in this country, continuing the tradition embodied by David Grange and Ferdinand Smith.[28] At the same time, in a maneuver that may have had Curran twisting in his grave, in 1998 the union placed "full page greetings" in the "program book" for a "banquet" designed to raise funds for the newspaper of the Communist Party.[29] The foundations of the nation were not shaken by this gesture, despite opinion to the contrary decades earlier.

Completing the historical circle, the party of Norman Manley—the PNP—sought to make amends to Richard Hart decades after the fact by expressing its contrition for his ouster. In so doing, they were also by implication making amends to Ferdinand Smith, who too had suffered when the PNP decided to climb aboard the bandwagon of the Red Scare. The continued plunge of the Jamaican currency, the violence that tore apart working-class communities in Kingston, and the extensive poverty that continued to scar this beautiful island all attested to the fact that few Jamaicans had gained when Smith's attempt to organize the workers was foiled. Indeed, by 2002 the sugar industry, to which Smith had given so much time and effort, was on life support. Finance Minister Omar Davies argued that the "government must now think seriously of shutting down the state sugar sector and turning its attention to more feasible ventures." This "would leave 40,000 people without jobs in a society where the official unemployment rate is 15 percent."[30]

David Brion Davis, the eminent historian, has remarked that "the deadly failure of communism in no way lessens the historical and contemporary crimes of capitalism."[31] Certainly, it is difficult to comprehend what Jamaicans or sailors gained when Ferdinand Smith was trounced because of his Red beliefs. For Smith was indeed punished—a punishment that continued to resonate long after he was sent to his grave. In 1964 a "secret" memorandum posted to the FBI revealed that "we have now received from our Jamaica office information from a secret and reliable source . . . that an additional contributor [to] the . . . widow fund [of Smith] is a man named Craig Vincent" of "San Cristobal, New Mexico who claimed to have been a good friend of [Smith] during the war when Vincent was in charge of the Atlantic Coast Manpower operations for the War Shipping Administration."[32] Long after Smith had passed away, the U.S. authorities continued to conduct surveillance against his widow and family as if they feared his ghost would reappear, like some apparition in the night, and seek once again to lead "Black and Red at Sea." There was little hope of this, of course, though "black labor," it seemed, was destined to remain "at sea," adrift, shorn of its moorings, as long as it turned its back on the radicalism, and the internationalism, of Ferdinand Smith.

Notes

NOTES TO THE PREFACE

1. "Proceedings of the Sixth National Convention," New York City, 22 September–15 October 1947, Box 90, **National Maritime Union Papers,** *Rutgers University, New Brunswick.*

2. Program for 20 September 1944 Testimonial Dinner for Ferdinand Smith, Box 97, **National Maritime Union Papers,** *Rutgers University, New Brunswick.* Hereinafter referred to **NMU Papers.**

3. **People's Voice,** 30 September 1944.

4. **The Pilot,** 22 September 1944. (I read this newspaper of the National Maritime Union at the main library of New York University, though it can be found elsewhere.) At this gathering Bethune thanked Smith in the name of "6,500,000 brown American women" for the "manly way you have represented us."

5. Message from President Franklin D. Roosevelt, 7 September 1944, Official File, 4177. See also Personal File, 6088, for an indication of the discussion that preceded the forwarding of this brief message. *Franklin D. Roosevelt Library, Hyde Park, New York.*

6. **New York World-Telegram,** 19 September 1944.

7. Sidney Hillman to "Dear Ferd," 9 June 1944, Reel 8, Part IV, #431, **National Negro Congress Papers,** *Schomburg Center, New York Public Library.* Hereinafter referred to as **NNC Papers.**

8. Dominic Capeci, **The Harlem Riot of 1943,** Philadelphia: Temple University Press, 1977, 103.

9. Ann Ksaloff to Ferdinand Smith, 15 November 1943, Box 42, **Vito Marcantonio Papers,** *New York Public Library;* **The Pilot,** 17 December 1943.

10. "Labor Leaders," **Ebony,** 11(Number 4, February 1947): 12–16, 12. Note, however, that a contemporary scholar has written about this era that "Randolph and [Willard] Townsend . . . sought the title of undisputed leader of black labor." See Eric Arnesen, **Brotherhoods of Color: Black Railroad Workers and the Struggle for Equality,** Cambridge: Harvard University Press, 2001, 115.

11. "The Quarter's Poll," **Public Opinion Quarterly,** 11(Number 1, Spring 1947): 138–171. This poll of "well-known labor leaders"—which included such luminaries as John L. Lewis, Harry Bridges, Walter Reuther, David Dubinsky, and others—also included Ferdinand Smith, who, with Randolph, had the lowest rating of disapproval.

12. "Approximate NMU Membership," NMU Research Department, 18 March 1952, Box 100, **NMU Papers.**

13. Richard Boyer, "Tidal Wave on the Waterfront," **New Masses,** 18 June 1946, Box 95, **NMU Papers.** As a possible NMU strike loomed, the writer noted, "for the first time in history striking American trade unions will be backed by the organized labor movement of the world. For the first time in history the newly formed World Federation of Trade Unions . . . will throw its earth-circling weight behind an American strike. For the first time in history a domestic strike will have profound repercussions on American foreign policy."

14. **New York Post,** 11 June 1946. Here it was noted that a proposed NMU strike would "cripple over 50 big ports, stall food and gas shipments inside the country and perhaps wind up as the first international strike."

15. At one point Smith and his West Coast counterpart, Harry Bridges, who was an Australian immigrant and leader of the stevedores and reputed Communist, advocated a merger of their respective unions, which would have given radicals an extraordinary impact on the national economy as the Cold War unfolded. **ILWU Dispatcher,** 9 January 1948, **Files of International Longshore and Warehousemen's Union,** *San Francisco.* Hereinafter referred to as the **ILWU Files.** Thanks to Gene Vrana, I read these files at the headquarters of the union.

16. **The Pilot,** 25 July 1941.

17. Interview, Terry Penman, 25 July 1999; interview, Paul Jarvis, 25 July 1999.

18. A'Leila Bundles, **On Her Own Ground: The Life and Times of Madam C. J. Walker,** New York: Scribner, 2001, 155. Of course, as the Introduction makes clear, this perception by U.S. Negroes often ignored deep-seated intersecting color and class biases in Jamaica. Still, as Winston James has observed, "the Afro-American experience is the anomaly of the Americas, the aberration, not the norm. . . . Only the United States has had on its statute books so-called anti-miscegenation laws" or "institutionalized racial segregation." Winston James, **A Fierce Hatred of Injustice: Claude McKay's Jamaica and His Poetry of Rebellion,** New York: Verso, 2000, 244.

19. Despite the earlier focus on sailors and the NMU as a major vector of spying and Soviet "penetration" of the United States, recent works on this phenomenon—based on research in recently opened Moscow archives—do not so much as mention this union in the index. See Harvey Klehr et al., **The Soviet World of American Communism,** New Haven: Yale University Press, 1998; Harvey Klehr et al., eds., **Venona: Decoding Soviet Espionage in America,** New Haven: Yale University Press, 1999. Though the NMU, unlike many unions and organizations so characterized, was actually led to a large degree by Communists, it has received short shrift from a number of writers who have analyzed the question of U.S. Communism. See Theodore Draper, **American Communism and Soviet Russia,** New York: Octagon, 1977; Harvey Klehr, **Communist Cadre: The Social Background of the American Communist Party Elite,** Stanford: Stanford University Press, 1978; Philip J. Jaffe, **The Rise and Fall of American Communism,** New York: Horizon Press, 1975; Aileen S. Kraditor, **"Jimmy Higgins": The Mental World of the American Rank and File Communist, 1930–1958,** New York: Greenwood, 1988; John Gates, **The Story of an American Communist,** New York: Thomas Nelson, 1958. Analysts of U.S. Communism are not alone. Those who have examined the Negro experience in port cities often have downplayed or ignored Smith's role and that of the NMU. See Earl Lewis, **In Their Own Interests: Race, Class and Power in Twentieth-Century Norfolk, Virginia,** Berkeley: University of California Press, 1991; Harold A. McDougall, **Black Baltimore: A New Theory of Community,** Philadelphia:

Temple University Press, 1993; Despite their importance to the nation's economy, world communism, and black liberation, Paul Buhle is no doubt correct when he writes, "As Marcus Rediker rightly complains, nearly all accounts of sailors' lives are about the nineteenth century." Paul Buhle, **Taking Care of Business: Samuel Gompers, George Meany, Lane Kirland and the Tragedy of American Labor,** New York: Monthly Review Press, 1999, 266.

20. William McFee, "Seagoing Soviets," **Saturday Evening Post,** 21 September 1940, Box 4, **National Maritime Union Papers,** *Cornell University.* Hereinafter referred to as **NMU Papers, Cornell.** This NMU collection has rich material on labor spies, minutes of meetings at sea, membership rolls, and the like, mostly from the Boston local of the union.

21. **New York Times,** 25 April 1940.

22. **The Pilot,** 12 November 1943.

23. Ferdinand Smith to Benjamin Fielding, circa 1945, Reel 2, Part IV, #670, **NNC Papers.**

24. **Hawsepipe,** 5(Number 4, December 1986): 3. This newsletter about NMU history can be found at NYU Library.

25. For an analysis of the impact of this middle-class leadership in a mostly working-class community, see Gerald Horne, **Fire This Time: The Watts Uprising and the 1960s,** Charlottesville: University Press of Virginia, 1995, passim.

26. Pamphlet on Ferdinand Smith, "For His Patriotic Service," circa 1948, Ferdinand Smith Vertical File, *Tamiment, New York University.*

27. **New York Times,** 16 August 1951.

28. Jon V. Kofas, "U.S. Foreign Policy and the World Federation of Trade Unions, 1944–1948," **Diplomatic History,** 26 (Number 1, Winter 2002): 21–60.

29. Report, 18 August 1955, 741h.00/8-1855, Box 3206, Decimal File, Record Group 59, *U.S. State Department, National Archives and Records Administration, College Park, Maryland.*

NOTES TO THE INTRODUCTION

1. Ferdinand Smith, "Jamaica: Paradise Isle," **World Trade Union Movement** (Number 9, 1–15 May 1953): 24–25, 24.

2. A'Leila Bundles, **On Her Own Ground: The Life and Times of Madam C. J. Walker,** New York: Scribner, 2001, 155. Gordon Lewis has spoken of "the remarkable unanimity with which travelers to the region, almost

from the very beginning, remarked on the stark contrast everywhere between the beauty of its natural habitat and the Gothic horrors of its social scene: where every prospect pleases and only man is vile." See Brian Meeks, **Radical Caribbean: From Black Power to Abu Bakr,** Kingston: University of the West Indies Press, 1996, 3.

3. File: Westmoreland, **Gleaner,** 21 August 1962, 24 August 1962, *National Library of Jamaica.* Pimento, coffee, honey, logwood, fishing, and cattle were the other props of the Westmoreland economy. See "Parish Profiles: Westmoreland," Kingston: Jamaica Information Service, 1991, *National Library of Jamaica.*

4. Philip Sherlock, **Norman Manley: A Biography,** London: Macmillan, 1980, 18, 64. "Some took the view that book education was not useful. . . . In St. Lucia the young poet Derek Walcott wrote of 'this malarial enervation, that nothing could ever be built among these rotting shacks, barefooted backyards and moulting shingles.'"

5. Interview, Earl Smith, 2 July 1999.

6. Carl Hamilton Senior, "Bountied European Immigration into Jamaica, 1834–1842," Ph.D. dissertation, University of West Indies, Mona, 1977, ix. Note that one of the leaders of the Jamaica Union of Teachers at the turn of the twentieth century was "A. J. Smith," a "white Moravian teacher who became a close associate of" the island's legendary Robert Love. See Joyce Mary Lumsden, "Robert Love and Jamaican Politics," Ph.D. dissertation, University of West Indies, Mona, 1987, 328.

7. See also George Eaton, **Alexander Bustamante and Modern Jamaica,** Kingston: Kingston Publishing Company, 1975, 197.

8. See Philip Sherlock and Hazel Bennett, **The Story of the Jamaican People,** Kingston: Ian Randle, 1998, 213.

9. O. Nigel Bolland, **The Politics of Labour in the British Caribbean: The Social Origins of Authoritarianism and Democracy in the Labour Movement,** Kingston: Ian Randle, 2001, 82.

10. O. Nigel Bolland, **On the March: Labour Rebellions in the British Caribbean, 1934–1939,** London: James Currey, 1995, 7.

11. Rupert Charles Lewis, **Walter Rodney's Intellectual and Political Thought,** Kingston: The Press, University of the West Indies, 1998, 27.

12. David Godfrey, **Reckoning with the Force: Stories of the Jamaica Constabulary Force in the 1950s,** Kingston: The Mill Press, 1998, 65.

13. Winston James, **A Fierce Hatred of Injustice: Claude McKay's Jamaica and His Poetry of Rebellion,** New York: Verso, 2000, 13.

14. James, **Fierce Hatred,** 16: "While less than one in every hundred black Jamaicans was eligible to vote, more than two of every hundred coloureds and seven of every hundred whites were registered to vote." See also George Eaton, **Alexander Bustamante and Modern Jamaica,** Kingston: Kingston Publishing Company, 1975, 19. Before 1944 "in a population of just under one million persons (with possibly half of them twenty-one and over) the island's electoral lists boasted no more than 40,000 electors, with some parishes having just about 1000 each."

15. Philip Sherlock and Hazel Bennett, **The Story of the Jamaican People,** Kingston: Ian Randle, 1998, 272. See also Jeffrey B. Perry, ed., **A Hubert Harrison Reader,** Middletown: Wesleyan University Press, 2001, 244.

16. Gladys Bustamante, **The Memoirs of Lady Bustamante,** Kingston: Kingston Publishing Company, 1997, 5, 8, 18, 22, 23, 30.

17. Susan Craig, **Smiles and Blood: The Ruling Class Response to the Workers' Rebellion of 1937 in Trinidad and Tobago,** London: New Beacon, 1988, 14.

18. Fitzroy L. Ambursley, "The Working Class in the Third World: A Study in Class Consciousness and Class Activism in Jamaica, 1919–1952," Thesis, Department of Sociology, Faculty of Social Sciences, University of West Indies, St. Augustine, Trinidad, 1978, 18, *British Library, London.*

19. **Freedom Newsletter,** August 1961, **Richard Hart Papers.**

20. **The Pilot,** 12 November 1937.

21. "Parish Profile: Westmoreland," Kingston: Jamaica Information Service, 1991, *National Library of Jamaica.*

22. Interview, Earl Smith, 2 July 1999.

23. Sherlock, **Norman Manley,** 12.

24. Eaton, **Alexander Bustamante,** 13.

25. Elizabeth McLean Peters, **Jamaican Labor Migration: White Capital and Black Labor, 1850–1930,** Boulder: Westview, 1988, 57. See also Aviva Chomsky, **West Indians and the United Fruit Company in Costa Rica, 1870–1940,** Baton Rouge: Louisiana State University Press, 1996.

26. Lancelot S. Lewis, **The West Indian in Panama: Black Labor in Panama, 1850–1914,**

Washington, D.C.: University Press of America, 1980.

27. Frank Hill, **Bustamante and His Letters,** Kingston: Kingston Publishing Company, 1976, 14, 17.

28. "Freedom's Assassins," **Spotlight,** 15(Number 4, April 1954): 14–16.

29. James, **Fierce Hatred,** 92.

30. Lord Oliver, **Jamaica: The Blessed Land,** London: Faber & Faber, 1936, 299, 300, 301.

31. Bolland, **The Politics of Labor,** 158, 159.

32. "Jim Crow Discrimination against U.S. Employees in the Canal Zone," circa 1948, Box 9, folder 9, **Ewart Guinier Papers,** Schomburg Center, New York Public Library: "They paid the white workers in gold. The colored workers were paid in silver. . . . For the past 42 years the 'silver-gold' system has degenerated into an economic and social pattern of racial segregation." In the Canal Zone "virtually all of the Negro employees and their families live in one or two room apartments. 90% of all the buildings provide toilet and washing facilities on a communal basis! Most of the buildings are dilapidated and infested with vermin. Many of them are firetraps with only one or two exits for five and six families!" See John Biesanz, "Race Relations in the Canal Zone," **Phylon,** 11(1950): 23–50; Frederic Haskin, **The Panama Canal,** New York: Doubleday, 1914; George W. Westerman, "Historical Notes on West Indians on the Isthmus of Panama," **Phylon,** 22(Winter 1961): 340–350.

33. "Strike of Silver Labourers," 1920, Box 919, **George Westerman Papers,** Schomburg Center, New York Public Library. See also Michael L. Conniff, **Black Labor on a White Canal: Panama, 1904–1981,** Pittsburgh: University of Pittsburgh Press, 1985.

34. Peters, **Jamaican Labor Migration,** 207.

35. M. Churchill, Brigadier General, General Staff, Director of Military Intelligence, to Frank Burke, Bureau of Investigation, Department of Justice, 26 February 1920, Reel 9, #925, **Federal Surveillance of Afro-Americans, 1917–1925.**

36. "Confidential" Memorandum from Major Norman Randolph, Infantry, Department of Intelligence Office, 22 May 1920, Reel 18, #957, **Federal Surveillance of Afro-Americans, 1917–1925.**

37. Bolland, **The Politics of Labour,** Kingston: Ian Randle, 2001, 158.

38. Aviva Chomsky, "'Barbados or Canada?' Race, Immigration and Nation in Early Twentieth-Century Cuba," **Hispanic American Historical Review,** 80(Number 3, August 2000): 415–462, 430, 439, 452.

39. **The Pilot,** 27 February 1948.

40. Peter Linebaugh and Marcus Rediker, **The Many-Headed Hydra: Sailors, Slaves, Commoners, and the Hidden History of the Revolutionary Atlantic,** Boston: Beacon, 2000, 312.

41. Alan J. Rice and Martin Crawford, "Triumphant Exile: Frederick Douglass in Britain, 1845–1847," in Alan J. Rice and Martin Crawford, eds., **Liberating Sojourn: Frederick Douglass and Transatlantic Reform,** Athens: University of Georgia Press, 1999, 1–12, 1.

42. **The Pilot,** 3 May 1940.

43. David Robertson, **Denmark Vesey,** New York: Random House, 1999.

44. Linebaugh and Rediker, **The Many-Headed Hydra,** 299.

45. Fred Lee McGhee, "The Black Crop: Slavery and Slave Trading in Nineteenth Century Texas," Ph.D. dissertation, University of Texas at Austin, 2000, 223.

46. See also David Cecelski, **The Waterman's Song: Slavery and Freedom in Maritime North Carolina,** Chapel Hill: University of North Carolina Press, 2001, 53.

47. **The Pilot,** 8 November 1940.

48. Linebaugh and Rediker, **The Many-Headed Hydra,** 113, 241, 321. "Othello was performed by African-American sailors in Dartmoor Prison in 1814." The confined nature of the sailing ship gave Negroes an opportunity to maximize their influence. Thus, in 1853 William Tell Coleman was on a ship from New York to San Francisco via Panama when yellow fever began spreading uncontrollably. His Negro "body servant, a free colored man . . . proved to be of genuine service throughout the voyage." See Narrative of William Tell Coleman, MS 419, California Historical Society, San Francisco.

49. Marcus Rediker, **Between the Devil and the Deep Blue Sea: Merchant Seamen, Pirates, and the Anglo-American Maritime World, 1700–1750,** New York: Cambridge University Press, 1987, 110. See also W. Jeffrey Bolster, **Black Jacks: African-American Seamen in the Age of Sail,** Cambridge: Harvard University Press, 1997.

50. See Martha Putney, **Black Sailors: Afro-American Merchant Seamen and Whalemen Prior to the Civil War,** Westport: Greenwood, 1987. See also Esther M. Douty,

Forten the Sailmaker: Pioneer Champion of Negro Rights, Chicago: Rand McNally, 1968.

51. Jonathan Rosenberg, "For Democracy, Not Hypocrisy: World War and Race Relations in the United States, 1914–1919," **International History Review,** 21(September 1999): 592–625, 592.

52. Langston Hughes, **The Big Sea,** New York: Hill and Wang, 1993. Hughes disputed the idea that labor at sea was somehow harsh. "There was nothing hard about a mess boy's work. You got up at six in the morning, with the mid-Atlantic calm as a sun-pool, served breakfast, made up the rooms, served luncheon, had all the afternoon off, served dinner, and that was all. The rest of the time you could lie on deck in the sun, play cards with sailors, or sleep. . . . When we got to Africa we took on a full African crew to supplement the regular crew. . . . Then I had an African boy to do my washing, my cleaning and almost all my work—as did everybody on board." See Peter Neill, ed., **American Sea Writing: A Literary Anthology,** New York: Library of America, 2000, 444. Negroes were not the only ones who drew on their experiences at sea for the benefit of literature. Joseph Conrad, a sailor, was one of the keenest critics of colonialism. See Arthur Pollard, ed., **The Representation of Business in English Literature,** London: Institute of Economic Affairs, 2000, 127.

53. Maryemma Graham and Amritjit Singh, eds., **Conversations with Ralph Ellison,** Jackson: University Press of Mississippi, 1995. Lawrence Jackson, **Ralph Ellison: Emergence of Genius,** New York: John Wiley, 2002, 282: "Ellison used his clout in Communist-influenced union circles to quickly muster into the National Maritime Union." See also John Charles Stoner, "Anti-Communism, Anti-Colonialism and African Labor: The AFL-CIO in Africa, l955–1975," Ph.D. dissertation, Columbia University, 2001, 101; St. Clair Drake, "Intellectual Climate among Black Americans between 1929 and 1945," Box 23, Folder 7, **St. Clair Drake Papers,** *Schomburg Center.*

54. As a young student in the United States, he had "belonged to the National Maritime Union." See June Milne, **Kwame Nkrumah: A Biography,** London: Panaf, 1999, 76.

55. J. Alexander Somerville, **Man of Colour: An Autobiography,** Kingston: Pioneer Press, 1951, 20.

56. Reed Ueda, "West Indians," in Stephan Thernstrom et al., eds., **Harvard Encyclopedia of American Ethnic Groups,** Cambridge: Harvard University Press, 1980, 1020–1027. By the 1930s, New York City contained 65 percent of all immigrant blacks.

57. David Cecelski argues that "the presence of West Indian roots in Beaufort [South Carolina] folk culture is a steady theme in local oral histories." See Cecelski, **The Waterman's Song,** 273.

58. Rupert Lewis and Maureen Warner-Lewis, eds., **Garvey: Africa, Europe, the Americas,** Trenton: Africa World Press, 1994, 3. Contrary to Du Bois, A. Philip Randolph was closely associated with the **Messenger,** which was said to embody "anti-West Indianism." Smith was the leading challenger to Randolph's preeminent position as the embodiment of black labor. See Theodore Kornweibel, **No Crystal Stair: Black Life and the** *Messenger,* **1917–1928,** Westport: Greenwood, 1975, 149.

59. See Dwight Morgan, "The Foreign Born in the United States," undated, Reel 1, Part III, #0491, **Civil Rights Congress Papers.**

60. Interview with W. A. Domingo, 18 January 1958, Series 1.2, Box 21, Folder 2, **Theodore Draper Papers,** *Emory University.*

61. Mark Solomon, **The Cry Was Unity: Communists   and   African-Americans, 1917–1936,** Jackson: University Press of Mississippi, 1998, 3.

62. See W. Burghardt Turner and Joyce Moore Turner, eds., **Richard B. Moore, Caribbean Militant in Harlem: Collected Writings, 1920–1992,** Bloomington: Indiana University Press, 76.

63. See Frances Henry, ed., **Ethnicity in the Americas,** The Hague: Mouton, 1976.

64. See Nancy Foner, "The Jamaicans: Race and Ethnicity among Migrants in New York City," in Nancy Foner, ed., **New Immigrants in New York City,** New York: Columbia University Press, 1987, 195–217; Clifton C. Hawkins, "Race First versus Class First: An Intellectual History of Afro-American Radicalism," Ph.D. dissertation, University of California, Davis, 2000, 243; Colin Powell, **My American Journey,** New York: Random House, 1995, 22; **New York Amsterdam News,** 16 April 1938.

65. R. B. Hudson, "The Fight of the Seamen for Militant Unionism," **The Communist,** 15(Number 3, March 1936): 220–229, 222.

66. Ferdinand Smith, "Why I Am a Communist," **Spotlight,** 14(No. 6–7, May–July 1953): 16–17. Former sailor Herman Ferguson

confirms that "once you get out to sea, the chief steward was more important" than the captain, particularly given his key role in the care and feeding of those on board. Interview, Herman Ferguson, 6 June 1999 (in possession of author).

67. See Alan Wald, **Exiles from a Future Time: The Forging of the Mid-Twentieth Century Literary Left,** Chapel Hill: University of North Carolina Press, 2002. One example among many of this trend among Negro sailors was Harold Donald Harper. He had a B.A. from the University of Edinburgh and an M.A. from the University of Berlin. He "reads and writes eight languages and speaks twelve, including French, German, Russian, English, Japanese, Arabic, Greek, Gaelic, Icelandic, Hindustani and Basuta, a Zulu dialect." In 1942, it was reported that he had been "torpedoed six times—five [during] the last war." He was born in Kansas City, Missouri, in 1888. The Ku Klux Klan "burnt down the house where his mother was living" on the night he was born. His mother was an escaped slave and his father was Irish. His father moved to Siberia and became a "wealthy fur trader" but "left behind" his son, though he would travel two or three times a year to Russia.

At twelve he was sent to boarding school in the United Kingdom: "He said no discrimination was shown toward Negroes in England until World War I." Then he enrolled in Edinburgh where he met his wife, the "daughter of a wealthy East Indian merchant." He went to Vienna to "study the piano." "I was always crazy to go to sea," he recalled later, so he traveled to Hamburg and shipped to Africa where he became a Muslim. During World War I he was stationed in Brussels as a translator for Thomas Cook. He moved on to become an aide to British Colonel Walter Marjoribanks, who was then High Commissioner for Foreign Trade with a broad transcontinental portfolio. The Colonel left him a tidy $50,000 when he died. After the war, he worked for Thomas Cook in Egypt, then Tokyo. But after the great 1923 earthquake, he left for his unforgettable love—the sea. See **The Pilot,** 20 November 1942.

68. Gerald Horne, **Class Struggle in Hollywood, 1930–1950: Moguls, Mobsters, Stars, Reds, and Trade Unionists,** Austin: University of Texas Press, 2001, 136–137.

69. Linebaugh and Rediker, **The Many-Headed Hydra,** 161.

70. Linebaugh and Rediker, **The Many-Headed Hydra,** 328.

71. Donald Edward Willett, "Joe Curran and the National Maritime Union, 1936–1945," Ph.D. dissertation, Texas A&M University, 1985, 34. See also Ralph W. Andrews and Harry A. Kirwin, **This Was Seafaring: A Sea Chest of Salty Memories,** Seattle: Superior, 1955.

72. Oral History, Hoyt Haddock, 23 December 1982, *Texas A&M University.*

73. Gerald Reminick, **Patriots and Heroes: True Stories of the U.S. Merchant Marine in World War II,** Palo Alto: Glencannon Press, 2000, xi. Another account of this era described ships thus: "Aboard most ships the food was lousy, the living quarters crowded and hot, reeking with the stench of unwashed bodies and ruined stomachs. . . . Vermin lined bunks, sharing the mean air that two small portholes let in, depending upon the weather." Beth McHenry and Frederick N. Myers, **Home Is the Sailor: The Story of an American Sailor,** New York: International Publishers, 1948, 34.

74. Richard H. Dillon, **Shanghaiing Days,** New York: Coward-McCann, 1961, 199, 240.

75. See John A. Butler, **Sailing on Friday: The Perilous Voyage of America's Merchant Marine,** Washington, D.C.: Brassey, 1997, 107.

76. See Joseph Curran, "Know the Score: On Seamen's Conditions before the NMU," New York: NMU, 1945, **Bertha Reynolds Papers,** *Smith College.*

77. Bertha C. Reynolds, **An Uncharted Journey: Fifty Years in Social Work by One of Its Great Teachers,** New York: Citadel, 1963, 250.

78. Peter Neill, ed., **American Sea Writing: A Literary Anthology,** New York: Library of America, 2000, 213, 287, 343–344, 659, 662. Seaman Thomas Rowe said that "the North Atlantic was the worst ocean I ever traveled, with ferocious storms and mountainous waves, the power and weight of which was really terrifying, especially at night when you could only see the fluorescence on the crests as they reared up alongside the ship. Nearing the coast of America or Canada you usually ran into fog, which added to the hazards of sailing in convoy. It was not uncommon to be fogbound for two or three days in that area." The northeast route to Russia posed a major challenge to sailors as the "perpetual daylight hours of summer and the ferocious weather and long nights of winter, when dawn and twilight were divided by an hour and when an

unseen 'growler' drifting from the icepack, could tear a hole in a ship below the waterline." Overhead there was "the eerie, multicoloured splendour of Aurora Borealis shimmering and flashing in the polar sky." Philip Kaplan and Jack Currie, **Convoy: Merchant Sailors at War, 1939–1945,** Annapolis: Naval Institute Press, 2000, 105, 136.

79. Paul S. Taylor, **The Sailors' Union of the Pacific,** New York: Ronald Press, 1923, 177.

80. **The Pilot,** 4 July 1947.

81. **The Pilot,** 9 July 1948.

82. **The Pilot,** 2 May 1947.

83. Rediker, **Between the Devil and the Deep Blue Sea,** 110, 161, 248.

84. "Seamen as Clients," undated, circa 1940s, Box 3, **Bertha Reynolds Papers,** *Smith College.*

85. Interview, Herman Ferguson, 6 June 1999 (in possession of author).

86. See Harry Kelsey, **Sir Francis Drake: The Queen's Pirate,** New Haven: Yale University Press, 1998, 20.

87. Herb Tank, **Communists on the Waterfront,** New York: New Century, 1946, 11, Box 105, #2, **Dorothy Healey Papers,** *California State University, Long Beach.*

88. Rediker, **Between the Devil and the Deep Blue Sea,** 174, 185, 229.

NOTES TO CHAPTER I

1. Maxine Silverstein, "Report on [NMU]," Spring 1944, Box 91, **NMU Papers.** See also John A. Butler, **Sailing on Friday: The Perilous Voyage of America's Merchant Marine,** Washington, D.C.: Brassey, 1997, 105, 108, 109.

2. Andrew Gibson and Arthur Donovan, **The Abandoned Ocean: A History of United States Maritime Policy,** Columbia: University of South Carolina Press, 2000, 181.

3. Gibson and Donavan, **The Abandoned Ocean,** 97.

4. Hyman Weintraub, **Andrew Furuseth: Emancipator of the Seamen,** Berkeley: University of California Press, 1959, 105, 112, 114, 160.

5. K. Jack Bauer, **A Maritime History of the United States,** Columbia: University of South Carolina Press, 1988, 255.

6. Weintraub, **Andrew Furuseth,** 112.

7. Butler, **Sailing on Friday,** 146.

8. Sterling D. Spero and Abram L. Harris, **The Black Worker: The Negro and the Labor Movement,** New York: Columbia University Press, 1931, 71.

9. Art Shields, **On the Battle Lines, 1919–1939,** New York: International Publishers, 1986, 203–204.

10. Gibson and Donavan, **The Abandoned Ocean,** 117.

11. Hugh Mulzac, **A Star to Steer By,** New York: International, 1963, 85.

12. Albert Ventere Lannon, "Second String Red: The Life of Al Lannon, an American Communist," M.A. thesis, San Francisco State University, 1997, 40.

13. Philip Taft, "Strife in the Maritime Industry," **Political Science Quarterly,** 54(Number 2, June 1939): 216–236, 216.

14. Steward R. Bross, **Ocean Shipping,** Cambridge, Maryland: Cornell Maritime Press, 1956, 8.

15. See **Bureau of Marine Inspection and Navigation, General Records Relating to the 1936 Maritime Strike Washington Star,** National Archives and Records Administration, College Park, Maryland, 27 December 1936.

16. Taft, "Strife in the Maritime Industry," 216–236, 216. See also Philip Taft, "Some Problems of the New Unionism in the United States," **American Economic Review,** 29(Number 2, June 1939): 313–324.

17. Gibson and Donavan, **The Abandoned Ocean,** 183, 184.

18. Herb Tank, **Communists on the Waterfront,** New York: New Century, 1946, 11, Box 105, #2, **Dorothy Healey Papers,** *California State University, Long Beach.* The "Sons of Liberty," preeminent in the American Revolution, were "in the main composed of . . . shipwrights, caulkers, seamen." See William Standard, **Merchant Seamen: A Short History of Their Struggles,** New York: International, 1947, 13. Shipping—particularly privateering—was essential to the formation of the United States, as the Yankees harassed the British, just as decades later the Confederates harassed the United States. See Jerome R. Garitee, **The Republic's Private Navy: The American Privateering Business as Practiced by Baltimore during the War of 1812,** Middletown, Connecticut: Wesleyan University Press, 1977.

19. T. H. Wintringham, **Mutiny: Being a Survey of Mutinies from Spartacus to Invergordon,** New York: Fortuny's Publishers, 1939, 348.

20. Irving Howe and Lewis Coser, **The American Communist Party: A Critical History,** New York: Praeger, 1962, 380: "From its inception [the NMU] had been dominated by

the Communists." Maurice Isserman, **Which Side Were You On? The American Communist Party during the Second World War,** Middletown: Wesleyan University Press, 1982, 132. From the attack on Pearl Harbor until the end of 1942 there were a "hundred" Reds in the NMU, many in leadership posts. See also Nathan Glazer, **The Social Basis of American Communism,** Westport: Greenwood, 1924, 119. The Communists had "great membership strength" in the NMU.

21. Clifton C. Hawkins, "'Race First versus Class First': An Intellectual History of Afro-American Radicalism, 1911–1928," Ph.D. dissertation, University of California, Davis, 2000, 124.

22. **Doghouse News,** 16 July 1934, Reel 286, delo 3688, **Communist Party—USA Papers,** *Library of Congress.* Hereinafter referred to as **CPUSA Papers.**

23. Philip S. Foner, **History of the Labor Movement in the United States, Volume X: The TUEL, 1925–1929,** New York: International Publishers, 1994, 237.

24. Minutes of TUEL, 5 September 1926, 28 December 1926, Box 28, **Theodore Draper Papers,** *Hoover Institute, California.*

25. Report, 25 November 1926, Reel 66, delo 914, **CPUSA Papers.** See also Bill Bailey, **The Kid from Hoboken: An Autobiography,** San Francisco: Circus Lithographic Prepress, 1993, 70.

26. **New Yorker,** 6 July 1946, Box 100, **NMU Papers.**

27. **New York Times,** 17 January 1926.

28. Scott Tadao Kurashige, "Transforming Los Angeles: Black and Japanese-American Struggles for Racial Equality in the 20th Century," Ph.D. dissertation, University of California, Los Angeles, 2000, 285.

29. Memorandum to "Comrade Rutherberg," 2 August 1926, Reel 59, delo 819, **CPUSA Papers.**

30. Jeffrey Perry, ed., **A Hubert Harrison Reader,** Middletown: Wesleyan University Press, 2001, 181; **Negro World,** 3 July 1920, 20 March 1920, 24 May 1920.

31. Report on ANLC Convention, 25–31 October 1925, Reel 39, delo 575, **CPUSA Papers.**

32. From Workers Party to UNIA, 14 August 1924, Reel 23, delo 359, **CPUSA Papers.**

33. Report on Negro Work to the CEC, 12 August 1926, Reel 59, delo 819, **CPUSA Papers.**

34. Report of Negro Committee, 20 September 1926, Reel 59, delo 819, **CPUSA Papers.**

35. Report of the Committee on Negro Work, circa 1926, Reel 83, delo 1108, **CPUSA Papers.**

36. Preliminary Report on Negro Labor Congress, 1 January 1926, Reel 59, delo 819, **CPUSA Papers.**

37. Internal Memorandum, 24 September 1924, Reel 39, delo 575, **CPUSA Papers.**

38. "Statement for the Minutes by Harold Williams," 4 August 1930, Reel 155, delo 2022, **CPUSA Papers.**

39. Otto Huiswood to James Ford, 14 November 1929, Reel 130, delo 1688, **CPUSA Papers.**

40. "Report on Party Registration," November 1931, Series 1.2, Box 6, Folder 9, **Theodore Draper Papers,** *Emory University.* "Foreign-born" membership was 5,766; there were 126 in the "marine" sector versus 1,073 in "metal." The "most important nationalities" included "Jews 1708" versus "Russians 761" and "Italians 285." In a speech at the Sixth World Congress of the Communist International in 1928, James W. Ford reported that there were no more than fifty Negro members in the CPUSA. "At the time the Party may have had no more than 12,000 members." James S. Allen, "Organizing in the Depression South: A Communist's Memoir," **Nature, Society and Thought: A Journal of Dialectical and Historical Materialism,** 13(Number 1, 2000): 1–145, 18.

41. "Minutes of the Political Committee Meeting," 6 November 1929, Series 1.2, Box 6, Folder 1, **Theodore Draper Papers,** *Emory University.*

42. Minutes of the Negro Committee of the Central Committee, CPUSA, 12 December 1929, Reel 130, delo 1686, **CPUSA Papers.**

43. Otto Huiswood to "Dear Comrades," 9 December 1929, Reel 130, delo 1688, **CPUSA Papers.**

44. "Draft proposals for initiating activities in the British West Indies," 1 February 1931, Reel 167, delo 2222, **CPUSA Papers.**

45. Minutes of TUEL, 4 March 1927, Box 29, **Theodore Draper Papers,** *Hoover Institute.*

46. Cyril Briggs to Theodore Draper, 5 June 1958, Box 31, **Theodore Draper Papers,** *Hoover Institute.*

47. Communist organizer James S. Allen, among others, has disputed the notion that

the Comintern in Moscow micromanaged the CPUSA. He cites a 1928 speech by Red leader James Ford in which he said, "During the last few years no less than 19 resolutions and documents upon the Negro question have been sent by the Comintern to the American Party, and not a single one of them has been carried into effect or brought before the party." See Allen, "Organizing in the Depression South," 19.

48. Cyril Briggs to Theodore Draper, 7 March 1958, Box 31, **Theodore Draper Papers,** *Hoover Institute.* Theodore Draper concluded that there was a connection between the significant West Indian influence on the Communists and their "Black Belt" thesis calling for self-determination for the Negroes. Theodore Draper to "Dear Jim," 21 February 1958, Series 1.2, Box 21, Folder 2, **Theodore Draper Papers,** *Emory University:* "Briggs was a West Indian. Now it seems that Huiswood and Richard Moore, as well as some others, were also West Indians. I have been told that the real drive for self-determination came from the West Indians, working in the American Party, rather than from native American Negroes, who were rather cool to the idea. I understand that West Indians always have taken a much greater interest in the 'national' question, owing to their immediate interest in struggling against colonialism. A number of former American Negro Communists have made this distinction for me." For his part, Briggs believed that "Negro nationhood sentiments are never quite absent from the Negro community. . . . Such sentiments were expressed as early as 1852. . . . They were also reflected, if obliquely, in the general rejoicing of the Darker Peoples of the world over Japan's crushing defeat of Tsarist Russia in 1905 and in the pro-Japanese movement among American Negroes during World War II." See Cyril Briggs to Theodore Draper, 24 March 1958, Box 31, **Theodore Draper Papers,** *Hoover Institute.*

Briggs also played a pivotal role in the African Blood Brotherhood, a "revolutionary secret order" formed "in the fall of 1917," and which "thrived six years" with "2500 members." It advocated "armed resistance against lynching" and "self determination" and was influential in the West Indies. See Folder 3, Box 21, **Theodore Draper Papers,** *Hoover Institute.* See also **The Worker,** 11 August 1923. Another study concludes that the ABB had about "3500 members" and was "dominated by emigrants from the Caribbean." See Mark Solomon, **The Cry Was Unity: Communists and African-Americans, 1917–1936,** Jackson: University Press of Mississippi, 1998, 61.

49. Solomon, **The Cry Was Unity,** 61.

50. Ira Reid, **Negro Membership in American Labor Unions,** New York: National Urban League, 1930, 21, 51, 127: As of 1920 "Longshoremen and stevedores" had one of the highest percentages of "male Negro workers." The headquarters of the Sailors Union of the Pacific, San Francisco, had 2,700 members, "none of whom are Negroes." The Sailors Union of the Great Lakes had more, while the Marine Cooks and Stewards of the Great Lakes had a "considerable number" of Negroes.

51. "The Communist Fight for the Negro Cause," no date, Reel 130, delo 1687, **CPUSA Papers.**

52. Allen, "Organizing in the Depression South," 24, 45.

53. Solomon, **The Cry Was Unity,** 132.

54. "Negro Trade Union Work in the Party since the 4th RILU Congress," no date, Reel 130, delo 1687, **CPUSA Papers.**

55. Minutes of meeting, 21 May 1934, Reel 284, delo 3657, **CPUSA Papers.**

56. **Doghouse News,** 29 October 1934, Reel 286, delo 3688, **CPUSA Papers.**

57. "Report to the Polcom," "Negro Department," 4 February 1930, Reel 155, delo 2024, **CPUSA Papers.**

58. "Draft Resolution on Negro Workers," February 1932, Reel 215, delo 2734, **CPUSA Papers.**

59. Report, 3 July 1932, Reel 231, delo 2984, **CPUSA Papers.**

60. Report on TUUL Negro Work in New York City, 3 December 1934, Reel 284, delo 3657, **CPUSA Papers.**

61. Solomon, **The Cry Was Unity,** 258.

62. To "Mrs. Sayer & Kettel," 24 December 1936, Box 2, Folder 10, **Gilbert Mers Papers,** *Houston Public Library.*

63. Robert Gurton to Follett, 25 November 1936, Box 2, Folder 11, **Gilbert Mers Papers.**

64. N. J. Nicholson to Follett, 12 December 1936, Box 2, Folder 11, **Gilbert Mers Papers.**

65. **Ship's Channel,** 2 May 1936, Box 3, Folder 22, **Gilbert Mers Papers.**

66. Memorandum, 5 November 1936, Box 3, Record Group 41, **Bureau of Marine Inspection and Navigation, General Records**

relating to the 1936 Maritime Strike, *National Archives, Washington, D.C.*

67. R. T. Moore to Hon. James A. Mott, 24 April 1936, Box 2, Record Group 41, **Bureau of Marine Inspection and Navigation, General Records relating to the 1936 Maritime Strike,** *National Archives, Washington, D.C.*

68. Oral History, Joseph Curran, 1964, Columbia University.

69. **The Pilot,** 7 March 1947.

70. Release, 18 January 1937, Reel 1, **Crusader News Agency Papers.**

71. Unit Minutes, January 1933, Box 1, **Clarina Michelson Papers,** *New York University.*

72. **ISU Pilot,** 5 June 1936.

73. W. D. Gelsleichter to Franklin D. Roosevelt, 16 April 1936, Box 2, Record Group 41, **Bureau of Marine Inspection and Navigation, General Records relating to the 1936 Maritime Strike,** *National Archives and Records Administration, College Park, Maryland.*

74. Ed Ballman to FDR, 12 November 1936, Box 1, Record Group 41, **Bureau of Marine Inspection and Navigation, General Records relating to the 1936 Maritime Strike.**

75. Biography of Ferdinand Smith, 16 September 1944, Box 9, **Nelson Frank Papers,** *New York University.* See also **ISU Pilot,** 20 November 1936.

76. Minutes of "Membership Meeting of Striking Maritime Workers Held at the Stuyvesant Casino, New York City, 3 December 1936," Box 53, **Vito Marcantonio Papers,** *New York Public Library.*

77. Minutes of "Closed Membership Meeting of Striking Maritime Workers Held at Manhattan Lyceum, Nov. 19, 1936," Box 2, Folder 14, **Gilbert Mers Papers,** *Houston Public Library.*

78. **People's Weekly World,** 10 February 2001.

79. **The Pilot,** 17 December 1937.

80. **New York World-Telegram,** 16 November 1936.

81. **The Hawsepipe,** May–June 1982.

82. **New York Amsterdam News,** 14 November 1936.

83. **New York Times,** 28 November 1936.

84. **New York World-Telegram,** 16 November 1936.

85. **New York World-Telegram,** 17 November 1936.

86. Winston James, **Holding Aloft the Banner of Ethiopia: Caribbean Radicalism in Early Twentieth-Century America,** New York: Verso, 1998, 72.

87. Clyde Deal, Oral History, University of Washington, no date, Acc. No. 1596-006, University of Washington, Seattle.

88. **New York World-Telegram,** 16 November 1936.

89. Oral History, Joseph Curran, 1964, Columbia University.

90. Undated Letter from William Follett, Box 2, Folder 10, **Gilbert Mers Papers.**

91. William Follett to Joint Strike Committee, 20 December 1936, Box 2, Folder 10, **Gilbert Mers Papers,** *Houston Public Library.*

92. **Houston Press,** 26 December 1936.

93. Undated Flyer, Box 1, Folder 1, **Gilbert Mers Papers,** *Houston Public Library.*

94. Minutes of the West Gulf Conference, 28 December 1936, Box 2, Folder 16, **Gilbert Mers Papers.**

95. C. W. Rice to Joseph Cullinan, 5 February 1937, Box 7, Folder 17, **Joseph Cullinan Papers,** *Houston Public Library.*

96. Lewis Valentine Ulrey to J. Evetts Haley, Box 17, Folder 7, **Joseph Cullinan Papers,** *Houston Public Library.*

97. Joseph Cullinan to Ernest B. Warriner, 25 September 1933, Box 7, Folder 17, **Joseph Cullinan Papers,** *Houston Public Library.*

98. Oral History, Joseph Curran, 1964, Columbia University.

99. Undated Flyer, "Strike Bulletin," 17 November 1936, 18 November 1936, Box 2, Folder 11, **Gilbert Mers Papers.**

100. Undated Report, Box 2, Folder 12, **Gilbert Mers Papers.**

101. **ISU Pilot,** 9 February 1937.

102. **The Pilot,** 5 February 1937.

103. See also Memorandum from Jerome King, 23 April 1936, **Bureau of Marine Inspection, General Records relating to the 1936 Maritime Strike,** Box 3, Record Group 41, *National Archives, Washington, D.C.*

104. **The Pilot,** 5 November 1937.

105. **The Pilot,** 19 August 1938.

106. Oral History, Joseph Curran, 1964, Columbia University.

107. See also John J. Daly to Director, Bureau of Marine Inspection and Navigation, 12 December 1936, Box 1, Record Group, **Bureau of Marine Inspection and Navigation, General Records relating to the 1936 Maritime Strike.**

NOTES TO CHAPTER 2

1. See review of book by David Milton, **The Politics of U.S. Labor: From the Great**

Depression to the New Deal, New York: Monthly Review Press, 1982. Box 1, **Stanley Postek Papers,** *New York University.* "At an early stage in the building of the [NMU] the Communist Party chose Joseph Curran for president of the NMU despite the angry opposition of left-wing seamen who knew better. Blackie Myers, the most popular avowed Communist on the waterfront, warned the party leadership that Curran was not to be trusted and that it would be a serious error to place the fate of the East Coast seamen in Curran's hands."

2. Oral History, M. Hedley Stone, Columbia University, No. 782, 1971.

3. Bill Bailey, **The Kid from Hoboken: An Autobiography,** San Francisco: Circus Lithographic Prepress, 1993, 269.

4. **New Yorker,** 6 July 1946, 13 July 1946, 20 July 1946, Box 100, **NMU Papers.**

5. Donald Edward Willett, "Joe Curran and the National Maritime Union, 1936–1945," Ph.D. dissertation, Texas A&M University, 1985, 42.

6. For analysis of a maritime leader whose persona was similar to that of Curran, see the profile of West Coast leader Harry Lundeberg in **Maui News,** 2 February 1957, Box 23, **International Longshore and Warehousemen's Union Papers,** *University of California, Berkeley,* and **North American Labor,** March 1948, Carton 10, **ILWU Papers.**

7. Oral History, Joseph Curran, 1964, Columbia University. For further insight on Curran as Machiavelli, see Oral Histories with Gilbert Mers at the Houston Public Library and at Texas A&M University.

8. Memorandum from Harry Bridges, 14 March 1945, Box 23, **ILWU Papers.** According to Gilbert Mers, a Gulf Coast maritime leader, Lundeberg "was probably under a lot of influence from the lady who was his personal secretary. . . . Her name was Norma Perry and I have considered her to be a [Trotskyite]. . . . A lot of people said that she was supposed to interpret Lundeberg's ideology for him." Oral History, Gilbert Mers, 11 May 1982, *Texas A&M University.* Hoyt Haddock says that Lundeberg's "main supporter was Eastern's Steamship Company and the Isthman Line of U.S. Steel." He was also "a very insecure person." See Oral History, Hoyt Haddock.

Mers was no friend of the Communists, referring to "faker Bridges" and adding, "I hate like the devil not to be able to get together on some program with the Lundebergites and

put it over in such a way that we could [send] all the CP over to Russia where Stalin could execute them for sabotaging his industries. But apparently Lundeberg & Co. are too busy baiting Bridges to have much time for thought on any plan to organize the East Coast." He also had strong opinions about John L. Lewis, the leader of the miners and the CIO: "I figure that he knows that he has enough power of his own to make it hot for the comrades any time he wants to and the CP knows it too. Therefore, he'll let them ride high just as long as he always has the opportunity to swing the weight of the organization when he needs it. They are content to have it that way because meantime there are lots of pie cards to make it unnecessary to soil their intellectual hands at ordinary labor and they can go right ahead with recruiting members. . . . They intend to go along as they are until his death, then have a 'strong man' ready to step into his shoes. Said persons being none other than Harry Bridges. . . . You know . . . this is damn good theorizing. I ought to be doing this for publication. . . . Publication of such a guess nationally would send the central committee into conference in a hurry—and into spasms along with it." See Gilbert Mers to W. B. Follett, 15 April 1938, Box 2, Folder 10, **Gilbert Mers Papers.**

9. Oral History, Hoyt Haddock, 23 December 1982, *Texas A&M University.* In this interview, Haddock expressed unrestrained hostility toward Ferdinand Smith. He said he was "an incompetent ass. He was put in the position solely because he was a Negro—the most prominent Negro in the group." Curran "supported" putting him in this post. Smith was a "pure figurehead—he had little ability. He really was an impediment to the union's growth. He was incompetent. . . . No expertise in anything. . . . He couldn't write a letter, he couldn't make a financial statement, he couldn't do anything. . . . [Communists] felt they needed a black person." As for Blackie Myers, he had a "great personality and a gift of gab. But that is really all he had. . . . The seamen liked him. He was well liked by the seamen. . . . Very personable." Jack Lawrenson, yet another Communist leader, "at that time was the best educated of the seafaring group . . . but he had some problems; drinking, being one." Stone "was an able person. He was good on raising ideas, he was a thinking person, he was an idea person . . . but he had family problems that ruined his career."

In short, said Haddock, "there were more Communists in the NMU leadership than there were non-Communists."

10. Oral History, Joe Stack, 1 January 1983, *Texas A&M University.*

11. "First Constitutional Convention," 19–30 July 1937, Box 90, **NMU Papers.**

12. Willett, "Joe Curran and the National Maritime Union," 84.

13. **The Pilot,** 14 October 1938. For a useful summary of the contretemps involving Smith and related matters, see the pamphlet "Labor Spies in the NMU," circa 1938, Box 95, **NMU Papers.**

14. **New Yorker,** 6 July 1946, Box 100, **NMU Papers.**

15. **The Pilot,** 14 October 1938.

16. **The Pilot,** 21 October 1938.

17. Transcript of hearing, September 1938, Carton 12, **International Longshore and Warehousemen's Union Papers,** *University of California, Berkeley.*

18. National Council meeting of NMU, 2 September 1938, Carton 11, **ILWU Papers.**

19. Letter from Wilford Caves, 26 August 1938, Carton 11, **ILWU Papers.**

20. Z. R. Brown to Frederick C. Phillips, 17 August 1938, Carton 10, **ILWU Papers.**

21. "Closing Remarks" by Joseph Curran, 1 January 1946, "Committee for Maritime Unity," **Vertical File,** *Tamiment, New York University.*

22. Joseph Curran to Harry Bridges, 6 October 1938, Box 4, **ILWU Files,** *San Francisco.*

23. **The Pilot,** 14 October 1938.

24. **The Pilot,** 28 October 1938.

25. **New York World-Telegram,** 19 September 1944.

26. **The Pilot,** 4 November 1938. Ray Carlucci, one of those who had brought charges against Smith, was later expelled from the union. Later he became "head of the criminal investigation unit for the American sector in Berlin." See **Hawsepipe,** March 1985.

27. Franklin D. Roosevelt to "P.A.," 1 November 1939, Personal Secretary File, Box 168, **Franklin D. Roosevelt Papers.**

28. **Daily Worker,** 11 April 1935.

29. **The Pilot,** 25 December 1942.

30. Account of Assault on NMU HQ, 28–29 July 1938, Roll 517, #1321, **Fiorello La Guardia Papers,** *Municipal Archives, New York City.*

31. **The Pilot,** 1 April 1938.

32. "Labor Spies in the NMU," circa 1938, **NMU File,** *Southern California Library for Social Studies and Research, Los Angeles.*

33. Richard Boyer, **The Dark Ship,** Boston: Little, Brown, 1947, 5, 122.

34. Oral History, Joseph Curran, 1964, *Columbia University.*

35. Oral History, Joseph Curran, 1964, *Columbia University.*

36. "Report of President Joseph Curran to the Second Biennial Convention of the National Maritime Union of America, New Orleans, July 1939," Box 95, **NMU Papers.**

37. Boyer, **The Dark Ship,** 98.

38. Willett, "Joe Curran and the National Maritime Union," 80.

39. "Maritime Workers Demand a New Deal," circa 1949, Box 23, **ILWU Papers.**

40. Oral History, M. Hedley Stone, 1971, *Columbia University.*

41. Willett, "Joe Curran and the National Maritime Union," 125.

42. Oral History, Paul Jarvis, 4 January 1983, *Texas A&M University.*

43. **The Pilot,** 9 June 1939.

44. **The Pilot,** 16 June 1939.

45. **The Pilot,** 15 December 1939.

46. **The Pilot,** 13 September 1940.

47. **The Pilot,** 7 February 1941.

48. Al Lannon, "Lessons of the Recent Maritime Struggles," **Political Affairs,** 26(Number 8, August 1947): 758–768, 758.

49. Alan W. Cafruny, **Ruling the Waves: The Political Economy of International Shipping,** Berkeley: University of California Press, 1987, xiii, 66, 67.

50. "The Forum," no date, Box 317, Subgroup III, Series 8, Folder 43, **American President Lines Records,** *J. Porter Shaw Library, Historic Documents Department, San Francisco Maritime National Historical Park.*

51. Andrew Gibson and Arthur Donovan, **The Abandoned Ocean: A History of United States Maritime Policy,** 123, 124, 125, 146.

52. Pamphlet by William Standard, circa 1941, Box 96, **NMU Papers.** See also William Standard, **American Merchant Marine: Under Britain's Heel: The Influence of British Financial Interests in Preventing the Development of American Shipping,** New York: NMU, 1941.

53. Greg Kennedy, "American and British Merchant Shipping: Competition and Preparation, 1933–1939," in Greg Kennedy, ed., **The Merchant Marine in International Affairs, 1850–1950,** London: Frank Cass, 2000, 107–154, 109.

54. Jerry Shields, **The Invisible Billionaire: Daniel Ludwig,** Boston: Houghton-Mif-

flin, 1986, 117, 125, 130, 143, 151. According to the **CIO News** of 17 June 1946, during the war "ship operators were getting fat ashore," as their "total assets grew from about $237 million in 1938 to more than $460 million in 1944. Net worth increased from about $125 million to $285 million." Box 95, **NMU Papers.**

55. United Fruit Company Brochure, Box 317, Subgroup III, Series 8, Folder 33, **American President Lines Records.**

56. Passenger Itinerary, Box 251, Subgroup I, Series 5, Folder 5, **American President Lines Records,** *J. Porter Shaw Records, Historic Documents Department, San Francisco Maritime National Historic Park.*

57. "Celebrity Photos," circa 1931, Box 302, Subgroup III Series 6, Folder 6, **American President Lines Records.** See also **Minneapolis Journal,** 21 May 1939.

58. **San Francisco News,** 9 December 1939.

59. **San Francisco Call-Bulletin,** 4 September 1939.

60. Pamphlet on W. R. Grace, undated, *Vertical File, Maritime Industry, Tamiment, New York University.*

61. American President Lines Stockholders, 1939, Box 329, Subgroup IV, Series 1, Folder 1, **American President Lines Records.**

62. Leo Robnett, Executive Secretary, National Laymen's Council Church League of America to Frederick Woltman, 29 May 1946, Box 9, **Nelson Frank Papers,** *New York University.*

63. U.S. Congress, House of Representatives, Committee on Un-American Activities, 75th Congress, 3rd Session, Volume 1, 111, August 1938, Washington, D.C.: GPO.

64. Flyer from "Rank and File Caucus," 25 September 1947, Box 20, **Counterattack Research Files,** *New York University.*

65. "An Interview with Paul Sweezy," **Monthly Review,** 5(Number 1, May 1999): 31–53, 42. Leo Huberman, a non-Communist, was also in the hierarchy of the NMU for a while.

66. Oral History, Hoyt Haddock, 23 December 1982, *Texas A&M University.*

67. **The Pilot,** 14 February 1936.

68. **The Pilot,** 29 March 1935.

69. **The Pilot,** 27 February 1939.

70. **The Pilot,** 3 February 1939.

71. **The Pilot,** 25 August 1939.

72. **The Pilot,** 8 September 1938.

73. **The Pilot,** 28 June 1940.

74. **The Pilot,** 8 July 1938.

75. **The Pilot,** 23 September 1938.

76. Merline Pitre, **In Struggle against Jim Crow: Lulu B. White and the NAACP, 1900–1957,** College Station: Texas A&M Press, 1999, 71.

77. James Ford to Roy Wilkins, 3 October 1936, Part II, Series B, #560, **NAACP Papers.**

78. James Ford to Walter White, 1 February 1937, Part II, Series B, #789, **NAACP Papers.**

79. Joe Ryan to Marvin McIntyre, 8 March 1940, Box, Official File, "Communism," *Franklin D. Roosevelt Library, Hyde Park, New York.*

80. **The Pilot,** 18 July 1941; **New York Times,** 14 July 1941, 15 July 1941.

81. **The Pilot,** 25 July 1941.

82. Letter from Josh Lawrence, circa 1941, *Vertical File, CPUSA, Waterfront Section, Tamiment, New York University.*

NOTES TO CHAPTER 3

1. Ronald H. Spector, **At War at Sea: Sailors and Naval Combat in the Twentieth Century,** New York: Viking, 2001, 129.

2. Adolph W. Newton with Winston Eldridge, **Better than Good: A Black Sailor's War, 1943–1945,** Annapolis: Naval Institute Press, 1999, 29.

3. Mary Pat Kelly, **Proudly We Served: The Men of the USS Mason,** Annapolis: Naval Institute Press, 1995, 45, 46.

4. Knut Weibust, **The Crew as Social System,** Oslo: Batgransking Norsk Sjofarstmuseum, 1958, 48, 55, 66.

5. Victor Silverman, **Imagining Internationalism in British and American Labor, 1939–1949,** Urbana: University of Illinois Press, 2000, 40, 77.

6. "What Is the International Trade Union Committee of Negro Workers?" RILU-F14, Hamburg: No date. *Working Class Movement Library, Salford, U.K.*

7. "The World Unity Congress of the International Water Transport Workers Union and Its Decisions," 21–24 May 1932, *Working Class Movement Library, Salford, U.K.*

8. "The International of Seamen and Harbour Workers and International Seamen's Clubs," Hamburg/London: ISH, No Date. *Working Class Movement Library, Salford, U.K.*

9. **The Pilot,** 15 November 1940.

10. Pamphlet, "The Silent Defense," Chicago: IWW, circa 1920, Box 2, **Peo Monoldi Collection,** *Labor Archives and Research Center, San Francisco State University.*

11. **The Pilot,** 8 November 1940.

12. Pamphlet, "Equality for All: The Stand of the NMU on Discrimination," undated, Box 91, **NMU Papers.**

13. Yvette Richards, **Maida Springer: Pan-Africanist and International Labor Leader,** Pittsburgh: University of Pittsburgh Press, 2001, 114, 310.

14. Document, April 1952, Box 9, Folder 1, **Ewart Guinier Papers,** *Schomburg Center, New York Public Library.*

15. **The Pilot,** 28 July 1939.

16. Interview, Vicki Lawrence, 27 June 1999 (in possession of author).

17. **New York Amsterdam News,** 19 October 1991.

18. **The Pilot,** 20 March 1940.

19. Immigration and Naturalization Service File on Ferdinand Smith, *Immigration and Naturalization Service, U.S. Department of Justice* (see note 60, chapter 9).

20. **The Pilot,** 27 March 1942.

21. **New York Times,** 1 February 1971.

22. Hugh Mulzac, **A Star to Steer By,** New York: International, 1963, 51, 55, 56, 90.

23. Immigration and Naturalization file on Ferdinand Smith, *U.S. Department of Justice.*

24. Bruce Nelson, **Workers on the Waterfront: Seamen, Longshoremen and Unionism in the 1930s,** Urbana: University of Illinois Press, 1988.

25. **The Pilot,** 19 February 1943.

26. Ira N. Brophy, "The Luxury of Anti-Negro Prejudice," **Public Opinion Quarterly,** 9(Number 4, Winter 1945–1946): 456–466, 463. See also John A. Davis, "Educational Programs for the Improvement of Race Relations: Organized Labor and Industrial Organizations," **Journal of Negro Education,** 13(Number 3, Summer 1944): 340–348; Clyde Summers, "Admissions Policies of Labor Unions," **Quarterly Journal of Economics,** 61(Number 1, November 1946): 66–107; Robert C. Weaver, "Recent Events in Negro Union Relationships," **Journal of Political Economy,** 52 (Number 3, September 1944): 234–249; Howard Kimeldorf, "Historical Studies of Labor Movements in the United States," **Annual Review of Sociology,** 18(1992): 495–517; Judith Stepan-Norris and Maurice Zeitlin, "'Red' Issues and 'Bourgeois' Contracts?" **American Journal of Sociology,** 96(Number 5, March 1991): 1151–1200.

27. **Hawsepipe,** 6(Number 1, March 1987).

28. Report of President Joseph Curran to the Second Biennial Convention of the National Maritime Union of America, New Orleans, July 1939, Box 90, **NMU Papers.**

29. **The Pilot,** 7 January 1938.

30. **The Pilot,** 14 January 1938.

31. **The Pilot,** 1 April 1938.

32. **The Pilot,** 8 April 1938.

33. **The Pilot,** 7 May 1943.

34. **The Pilot,** 4 February 1938.

35. **The Pilot,** 27 May 1938.

36. Gilbert Mers, President of Maritime Federation of the Gulf Coast to K. C. Krolek, Secretary-Treasurer, Maritime Federation of the Pacific, 26 March 1936, Box 37, **Papers of the Maritime Federation of the Pacific,** *Labor Archives and Research Center, San Francisco State University.*

37. Gilbert Mers to Harry Bridges, 13 August 1936, Box 37, **Papers of Maritime Federation of the Pacific.**

38. Gilbert Mers to F. M. Kelley, Maritime Federation of the Pacific, 1 September 1936, Box 37, **Papers of Maritime Federation of the Pacific.**

39. A. Thomas to Jerry King, 29 June 1937, Box 37, **Papers of Maritime Federation of the Pacific.**

40. Gilbert Mers to "All District Councils," 12 November 1936, Box 37, **Maritime Federation of the Pacific.**

41. **The Pilot,** 5 February 1943.

42. Oral History, Paul Jarvis, 4 January 1983, *Texas A&M University.*

43. Oral History, M. Hedley Stone, 1971, *Columbia University.*

44. **The Pilot,** 23 June 1939.

45. **The Pilot,** 23 February 1940.

46. **The Pilot,** 14 April 1939.

47. **The Pilot,** 31 May 1940.

48. **The Pilot,** 24 October 1941.

49. **The Pilot,** 24 May 1936.

50. **The Pilot,** 17 June 1938.

51. **The Pilot,** 8 July 1938.

52. **The Pilot,** 19 May 1936.

53. **The Pilot,** 26 September 1941.

54. **The Pilot,** 10 October 1941.

55. **The Pilot,** 17 October 1941.

56. Regular Membership Meeting, New York City, 4 March 1940, Carton 9, **ILWU Papers.**

57. **The Pilot,** 19 July 1940.

58. **The Pilot,** 8 July 1938.

59. **The Pilot,** 8 July 1938.

60. **The Pilot,** 8 July 1938.

61. Membership Meeting, 8 August 1940, New York City, Carton 9, **ILWU Papers.**

62. Regular Membership Meeting, 29 August 1940, Carton 9, **ILWU Papers.**

63. **The Pilot,** 26 July 1940.

64. **The Pilot,** 5 May 1939.

65. **The Pilot,** 14 July 1939.

66. **The Pilot,** 7 April 1939.

67. **The Pilot,** 23 June 1939.

68. **The Pilot,** 31 March 1939.

69. **The Pilot,** 26 July 1940.

70. **The Pilot,** 31 July 1942; "Clarence Brown, et al. vs. Atlantic Coast Line Railroad Company," No. 28898, Interstate Commerce Commission, 4670, Box 7, **William Standard Papers,** *Cornell University.*

71. **The Pilot,** 19 February 1943.

72. **Hawsepipe,** 12(Number 2, April–May 1993).

73. **The Pilot,** 8 August 1941.

74. **The Pilot,** 19 September 1941.

75. **The Pilot,** 19 April 1940.

76. **The Pilot,** 19 September 1941.

77. **The Pilot,** 10 January 1941.

78. **The Pilot,** 7 March 1941. A few weeks after that, "backed by the NMU in Mobile, the crew of the river steamer Dempolis, Negro and white, stuck together. . . . The captain tried to divide Negro and white crew members by browbeating the colored brothers—but it was no go. They all stuck together. Finally, the company gave up and agreed." **The Pilot,** 18 April 1941.

79. **The Pilot,** 26 September 1941.

80. **The Pilot,** 28 August 1942.

81. **The Pilot,** 15 August 1941.

82. **The Pilot,** 9 January 1942.

83. **The Pilot,** 8 May 1942.

84. **The Pilot,** 13 February 1942.

85. **The Pilot,** 13 March 1942.

86. **The Pilot,** 30 January 1942. R. E. Himmaugh, a union organizer, noted in January 1942, "Several months ago I watched with interest the efforts of Brother W. F. Wilson to secure extra clerk's work for some of our Negro workers at the Vicksburg Terminal. I was rather surprised at the reaction of some of our boat crews, for the boatmen, of all workers, have known more about just how little the shipowner thinks of all workers than anyone else. All of us know the important part the Negro boatmen played in organizing the Inland waters and how faithfully they struck in the Federal Barge Lines' strike in '39. Not one of them scabbed and in New Orleans women served as faithfully as men. One of our best picket captains was a Negro, Brother Ben

Hawkins, who didn't miss a watch during the whole strike. If crews could be checkerboarded on the river boats we would have a much better weapon to fight with than Jim Crow boats where Negroes are not even accepted in the galley."

87. **The Pilot,** 2 November 1945.

88. **The Pilot,** 10 December 1943.

89. **The Pilot,** 21 January 1944.

90. **The Pilot,** 18 June 1943. Note, however, that as the end of the war neared, "because Negro seamen [could not] purchase cigarettes at the Catholic Maritime Club here in Mobile, membership voted May 7th not to support this club." **The Pilot,** 18 May 1945.

91. **The Pilot,** 13 March 1942.

92. **The Pilot,** 20 March 1942.

93. **The Pilot,** 16 July 1943.

94. **The Pilot,** 18 February 1944.

95. **New York Herald Tribune,** 25 August 1944.

96. Donald Edward Willett, "Joe Curran and the National Maritime Union, 1936–1945," Ph.D. dissertation, Texas A&M University, 1985, 82. See also Joe H. Roach, "Women in the American Communist Party and How Their Party Activities Affected Their Home Lives as Wives and Mothers," Ph.D. dissertation, New York University, 2000.

97. Marcus Rediker, **Between the Devil and the Deep Blue Sea: Merchant Seamen, Pirates, and the Anglo-American Maritime World, 1700–1750,** New York: Cambridge University Press, 1987, 182, 250.

98. David Cordingly, **Women Sailors and Sailors' Women,** New York: Random House, 2001, 139.

99. Ulrike Klausmann et al., **Women Pirates and the Politics of the Jolly Roger,** Montreal: Black Rose, 1997, 8, 182.

100. Harry Kelsey, **Sir Francis Drake: The Queen's Pirate,** New Haven: Yale University Press, 1998, 256.

101. Interview, Bill Penman, 5 July 1999 (in possession of author).

102. **The Pilot,** 9 May 1941.

103. **The Pilot,** 12 February 1943.

104. **The Pilot,** 11 June 1943.

105. "From Kitchen to Congress," 1944, NMU pamphlet, Box 19, **ILWU Papers.**

106. **The Pilot,** 16 April 1943.

107. "Proceedings of the Fourth National Convention of America," New York City, 6–12 July 1943, Box 90, **NMU Papers.**

108. Report on the Fifth Convention of the

NMU, New York City, July 1945, Box 90, **NMU Papers.**

109. Memorandum, 8 January 1946, NMU Research Department, Carton 12, **ILWU Papers.**

110. **ISU Pilot,** 25 March 1935.

111. Beth McHenry and Frederick N. Myers, **Home Is the Sailor: The Story of an American Sailor,** New York: International, 1948, 76.

112. **New York Amsterdam News,** 15 August 1936.

113. Interview, Carl Pandover, 7 May 2001 (in possession of author).

114. From American Consulate in Liverpool to Secretary of State, "Strictly Confidential," 17 June 1944, U.S. State Department, Record Group 59, Decimal Files, Box 995, 196.7/3643, 196.7/6-1744, *National Archives and Records Administration, College Park, Maryland.*

NOTES TO CHAPTER 4

1. **The Pilot,** 1 May 1942.

2. Gerald Horne, **Black Liberation/Red Scare: Ben Davis and the Communist Party,** Newark: University of Delaware Press, 1994.

3. **Life,** 24 August 1942, Box 96, **NMU Papers.** See **The Pilot,** 12 June 1942, which includes a picture of Smith with "torpedoed NMU members." See Leo Huberman, "Sailors in Mufti: Test Case in Cooperation," **Public Opinion Quarterly,** 7(Number 3, Autumn 1943): 431–442, 431: "In the first year of the war, casualties among the men who sail the merchant ships were four times greater, proportionately, than the combined losses of the Army, Navy, Marines and Coast Guard." See also **The Pilot,** 1 May 1942, which features a picture of eleven Negroes and Latinos, including one Latina steward, who survived when their ship was torpedoed in the Atlantic. As early as February 1942 the Greater New York Industrial Council was "paying tribute to 'American seamen' who have given their lives" in war: **The Pilot,** 13 February 1942. The losses among U.S. sailors were matched by those of British sailors. British "seamen's losses totaled more than 12 percent of all civilian deaths in the war." Victor Silverman, **Imagining Internationalism in British and American Labor, 1939–1949,** Urbana: University of Illinois Press, 2000, 110. War "tales of leaking lifeboats with rusted out bottoms

and outdated emergency supplies, along with stories of rotted cork life preservers and almost non-existent naval protection, tended to dampen spirits and raise questions about high casualty rates." Donald Edward Willett, "Joe Curran and the National Maritime Union, 1936–1945," Ph.D. dissertation, Texas A&M University, 1985.

4. Gerald Reminick, **Patriots and Heroes: True Stories of the U.S. Merchant Marine in World War II,** Palo Alto: Glencannon Press, 2000, xv. Eisenhower's comment can be found on the back cover of this book.

5. **The Pilot,** 13 November 1942.

6. Mary Pat Kelly, **Proudly We Served: The Men of the U.S. Mason,** Annapolis: Naval Institute Press, 1995, 9. See also Mary Malloy, ed., **African Americans in the Maritime Trades: A Guide to Resources in New England,** Sharon, Massachusetts: Kendall Whaling Museum, 1990.

7. See also Paul S. Taylor, **The Sailors' Union of the Pacific,** New York: Ronald Press, 1923, 176–177.

8. Constance Kyle, "Case Work in the National Maritime Union," **The Family: Journal of Case Work,** 25(Number 6, October 1944): 217–223, 218, Box 97, **NMU Papers.**

9. See also "3 East Coast Operators, Pacific American Shipowners, General Agents et al." vs. NMU et al., 19–20 July 1945, "National War Labor Board Verbatim Transcript," Box 138, **Clark Kerr Papers,** *Labor Archives and Research Center, San Francisco State University.*

10. Democratic National Committee, "The Ships and Sailors That Licked Hitler," circa 1944, Box 97, **NMU Papers.**

11. Memorandum, Box 1, circa 1944, **Robert S. Lynd Papers.**

12. **The Pilot,** 6 June 1941.

13. **The Pilot,** 6 September 1940.

14. **The Pilot,** 4 July 1941.

15. **The Pilot,** 14 November 1941.

16. **The Pilot,** 11 June 1943.

17. **The Pilot,** 24 July 1942.

18. Kurt Singer, **Spies and Traitors of World War II,** New York: Prentice-Hall, 1945, 146, 186.

19. **The Pilot,** 13 March 1942.

20. Pearl Buck, **American Unity and Asia,** New York: John Day, 1942, 40.

21. **Hawsepipe,** 2(Number 3, March–April 1983).

22. **The Pilot,** 14 August 1942.

23. **The Pilot,** 21 August 1942.

24. **The Pilot,** 17 January 1941.

25. **The Pilot,** 21 March 1941.

26. Gus Alexander, "Society's Stepchildren Fight Back! The Story of the Scandinavian Seamen in America," Box 97, **NMU Papers.**

27. Hoyt Haddock to the Honorable Joseph Starnes, 16 February 1943, Box 6 #5234, **William Standard Papers,** *Cornell University.*

28. Pamphlet, "Lest We Forget," no date, Box 96, **NMU Papers.**

29. **The Pilot,** 20 September 1935.

30. Bill Bailey, **The Kid from Hoboken: An Autobiography,** San Francisco: Circus Lithographic Prepress, 1993, 218, 257. See also **Brooklyn Daily News,** 27 July 1935. See also Louis Colman, "Lawrence Sampson's Treason," New York: National Committee for the Defense of Political Prisoners, 1936, *NMU File, Southern California Library for Social Studies and Research, Los Angeles.*

31. Letter to the White House, 7 June 1939, Official File, 4177, *Franklin D. Roosevelt Library.*

32. Richard Boyer, **The Dark Ship,** Boston: Little, Brown, 1947, 97–98.

33. Willett, "Joe Curran and the National Maritime Union," 68.

34. Roy Hudson, "True Americans," February 1939, OF, *Vertical File, Tamiment, New York University.*

35. Richard Boyer, "Tidal Wave on the Waterfront," **New Masses,** 18 June 1946, Box 95, **NMU Papers.**

36. **The Pilot,** 4 November 1938.

37. **The Pilot,** 19 March 1943. Another analyst claimed that eight hundred NMU members fought in Spain. See Boyer, **The Dark Ship,** 97.

38. **The Pilot,** 7 May 1943.

39. **The Pilot,** 28 May 1937.

40. **The Pilot,** 21 August 1942.

41. **The Pilot,** 10 April 1942.

42. **The Pilot,** 2 June 1944.

43. Regular Membership Meeting of NMU, 4 March 1940, New York City, Carton 9, **ILWU Papers.**

44. Ferdinand Smith to Department of State, 20 February 1941, Record Group 59, Decimal File, 1940–1944, Box 981, 196/780, *National Archives and Records Administration, College Park, Maryland.*

45. Ferdinand Smith to Department of State, 16 April 1941, Record Group 59, Decimal File, Box 981, 196/787, *National Archives and Records Administration, College Park, Maryland.*

46. **The Pilot,** 30 August 1940.

47. **The Pilot,** 12 February 1943.

48. **The Pilot,** 18 September 1942.

49. **The Pilot,** 12 December 1947.

50. **The Pilot,** 6 September 1940.

51. Emory Land to Ferdinand Smith, 16 June 1941, Box 90, **NMU Papers.**

52. **People's Voice,** 6 May 1944.

53. **The Pilot,** 10 January 1941.

54. A. A. Adio-Moses to Council on African Affairs, 14 November 1946, Reel 27, Part II, #431, **National Negro Congress Papers.**

55. **The Pilot,** 25 April 1947.

56. **The Pilot,** 7 February 1941.

57. **The Pilot,** 10 March 1944.

58. George Padmore, ed., **Colonial and Coloured Unity: A Program of Action; History of the Pan-African Congress,** Manchester: Pan-African Federation, 1945, 28.

59. **The Pilot,** 1 September 1944.

60. **The Pilot,** 6 February 1942.

61. **People's Voice,** 15 April 1944.

62. **The Pilot,** 24 March 1944.

63. William Mandel, **Saying No to Power: Autobiography of a 20th Century Activist and Thinker,** Berkeley: Creative Arts, 2001, 132.

64. **The Pilot,** 22 January 1943.

65. Interview, Terry Penman, 5 July 1999 (in possession of author).

66. **The Pilot,** 22 January 1943.

67. Press Release, circa 9 November 1946, *Vertical File, NMU 1946, file TF, Tamiment, New York University.* On NMU funding for the NNC, see Neal Hanley to Thelma Dale, 27 December 1944, Reel 13, Part II, #0300, **National Negro Congress Papers.**

68. **The Pilot,** 5 June 1942.

69. John Davis to Ferdinand Smith, 4 March 1940, Reel 17, Part III, #702, **National Negro Congress Papers.**

70. Resolution on Ferdinand Smith, July 1944, Reel 6, Part III, #720, **National Negro Congress Papers.**

71. Mayme Brown to Jacob Green, 16 June 1944, Reel 13, Part II, #0279, **National Negro Congress Papers.**

72. Receipt from NNC to Ferdinand Smith, 14 July 1944, Reel 13, Part II, #308, **National Negro Congress Papers.** (On this point, see also #310 and #361.)

73. Thelma Dale to Gene Birch, 9 October 1946, Reel 30, Part II, #24, **National Negro Congress Papers.**

74. Speech by Ferdinand Smith, 27 June 1942, Reel 1, Part IV, #803, **National Negro Congress Papers.**

75. William R. Henderson, Jr., Memphis agent, Inland Boatmen's Division, NMU, to John Davis, 19 July 1940, Reel 20, Part II, #0172, **National Negro Congress Papers.**

76. **The Pilot,** 14 January 1944.

77. See U.S. War Department, "Office of the Chief of Engineers, in re: Labor Conditions in the Memphis District. Transcript of Report of Hearing Held at Memphis, Tn." 8 June 1940, Reel 20, Part II, #0241, **National Negro Congress Papers.**

78. Ferdinand Smith to National Negro Congress, 11 July 1942, Reel 27, Part I, #0193, **National Negro Congress Papers.**

79. Ferdinand Smith to John Davis, 14 November 1941, Reel 27, Part I, #0545, **National Negro Congress Papers.**

80. Ferdinand Smith to John Davis, 2 April 1940, Reel 20, Part II, #0446, **National Negro Congress Papers.**

81. John Davis to Ferdinand Smith, 4 April 1940, Reel 20, Part II, #445, **National Negro Congress Papers.**

82. Ferdinand Smith to John Green, 14 April 1944, Reel 12, Part II, #325, **National Negro Congress Papers.**

83. **The Pilot,** 30 October 1942. Curran was also a member of this body, along with Congressman Vito Marcantonio and Max Yergan.

84. **The Pilot,** 21 August 1942.

85. Ferdinand Smith to Dorothy Funn, 11 August 1942, Reel 4, Part IV, #373, **National Negro Congress Papers.**

86. "Proceedings of the Fourth National Convention," New York City, 6–12 July 1943, Box 90, **NMU Papers.**

87. Charles Collins to Sinclair Bourne, 21 July 1943, Reel 3, Part IV, #416, **National Negro Congress Papers.** Smith helped a group of black miners form a "Negro Labor Committee of District 50, United Mine Workers." See **The Pilot,** 14 November 1941.

88. **The Pilot,** 12 June 1942.

89. Ferdinand Smith to Dorothy Funn, 22 October 1942, Reel 4, Part IV, #371, **National Negro Congress Papers.**

90. **Chicago Defender,** 29 September 1945.

91. Moran Weston to Isidore Rosenberg, no date, Reel 4, Part IV, #307, **National Negro Congress Papers.**

92. **People's Voice,** 29 July 1944.

93. **People's Voice,** 14 October 1944.

94. Helene Powell to Ferdinand Smith, 18 June 1943, Reel 4, Part IV, #453, **National Negro Congress Papers.**

95. Ferdinand Smith and Charles Collins to Ben Davis, 28 March 1945, Reel 2, Part IV, #699, **National Negro Congress Papers.**

96. Benjamin Fielding to Ferdinand Smith, 10 October 1945, Reel 2, Part IV, #671, **National Negro Congress Papers.**

97. J. Edgar Hoover to Jonathan Daniels, 11 August 1943, Official File, Box 4245g, *Franklin D. Roosevelt Library.*

NOTES TO CHAPTER 5

1. Nat Brandt, **Harlem at War: The Black Experience in World War II,** Syracuse: Syracuse University Press, 1996, 194–195.

2. **The Pilot,** 6 August 1943.

3. Press Release, 6 August 1943, Reel 27, Part 18, Series C, #626, **NAACP Papers.**

4. Claude Barnett to Congresswoman Frances Payne Bolton, 7 August 1943, Box 80, #1425, **Frances Payne Bolton Papers,** *Western Reserve Historical Society, Cleveland.*

5. "A Group of White People" to Mayor La Guardia, 3 August 1943, Reel 77, #998, **Fiorello La Guardia Papers,** *New York City Municipal Archives.*

6. Memorandum, War Department, Army Service Forces Second Service Command, 7 August 1943, **FBI,** 100-19713-43. See also Fletcher C. Smith, "Clyde Johnson, American Communist: His Life in the Labor Movement," Ph.D. dissertation, University of Arkansas, 1999.

7. From Department of the Army, U.S. Army Military Intelligence and Security Command to J. Edgar Hoover, 8 October 1943, **FBI,** 100-19713. Smith—along with Richard Wright, Paul Robeson, et al.—was a member of the leadership of the International Labor Defense, which had caused such consternation with its aggressive defense of the Scottsboro defendants in the 1930s. See Memorandum, circa 1944, Reel 10, Part II, #0429, **National Negro Congress Papers.**

8. J. Edgar Hoover to A. A. Berle, 4 December 1942, Record Group 59, Decimal Files, Box 3163, 800.20211/1006, *National Archives and Records Administration, College Park, Maryland.*

9. J. Edgar Hoover to A. A. Berle, 2 October 1943, Record Group 59, Reel 36, M 1284, 840.48/4677, *National Archives and Records Administration, College Park, Maryland.*

10. Ferdinand Smith to Cordell Hull, 15 March 1943, Record Group 59, LM 142, Reel 4, 865.00/2221, *National Archives and Records Administration, College Park, Maryland.*

11. Ferdinand Smith to Cordell Hull, 20

November 1940, Record Group 59, LM 65, Reel 35, 893.248, *National Archives and Records Administration.*

12. Franklin D. Roosevelt to Joseph Curran, 19 November 1940, Official File, 4177, *Franklin D. Roosevelt Library.*

13. Letter to President Roosevelt, 22 April 1940, Official File, 4177, *Franklin D. Roosevelt Library.*

14. Ferdinand Smith to Mayor La Guardia, 27 July 1945, Reel 27, Part II, #393, **National Negro Congress Papers.** See also **New York Daily News,** 23 July 1945.

15. See Flyer, Reel 5, #160, **Universal Negro Improvement Association Papers,** *Schomburg Center, New York Public Library.*

16. **The Pilot,** 1 November 1940.

17. Flyer, 11 May 1944, Reel 13, Part II, #0499, **National Negro Congress Papers.** See also joint letter signed by Smith and Powell for Negro Freedom Rally and "parade" in Harlem: Letter, 7 June 1944, Reel 6, Part IV, #820, **National Negro Congress Papers.** In this capacity, Smith worked closely with Powell, C. B. Powell (powerful owner of a local black newspaper), and Ed Lewis of the National Urban League. See Letter, circa 1944, Reel Part IV, #164, **National Negro Congress Papers.**

18. Press Release, 21 July 1944, Reel 13, Part II, #533, **National Negro Congress Papers.**

19. **The Pilot,** 28 July 1944.

20. **The Pilot,** 28 May 1943.

21. Memorandum, circa 1944, Reel 9, Part II, #0371, **National Negro Congress Papers.**

22. **The Pilot,** 4 August 1944.

23. Ferdinand Smith to James J. Conroy, 25 February 1944, Reel 15, Part II, #9538, **National Negro Congress Papers.**

24. Ferdinand Smith to Thelma Dale, 24 April 1944, Reel 13, Part II, 0279, **National Negro Congress Papers.**

25. Ferdinand Smith et al. to "all Board Members," 31 October 1944, Reel 6, Part IV, #184, **National Negro Congress Papers.**

26. **The Pilot,** 21 July 1944.

27. **The Pilot,** 7 January 1944.

28. **The Pilot,** 19 November 1943.

29. **The Pilot,** 26 November 1943.

30. **The Pilot,** 3 December 1943.

31. **The Pilot,** 5 February 1943.

32. **The Pilot,** 31 March 1944.

33. Ferdinand Smith to Charles Collins, 4 April 1944, Reel 13, Part II, #563, **National Negro Congress Papers.**

34. Open Letter from Ferdinand Smith, 4 April 1944, Reel 2, Part II, #900, **National Negro Congress Papers.**

35. Speech by Ferdinand Smith, April 1944, Reel 27, Part II, #398, **National Negro Congress Papers.**

36. Ferdinand Smith to "Brother Jackson," 18 August 1944, Reel 2, Part II, #0040, **National Negro Congress Papers.**

37. Letter from Ferdinand Smith, 2 May 1945, Box 90, **NMU Papers.**

38. **The Pilot,** 12 February 1943.

39. **The Pilot,** 28 July 1944.

40. Harry S Truman to Ferdinand Smith, 16 May 1945, Box 500, **Harry S Truman's Personal File,** *Harry S Truman Library, Independence, Missouri.* See also in same box, Ferdinand Smith to Harry Truman, 19 June 1945.

41. Memorandum on President's Committee on FEPC re. the Seafarers International Union turning down "qualified Negro [seamen]," September 1944, Reel 8, Part II, #0192, **National Negro Congress Papers.**

42. Memorandum, circa June 1945, Reel 3, Part V, #354, **National Negro Congress Papers.**

43. Ferdinand Smith and Adam Clayton Powell to President Roosevelt, 7 June 1944, Reel 3, Part IV, #354, **National Negro Congress Papers.**

44. Ferdinand Smith and Adam Clayton Powell to Alben Barkley, 7 June 1944, Reel 3, Part IV, #354, **National Negro Congress Papers.**

45. Ferdinand Smith to Thelma Dale, 11 May 1943, Reel 2, Part II, #0218, **National Negro Congress Papers.**

46. **The Pilot,** 30 May 1941.

47. **The Pilot,** 27 September 1940.

48. Ferdinand Smith to Phil Murray, 18 June 1943, Reel 9, Part IV, #794, **National Negro Congress Papers.**

49. Sidney Hillman to "Dear Ferd," 9 June 1944, Reel 8, Part IV, #431, **National Negro Congress Papers.**

50. Ferdinand Smith to Jeanne Pastor, 24 April 1944, Reel 13, Part II, #0362, **National Negro Congress Papers.**

51. Ferdinand Smith to Jeanne Pastor, 28 April 1944, Reel 14, Part II, #0140, **National Negro Congress Papers.** See also Ferdinand Smith to Charles Collins, 6 December 1943, Reel 6, Part IV, #825, **National Negro Congress Papers.**

52. **The Pilot,** 18 August 1944.

53. Sidney Hillman to Charles Collins, 6

April 1944, Reel 6, Part IV, #165, **National Negro Congress Papers.**

54. **The Pilot,** 12 November 1943.

55. **The Pilot,** 5 May 1944.

56. **The Pilot,** 16 June 1944.

57. **The Pilot,** 7 July 1944.

58. **The Pilot,** 4 August 1944.

59. Ferdinand Smith and Charles Collins to Governor Harry Kelly, undated, circa 1943, Reel 2, Part IV, #789, **National Negro Congress Papers.**

60. **The Pilot,** 10 April 1942.

61. **The Pilot,** 15 May 1942.

62. **The Pilot,** 13 November 1942.

63. Charles Houston to Walter White, 29 February 1936, Reel 16, Part II, Series B, #980, **NAACP Papers.**

64. Roy Wilkins to John Davis, 3 March 1936, Reel 16, Part II, Series B, #981, **NAACP Papers.**

65. Nuffie to Walter White, 17 March 1936, Reel 16, Part II, Series B, #994, **NAACP Papers.**

66. A. Philip Randolph to Frank Gell, 1 October 1941, Reel 18, Part XVI, Series B, #667, **NAACP Papers.**

67. Memorandum from A. Philip Randolph, 4 May 1940, Series C, Part XVIII, Reel 16, #483, **NAACP Papers.**

68. Helene Powell to Moran Weston, 7 February 1944, Reel 5, Part V, #496, **National Negro Congress Papers.**

69. Ferdinand Smith to A. Philip Randolph, 7 June 1944, Reel 3, Part IV, #10, **National Negro Congress Papers.**

70. NLVC to Benjamin McLaurin, 1 August 1945, Reel 13, Part III, #978, **National Negro Congress Papers.**

71. Robert Haskins to NAACP, 22 August 1938, Group I, Box C-284, **NAACP Papers,** *Library of Congress, Washington, D.C.*

72. "Confidential" memorandum from George B. Murphy, 16 November 1938, Group I, Box C-284, **NAACP Papers.**

73. William O. Sims to Walter White, 20 July 1939, Group I, Box C-284, **NAACP Papers.**

74. Roy Wilkins to Walter White, 20 July 1939, Group I, Box C-284, **NAACP Papers.**

75. Walter White to George Backer, 18 September 1939, Group I, Box C-284, **NAACP Papers.**

76. Thurgood Marshall to Walter White, 27 July 1939, Group I, Box C-284, **NAACP Papers.**

77. Ferdinand Smith to Walter White, 20 September 1939, Group I, Box C-284, **NAACP Papers.**

78. Daniel Ring to Walter White, 6 January 1939, Reel 13, Part 10, #452, **NAACP Papers.**

79. Thurgood Marshall to Daniel Ring, 26 January 1939, Reel 13, Part 10, #456, **NAACP Papers.**

80. Charles A. Collier to Thurgood Marshall, 10 February 1939, Reel 13, Part 10, # 458, **NAACP Papers.**

81. Bernard Soothcage to George Murphy, 15 June 1939, Reel 13, Part 10, #464, **NAACP Papers.**

82. Thurgood Marshall to Joseph Ryan, 10 April 1940, Reel 7, Part 13, Series A, #0001, **NAACP Papers.**

83. Memorandum from Roy Wilkins, 9 March 1936, Series A, Part XVI, Reel 5, #325, **NAACP Papers.**

84. Secretary's Monthly Report, December 1943, Reel 6, Part I, #686, **NAACP Papers.**

85. Secretary's Monthly Report, July 1944, Reel 6, Part I, #944, **NAACP Papers.**

86. Interview, Kenneth Janken, 10 December 1998. See also Kenneth Janken, *Rayford W. Logan and the Dilemma of the African-American Intellectual,* Amherst: University of Massachusetts Press, 1993, p. 193.

87. Roy Wilkins to Harry Davis, 20 March 1944, Reel 6, Part 16, Series B, #543, **NAACP Papers.**

88. **The Pilot,** 24 January 1941.

89. Leo Huberman, "Sailors in Mufti: Test Case in Cooperation," **Public Opinion Quarterly,** Fall 1943, Box 97, **NMU Papers.**

90. Huberman, "Sailors in Mufti," **Public Opinion Quarterly,** 7(Number 3, Autumn 1943): 431–442, 431.

91. See Exhibition of "Merchant Seamen's Water Colors and Drawings", 6–25 August 1945 at ACA Gallery, 63 East 57th Street, Manhattan, Box 96, **NMU Papers.** The catalogue for this exhibit refers to the "vogue of the primitive" and notes that the exhibit was selected from "almost 600 works by some 175 seamen."

92. **The Pilot,** 30 June 1939.

93. **The Pilot,** 28 February 1941; **The Pilot,** 18 April 1941; **The Pilot,** 11 July 1941.

94. **The Pilot,** 24 November 1939.

95. **The Pilot,** 13 September 1940.

96. A. F. Hinrichs to Ben L. Owens, 5 April 1941, Box 2E304, **Labor Movement in Texas Collection,** *University of Texas, Austin.*

97. **Houston Chronicle,** 12 May 1939.

98. **Houston Chronicle,** 13 May 1939.

99. **Houston Chronicle,** 10 May 1939.

100. Open Letter from Boycott Committee of Seattle, 10 October 1939, Box 13, Folder 72,

Cannery Workers and Farm Laborers Local 7 Papers, *University of Washington, Seattle.*

101. Ralph Rogers to "Dear Sisters and Brothers," 13 March 1944, Box 13, Folder 72, Cannery Workers and Farm Laborers Local 7 Papers, *University of Washington, Seattle.*

102. Gethy Lyons to John L. Lewis, 1 July 1937, Reel 7, #0736, CIO Files of John L. Lewis.

103. Al Lannon to "Dear Brothers," 28 October 1937, Reel 7, #0736, CIO Files of John L. Lewis.

104. The Pilot, 28 May 1943.

105. Washington Post, 9 July 1943.

106. Oral History, Joseph Curran, 1964, Columbia University.

107. Memorandum, undated, Stanley Postek Papers, *New York University.*

108. Memorandum for General Watson, 17 August 1943, Official File, 4177, *Franklin D. Roosevelt Library.*

109. "Report of National Council of Subcommittee on Policy Enforcement," 18 February 1946, *Vertical File, NMU, Tamiment, New York University.*

110. The Pilot, 22 March 1946.

111. Joseph Curran to President Roosevelt, 3 November 1939, Official File, 4177, *Franklin D. Roosevelt Library.*

NOTES TO CHAPTER 6

1. New York World-Telegram, 19 September 1944.

2. The Pilot, 22 September 1944.

3. Washington Times-Herald, 26 September 1944.

4. New York World-Telegram, 21 September 1944.

5. The Pilot, 5 March 1945.

6. New York Field Office to Headquarters, 21 September 1944, 100-14347, FBI.

7. Memorandum, 9 March 1944, 100-14347, FBI, *New York Field Office.*

8. J. Edgar Hoover to SAC, 25 March 1944, 100-14347, FBI, *New York Field Office.*

9. FBI to Harry Hopkins, 18 September 1944, 100-14347, FBI.

10. From New York Field Office to Headquarters, 16 September 1944, 100-14347, FBI.

11. Transcript of conversation, 20 September 1944, 100-14347, FBI.

12. Transcript of conversation, 10 October 1944, 100-14347, FBI.

13. Transcript of conversation, 13 November 1944, 100-14347, FBI.

14. Transcript of conversation, 13 November 1944, 100-14347, FBI.

15. Transcript of conversation, 13 November 1944, 100-14347, FBI.

16. Transcript of conversation, 13 November 1944, 100-14347, FBI.

17. Report, 16 October 1945, 100-14347, FBI.

18. The Pilot, 17 November 1944.

19. The Pilot, 17 November 1944.

20. Transcript of conversation, 6 March 1945, FBI.

21. The Pilot, 20 February 1948.

22. The Pilot, 30 March 1945.

23. The Pilot, 15 March 1946.

24. Washington Times-Herald, 17 February 1948.

25. Richard M. Freeland, The Truman Doctrine and the Origins of McCarthyism: Foreign Policy, Domestic Politics and Internal Security, 1946–1948, New York: Knopf, 1972, 218. See also Gerald Horne, Black & Red: W. E. B. Du Bois and the Afro-American Response to the Cold War, 1944–1963, Albany: State University of New York Press, 1986, 61.

26. Max Yergan and Thelma Dale to Ferdinand Smith, 17 April 1945, Reel 18, Part II, #632, National Negro Congress Papers.

27. Max Yergan and Thelma Dale to Ferdinand Smith, 21 August 1945, Reel 18, Part II, #628, National Negro Congress Papers.

28. Ferdinand Smith to Max Yergan, 14 March 1946, Reel 27, Part II, #800, National Negro Congress Papers.

29. Revels Cayton to Ferdinand Smith, 19 November 1946, Reel 22, Part II, #907, National Negro Congress Papers.

30. Ferdinand Smith to National Negro Congress, 7 November 1946, Reel 22, Part II, #907, National Negro Congress Papers.

31. The Pilot, 19 April 1946.

32. Daily Worker, 13 October 1942.

33. Daily Worker, 11 March 1942.

34. Daily Worker, 9 July 1943.

35. New York Times, 22 December 1943.

36. Max Yergan to Ferdinand Smith, 18 February 1946, Reel 27, Part II, #800, National Negro Congress Papers.

37. Undated Memorandum, Reel 7, Part II, #0136, National Negro Congress Papers.

38. The Pilot, 15 February 1946.

39. The Pilot, 1 November 1946.

40. The Pilot, 12 April 1946.

41. The Pilot, 11 January 1946.

42. The Pilot, 11 October 1946. Perhaps be-

cause of their difficult experiences in South African ports, NMU sailors spent a lot of time protesting racial policies in that country. **The Pilot,** 29 November 1946.

43. **The Pilot,** 22 March 1946.

44. **The Pilot,** 8 March 1946.

45. "Report of the Conference of Negro Trade Unionists and Their Supporters," 23 March 1947, Reel 36, Part II, #144, **National Negro Congress Papers.**

46. **New York Times,** 11 May 1947. See also David Dubinsky, "A Warning against Communism in Unions," in Melvyn Dubofsky, **American Labor since the New Deal,** Chicago: Quadrangle, 1971, 152–163.

47. Ruth Jett to Ferdinand Smith, undated, Reel 27, Part II, #352, **National Negro Congress Papers.**

48. **Baltimore Post,** 1 March 1946.

49. Undated Memorandum, Reel 38, Box 4, Folder 4, **National Republic Papers,** *Hoover Institute, Stanford University.*

50. **New York Journal-American,** 8 April 1948.

51. **The Pilot,** 1 September 1939.

52. **The Pilot,** 1 August 1941.

53. **The Pilot,** 9 February 1940.

54. Memorandum, circa 1943, Record Group 233, Box 1005, **Records of the House Committee on Un-American Activities.**

55. Undated memorandum, circa 1940, Record Group 233, Box 1006, **Records of the House Committee on Un-American Activities.**

56. Letter to Martin Dies, 25 September 1939, Record Group 233, Box 1006, **Records of the House Committee on Un-American Activities.**

57. Undated material on CP and NMU, Reel 43, Box 38, Folder 7, **National Republic Papers.**

58. Thomas Abello to Ernie Adamson, 9 November 1946, Record Group, Box 1005, **Records of Committee on Un-American Activities.**

59. Memorandum from Louis Russell, 25 June 1946, Record Group 233, Box 1005, **Records of Committee on Un-American Activities.**

60. Memorandum, 28 January 1946, Record Group 233, Box 1005, **Records of the Committee on Un-American Activities.**

61. Joseph R. Walsh to Hon. John S. Wood, 22 January 1946, Record Group 233, Box 1005, **Records of the Committee on Un-American Activities.**

62. **Washington Daily News,** 18 November 1947.

63. **New York Times,** 29 November 1947.

64. Charles H. Wright, **Robeson: Labor's Forgotten Champion,** Detroit: Balamp, 1975, 31.

65. "Proceedings of the Fourth National Convention" of NMU, New York City, 6–12 July 1943, Box 90, **NMU Papers.**

66. Union leaders Mike Quill, Irving Potash, and Saul Mills joined the chorus of praise for this film, as did Leo Huberman. See **The Pilot,** 28 May 1943.

67. **The Pilot,** 31 October 1941.

68. Joseph Curran to President Roosevelt, 27 January 1942, Official File, 4177, *Franklin D. Roosevelt Library.* At the same time the "crew of the Sizaola" demanded the "immediate release of Earl Browder from prison," calling him "one of the outstanding leaders for years against Nazism and Fascism." **The Pilot,** 20 March 1942.

69. **The Pilot,** 20 September 1940. See also **The Pilot,** 8 November 1940: Curran received 4,635 votes in the general election to the victor's 26,113.

70. Len De Caux, **Labor Radical: From the Wobblies to CIO, A Personal History,** Boston: Beacon, 1970, 422.

71. **New York Sun,** 20 December 1940.

72. Joseph Curran to Jerry Voorhis, 17 August 1940, Box 2, Folder 10, **Jerry Voorhis Papers,** *Claremont Colleges, California.*

73. Joseph Curran to Martin Dies, 17 August 1940, Record Group 233, Box 1005, **U.S. House of Representatives, Records of Committee on Un-American Activities,** Box 1005, *National Archives, Washington, D.C.*

74. Testimony of John Frey, 13 August 1938, Reel 36, Part I, #0049, **Civil Rights Congress Papers,** *Schomburg Center, New York Public Library.*

75. **The Pilot,** 25 February 1938.

76. Joseph Curran to President Roosevelt, 3 November 1939, Official File, 4177, *Franklin D. Roosevelt Library.*

77. Joseph Curran to "Honorable Sir," 26 March 1941, Record Group 233, Box 1005, **Records of Committee on Un-American Activities,** Box 1005.

78. **Congressional Record,** 25 March 1941, Record Group 233, Box 1005, Records of the Committee on Un-American Activities.

79. **New Leader,** October 1943, Record Group 233, Box 1005, **Records of the Committee on Un-American Activities.**

80. Immigration File of Ferdinand Smith.

81. De Caux, **Labor Radical,** 422.

82. Johnny Gladstone to Marine Workers Historical Association, 11 September 1982, **Stanley Postek Papers,** *New York University.*

83. Interview, Terry Penman, 5 July 1999.

84. **Hawsepipe,** 15(Number 2, May–June 1996).

85. Debate on William Z. Foster challenge to Earl Browder, February 1944, Series 1.2, Box 8, Folder 11, **Theodore Draper Papers,** *Emory University.*

86. Harry Haywood, **Black Bolshevik: Autobiography of an Afro-American Communist,** Chicago: Liberator Press, 1978, 509.

87. Report on Election, 1944, Series 1.2, Box 8, Folder 12, **Theodore Draper Papers,** *Emory University.*

88. Ferdinand Smith to Thelma Dale, 7 February 1944, Reel 6, Part II, #0612, **National Negro Congress Papers.**

89. **The Pilot,** 3 April 1942.

90. Article, 20 March 1943, Box 12, **Counterattack Papers,** *Tamiment, New York University.*

91. Ben Davis to Charles Collins, 6 June 1944, Reel 8, Part IV, #433, **National Negro Congress Papers.**

92. Charles Collins to Ben Davis, 9 June 1944, Reel 8, Part IV, #494, **National Negro Congress Papers.**

93. **Hawsepipe,** 1(Number 5, July–August 1982).

94. **Hawsepipe,** 4(Number 1, January 1985).

95. Undated Memorandum from Earl Browder, Box 10, Series II, **Earl Browder Papers,** *Syracuse University.*

96. Memorandum, circa 1945, Reel 3, Part IV, #707, **National Negro Congress Papers.**

97. Undated Memorandum, 100-19713, **FBI,** *Washington, D.C.* (FBI documents on Smith were released to me pursuant to the Freedom of Information Act and thus can be obtained from their headquarters. But I was not able to obtain corroboration of the points the FBI alleges about conflict between Smith and the C.P.)

98. Memorandum, 8 June 1942, 100-19713, **FBI.**

99. Membership Roster of Communist Party, 26–29 July 1945, Box 11, **Counterattack Papers,** *New York University.*

100. Confidential Report, 4 September 1946, Box 11, **Counterattack Papers,** *New York University.*

101. Vernon Pedersen, **The Communist Party in Maryland, 1919–1957,** Urbana: University of Illinois Press, 2001, 121.

102. De Caux, **Labor Radical,** 423, 497–498.

103. "Sixth Biennial Convention," Report of **The Pilot,** Education and Publicity Department, 22 September 1947, Box 100, **NMU Papers.**

104. Ferdinand Smith to "Dear Sirs and Brothers," 21 November 1946, *Vertical File, NMU, Tamiment, New York University.*

105. Beatrice Lumpkin, **"Always Bring a Crowd!" The Story of Frank Lumpkin,** New York: International, 1999, 55.

NOTES TO CHAPTER 7

1. **Time,** 25 March 1946.

2. **Time,** 17 June 1946.

3. **The Pilot,** 10 August 1945.

4. **The Pilot,** 27 April 1945.

5. **The Pilot,** 19 October 1945.

6. **The Pilot,** 26 October 1945.

7. **New York Times,** 18 August 1947.

8. **The Pilot,** 4 July 1947. See letter from F. M. D. Paynter of the SS *Martin Behrman:* "Seamen are not accustomed to gaze on the poverty and shameful oppression of the proletariat of many lands. The Dutch beast in Java, however has reached a new level in exploitation of the masses. It causes your blood to boil when you see those poor innocent children, whose only fault was to have a copper-tinged skin, lying on the streets of Dutch controlled Java their stomachs distended from starvation, ulcerous sores on their limbs that are the result of malnutrition. Every morning at about nine o'clock, the gatherer of the dead goes from street to street of the cities. . . . His task, to collect the bodies early in the morning so that the sensitive aesthetic spirit of the Dutchman will not be shocked during his morning constitutional."

9. **The Pilot,** 26 July 1946.

10. **The Pilot,** 15 February 1946.

11. **The Pilot,** 6 September 1946.

12. Ferdinand Smith to U.S. State Department, 18 April 1947, Record Group 59, Decimal Files, Box 1596, 196/4-1847, *National Archives and Records Administration, College Park, Maryland.*

13. L. James Falck, Assistant Chief, Shipping Division, to Ferdinand Smith, 11 July 1947, Record Group 59, Decimal Files, Box 1596, 196/4-1847, *National Archives and Records Administration, College Park, Maryland.*

14. **The Pilot,** 15 August 1947.

15. Emmanuel Fitharoulis and Nicholas Kaloudis to Vito Marcantonio, 17 July 1947, Box 52, **Vito Marcantonio Papers,** *New York Public Library.* See Telegram from Ferdinand Smith to President Truman, 18 December 1947, Box 500, President's Personal File, *Harry S Truman Library.* This telegram protested the "death sentence imposed by Greek government on strikers." See also Ferdinand Smith to President Truman, 1 October 1946, Box 500, President's Personal File, *Harry S Truman Library.* Smith was "horrified at the demand for withdrawal of UNRRA supplies from the people of Yugoslavia." He said that "those who formerly out of enmity for the Partisans gave their support to the war time traitor Mihilovitch. . . . They feel that we are not in possession of all the facts."

16. Ferdinand Smith to George C. Marshall, 12 June 1947, Record Group 59, Box 1606, 196.7/6-1247, *National Archives and Records Administration, College Park, Maryland.* The consulate was unmoved by the sailors' pleas. See Walter A. Radius, Director, Office of Transport and Communication, State Department, to Ferdinand Smith, 10 July 1947, Record Group 59, Box 1606, 196.7/7-1047, *National Archives and Records Administration:* "The consulate is not aware that seamen who report to the Consulate after failure to join their ships are the objects of mirth."

17. Ferdinand Smith to State Department, 18 September 1947, Record Group 59, Decimal Files Box 1263, 125.1616/9-1847, *National Archives and Records Administration, College Park, Maryland.*

18. Ferdinand Smith to State Department, 9 September 1947, Record Group 59, Decimal Files, Box 1601, 196.33/9-2047, *National Archives and Records Administration.*

19. Ferdinand Smith to State Department, 6 September 1947, Record Group 59, Decimal Files, Box 1601, 196.33/9-2047, *National Archives and Records Administration.* This was a common case. In the postwar era Ed King of the SS *Bear Paw* was being taken "ashore in Aruba. He has been brought up on three separate charges of disobedience to orders and intoxication. . . . He was chained . . . in the open. . . . Finally about three days later they put him inside the hospital after he got good and sick." See Ferdinand Smith to State Department, 7 October 1946, Record Group 59, Decimal Files, Box 1601, 196.33/10-746, *National Archives and Records Administration.* See

also Ferdinand Smith to State Department, 26 September 1947, Record Group 59, Decimal Files, Box 1601, 196.33/11-447, *National Archives and Records Administration.* The crew of the SS *Fort Mims* complained to Smith while still "at sea" about "mistreatment . . . in . . . Venezuelan ports. . . . For no obvious reason, members of the crew of the Fort Mims and other tankers that load at these ports, have been fined, beaten and jailed. The amount of the personal fines usually amounts to the capital in the victim's pocket. The jailing is the consequence of being ashore broke."

20. Ferdinand Smith to State Department, 3 August 1947, Record Group 59, Decimal Files, Box 1606, 196.7/8-347, *National Archives and Records Administration.*

21. Ferdinand Smith to J. Godfrey Butler, 18 October 1946, Record Group 59, Decimal Files, Box 1601, 196.33/10-1846, *National Archives and Records Administration, College Park, Maryland.* The consul there disagreed with the sailors' position. "The Consulate General is unable to give any authoritative or detailed information on this subject as no complaints have been filed with this office. . . . The newspaper version was that the two crew members had gone to an uptown tearoom and when they were leaving, a waiter noticed that they were carrying away a glass tumbler belonging to the place. The waiter is said to have called a policemen who attempted to induce them to return the glass. . . . The crewman then treacherously assaulted the policeman, knocking him down and making an attempted escape. Whereupon another policeman nearby caught the seamen who are said to have resisted arrest and, as a result, one of them was knocked down receiving injuries, which required first aid treatment at the hospital. Finally, the two seamen were lodged in jail. . . . The Consulate General has also heard rumors that American seamen on Christmas night were so badly beaten up by the police at a cabaret in Beira, that women witnessing the assault fainted. . . . Seamen on whole (not only American) have a reputation for excessive drunkenness and consequent bad behavior in this port. . . . The exceptions to this are the cases of men who refuse pay taxi-drivers excessive fares and thus become embroiled with the drivers and the police. As a consequence, public opinion is generally against them. However, the Consulate General is of the opinion that the tactics of the local Portuguese police (immediate rough and ready use of po-

lice batons upon arriving at scene of arrest) is very largely due to ignorance of civilized police methods. . . . Tendency for the police to immediately resort to force and intimidation upon being called, without making preliminary inquiries as to the cause of the trouble. Added to this is the fact that American seamen have no knowledge of Portuguese and the local police have no knowledge of English."

This was the dilemma of NMU members abroad—a reputation for rowdiness, excessive use of force by the authorities, no knowledge of local languages and cultures. When U.S. diplomats became more restrained—or appeared to be more restrained—in defending the seamen, this sounded the death knell for Communist leadership of the union. See Leland C. Altaffer, Vice Consul, Lourenco Marques, to State Department, circa October 1947, Record Group 59, Decimal Files, Box 1601, 196.33/1-1047, *National Archives and Records Administration, College Park.*

22. **The Pilot,** 14 January 1949. A number of complaints, major and minor, from sailors came from Africa. See Ferdinand Smith to State Department, 18 July 1947, Record Group 59, Decimal Files, Box 1595, 195.98/7-1847. Aboard the SS *Spirit Lake,* "the ship ordered cigarettes from the Ship's chandler in the port of Port Said, Egypt. These cigarettes cost the ship $2.36 per carton and were sold to us for $2.60 per carton. We found out the cigarettes have the tax free stamp understanding to be sea stores. . . . We are under the impression that these cigarettes are to be sold by the U.S. government only. We can understand why the crew feels this is an unjust situation," said Smith. "We would appreciate your investigation and action."

23. **The Pilot,** 2 April 1948.

24. **Smith's Weekly,** circa 1946, Reel 34, Part II, #071, **National Negro Congress Papers.** "We have tried to reason with the girls who have been frenziedly embracing their black lovers, begging them not to go. But they have no reasoning power. . . . During war we had wide experience with American Negroes. . . . [U.S. whites] pointed out that in the States no black man would dare approach a white woman. . . . The Negroes were at first amazed by the attention paid them by Sydney girls. Then they became arrogant. . . . We quickly discovered that all Negroes carried clasp knives . . . many half-caste children running around. . . . Negro troops came on leave from the north, with plenty of spending

money, they were rushed. . . . Degraded spectacle of Australian white girls rushing the wharf to vie for the attentions of the Negro members of the crew. . . . According to white Americans in no other Pacific port do white women behave in such a depraved and abandoned fashion. And for this reason Sydney has become the favorite port of call for Negro seamen . . . some of our 'Boong molls,' as we term it in the police force, reserve themselves exclusively for the black men. They watch the shipping news carefully for arrival dates of American ships."

25. Ferdinand Smith to "Gentlemen," 23 December 1946, Reel 34, Part II, #071, **National Negro Congress Papers.**

26. Ferdinand Smith to Honorable N. J. O. Makin, 20 November 1946, Reel 34, Part II, #071, **National Negro Congress Papers.**

27. Australian Ambassador to Revels Cayton, 13 January 1947, Reel 34, Part II, #50, **National Negro Congress Papers.**

28. **The Pilot,** 11 April 1947.

29. **The Pilot,** 28 May 1948.

30. **New York Post,** 11 June 1946. For useful background on the CMU and the issues involved, see Reports, circa 1946, Reel 9084, **Federated Press Papers.**

31. "Statement of Vice President McKenzie to National Council on Unity of the Maritime Unions for Pork Chops in 1947," 21 January 1947, *Vertical File, Committee for Maritime Unity, Tamiment, New York University.*

32. Research Department Publications, "NMU Research Department Notes," No.39, 22 April 1946, Carton 12, **ILWU Papers,** *University of California, Berkeley.*

33. **Journal of Commerce,** 22 April 1947.

34. "Proceedings of the Sixth National Convention" of the NMU, New York City, 22 September–15 October 1947, Box 90, **NMU Papers.**

35. **The Pilot,** 7 November 1947.

36. Minutes, 15–16 June 1947, Box 98, **NMU Papers.**

37. **PM,** [New York City], 7 June 1946.

38. **The Pilot,** 5 April 1946.

39. "Introduction" to CMU Finding Aid, undated, Officers' Correspondence, Box 14, **Files of International Longshore and Warehousemen's Union,** *San Francisco.* Hereinafter referred to as **ILWU Files.**

40. Examination of Victor Michael Campbell, 2 July 1948, Record Group 85, Box 2, File 36, **Harry Bridges Civil Trial, Communist Party Meeting Files,** *National Archives and Records*

Administration—San Bruno, California (hereinafter noted as "Harry Bridges Trial File").

41. "Proceedings of the National Convention of Maritime Unions . . . San Francisco, May 6–11, 1946," **ILWU Files.**

42. Ferdinand Smith to Norma Moody, 23 September 1946, Reel 24, Part II, #0051, **National Negro Congress Papers.**

43. Open Appeal, circa 1946, Reel 24, Part II, #103, **National Negro Congress Papers.**

44. Ferdinand Smith to Norma Moody, 3 October 1946, Reel 23, Part II, #601, **National Negro Congress Papers.**

45. Transcript, 15 May 1947, CMU meeting, **CIO Maritime Committee Papers,** *Cornell University.*

46. **The Pilot,** 27 September 1946.

47. Louis Saillant to Joseph Curran and Harry Bridges, 5 June 1946, Box 9, **ILWU Files.**

48. Louis Goldblatt to "Federation de Triuplantes del Peru Adherida a la Confederacion de Trabajadoras del Peru y la Union de Maritimos y Portuarios," 22 January 1947, Box 9, **ILWU Files.**

49. Virginia Woods to Louis Goldblatt, 6 June 1946, Box 9, **ILWU Files.**

50. Philippine Seamen's Federation to Joseph Curran, 28 May 1946, Box 9, **ILWU Files.**

51. Danilo Jiminez to Joseph Curran, 3 June 1946, Box 9, **ILWU Files.**

52. Jack Vinocur to CMU, 12 June 1946, Box 9, **ILWU Files.**

53. Bill Gettings to Harry Bridges, 28 April 1946, Box 9, **ILWU Files.**

54. Cintron Rivera, Union de Empleados de Muelles de Puerto Rico, to ILWU, 6 June 1946,**ILWU Files.**

55. **New York Times,** 4 June 1946.

56. **New York Post,** 8 June 1946.

57. "Crackpot File," circa 1946, Box 1, **ILWU Files.**

58. "Auditor's Report," 27 May–30 November 1946, Box 1, **ILWU Files.**

59. Statement of Joseph Curran, 26 December 1946, Box 1, **ILWU Files.**

60. Statement by Ferdinand Smith, 26 December 1946, Box 1, **ILWU Files.**

61. Joseph Curran to Louis Goldblatt, 28 December 1946, Box 1, **ILWU Files.**

62. Transcript, CIO Maritime Committee Meeting, New York City, 15 June 1947, Box 92, **NMU Papers.**

63. Minutes of Committee on Maritime Unity, 17 December 1946, Box 20, **Counterattack Research Files,** *New York University.*

64. CMU Executive Committee Meeting, 19 September 1946, Box 3, **ILWU Files.**

65. Minutes of Meeting, 7–8 February 1947, Box 4, **ILWU Files.**

66. **The Pilot,** 27 December 1946.

67. **The Pilot,** 3 January 1947.

68. **The Pilot,** 14 February 1947.

69. **The Pilot,** 26 December 1947.

70. **The Pilot,** 14 March 1947.

71. **The Pilot,** 7 March 1947.

72. **The Pilot,** 4 April 1947. Emphasis in original.

73. **The Pilot,** 11 April 1947.

74. **The Pilot,** 9 May 1947.

75. **The Pilot,** 25 July 1947. Emphasis in original.

76. **The Pilot,** 21 March 1947.

77. **The Pilot,** 5 March 1948.

78. **The Pilot,** 23 April 1948.

79. **The Pilot,** 23 April 1948.

80. Report on New Orleans, circa 1947, Box 97, **NMU Papers.**

81. **The Pilot,** 15 August 1947.

82. **The Pilot,** 15 August 1947.

83. "Proceedings of the National Council Meeting," March 17th–April 7th, 1947, Box 90, **NMU Papers.**

84. Circular from Rank and File Caucus issued at Convention, 25 September 1947, Box 20, **Counterattack Research Files.**

85. "Proceedings of the Sixth National Convention," New York City, 22 September–15 October 1947, **NMU Papers.**

NOTES TO CHAPTER 8

1. Harry Haywood, **Black Bolshevik: Autobiography of an Afro-American Communist,** Chicago: Liberator, 1978, 501. Simultaneously the Marine Firemen chose to "elect anti-Reds," as "affiliation with the Committee for Maritime Unity was defeated 3679 to 732." See **New York Times,** 12 February 1947.

2. **The Pilot,** 17 October 1947.

3. Memorandum from Paul Palazzi, 23 July 1948, Box 95, **NMU Papers.**

4. Ferdinand Smith to President Truman, 16 October 1945, Box 1552, Official File, **Harry S Truman Papers,** *Harry S Truman Library.*

5. Undated Circular, Box 1, Folder 25, **Bill Dunne Papers,** *New York University.*

6. **The Pilot,** 11 June 1948.

7. **The Pilot,** 11 June 1948.

8. **The Pilot,** 2 July 1948.

9. **The Pilot,** 16 July 1948.

10. Report, circa 1948, Box 95, **NMU Papers.**
11. **The Pilot,** 16 July 1948.
12. **The Pilot,** 1 October 1948.
13. **The Pilot,** 30 July 1948.
14. **The Pilot,** 9 May 1947.
15. **The Pilot,** 23 May 1947.
16. **New York Times,** 9 October 1947
17. Article by Joe Johnson, circa 1948, Box 54, Folder 3, **Ewart Guinier Papers,** *Schomburg Center.*
18. **New York Times,** 16 March 1947.
19. Oral History, Joseph Curran, 1964, *Columbia University.*
20. "Proceedings of the National Council Meeting, March 17th–April 7th, 1947," Box 90, **NMU Papers.**
21. **The Pilot,** 7 November 1947.
22. **The Pilot,** 2 May 1947.
23. **Daily Worker,** 6 January 1947.
24. Resolution, 14 December 1947, Box 95, **NMU Papers.**
25. **The Pilot,** 7 March 1947.
26. **The Pilot,** 23 May 1947.
27. **CIO News,** 17 June 1946, Box 95, **NMU Papers.**
28. Mary Dudziak, **Cold War Civil Rights: Race and the Image of American Democracy,** Princeton: Princeton University Press, 2000.
29. **The Pilot,** 9 May 1947.
30. Letter from Ferdinand Smith, 16 December 1946, Reel 27, Part II, #711, **National Negro Congress Papers.** Smith spent a considerable amount of time in Texas, which, he thought, had great national importance. Just after the war ended, he sent Thelma Dale, his colleague in the NNC, an "excerpt of a letter received by my office from Morris Carzine, our port agent in Houston. 'I made contact with a very progressive Negro fellow by the name of G. W. Williams. He is the controlling factor in Fort Worth, Texas among the Negro population. He has a magazine called "Opinion" and will print anything progressive. . . . There is also a Negro lady there, a Mrs. Charles H. Robinson who is very good and works closely with Williams. . . . I had a long talk with Williams and he went down the line with us. . . . I mentioned your name to him and he told me he had heard of you, did not know you personally but that he did know Paul Robeson personally.'" See Ferdinand Smith to Thelma Dale, 27 August 1945, Reel 27, Part II, #390, **National Negro Congress Papers.**
31. "Report of Mandell and Wright," 5th Biennial Convention of the NMU, July 1945, Box 90, **NMU Papers.**
32. **The Pilot,** 2 July 1948.
33. **The Pilot,** 9 July 1948.
34. Don E. Carleton, **Red Scare! Right Wing Hysteria, Fifties Fanaticism and Their Legacy in Texas,** Austin: Texas Monthly Press, 1985, 48, 51.
35. Griffin Fariello, **Red Scare: Memories of the American Inquisition; An Oral History,** New York: Norton, 1995, 415.
36. **The Pilot,** 16 July 1948.
37. **The Pilot,** 28 June 1948.
38. **The Pilot,** 9 July 1948.
39. **The Pilot,** 6 September 1946.
40. **The Pilot,** 7 March 1947.
41. **The Pilot,** 16 May 1947.
42. Arthur Selwyn Miller, **A "Capacity for Outrage": The Judicial Odyssey of J. Skelly Wright,** Westport: Greenwood, 1984, 129.
43. See Lee Brown with Robert L. Allen, **Strong in the Struggle: My Life as a Black Labor Activist,** Lanham, Maryland: Rowman & Littlefield, 2001, 83, 84.
44. **The Pilot,** 31 October 1947.
45. Memorandum, 17 January 1947, 100-5000, **FBI.**
46. From SAC, Birmingham to FBI Director, 13 January 1947, 100-120, 818-2316, **FBI.**
47. Memorandum, 29 January 1947, 100-2622, **FBI.**
48. Memorandum, 4 March 1947, 100-1945, **FBI.**
49. Memorandum to J. Edgar Hoover, 20 January 1947, 100-120818-232, **FBI.**
50. Memorandum to J. Edgar Hoover, 22 March 1948, 100-19713-169, **FBI.**
51. **The Pilot,** 11 April 1947.
52. Press Release, 10 May 1948, Box 9, **Nelson Frank Papers,** *New York University.*
53. Hans J. Massaquoi, **Destined to Witness: Growing Up Black in Nazi Germany,** New York: Morrow, 1999, 297.
54. Report, 18 August 1948, Box 76, **NMU Papers.**
55. **The Pilot,** 3 September 1948.
56. **The Pilot,** 3 December 1948.
57. **Saturday Evening Post,** 25 December 1948. Carton 9, **ILWU Papers,** *University of California, Berkeley.*
58. **The Reporter,** 28 March 1950, Carton 9, **ILWU Papers.**
59. Letter from Donald Henderson of Food, Tobacco, Agricultural and Allied Workers-CIO, to White House, 17 February 1948, Box 500, President's Personal File, *Harry S Truman Library.*
60. **CIO** News, 26 January 1948, Box

7, **Nelson Frank Papers,** *New York University.*

61. Lester Granger to Max Yergan, undated, circa 1948, Reel 14, Part II, #712, **National Negro Congress Papers.**

62. Gerald Horne, **Black and Red: W. E. B. Du Bois and the Afro-American Response to the Cold War, 1944–1963,** Albany: State University of New York Press, 1986.

63. Press Release, 10 April 1948, Reel 10, Part 18, Series C, #325, **NAACP Papers.**

64. Letter from John Owen, 30 September 1946, Box 500, President's Personal File, *Harry S Truman Library, Independence, Missouri.*

65. Marian Wynn Perry to Ewart Guinier, 15 September 1947, Box 9, Folder 2, **Ewart Guinier Papers.**

66. **Baltimore Afro-American,** 6 August 1949.

67. Memorandum, 20 December 1946, Box 20, **Counterattack Research Files.**

68. **The Pilot,** 23 January 1948.

69. Press Release, 26 February 1948, Box 2, Folder 13, **Saul Mills Papers,** *New York University.* See also **New York Times,** 19 July 1948.

70. **New York Mirror,** 15 October 1948.

71. "Transcript of Proceedings," "In the Matter of Hearings on Charges Preferred against Greater New York CIO Council," 14–15 October 1948, Box 4, Folder 4, **Saul Mills Papers.** Cf. Robert H. Zieger, "Nobody Here But Us Trade Unionists: Communism and the CIO," **Reviews in American History,** 10(Number 2, June 1982): 245–249.

72. Circular, circa 1948, Box 95, **NMU Papers.**

73. Press Release, 11 June 1948, Box 95, **NMU Papers.**

74. Letter from Ferdinand Smith, 10 May 1948, Carton 12, **ILWU Papers,** *University of California, Berkeley.*

75. **The Pilot,** 14 May 1948.

76. **The Pilot,** 21 May 1948.

77. Letter from Anthony Lucio, 10 July 1948, Carton 12, **ILWU Papers,** *University of California, Berkeley.*

78. Press Release, 22 May 1948, Carton 12, **ILWU Papers.**

79. Undated internal Memorandum, circa 1956, *Vertical File, Niebyl-Procter Library, Oakland, California.*

80. **The Militant,** 14 June 1948. Cf. Jim Green, **Against the Tide: The Story of the Canadian Seamen's Union,** Toronto: Progress, 1986.

81. **Daily Worker,** 29 July 1948.

82. **San Francisco Chronicle,** 18 May 1955.

83. C. Wright Mills, **The New Men of Power: America's Labor Leaders,** Urbana: University of Illinois Press, 2001, 95, 165.

84. "Persons Present at CP meetings with Harry Bridges," undated, Record Group 85, Box 2, **Harry Bridges Civil Trial, Miscellaneous Records,** *National Archives and Records Administration, San Bruno, California.*

85. "Complete List of Convention Delegates," NMU, Cleveland, 5–15 July 1941, Record Group 85, Box 4, **Harry Bridges Criminal Trial, Miscellaneous Investigative Records.**

86. Oral History, M. Hedley Stone, 1971, Columbia University.

87. **The Pilot,** 14 November 1947.

88. **Daily Worker,** 16 June 1948.

89. Open Letter from Josh Lawrence, Paul Palazzi, et al., circa 1948, Box 95, **NMU Papers.**

90. **The Reporter,** 28 March 1950, Carton 9, et al. **ILWU Papers,** *University of California, Berkeley.*

91. **New York World-Telegram,** 14 September 1949.

92. **New York Times,** 14 September 1949.

93. **New York Times,** 25 September 1949.

94. "Proceedings of Seventh National Convention, National Maritime Union of America, CIO," New York City, 12–26 September 1949, Box 90, **NMU Papers.**

95. Robert Lienhard, "Communism: A Problem Confronting American Trade Unionism. How the National Maritime Union Solved It," 1958, Box 95, et al. **NMU Papers.**

96. **The Reporter,** 28 March 1950, Carton 9, et al. **ILWU Papers.**

97. Oral History, M. Hedley Stone, 1971, Columbia University.

98. "Hearings before the Committee to Investigate Charges against National Union of Marine Cooks and Stewards," "Transcript of Hearing Held by the Committee, Commencing on May 22, 1950 at National CIO Headquarters," Washington, D.C., Carton 5, **ILWU Papers.**

99. **New York Mirror,** 18 November 1949; **New York Times,** 17 November 1949; **New York Daily News,** 17 November 1949.

NOTES TO CHAPTER 9

1. Smith's Socialist Party counterpart—Frank Crosswaith—also hailed from the Caribbean, in his case St. Croix. He was born there in 1892. He arrived in the United States

during his teenage years and began working as an elevator operator. He graduated from the Rand School of Social Science, where he also taught. With his comrade A. Philip Randolph he was an organizer for the Brotherhood of Sleeping Car Porters and later with the International Ladies Garment Workers Union. See Biographical Information, Box 1, **Frank Crosswaith Papers,** *Schomburg Center.*

2. Memorandum from Ferdinand Smith, 24 March 1948, Reel 6, Part 13, Series C, **NAACP Papers.**

3. **New York Amsterdam News,** 9 April 1949. For insight on the HTUC, this section draws heavily on Martha Biondi, "The Struggle for Black Equality in New York City," Ph.D. dissertation, Columbia University, 1997, 485, 494, 503; see Martha Biondi, **To Stand and Fight: The Struggle for Civil Rights in Postwar New York City,** Cambridge: Harvard University Press, 2003.

4. **New York Amsterdam News,** 10 June 1950, 12 August 1950. See also **Daily Worker,** 11 June 1950.

5. Biondi, "Struggle for Black Equality," 494; **New York Amsterdam News,** 11 June 1949, 18 June 1949.

6. Colin Davis, "'All I Got's a Hook': New York Longshoremen and the 1948 Dock Strike," in Calvin Winslow, ed., **Waterfront Workers: New Perspectives on Race and Class,** Urbana: University of Illinois, 1999, 131–154, 133.

7. Ferdinand Smith to Harry Bridges, 2 June 1949, **ILWU Files,** *San Francisco.*

8. Biondi, "Struggle for Black Equality," 494.

9. **New York Amsterdam News,** 18 June 1949.

10. Biondi, "Struggle for Black Equality," 494.

11. **Daily Worker,** 17 March 1950.

12. Jackie Robinson to Max Yergan, 23 May 1946, Reel 23, Part II, #813, **National Negro Congress Papers.**

13. Affidavit in New York state court by Herbert Hill, 1952, Reel 6, Part 18, Series B, #552, **NAACP Papers.**

14. **New York World-Telegram,** 17 April 1950.

15. **The Pilot,** 13 May 1949.

16. **The Pilot,** 13 May 1949.

17. **The Pilot,** 20 October 1949.

18. Hazel Clarke et al. to Dr. Louis Wright, circa 1950, Reel 29, Part 17, #223, **NAACP Papers.**

19. George Morris, **The CIA and American Labor: The Subversion of the AFL-CIO's Foreign Policy,** New York: International, 1967, 67.

20. **New York Amsterdam News,** 10 April 1954.

21. Press Release, circa 1954, Reel 16, Part 13, Series A, #378, **NAACP Papers.**

22. **New York Times,** 20 August 1950.

23. Statement, circa 1950, Reel 14, Part III, #029, **Civil Rights Congress Papers,** *Schomburg Center.*

24. Juan Mendoza to NAACP, 12 January 1954, Reel 16, Part 13, Series A, #343, **NAACP Papers.** See also **The Pilot,** 24 December 1953.

25. Herbert Hill to Walter White, 18 February 1958, Reel 16, Part 13, Series, A, #359, **NAACP Papers.**

26. Biondi, "Struggle for Black Equality," 413; **New York Amsterdam News,** 15 March 1952.

27. **New York Times,** 24 April 1950.

28. Release, Federated Press, 2 November 1949, Carton 1, **ILWU Papers.**

29. Press Release from Economic Cooperation Administration, 3 August 1950, Carton 1, **ILWU Papers.**

30. **New York Times,** 18 December 1951.

31. **New York Times,** 17 December 1951.

32. **New York Times,** 3 April 1951.

33. Article by Jesse Gray, **March of Labor,** October 1950, Carton 12, **ILWU Papers.**

34. **National Guardian,** 8 March 1950.

35. **Voice of the Membership,** 9 September 1949, *Tamiment, New York University.*

36. Pamphlet in possession of author on case of Jake Green, given to author by Herb Kransdorf in July 1999.

37. Neal Hanley to "all ports," 6 February 1950, Box 95, **NMU Papers.**

38. Article, 3 February 1955, Box 23, **ILWU Papers,** *University of California, Berkeley.*

39. "CIO Trial 1950," Box 18, **ILWU Papers.**

40. **Voice of the Membership,** 14 November 1949, Carton 12, **ILWU Papers.**

41. Open Letter from Cecil Brooks, 5 February 1951, Carton 12, **ILWU Papers.**

42. Leaflet from "United Rank and File Committee," undated (circa 1952), Carton 12, **ILWU Papers.**

43. Ann Fagan Ginger, **Carol Weiss King: Human Rights Lawyer, 1895–1952,** Niwot: University Press of Colorado, 1993, 104.

44. **ILWU Dispatcher,** 14 April 1950, **ILWU Files,** *San Francisco.*

45. Ferdinand Smith, "From Worker's

Overalls to Soldier's Uniform," **World Trade Union Movement,** (Number 23, 5 December 1951): 9–15.

46. **Compass** (New York), 12 August 1949.

47. Memorandum, 14 September 1950, Box 27, **Counterattack Research Files,** *New York University.*

48. **New York Times,** 16 July 1949.

49. Gerald Horne, **Communist Front? The Civil Rights Congress, 1946–1956,** London: Associated University Presses, 1988.

50. Memorandum, 14 September 1950, Box 27, **Counterattack Research Files.**

51. **Brooklyn Eagle,** 3 March 1948.

52. **Compass,** 16 August 1949.

53. Pamphlet, "Five Men on a Hunger Strike," circa 1948, Reel 6, Part II, #0805, **Civil Rights Congress Papers.**

54. **The Pilot,** 5 March 1948.

55. **The Pilot,** 5 March 1948.

56. **The Pilot,** 5 March 1948.

57. Paul Palazzi to "All Ships," 15 March 1948, Box 95, **NMU Papers.**

58. **New Orleans Times-Picayune,** 2 March 1948.

59. Ferdinand Smith to Paul Robeson, 26 July 1949, File A 5813 535, Part IV, FBI File, 100-14347, *Immigration and Naturalization Service, New York City.*

60. William F. Watkins, District Director to T. Avery, Chief, Status Section, 2 April 1945, File A 5813 535, Part I, 0300-23358 DD, *Immigration and Naturalization Service, New York City.* The following pages about Smith's immigration problems are based on this immigration file, which can be found at the INS offices at 26 Federal Plaza in Manhattan.

61. Harry Alexander to J. F. Delany, 2 March 1948, Part III, *Immigration and Naturalization Service.*

62. Testimony of Enrique Gonzales, *INS.*

63. "In the Matter of Application of Ferdinand Smith for a Certificate of Lawful Entry," 10 July 1946, 0300-23558 R-250353, AR-5813536, *INS.*

64. Charles Rosenberg to Robert Smith, 18 July 1949, *INS.* It is possible that as a trade union leader, Smith had an arrangement with the Communist Party that allowed him to avoid paying dues and thus credibly deny that he was a party "member."

65. "Duplicate Record, Exhibit #3, Expulsion Hearing," 7 April 1948, *INS.*

66. Memorandum, 5 October 1945, 0300-23358, *INS, New York City.*

67. Report, 26 March 1940, 100-19713, **FBI.**

68. Memorandum to FBI Director, 21 January 1948, 100-17000, **FBI.**

69. Report from New York Field Office, 11 October 1943, 100-14347, **FBI.**

70. Memo from J. Edgar Hoover, 29 May 1944, 100-14347, **FBI.**

71. Memorandum, 1 February 1945, 100-14347, **FBI.**

72. Report, 14 April 1945, 100-17000, **FBI.**

73. Report, circa May 1947, 100-17000, **FBI.**

74. Report, 12 April 1950, 100-17000, **FBI.**

75. **Daily Worker,** 23 December 1949.

76. Director to SAC, New York, 8 April 1948, 100-17000, **FBI.**

77. Report, 12 April 1950, 100-17000, **FBI.**

78. Statement Furnished to Immigration and Naturalization Service, New York, undated, 100-14347, **FBI.**

79. Press Release, 7 November 1950, Box 7, Folder 7, **American Committee for the Protection of the Foreign Born Papers,** *Southern California Library for Social Studies and Research, Los Angeles.*

80. **Compass,** 16 August 1949.

81. **New York Times,** 16 August 1949.

82. Memo to Vincent Quinn, 11 March 1948, 100-19713, **FBI.** Reference in text to "deleted" refers to material excised in this document on its release by the FBI.

83. Memorandum, 3 May 1948, 100-19713-178, **FBI.**

84. **The Pilot,** 9 April 1948.

85. **New York World-Telegram,** 17 March 1950.

86. **New York Herald Tribune,** 5 March 1948.

87. "Secret" Report, 12 April 1950, 100-19713, **FBI.**

88. **Compass,** 16 August 1949.

89. **Daily Worker,** 4 June 1951; SAC, New York to FBI Director, 15 September 1951, 100-17000, **FBI.**

90. **New York World-Telegram,** 20 August 1951.

91. From Vienna to U.S. State Department, 23 August 1951, 100-19713, **FBI.**

92. **New York Herald Tribune,** 16 August 1951.

93. SAC, New York to Director, FBI, 15 September 1951, 100-17000, **FBI.**

94. See Siegfried Hesse, "The Constitutional Status of the Lawfully Admitted Permanent Resident Alien: The Inherent Limits of the Power to Expel," **Yale Law Journal,** 69(Number 2, December 1959): 262–297, 262. "Prior to 1917 no statute authorized the expul-

sion, for post entry conduct, of aliens not considered initially excludable."

1. **Chicago Defender,** 29 September 1945.

2. Hakim Adi and Marika Sherwood, **The 1945 Manchester Pan African Congress Revisited,** London: New Beacon, 1995, 24, 32, 76, 140.

3. Report, 17 December 1945, CO 968/164/5, *Public Records Office, London, U.K.*

4. **The Economist,** 17 October 1953.

5. Undated Report, circa 1953, RG 18-005, Box 11, **George Delaney Files,** *George Meany Center, Silver Spring, Maryland.*

6. Press Release, 10 October 1946, Reel 3, Part III, #151, **National Negro Congress Papers.**

7. A. Bennett, British Embassy, Vienna, to A. Greenhough, Ministry of Labour, 29 February 1952, MS292/918/3, **Trade Union Congress Papers,** *University of Warwick, U.K.*

8. F. C. Mason, Foreign Office, to A. E. Carthy, TUC, 27 November 1952, MS292/918/3, **Trade Union Congress Papers.**

9. Foreign Office to E. A. Bell, TUC, 24 May 1951, MS292/918/3, **Trade Union Congress Papers,** *University of Warwick, U.K.*

10. Ferdinand Smith to William Patterson, 21 September 1951, Reel 2, Part II, #0192, **Civil Rights Congress Papers,** *Schomburg Center.*

11. William Patterson to Ferdinand Smith, 17 October 1951, Reel 2, Part II, #0191, **Civil Rights Congress Papers,** *Schomburg Center.*

12. Ferdinand Smith to William Patterson, 28 November 1951, Reel 2, Part II, #0196, **Civil Rights Congress Papers.**

13. William Patterson to Ferdinand Smith, 10 November 1951, Reel 2, Part II, #0240, **Civil Rights Congress Papers.**

14. Ferdinand Smith to William Patterson, 28 January 1952, Reel 2, Part II, #0307, **Civil Rights Congress Papers.**

15. Memo from "Civil Censorship Group Austria (U.S.)," 4 December 1951, 100-19713-212, **Department of the Army, U.S. Army Intelligence and Security Command** (in possession of author pursuant to Freedom of Information request).

16. Ferdinand Smith to Louis Weinstock, 9 October 1951, Record Group 59, Decimal Files, Box 4359, 800.062 WFTU 10-951, *National Archives and Records Administration, College Park, Maryland.*

17. Report by Harold V. Cates, 29 April 1952, 100-19713-213, **FBI.**

18. Unpublished manuscript by Richard Hart, chapter 19, **Richard Hart Papers.** Fortunately, Richard Hart, an octogenarian and Smith's closest comrade in Jamaica, allowed me to examine his voluminous papers. There is a microfilm version of this important collection at the University of London, though the citations of this collection herein are from the originals in Hart's possession.

19. Speech by Ferdinand Smith, 20 May 1952, **Richard Hart Papers.**

20. C. E. Hennrich to A. H. Belmont, 26 May 1952, 100-17000, **FBI.**

21. Report, 20 April 1952, CO 1031/14, *Public Records Office, London, U.K.*

22. From Kingston Consulate of U.S. to Secretary of State, 20 May 1952, 100-19713, **FBI.**

23. Report, May 1952, CO 1031/132, **Richard Hart Papers** (the designation "CO" indicates that such documents are copies from the Public Records Office in Kew Gardens, London, U.K.)

24. Acting Administrator of St. Luica to Secretary of State, 26 April 1952, CO 968/302, **Richard Hart Papers.**

25. Memorandum to Secretary of State and Governor of Barbados, 27 April 1952, CO 968/302, **Richard Hart Papers.**

26. Memorandum, 7 May 1952, CO 1031, File WIS 22/12/07, **Richard Hart Papers.**

27. Governor Rance to Secretary of State for Colonies, 23 April 1952, CO 137/864 File 69233, **Richard Hart Papers.**

28. Memorandum, 25 April 1952, CO 1031/ 14 File WIS 22/12/07, **Richard Hart Papers.**

29. Deputy Acting Governor Windward Islands to Secretary of State for Colonies, April 1952, CO 1031/14 File WIS 22/12/07, **Richard Hart Papers.**

30. Governor Rance to Secretary of State for Colonies, 26 May 1952, CO 968/302, **Richard Hart Papers.**

31. Memorandum, April 1952, CO 031/132 File WIS 22/12/07, **Richard Hart Papers.**

32. Memorandum with attaching clipping, 17 April 1950, CO 537/6152 File 71368/1, **Richard Hart Papers.**

33. "Findings of the Tribunal," 2 March 1952, MSS292/972.1/3, **Trade Unions Congress Papers,** *University of Warwick, U.K.* Hereinafter referred to as **TUC Papers.**

34. Clipping, circa 1952, MSS292/972.1/3, **TUC Papers.**

35. Richard Hart to "Dear Bertie" (Albert

Gomes), 23 December 1947, File 14, **Richard Hart/Caribbean Labour Congress Papers,** *University of the West Indies, Jamaica.* Hereinafter referred to as **Caribbean Labour Congress Papers.**

36. Joseph N. France to Secretary, St. Kitts-Nevis Chamber of Commerce, 14 September 1950, File 12, **Caribbean Labour Congress Papers.**

37. Richard Hart to "Dear Comrade," 13 May 1949; Richard Hart to Harris Davis, President, Canadian Seamen's Union, 14 April 1949; Report by A. J. MacGlashan, 11 September 1947, File 17, **Caribbean Labour Congress Papers.**

38. Ralph E. Gonsalves, "The Role of Labour in the Political Process of St. Vincent (1935–1970)," M.Sc., University of West Indies, Jamaica, 1971, 61, 62, 63, 76, 84.

39. Press Release, circa December 1953, File 1, **Caribbean Labour Congress Papers.**

40. Mansraj Ramphal, "Trade Unionism in the Sugar Industry of St. Vincent: 1951–1962," M.Sc., University of West Indies, Jamaica, 1977.

41. Memo to the Secretary of State for the Colonies and certain Caribbean governments from the Caribbean Labour Congress et al., 23 April 1952, **Richard Hart Papers.**

42. William Patterson to Ferdinand Smith, 7 May 1952, Reel 5, Part II, #0484, **Civil Rights Congress Papers.**

43. Frank Elliott to Gordon Corbaley, 27 April 1950, Record Group 59, Box 3544, 741h.00/4-2750, *National Archives and Records Administration, College Park, Maryland.*

44. **Jamaica Express,** 30 August 1950; R. Palme Dutt, **The Crisis of Britain and the British Empire,** New York: International, 1953, 65.

45. Peter Stone, "Special Enquiry: Colour Bar, 1954–1955," 16 December 1954, T4/55, **BBC Written Archives,** *Reading, U.K.*

46. **New York Amsterdam News,** 6 June 1950.

47. Clive Harris, "Post-War Migration and the Industrial Reserve Army," in Winston James and Clive Harris, eds., **Inside Babylon: The Caribbean Diaspora in Britain,** London: Verso, 1993, 22–23, 39–55. Upholding the colour bar was a principle for certain elements within the labor movement as well. See Partha Sarathi Gupta, **Imperialism and the British Labour Movement,** London: Macmillan, 1975. Some employers refused to accept "coloured labour." When a "coloured family

in Liverpool—natives" of the United Kingdom showed their faces in their hometown, "people in the street shout[ed] . . . get back to your own country.' [A] fifteen year old daughter who has never been out of England, was told in a shop to 'go back to Mau Mau land.' . . . [Children come home crying because [other] children have been dancing around them, shouting 'Nigger.' . . . There are shops that leave coloured people to wait until everyone else has been served and cafes where Negro customers are ignored." See Peter Stone, "Special Enquiry: Colour Bar, 1954–1955," 16 December 1954, T4/55, **BBC Written Archives,** *Reading, U.K.*

See also Memorandum from Peter Stone, 14 December 1954, T4/55, **BBC Written Archives:** "The most talked about coloured man in Birmingham is Dr. C. J. K. Piliso. . . . He has also been in practice there since about 1936 and most of his patients are white. He is also the President of the Afro-Caribbean Organization, which is said to be Communist. . . . His house seemed to be full of coloured people who were coming to see him on various problems. . . . He comes from Johannesburg. . . . He said the big hotels have no colour bar but many commercial hotels have, so as not to offend their regular customers. The excuse frequently given is that they have only one bathroom and the white gentlemen would not care to use it after the black gentleman had. . . . It is seldom that the white wife is as friendly" as her spouse. "There is a good deal of concubinage with coloured men and Irish or country girls. . . . There are several dance halls that will not take coloured men. . . . [They] would take a coloured man if he was accompanied by a coloured woman, but not if they thought he was out to get a white girl. . . . Conclusion: At the national official written level there is no colour bar whatever. At the local personal tacit level there is a hell of a lot."

48. R. Palme Dutt, **The Crisis of Britain and the British Empire,** New York: International, 1953, 19.

49. Jack Woddis, **The Mask Is Off: An Examination of the Activities of Trade Union Advisers in the British Colonies,** England: Thames Publications, 1954, *British Library, London.*

50. Jervis Anderson, "England in Jamaica: Memories from a Colonial Boyhood," **American Scholar,** 69(Number 2, Spring 2000): 15–34, 15.

51. Gladys Bustamante, **The Memoirs of**

Lady Bustamante, Kingston: Kingston Publishing Company, 1997, 22, 23, 30.

52. Linda D. Cameron, ed., **The Story of the Gleaner: Memoirs and Reminiscences,** Kingston: Gleaner, 2000, 145.

53. Mary Turner, "Chattel Slaves into Wage Slaves: A Jamaican Case Study," in Malcolm Cross and Gade Heuman, eds., **Labour in the Caribbean,** London: Macmillan, 1988, 14–31.

54. Fitzroy L. Ambursley, "The Working Class in the Third World: A Study in Class Consciousness and Class Action in Jamaica, 1919–1952," Department of Sociology: Faculty of Social Sciences, University of the West Indies, St. Augustine, Trinidad, 1978, 18, *British Library, London.*

55. Susan Craig, **Smiles and Blood: The Ruling Class Response to the Workers Rebellion of 1937 in Trinidad and Tobago,** London: New Beacon, 1988, 36.

56. Jeffrey Harrod, **Trade Union Foreign Policy: A Study of British and American Trade Union Activities in Jamaica,** London: Macmillan, 1972, 232; Zin Henry, **Labour Relations and Industrial Conflict in Commonwealth Caribbean Countries,** Port of Spain, Trinidad & Tobago: Columbus, 1972.

57. O. Nigel Bolland, **On the March: Labour Rebellions in the British Caribbean, 1934–1939,** London: James Currey, 1995, 84, 121, 141.

58. Bolland, **On the March,** 146.

59. Richard Hart, **Rise and Organize: The Birth of the Workers and National Movements in Jamaica (1936–1939),** London: Karia, 1989, 45.

60. **The Pilot,** 1 January 1943.

61. **The Pilot,** 30 July 1943. See also the photo of Curran and Felix Cummings, General Secretary of the Marine Workers Union of Trinidad at the NMU convention in **The Pilot,** 10 September 1943.

62. Ronald Harpelle, "Racism and Nationalism in the Creation of Costa Rica's Pacific Coast Banana Enclave," **The Americas: A Quarterly of Inter-American Cultural History,** 56(Number 3, January 2000): 29–51, 42.

63. Anthony P. Maingot, **The United States and the Caribbean,** London: Macmillan, 1994, 41, 52, 63. See also Richard Fagen, ed., **The State and Capitalism in U.S.–Latin American Relations,** Stanford: Stanford University Press, 1979.

64. Richard Hart, "Onward to Independence: Political, Labour and Economic Developments in Jamaica and the Caribbean Region, 1944–1966," Manuscript copy, **Richard Hart Papers.**

65. Ted Morgan, **A Covert Life: Jay Lovestone; Communist, Anti-Communist and Spymaster,** New York: Random House, 1999, 175.

66. See Marjorie Nicholson, **The TUC Overseas: The Roots of Policy,** London: Allen & Unwin, 1986; George Meany to Sir Vincent Tewson, 24 December 1957, Box 9, **Marjorie Nicholson Papers,** *University of North London;* **London Times,** 12 April 1957.

67. T. F. McWhinnie, "The State Department Buys Itself an International," **World Trade Union Movement,** 9–10(Number 1–2, January–February 1950): 19–23, 19.

68. Claudia Jones, "American Imperialism and the British West Indies," **Political Affairs,** 36(Number 4, April 1958): 9–18, 11.

69. Trevor Munroe, **The Politics of Constitutional Decolonization: Jamaica, 1944–1962,** Mona: Institute of Social and Economic Research, 1984, 61.

70. Manley, a top-flight lawyer, was once asked to intervene in the "domestic trouble" involving "your cousin Alec Bustamante's wife." See Sophie May Bustamante to Norman Manley, 15 February 1934, 4/60/11/162, **Norman Manley Papers,** *National Archives of Jamaica.*

71. See Richard Hart, compiler and editor, **The Ouster of the 4Hs from the Peoples National Party in Jamaica in 1952,** London: Caribbean Labour Solidarity, 1999.

72. Richard Hart, **Rise and Organize: The Birth of the Workers and National Movements in Jamaica (1936–1939),** London: Karia, 1989, 110, 147. Trevor Munroe, the leading Jamaican scholar and activist, confirms this opinion. See Trevor Munroe, **Jamaican Politics: A Marxist Perspective in Transition,** Boulder: Lynne Rienner, 1990, 5, 131: Jamaican Marxists were influenced by Lenin and Stalin but had "extremely . . . limited contacts with the international communist movement." What contacts Jamaicans had with the global left often came from seamen. Says Richard Hart, "We had no direct contact either with the American Communist Party or with the Comintern."

73. Frances Grant to Serafino Romauldi, 3 March 1954, Box 2, **Frances Grant Papers,** *Rutgers University, New Brunswick.*

74. Memorandum, 14 January 1946, Reel 10, Part XIV, #787, **NAACP Papers.**

75. Invitation, 14 February 1951, 4/60/11/118, **Norman Manley Papers.**

76. H. F. Edwards to Norman Manley, 1 May 1961, 4/60/2A/40, **Norman Manley Papers.**

77. Paul Blanshard to "Dear Norman and Edna," undated, 4/60/11/160, **Norman Manley Papers.**

78. Norman Manley to Eric Williams, 11 December 1956, 4/60/2A/18, **Norman Manley Papers.**

79. Munroe, **The Politics of Constitutional Decolonization,** 82.

80. N. N. Nethersole to James Watson, 27 June 1941, Box 12, Folder 3, **James Watson Papers,** *Schomburg Center.*

81. Alfred Baker Lewis to NAACP, 23 January 1945, Reel 9, Part XVI, Series B, #468, **NAACP Papers.**

82. Undated Memorandum from W. A. Domingo, File 4/60/2A/2, **Norman Manley Papers,** *National Archives of Jamaica, Spanishtown, Jamaica.*

83. Consul General of U.K. in New York City to U.K. Embassy in Washington, D.C., 29 March 1945, CO 968/164/5, *Public Records Office, London.*

84. Memorandum, 21 February 1946, CO137/864 File 69233, **Richard Hart Papers.**

85. **Gleaner** (Jamaica), 22 May 1938.

86. Rex Nettleford, ed., **Norman Washington Manley and the New Jamaica: Selected Speeches and Writings, 1938–1968,** London: Longman, 1971, liii.

87. Report, 18 August 1955, Record Group 59, Decimal Files, Box 3206, 741h.00/8-1855, *National Archives and Records Administration.*

88. Paul Blanshard, **Democracy and Empire in the Caribbean: A Contemporary Review,** New York: Macmillan, 1947, 96.

89. Michael Manley, **A Voice at the Workplace: Reflections on Colonialism and the Jamaican Worker,** London: Andre Deutsch, 1975, 34, 104.

90. Article by Esther Chapman, **West Indian Review,** January 1957, Vertical File, **West Indies Collection,** *University of West Indies, Jamaica.*

91. Bustamante, **The Memoirs of Lady Bustamante,** 161, 163.

92. David Godfrey, **Reckoning with the Force: Stories of the Jamaica Constabulary Force in the 1950s,** Kingston: The Mill Press, 1998, 58.

93. Trevor G. Munroe, "Political Change and Constitutional Development in Jamaica, 1944–1962," Ph.D. dissertation, Oxford University, 1969, 65.

94. George Eaton, **Alexander Bustamante**

and **Modern Jamaica,** Kingston: Kingston Publishing Company, 1975, 147.

95. Rupert Lewis, "A Political Study of Garveyism in Jamaica and London: 1914–1940," M.Sc., University of the West Indies, Jamaica, 1971, 122, 136, 145–146, 160, 182. See also Paul D. Robertson, "Political Behaviour at the Grass Roots Level: A Study of Electoral and Party Politics in Jamaica," M.Sc., University of the West Indies, Jamaica, 1971; Harold De Costa Goulbourne, "Teachers and Pressure Group Activity in Jamaica, 1894–1967," Ph.D. Dissertation, University of Sussex, 1975; Derwin St. B. Munroe, "Riots in Post Colonial Jamaica," M. Phil., University of the West Indies, Jamaica, 1989; Obika Gray, **Radicalism and Social Change in Jamaica, 1960–1972,** Knoxville: University of Tennessee Press, 1991; Ivy J. Mitchell, "Race in the Jamaican Novel," M. Phil., University of the West Indies, Jamaica, 1980. Frank Hill, ed., **Bustamante and His Letters,** Kingston: Kingston Publishing Company, 1976; William Richard Jacobs, "The Role of Some Labour Movements in the Political Process in Trinidad, 1937–1950," M.Sc., University of the West Indies, Jamaica, 1969.

96. Trevor Munroe, **The Marxist 'Left' In Jamaica, 1940–1950,** Mona, Jamaica: University of West Indies, Institute of Social and Economic Research, 1978, 3.

97. Cary Fraser, **Ambivalent Anti-Colonialism: The United States and the Genesis of West Indian Independence, 1940–1964,** Westport: Greenwood, 1994, 125.

98. Norman Manley, "Autobiography," Vertical File, **West Indies Collection,** *University of West Indies, Jamaica.*

99. Trevor Munroe, **Jamaican Politics: A Marxist Perspective in Transition,** Kingston, Jamaica: Heinemann, 1990, 139.

100. "Probate" of Ferdinand Smith, 10 November 1962, **Richard Hart Papers.**

101. Ferdinand Smith to William Patterson, 14 August 1952, Reel 5, Part II, #0490, **Civil Rights Congress Papers.**

102. Analysis of History of Trade Unions in Jamaica since 1938, undated, **Richard Hart Papers.**

103. Norman Manley to F. A. Glasspole, 20 March 1947, 4/60/2B/12, **Norman Manley Papers.**

104. Norman Manley to "Comrade Arnett," 9 May 1947, 4/60/2B/12, **Norman Manley Papers.**

105. Norman Manley to C. A. Neita, 13

February 1947, 4/60/2B/12, **Norman Manley Papers.**

106. Norman Manley to "Domingo," 19 July 1948, 4/60/2B/13, **Norman Manley Papers.**

107. Norman Manley to W. A. Domingo, 28 July 1948, 4/60/2B/13, **Norman Manley Papers.**

108. Manley, **A Voice at the Workplace,** 25.

109. Report, 1 March 1952, 4/60/2A/5, **Norman Manley Papers.**

110. Norman Manley to F. L. Walcott, 11 June 1952, 4/60/2B/15, **Norman Manley Papers.**

111. **Gleaner** (Jamaica), 18 September 1998.

112. Interview, Douglas Manley, 23 July 2000.

113. George Woodcock to Vincent Tewson, 14 March 1952, MSS292/972.1/5, **TUC Papers,** *University of Warwick.*

114. Undated Report by George Woodcock, MSS292/972.1/5, **TUC Papers.**

115. Munroe, "Political Change and Constitutional Development in Jamaica, 1944–1962," 131.

116. Letter from Richard Hart, 31 August 1953, **Richard Hart Papers.**

117. Chapter 19 of draft manuscript by Richard Hart, **Richard Hart Papers.**

118. "Foreign Service Despatch," 23 December 1952, "Confidential File," Record Group 59, Decimal Files, 741h.00/12-2362, *National Archives and Records Administration, College Park, Maryland.*

119. Political Report of Governor of Jamaica, November 1952, CO 1031/132, **Richard Hart Papers.**

120. Political Report of the Governor, September 1952, CO 1031/132, **Richard Hart Papers.**

121. Clipping, 26 February 1953, **Richard Hart Papers.**

122. Jack Woddis, **The Mask Is Off,** 6.

123. See Robert Murray, **The Split: Australian Labor in the Fifties,** Melbourne: Cheshire, 1970.

124. Ken Jones, ed., **The Best of Bustamante: Selected Quotations, 1935–1974,** Red Hills, Jamaica: Twin Guinep, 1977, 34.

125. Roger Mais, **The Hills Were Joyful Together,** London: Heinemann, 1953, 238.

NOTES TO CHAPTER 11

1. Hakim Adi and Marika Sherwood, **The 1945 Manchester Pan-African Congress Revisited,** London: New Beacon, 1995, 93.

2. Arthur Lewis, **Labor in the West Indies: The Birth of a Workers Movement,** London: New Beacon, 1977, 33.

3. Tough and complicated negotiations regularly occurred between the transnational corporations that controlled the bauxite industry and their Jamaican interlocutors. See Files 4/60/2A11; 12; and 13, **Norman Manley Papers.**

4. "Discussion Document," October 1950, CP?CENT/INT/31/07, **Communist Party of Great Britain Archives,** *National Labour History Museum, Manchester, U.K.*

5. Frank Hill, ed., **Bustamante and His Letters,** Kingston: Kingston Publishing Company, 1976, 25.

6. Report, 26 December 1952, Record Group 59, Decimal Files, Box 3545, 741h.001/12-2652, *National Archives and Records Administration.*

7. Report, 1 May 1953, Record Group 59, Decimal Files, Box 3544, 741h.00/5-153, *National Archives and Records Administration.*

8. Report, 6 November 1953, Record Group 59, Decimal Files, Box 3544, 741h.00/11-653, *National Archives and Records Administration.*

9. Report, 14 October 1953, Record Group 59, Decimal Files, Box 3545, 7441h.001/10-1453, *National Archives and Records Administration.*

10. **Jamaica Times,** 20 March 1954.

11. **Spotlight** (Jamaica), 15 (Number 4, April 1954): 14–16.

12. **Spotlight,** 14(Numbers 6–7, May–July 1953): 16–17.

13. Report, 22 May 1953, Record Group 59, Decimal Files, Box 3544, 741h.00/5-2253, *National Archives and Records Administration.*

14. Report 1 May 1953, Record Group 59, Decimal Files, Box 3544, 741h.00/5-153, *National Archives and Records Administration.*

15. Report, 14 August 1953, Record Group 59, Decimal Files, Box 3544, 741h.00/9-1453, *National Archives and Records Administration.*

16. **Spotlight,** 14 (Numbers 6–7, May–July 1953): 16–17.

17. Proceedings of SAWU, 21 November 1954, **Richard Hart Papers.**

18. **Jamaica Times,** 2 April 1953.

19. Draft of chapter 19 of Richard Hart manuscript, **Richard Hart Papers.**

20. Quintin O'Connor, Secretary Trinidad & Tobago Trades Union Council, to Richard Hart, 17 August 1953, **Richard Hart Papers.**

21. Speech by Ferdinand Smith, circa 1952, **Richard Hart Papers.**

22. Report, 28 December 1953, CO 968/302, **Richard Hart Papers.**

23. Colonial Office Minute, 19 December 1953, CO 968/302, **Richard Hart Papers.**

24. Memorandum to Secretary of State for Colonies, 4 August 1953, CO 859/425, File SSD 176/01, **Richard Hart Papers.**

25. Report, 23 December 1953, Record Group 59, Decimal Files, Box 3544, 741.00/12-2353, *National Archives and Records Administration.*

26. Report, 8 January 1954, Record Group 59, Decimal Files, Box 3545, 741h.00/2-2654, *National Archives and Records Administration.*

27. Report, 30 October 1953, Record Group 59, Decimal Files, Box 3544, 741h.00/10-3053, *National Archives and Administration.*

28. Flyer, circa 1954, **Richard Hart Papers.**

29. Report by Richard Hart, 16 November 1953, **Richard Hart Papers.**

30. Memorandum on meeting, 13 October 1953, **Richard Hart Papers.**

31. Colonial Office Minute, 2 November 1953, CO 968/302, **Richard Hart Papers.** See also Colonial Office Minute, 4 January 1954, CO 968/302, **Richard Hart Papers.**

32. **Gleaner,** 8 March 1954.

33. **Express** (U.K.), 25 March 1954.

34. Report, 22 December 1953, Record Group 59, Decimal Files, Box 3544, 741h.00/12-2253, *National Archives and Records Administration.*

35. Report, 30 October 1953, Record Group, Decimal Files, Box 3544, 741h.00/10-3053, *National Archives and Records Administration.*

36. **Star** (Jamaica), 1 July 1953.

37. Memorandum, 2 April 1954, CO 1031/1961, *Public Records Office, London, U.K.*

38. **Daily Telegraph,** 23 March 1954.

39. **Yorkshire Observer,** 3 April 1954.

40. Ferdinand Smith to "Dear Al," Box 2, Folder 74, **William Patterson Papers,** *Howard University, Washington, D.C.*

41. David Godfrey, **Reckoning with the Force: Stories of the Jamaica Constabulary Force in the 1950s,** Kingston: The Mill Press, 1998, 166, 199, 200, 202.

42. Clipping, circa 1953, Box 2, Folder 74, **William Patterson Papers.** Emphasis original.

43. Report, "Communism in Jamaica," 21 January 1954, CO 1031/1961, *Public Records Office.* See also CO 859/891, undated, circa 1950s: "Communist influences have been strong in the trade union in Trinidad."

44. **Gleaner,** 12 March 1954.

45. Draft of chapter 22 of Richard Hart manuscript, **Richard Hart Papers.**

46. Richard Hart, pamphlet, "Keep Left," 1953, **West Indies Collection,** *University of West Indies, Jamaica.*

47. Manley, **A Voice in the Workplace,** 25.

48. Undated Statement by Ferdinand Smith, MSS292/972.1/5, **TUC Papers.**

49. 1954 Flyer including excerpt from **London Times,** 4 April 1954, **Richard Hart Papers.**

50. Open Letter from Ferdinand Smith, 15 March 1955, **Richard Hart Papers.**

51. Press Release, 10 March 1955, **Richard Hart Papers.**

52. Ferdinand Smith to General Secretary of NWU, 9 March 1955, **Richard Hart Papers.**

53. Proceedings of SAWU, 21 November 1954, **Richard Hart Papers.**

54. Brochure, "Unemployed Organizing Committee," 2 February 1954, **Richard Hart Papers.**

55. Leaflet re. unemployment march, circa July 1954, **Richard Hart Papers.**

56. Programme of Activities for Peoples Education Organization, circa 1954, **Richard Hart Papers.**

57. "Proceedings of the Second Annual Conference" of JFTU, 6 February 1955, **Richard Hart Papers.**

58. Report, 26 February 1954, Record Group 59, Decimal Files, Box 3545, 741h.00/2-2654, *National Archives and Records Administration.*

59. Report, 26 August 1954, Record Group 59, Decimal Files, Box 3545, 741h.00/8-2654, *National Archives and Records Administration.*

60. Ferdinand Smith to William Patterson, 12 February 1954, Box 2, Folder 74, **William Patterson Papers.**

61. **JFTU News,** circa June 1954, **Richard Hart Papers.**

62. General Secretary, TUC, to Ken Stirling, NWU, 4 January 1955, MSS292/972.1/5, **TUC Papers,** *University of Warwick.*

63. T. A. Kelly, Acting President, NWU, to "Sir Vincent Tewson," General Secretary, TUC, 1 October 1955, MSS292/972.1/5, **TUC Papers.**

64. TUC General Secretary to P. Belcher, Tobacco Workers Union, Reading, 6 October 1954, MSS292/972.1/5, **TUC Papers.** Letter

from Ferdinand Smith, circa October 1954, MSS292/972.1/5, **TUC Papers.**

65. F. A. Glasspole to Vincent Tewson, 14 April 1954, MS292/972.1/5, **TUC Papers.**

66. F. A. Glasspole to "Bro. Tewson," 9 July 1954, MSS292/972.1/5, **TUC Papers.**

67. F. A. Glasspole to Vincent Tewson, 14 June 1954, MSS292/972.1/5, **TUC Papers.**

68. Ferdinand Smith to National Union of Public Employee, 22 April 1954, MSS292/972.1/5, **TUC Papers.**

69. **Gleaner,** 12 March 1954.

70. Sir Hugh Foot to Secretary of State for Colonies, 29 March 1954, CO1031/1961, *Public Records Office.*

71. "Note of a Meeting Held in Mr. Rogers' Room at the Colonial Office on Tuesday, 22nd June, 1954," CO 1031/1961, *Public Records Office, London.*

72. **Gleaner,** 12 March 1954.

73. "Colonial Trade Unions in the WFTU," circa 1954, CO 537/6559, *Public Records Office.*

74. "Minutes of a Meeting of World Federation of Trade Unions," circa 1954, FO 1110/632, *Public Records Office.*

75. "Industrial Relations in the Sugar Industry," circa 1955, CO 1031/1448, *Public Records Office.*

76. "Annual Report of the Sugar Industry Labour Welfare Board, Jamaica," CO 1031/65, *Public Records Office.*

77. Memorandum from British Embassy, 2 March 1955, CO 1031/1961, *Public Records Office.* See also **Boston Globe,** 12 November 1953. **The New Counterattack,** 1 March 1954.

78. Ted Morgan, **A Covert Life: Jay Lovestone; Communist, Anti-Communist and Spy-Master,** New York: Random House, 1999, 307.

79. Report, 13 March 1953, Record Group, Decimal Files, Box 3543, 741h.00/3-1353, *National Archives and Records Administration.*

80. Report, 18 August 1955, Record Group 55, Decimal Files, Box 3106, 741h.00/8-1855, *National Archives and Records Administration.*

81. "Political and Economic Report on the [British] West Indies," December 1952, CP/CENT/INT/31/07, **Communist Party of Great Britain Archives,** *National Labour History Museum, Manchester, U.K.*

82. **Spotlight,** 15(Number 4, April 1954): 14–16.

83. Draft of chapter 22 of Richard Hart manuscript, **Richard Hart Papers.**

84. Richard Hart, undated, "The Situation in Jamaica," **Richard Hart Papers.**

85. Colonial Office Minute, P. Rogers to Bourdillon, CO 859/776, **Richard Hart Papers.**

86. Secretary of State of Colonies to Officer Administering Government of Jamaica, 14 September 1956, CO 859/776, **Richard Hart Papers.**

87. Colonial Office Minute relating to Jamaican Government's "No Dealing with Communist Unions," 9 August 1956, CO 859/776, **Richard Hart Papers.**

88. Report, 28 April 1955, Record Group 59, Decimal Files, Box 4454, 841h.062/4-2855, *National Archives and Records Administration.*

89. Report, 6 October 1955, Record Group 59, Decimal Files, Box 4454, 841h.062/10-655, *National Archives and Records Administration.*

NOTES TO CHAPTER 12

1. Minutes of the First Annual Conference of PFM, 21–25 July 1956, **Richard Hart Papers.**

2. Ferdinand Smith to "Dear Las," 9 November 1956, **Richard Hart Papers.**

3. Ferdinand Smith to William Patterson, 12 May 1958, **Richard Hart Papers.**

4. Report, 5 December 1955, CO 1031/1961, *Public Records Office.*

5. **Freedom Newsletter,** 1 July 1956, **Richard Hart Papers.**

6. Colonial Office Minute, Nixon Barton to Phillips, 28 October 1956, CO 1031/1958, File WIS 472/1025/01, Public Records Office.

7. Report, 23 March 1956, Record Group 59, Decimal Files, Box 3207, 741.h00/3-2356, *National Archives and Records Administration.*

8. Richard Hart, Analysis of History of Trade Unions in Jamaica since 1938, undated, **Richard Hart Papers.**

9. Report, 29 March 1956, Record Group 59, Decimal Files, Box 4454, 841h.062/3-2956, *National Archives and Records Administration.*

10. Report, 27 January 1955, Record Group 59, Decimal Files, Box 3206, 741h.00/1-2755, *National Archives and Records Administration.*

11. Report, 19 February 1957, Record Group 59, Decimal Files, Box 3207, 741h.00/2-1957, *National Archives and Records Administration.*

12. Ferdinand Smith to Secretary, TUC, 12 April 1956, MS292/972.1/5, **TUC Papers.** See also **Daily Telegraph,** 11 April 1956.

13. Report, 24 February 1955, Record 59,

Decimal Files, Box 3206, 741h.00/1-2755, *National Archives and Records Administration.*

14. Richard Hart, **Michael Manley: An Assessment and Tribute,** London: Caribbean Labour Solidarity, 1997, 2.

15. "The British Caribbean," April 1955, published by the Royal Institute of International Affairs, London, **Labour Party Archives,** *National Labour History Museum, Manchester.*

16. Norman Manley to John Hatch, 18 February 1956, **Labour Party Archives.**

17. Norman Manley to John Hatch, 11 May 1956, **Labour Party Archives.**

18. John Hatch to Norman Manley, 27 April 1956, **Labour Party Archives.**

19. John Hatch to Maurice Mason, 12 September 1958, **Labour Party Archives.**

20. S. O. Veith to David Emalls, 11 January 1962, **Labour Party Archives.**

21. "Stephanie," to Ferdinand Smith, 20 May 1955, **Richard Hart Papers.**

22. "Stephanie," to Ferdinand Smith, 25 March 1955, **Richard Hart Papers.**

23. "Stephanie," to Ferdinand Smith, 16 November 1954, **Richard Hart Papers.**

24. Paul Robeson, Jr. to Ferdinand Smith, 28 July 1955, **Richard Hart Papers.**

25. William Patterson to Ferdinand Smith, 15 August 1955, **Richard Hart Papers.**

26. Ben Davis to Ferdinand Smith, 26 August 1955, **Richard Hart Papers.**

27. Ferdinand Smith to Ben Davis, 22 October 1956, **Richard Hart Papers.**

28. Ben Davis to Ferdinand Smith, 17 October 1956, **Richard Hart Papers.**

29. Ben Davis to Ferdinand Smith, 28 October 1956, **Richard Hart Papers.**

30. Gerald Horne, **Black Liberation/Red Scare: Ben Davis and the Communist Party,** Newark: University of Delaware Press, 1994.

31. Ferdinand Smith to William Patterson, 26 January 1958, Box 2, Folder 74, **William Patterson Papers.**

32. Ferdinand Smith to William Patterson, 31 December 1956, **Richard Hart Papers.**

33. Ferdinand Smith to Ben Davis, 22 October 1956, **Richard Hart Papers.**

34. Horace Mitchell to F. A. Glasspole, 5 July 1955, Box 5, Folder 8, **Serafino Romualdi Papers,** *Cornell University.*

35. Report, 1 February 1955, Record Group 59, Decimal Files, Box 4454, 841h.06/2-155, *National Archives and Records Administration.*

36. Report, 6 January 1956, Record Group

59, Decimal Files, Box 3207, 741h.00/1-656, *National Archives and Records Administration.*

37. See Gerald Horne, **Black and Red: W. E. B. Du Bois and the AfroAmerican Response to the Cold War, 1944–1963,** Albany: State University of New York Press, 1986.

38. **Star** (Jamaica), 1 October 1956; Report, 29 November 1956, Record Group 59, Decimal Files, Box 3207, 741h.00/11-2952, *National Archives and Records Administration.*

39. Report, 23 January 1957, Record Group 59, Decimal Files, Box 3207, 741h.00/1-2357, *National Archives and Records Administration.* See also Mark Phythian and Jonathan Jardine, "Hunters in the Backyard? The U.K., the U.S. and the Question of Arms Sales to Castro's Cuba, 1959," **Contemporary British History,** 13(Number 1, Spring 1999): 32–61. Differences between London and Washington were also arising over Cuba, and were becoming sharper over Jamaica.

40. Ben Davis to Ferdinand Smith, 17 October 1956, **Richard Hart Papers.**

41. Undated letter from Ferdinand Smith, circa 1955, **Richard Hart Papers.**

42. Ferdinand Smith to Ben Davis, 22 October 1956, **Richard Hart Papers.** Emphasis in original.

43. William Patterson to Ferdinand Smith, 7 December 1960, **Richard Hart Papers.**

44. William Patterson to Ferdinand Smith, undated, **Richard Hart Papers.**

45. Minutes of Executive of West Indian Federal Labour Party, 16 June 1960, **C. L. R. James Papers,** *Institute of Commonwealth Studies, University of London, U.K.*

46. Norman Manley to C. L. R. James, 17 November 1960, **C. L. R. James Papers.**

47. Norman Manley to C. L. R. James, 1 April 1959, 4/60/2B/21, **Norman Manley Papers.**

48. Norman Manley to C. L. R. James, 19 September 1958, **C. L. R. James Papers.** See also Joyce Toney, "West Indian Response to Race in the U.S.," **Journal of Caribbean Studies,** 14(Number 3, Summer 2000): 199–214.

49. Norman Manley to A. E. Issa, 24 February 1961, 4/60/2B/24, **Norman Manley Papers.**

50. C. Walker to Norman Manley, 6 March 1961, 4/60/2B/25, **Norman Manley Papers.** See also Ralph Crowder, "Fidel Castro and Harlem: Political, Diplomatic and Social Influences of the 1960 Visit to the Hotel Theresa," **Afro-Americans in New York Life**

and History, 24(Number 1, January 2000): 79–92.

51. Flyer issued by JFTU for WFTU Congress, 4–15 October 1957, Leipzig, East Germany, **Richard Hart Papers.**

52. Ferdinand Smith to W. A. Bustamante, 18 March 1958, **Richard Hart Papers.**

53. Ferdinand Smith, letter to editor of the **Gleaner,** 17 July 1958, **Richard Hart Papers.**

54. **Freedom Newsletter,** 25 August 1956, **Richard Hart Papers.**

55. Ferdinand Smith to Giuseppe Casadei, 7 November 1960, **Richard Hart Papers.**

56. Ferdinand Smith to "Sister Xemtsova," 29 March 1958, **Richard Hart Papers.**

57. See Ken Jones to Norman Manley, 12 September 1960; W. M. Seivright to Norman Manley, 29 September 1960; Norman Manley to Robert McGregor, 5 October 1960, 4/60/2B/23, **Norman Manley Papers.**

58. "Communism on the World Scene," pamphlet, circa 1961, File—Communism, *National Library of Jamaica.*

59. **Gleaner,** 5 July 1960. See also **Jamaica Times,** 3 December 1960, 19 November 1960.

60. **Gleaner,** 31 August 1960.

61. **Gleaner,** 7 October 1960.

62. **Jamaica Times,** 12 November 1960. For more on this point, see **Gleaner,** 5 September 1960, 22 December 1960, 20 May 1961, 5 June 1961, 20 June 1961, 30 June 1961.

63. **Freedom Newsletter,** 27 April 1957, **Richard Hart Papers.**

64. **Freedom Newsletter,** 2 February 1957, **Richard Hart Papers.**

65. **Freedom Newsletter,** 23 August 1958, **Richard Hart Papers.**

66. See Ferdinand Smith to "Dear Mr. President," Kwame Nkrumah, 18 July 1960, BAA/4, **Archives of Ghana,** *Accra.*

67. Richard Hart to "Dear Reader," 20 January 1961, **Richard Hart Papers.**

68. **Freedom Newsletter,** February 1961, **Richard Hart Papers.**

69. **Freedom Newsletter,** February 1961.

70. **Freedom Newsletter,** August 1961, **Richard Hart Papers.**

NOTES TO THE EPILOGUE

1. **Hawsepipe,** 12 October 1995.

2. Rene De La Pedraja, **The Rise and Decline of U.S. Merchant Shipping in the Twentieth Century,** New York: Twayne, 1993, 156, 17. See also John Wenlock Welch, "Our Oceanic Ills," **United States Naval Institute Proceedings,** 65(Number 440, October 1939): 1417–1530.

3. **People's Weekly World,** 24 July 1999.

4. **New York Times,** 24 December 1999.

5. **Financial Times,** 7 March 2001.

6. **The Economist,** 18 May 2002.

7. **Los Angeles Times,** 29 May 2001.

8. **New York Times,** 23 June 1961.

9. Joshua B. Freeman, **Working-Class New York: Life and Labor in New York since World War II,** New York: New Press, 2000, 164.

10. Freeman, **Working-Class New York,** 240.

11. Jim Green, **Against the Tide: The Story of the Canadian Seamen's Union,** Toronto: Progress, 1986, 242.

12. **New York Times,** 1 February 1971.

13. Freeman, **Working-Class New York,** 185–186.

14. Griffin Fariello, **Red Scare: Memories of the American Inquisition; An Oral History,** New York: Norton, 1995, 402–417.

15. **Hawsepipe,** May 1986.

16. **Hawsepipe,** July 1984.

17. Interview, Paul Palazzi, 1 August 1999 (in possession of author).

18. **Wall Street Journal,** 13 July 1981.

19. **Wall Street Journal,** 13 July 1981. See also James R. Prickett, "Anti-Communism and Labor History," **Industrial Relations,** 13(October 1974): 219–227. Cf. Robert H. Zieger, "Nobody Here But Us Trade Unionists: Communism and the CIO," **Reviews in American History,** 10(Number 2, June 1982): 245–249.

20. Undated Letter, **NMU Vertical File,** TF, *Tamiment, New York University.*

21. Undated Letter, **NMU Vertical File.** See also **New York Times,** 28 July 1979.

22. John A. Butler, **Sailing on Friday: The Perilous Voyage of America's Merchant Marine,** Washington, D.C.: Brassey, 1997, 11.

23. Harold C. Nystrom to James Mitchell, 30 September 1960, LR-23, Box 115, **James Mitchell Papers,** *Dwight D. Eisenhower Library, Kansas.*

24. Memorandum from James Mitchell, 3 October 1960, LR-23, Box 115, **James Mitchell Papers.**

25. Clipping, **Panama Star Herald,** 29 November 1980, Box 923, **George Westerman Papers.**

26. Yvette Richards, **Maida Springer: Pan-Africanist and International Labor Leader,** Pittsburgh: University of Pittsburgh Press, 2000, 147.

27. George Morris, **The CIA and American Labor: The Subversion of the AFL-CIO's Foreign Policy,** New York: International, 1967, 16, 126.

28. **The Pilot,** June 1999.

29. **People's Weekly World,** 5 December 1998.

30. **Financial Times,** 3 January 2002.

31. **New York Review of Books,** 20 September 2001.

32. Memorandum, 7 February 1964, 100-19713, **FBI.**

Index

To conserve space, Ferdinand Smith is referred to as "FS" in subheadings. Also to save space, acronyms and initialisms generally used in the text are also used in subheadings. For example: the International Confederation of Free Trade Unions is generally referred to by its initialism (ICFTU), which is also used in subheadings. All acronyms and initialisms in subheadings also appear as main headings, along with their translations.

About the Author

GERALD HORNE is Moores Professor of History and African American Studies at the University of Houston. He is also is the author of *Race Woman: The Lives of Shirley Graham Du Bois*, *Race War! White Supremacy and the Japanese Attack on the British Empire*, and *Black and Brown: African Americans and the Mexican Revolution, 1910–1920* (all available from NYU Press).